LSAT® FOR DUMMIES®

by Amy Hackney Blackwell

Wiley Publishing, Inc.

LSAT® For Dummies®

Published by
Wiley Publishing, Inc.
111 River St.
Hoboken, NJ 07030-5774
www.wiley.com

About the Author

Amy Hackney Blackwell is an attorney and writer. She holds a JD from the University of Virginia School of Law, an MA in history from Vanderbilt University, and an AB from Duke University. Her past occupations include various teaching jobs — LSAT test-prep, paralegal training, and two years of teaching English in Japan on the JET Program; several years as a researcher in the UVA Law Library; and a stint as a theatrical technician and lighting designer. Oh, yes, and she is a member of the South Carolina Bar and worked as a lawyer for several years, but doesn't do that now. Her writing credits include *Mythology For Dummies* (written with her husband, Christopher W. Blackwell, and published by the folks bringing you this volume), *The Everything Book of Irish History and Heritage* (Adams Media, 2004), and *The Essential Dictionary of Law* (Barnes & Noble Books, 2004).

Her extracurricular accomplishments include winning second place in a Japanese calligraphy contest, certification as a coral reef assessor and an expert parachutist, and Arbitrator of the Year of the local Better Business Bureau. She speaks French, Japanese, German, Italian, and Spanish with varying degrees of competence. For fun, she enjoys hurling herself from airplanes, moving sea urchins around the ocean floor, riding horses through sugarcane fields in small island nations, copying Byzantine icons, and pedaling her various bicycles across entire states. She shares an old house in Greenville, S.C., with her husband, two children, and cat (and for the space of one spring weekend, an entire swarm of honeybees).

Dedication

To Slick, who knows all about law school and the LSAT.

Author's Acknowledgments

Thanks are in order to the many people who worked their way through the multitude of LSAT problems and massaged this book into user-friendly form. Project editor Chrissy Guthrie, copy editor Chad Sievers, acquisitions editor Kathy Cox, technical reviewer Theresa Gheen, and the other hardworking souls at Wiley deserve kudos for their endless patience and attention to detail, as well as their contribution of humor to what some might think is a pretty dry subject. Many thanks to my agent, Grace Freedson, for her continuing hard work and advocacy on my behalf. Infinite gratitude to Ryan and Chris for their contributions and to Mom and Dad for facilitating this whole thing in the first place. And thanks as always to Favignana for her constant and immediate presence.

Publisher's Acknowledgments

We're proud of this book; please send us your comments through our Dummies online registration form located at www.dummies.com/register/.

Some of the people who helped bring this book to market include the following:

Acquisitions, Editorial, and Media Development

Project Editor: Christina Guthrie

Acquisitions Editor: Kathy Cox

Copy Editor: Chad Sievers

Assistant Editor: Holly Gastineau-Grimes

Technical Editor: Theresa Gheen

Editorial Manager: Christine Meloy Beck

Editorial Assistants: Courtney Allen, Melissa Bennett, Elizabeth Rea

Cover Photo:
© Steve Dunwell/Getty Images/The Image Bank

Cartoons: Rich Tennant, www.the5thwave.com

Composition

Project Coordinator: Nancee Reeves

Layout and Graphics: Lauren Goddard, Denny Hager, Joyce Haughey, Stephanie D. Jumper, Barry Offringa, Jacque Roth

Proofreaders: John Greenough, Betty Kish, Susan Moritz, Brian H. Walls

Indexer: Joan Griffitts

Publishing and Editorial for Consumer Dummies

> **Diane Graves Steele,** Vice President and Publisher, Consumer Dummies
>
> **Joyce Pepple,** Acquisitions Director, Consumer Dummies
>
> **Kristin A. Cocks,** Product Development Director, Consumer Dummies
>
> **Michael Spring,** Vice President and Publisher, Travel
>
> **Brice Gosnell,** Associate Publisher, Travel
>
> **Kelly Regan,** Editorial Director, Travel

Publishing for Technology Dummies

> **Andy Cummings,** Vice President and Publisher, Dummies Technology/General User

Composition Services

> **Gerry Fahey,** Vice President of Production Services
>
> **Debbie Stailey,** Director of Composition Services

Contents at a Glance

Table of Contents

Introduction

Welcome to *LSAT For Dummies*. You may have heard horror stories about the Law School Admission Test (LSAT), especially about the infamous "logic games," formally known as Analytical Reasoning problems. Yes, the LSAT is no walk in the park, but it's not the hardest test in the universe. It doesn't require you to brush off your rusty math and science; it doesn't expect you to remember anything from your history classes; it really just expects you to be able to read. If you can read carefully and quickly and then apply what you've read, you already have the skills you need to succeed on the LSAT.

This book helps you refine those skills and apply them to the particular tasks on the LSAT. If you go through this book and do at least some of the practice questions, you should have a pretty good idea of what awaits you on test day.

About This Book

First, allow me to tell you what this book *can* do: This book introduces you to the LSAT and helps you get a handle on how to take it. It describes the three types of multiple-choice sections — Analytical Reasoning, Logical Reasoning, and Reading Comprehension and provides guidance on how to handle them as well as plenty of practice with explanations. It also touches on the Writing Sample, which at the moment is unscored but still merits a bit of attention. The first three chapters discuss some basics of law school admissions, test-taking strategy, and other logistical entertainment.

Now, on to what the book *can't* do: This book doesn't give you a bunch of tricks to help you "crack" the LSAT. It's not a nut; it's a test, and to do well on it you have to take it the same way everyone else does. The LSAT is pretty hard, and the only way to succeed is to work through the questions and answer most of them correctly. I do provide some techniques you can use to help you, but they're generally on the lines of "budget your time" and "make sure you read the questions carefully." Anyone who promises you the key to unlock the test is lying to you — there's no such thing.

One topic of some interest to people buying LSAT-prep books is the source of the questions used in the book. Reviews of other LSAT books on certain bookselling Web sites mention that some books are flawed because the writers made up the questions. A certain LSAT-prep book insists that its questions are best because they are made according to the same principles used by the real LSAT-makers. That's all well and good, but the fact is, no one makes real LSAT questions but the real Law School Admissions Council (LSAC). If you want real LSAT questions, get yourself some LSAT PrepTests, which are real LSATs administered in previous years. That's the most authentic practice you can find, and I highly recommend it. (You can order these PrepTests from the LSAC Web site (www.lsac.org); they come with answers but not explanations, so they're great practice, but if you have trouble figuring out why your answers are right or wrong, you should work through this book first to get a sense of how the questions work.)

So where did the questions in this book come from? I made them up. I didn't pull them out of the air, though. I made them up based on actual LSATs. The difficulty and thought patterns are the same as those on real LSATs. *For Dummies* editors and actual LSAT test-prep instructors and LSAT-takers assisted me by massaging and tweaking the questions to make sure that they're equivalent to the real LSAT questions. You can get real and valuable practice by using the questions in this book. And the fact remains, not even LSAT PrepTests are going to let you practice the questions you have to answer on test day for the simple reason that no one ever gets to work those until the test is upon them.

Conventions Used in This Book

While writing this book, I used a few conventions that you should be aware of:

- ✔ I relegate topics that are complementary to the subject at hand but not essential to sidebars. They appear in gray boxes throughout the book.
- ✔ I style Web sites and email addresses in monofont to help them stand out in the text.
- ✔ I *italicize* any new LSAT-related terms that you're likely to be unfamiliar with.

Foolish Assumptions

I make a few assumptions about you, the reader (I hope you don't mind):

- ✔ My first assumption is that you've either signed up to take the LSAT or you're at least seriously considering taking the LSAT.
- ✔ My second assumption is that, of course, you're not a dummy; the LSAT is too hard for real dummies. You're a normal person who wants to succeed at the LSAT but who knows little about the test at this point.
- ✔ My third and final assumption is that you've chosen this book for one of several reasons — the fabulous *For Dummies* reputation, the price, or maybe the elegant typeface and the page layout — but primarily because you think you want to go to law school, and the LSAT is the only way to that destination.

What You're Not to Read

Because this book is a test-prep, you probably want to read most everything here. Besides, I worked really hard on this book! However, if you're pressed for time or just have a short attention span, you can skip the sidebars and any text marked with a Technical Stuff icon without missing out on too much.

How This Book Is Organized

This book is divided into seven parts. Each part has been carefully calibrated to introduce you to an aspect of the LSAT. Go through the whole thing, and you should have a pretty good idea of what you're up against.

Part 1: Taking the LSAT Plunge

So you think you want to go to law school. Well, you won't get there without taking the LSAT. This part introduces the LSAT and the people who make the LSAT, explains some basic test-taking techniques, and briefly describes the nuts and bolts of law school admissions.

Part II: Analytical Reasoning: Players, Rules, and Logic

The Analytical Reasoning section strikes terror into the hearts of thousands of students every year. It consists entirely of those logic problems in which you have to arrange performers on a stage, or schedule swimmers for a swim meet, or plan the courses of a complicated menu, applying totally random and arbitrary rules to an arbitrary and random set of players. The good news: You can figure out how to do these problems. It's just a matter of relaxing and going with the analytical flow.

Part III: Logical Reasoning: Arguing Well

Logical Reasoning makes up half your score on the LSAT. How does that work? Well, you get to work not one but two sections of these lovely little questions. Logical Reasoning questions are designed to test your ability to read short paragraphs and then figure out how and why they're put together. The questions ask you to do things like strengthen or weaken arguments, spot assumptions and flaws, figure out patterns of reasoning, and other fun stuff like that. It's all meant to spot people who are likely potential lawyers. Could that group include you? Of course!

Part IV: Reading Comprehension: Read 'Em but Don't Weep

In Reading Comprehension, you get to read short passages — 450 words or so — on completely random topics, and then answer questions about them. Some of the passages are kind of interesting; others most definitely aren't. The questions are designed to test your understanding of how the passage is put together — what the main idea is, why the author wrote it, why she uses particular phrases, and other similar questions. What's the trick to this section? Keep concentrating.

Part V: The Writing Sample: No Score but Can Count

To complete your LSAT experience, you get to write a short essay on a topic provided for you. The topic always requires you to pick one of two sides and argue in support of the side you've chosen. The bad news is you have to write it by hand. The good news? It doesn't count toward your score. It's kind of like a calorie-free dessert! (Do take it seriously, though — the LSAT folks send a copy of your essay to every law school that receives your LSAT scores, so there's a good chance that some admissions guru will read it.)

Part VI: The Real Deal: Full-Length Practice LSATs

Good scores come to those who practice. This part contains two full-length practice tests in the same format as the real LSAT. It also includes the answers and explanations to help you if you answered a question incorrectly.

Part VII: The Part of Tens

Like every *For Dummies* book, this part includes some interesting lists to help make your LSAT experience a little less boring. This part contains useful information that's fun and useful, like a list of myths about the LSAT and secrets of highly successful LSAT-takers.

Icons Used in This Book

This book, like all *For Dummies* books, uses icons to help you spot important tidbits of information, and to break up the monotony of otherwise plain and ordinary pages. Here are the icons I use in this book:

This icon marks useful bits of information that may come in handy when you study for or take the LSAT.

This icon marks stuff you should try to remember.

This icon marks stuff to avoid, potential mistakes, and traps for the unwary.

This icon identifies questions resembling those on the actual LSAT.

This icon highlights extra tidbits of info that enhance your reading but aren't essential to preparing for the LSAT. You can skip over these icons if you really want to, but just because they aren't essential doesn't mean that you can't learn from them.

Where to Go from Here

If you bought this book, you must have some plan — definite or tentative — to take the LSAT. But just buying the book alone won't help you much. To get the full benefit, you have to open it up, read it, and work the problems

There are two approaches you can take:

- ✔ Read all the explanatory materials and work your way through all the practice problems, then take the practice tests at the end and see how you did.
- ✔ Pick and choose the sections that most concern you, concentrating on the questions you find difficult.

It's up to you. You're the one taking the test, and you're the one who has to decide what you need to study and how much time you want to allocate to the process.

Also, don't forget to visit this book's Web site for bonus content and extra Analytical Reasoning practice. Go to www.dummies.com and search for this book's title.

Part I
Taking the LSAT Plunge

In this part . . .

What is the LSAT? Who thinks it up? Who would want to do a thing like that? Look into this part to find the answers to these questions, plus a few more interesting tidbits — suggestions of how you can maximize your LSAT score and a short chapter all about law school admissions, a topic that you'll probably figure out how to love over the next few months.

Chapter 1

The L Team: The LSAT and Its Sponsors

*I*f you want to go to law school, you must take the *Law School Admission Test,* a.k.a. the LSAT. All 201 law schools that belong to the Law School Admission Council (LSAC) (see the section, "What Have You Done for Me Lately? The LSAC" at the end of this chapter) require it. Law schools that don't require it may not be approved by the American Bar Association (ABA), which in turn may not qualify you for admission to a state bar, so be careful about choosing a school that doesn't.

The LSAT, annoying though it can be, is the only means law schools have of evaluating all their applicants on the same playing field. Colleges are different, backgrounds are different, cultures are different, but the LSAT is the same for everyone. The LSAT is carefully designed so that the testing experience of test-takers is virtually identical. Everyone has the same time per section, the same rules, and the same testing environment. And each LSAT test is crafted so that test-takers have a 90 percent chance of scoring the same on a different version. So, each school feels pretty confident that the LSAT is an objective measure of student ability.

Grade point averages, unlike the LSAT, are highly subjective; they vary depending on the difficulty of a school, the difficulty of particular courses, and other totally random and unpredictable factors (like how often a student decides to go out instead of staying in to study). Law school applications include other information like personal statements that can give them an idea of a student's abilities, but still the schools can't know for sure that they're getting the real goods — plenty of students get help writing those essays. That leaves the LSAT as one of the most reliable and objective means to compare candidates.

In this chapter, I introduce you to the LSAT and its various parts, and then tell you all about registering and preparing for the big day. Finally, I talk about the organization behind all this madness, the LSAC.

Getting to Know the Enemy

If you want to get a decent score on the LSAT, you need to know the test. You can't expect to walk into a test center cold, never having encountered an LSAT in your life and just ace the questions.

You don't necessarily have to study for a long time. If you're good at standardized tests, you may be able to flip through one or two sample tests, work a few of the problems, get the idea, and score in the 95th percentile. Some people can. If, on the other hand, you find standardized tests in general difficult, and the LSAT particularly difficult, you probably need to practice a bit more. Whatever your situation, keep your motivation and prepare with the notion that you can and will improve with practice.

The LSAT consists of four parts:

- Analytical Reasoning section
- Logical Reasoning section
- Reading Comprehension section
- Writing Sample section

The Writing Sample section is always last, but the other three sections can come in any order. You take six different test sections, which include two scored sections of Logical Reasoning and one unscored section that can be any of the three multiple-choice tests. You don't know which section is unscored, and it looks just like any other LSAT test section. Every section except for the Writing Sample is a 35-minute multiple-choice test; the Writing Sample lasts 30 minutes.

Remember, on the LSAT, all the multiple-choice questions have five possible answers: A, B, C, D, and E.

The unscored section that you take is a collection of questions that the LSAC is considering using on a future LSAT. The LSAC wants to see how well these new questions work when presented to actual LSAT-takers. This section can be Analytical Reasoning, Logical Reasoning, or Reading Comprehension; you don't know which section is unscored.

The quickest way to get your hands on an actual LSAT is to download the sample test available at the LSAC Web site (www.lsac.org). Downloading the sample is a good way to familiarize yourself with the test and its format.

Taking a Quick Look at the Types of Questions

The LSAT has three different kinds of multiple-choice questions. Each of them has its own virtues and vices, and you will come to know and love them all (though I won't blame you if you pick a favorite).

Analytical reasoning — playing games with your head

The Analytical Reasoning section consists of four logic problems — the infamous "logic games" — each of which is followed by between five and eight questions. These problems involve a group of players that need to be arranged and the rules that govern how you can arrange them.

Many people call Analytical Reasoning problems "logic games." This book doesn't use the term "logic games"; it calls them "Analytical Reasoning problems." The reason for this is that there's another section on the LSAT called Logical Reasoning, and it gets terribly confusing if two different sections of the LSAT have almost identical-sounding names.

You may get something like: Five college students, B, C, D, E, and F, must share three rooms in a house. B can't stay with D. E must stay with F. This fact pattern is followed by several questions that allow you to explore your understanding of the relationships between the students and the dorm rooms. One question may propose five possible roommate arrangements, and ask you to choose which one is the only one that could work.

This kind of puzzle commonly appears on IQ tests or in books of games to amuse travelers on airplanes. What they have to do with law school is a mystery to many people. The LSAC PrepTest booklets say that these types of problems "simulate the kinds of detailed analyses of relationships that a law student must perform in solving legal problems." That may be exaggerating the amount of logical analysis that law students must perform. When I was in law school, I was never called upon to work a logic problem. Nor, to the best of my knowledge, were any of my classmates.

Still, the skills that the Analytical Reasoning section tests are important in law school. To answer these questions correctly, you must read carefully and accurately. You have to apply rules to a system, which is similar to applying statutes or case law to a problem. You have to restrict your analysis to what is directly stated or that can be logically inferred. So the Analytical Reasoning section is fairly useful at predicting who might succeed in law school.

The Analytical Reasoning section is worth 25 percent of your LSAT score. See Chapters 4 through 7 for more on analytical reasoning.

Logical reasoning — putting your arguing skills to good use

The Logical Reasoning section consists of about 25 short (for example, three or four sentences) passages about various topics. Each of them is followed by one or two questions. The questions ask you to identify the point of an argument, to make deductions about what the author is assuming, to draw conclusions, to identify principles or argument structures, to spot logical errors, and so forth.

You don't need to know any formal logic to answer these questions. All you have to do is read carefully (and quickly) and think clearly. Sometimes the wording is tricky, and you have to concentrate to avoid getting confused. Sometimes jotting down some notes or paraphrasing the passage in your own words can help you focus.

Every LSAT has two Logical Reasoning sections. Together, they're worth 50 percent of your LSAT score. Chapters 8 through 13 are full of information and practice for logical reasoning.

This point may seem obvious. Because the Logical Reasoning section is with 50 percent of your total LSAT score, work hard on your technique for these problems. You get twice the benefit if you do well on this section!

Reading comprehension — concentrating and remembering what you read

In the Reading Comprehension section, you read four fairly long passages on particular topics and answer several questions about them. The questions ask about the author's conclusion, the author's tone, the meaning of words, how the passage is organized, and other points designed to test your ability to understand what you read. The good news: The LSAT uses a limited pool of question types over and over again. Because you can predict the types of questions being asked, you can practice reading to answer the questions you know you'll see.

Topics range from humanities and science and social science disciplines to political writing. You don't need any expertise in any particular area; in fact, if you have expertise in the subject of a passage, try to forget your outside knowledge. You want to answer all the questions from the information given to you in the passage. Outside knowledge may actually distract you!

This section tests your ability to read and understand a fairly long reading passage. Reading and understanding a long passage is applicable to law school because most law classes consist of reading long, densely worded passages on obscure topics and then answering questions about them.

The Reading Comprehension section accounts for 25 percent of your LSAT score. See Chapters 14 through 17 for the lowdown.

The writing sample — jumping the final hurdle

The last part of the LSAT is the Writing Sample section. You receive one sheet of lined paper, and you get 30 minutes to write your essay on it. (Yep, that means you write it by hand.) The essay topic lets you exhibit your skills at arguing one side or the other of a proposition.

For example, your question may ask you to decide which dog a widow should buy: a German shepherd, who would be a good guard dog but eat a lot of food and not be very affectionate; or a Pekingese, who would make a good companion and be cheap to feed but would be utterly useless for home defense. (Actually, my mother's Pekingese was a fierce little demon and terrorized the whole neighborhood. You can explore this question further in Chapter 20.)

Your selection doesn't matter. There's no right or wrong answer. All you have to do is pick a side and justify your decision. Chapters 18 and 19 go over this process in detail.

You don't get a score on the writing sample, but the Law School Data Assembly Service (LSDAS) (see "What Have You Done for Me Lately? The LSAC" later, in this chapter) sends a copy of your essay to every law school that receives your LSAT score.

Some folks wonder why they should prepare for the Writing Sample section if it's unscored. Law schools often read essays in deciding borderline cases or comparing similar applicants. If your profile is substantially similar to hundreds of others, law schools often look at the essays to compare like candidates.

You Gotta Score!

The LSAT is scored on a scale from 120 to 180; every year a few people attain the Everest-like peak of 180, and they can pretty much write their own tickets to law school. The average score is a little higher than 150 (around 153). Any score higher than 160 is quite good, and puts you in the top 10 to 12 percent of test-takers. A score of 166 puts you near the 95th percentile, and a score more than 170 is rare.

To get a 160, you need to get more than 80 percent of the answers correct. To get a 150, you need to get about 65 percent correct. If you get 95 percent or more right, you'll be up in the stratospheric 170 or even 180.

The LSAT of the future

The Law School Admission Council (LSAC) is constantly working to develop the LSAT, testing new questions and considering ways to make the test more accurate. One potential new addition is a scored writing test. The LSAC realizes that many people and schools currently ignore the Writing Sample section, and the LSAC believes that a scored writing test would better reflect the abilities of test-takers, which makes sense, because law students and lawyers do a lot of writing. The LSAC is also considering a listening comprehension test, which would test a student's ability to take notes on a dialog and answer questions about it. Other possible modifications to the LSAT include revisions in the Analytical Reasoning and Reading Comprehension sections, perhaps requiring students to use two related passages to answer questions, which would be similar to the law school skill of applying principles from several different cases to a legal problem. All potential changes would be intended to make the test a more reliable method of identifying students with the skills that would make them successful law students.

The LSAT scoring is straightforward. Your raw score is the number of questions you get right; no points are deducted for wrong answers. You plug that raw score into the score chart to determine what your LSAT score would be. So if, say, your test has 100 questions on it, and you get 75 of them right, your raw score is 75 and your LSAT score would be 161. If you get 44 right, you'd get a 142.

The LSAT-writers work hard to ensure that the test is reliable. That means the same test-taker should get scores in a similar range on two or three different tests, and that luck in getting an easy test shouldn't be a factor in scores. In practice, luck will always be something of a factor, but it shouldn't be a major one.

Still, you've probably taken a metric ton of tests by now, and you know that everyone has good days and bad days, good tests and bad tests (hey, even good hair days and bad hair days!). The combination of a bad test and a bad mood (say, for instance, despite my advice to the contrary you showed up at the test center with a killer hangover) can lead to a misleadingly bad score. If that happens, you can cancel your score and try again (see more about doing this in Chapter 2). On the other hand, you may be in the test-taking zone on test day, and every question seems laughably easy to you. It can happen that way. If you have a good day, thank your lucky stars because that'll probably result in a good LSAT score and law school admission.

What if you get a 160 and your friend gets a 163? Does that mean your friend is a better law school prospect than you? Probably not. Small differences between test-takers aren't usually due to actual differences of ability. Your score will be in the range of scores you're capable of, but if you take the LSAT several times within a short period of time, you probably won't get the same score every time. It may go up slightly; it may go down slightly, but it should be within 3 points up or down of your original score (though your mileage may vary).

Registering for the LSAT

The LSAT happens four times a year: in June, October, December, and February. If you want to enter law school the next fall, you must take the LSAT by December at the latest, though I highly recommend taking it earlier. October and December are the most popular test dates because some law schools start taking applications in the fall and begin accepting applicants early in the winter; the earlier you apply, the better your odds of acceptance. The October, December, and February tests are scheduled for Saturdays. The June test is on a Monday.

If you observe the Sabbath on Saturday, you can request to take the test on another day, usually the Monday following the Saturday test date. To do this, have your rabbi or minister write a letter on official stationery, confirming your religious obligations, and send it to the LSAC.

The registration fee for the LSAT is currently $112. If you miss the first deadline and must register late, there is an additional charge of $56. (All prices are subject to change; be sure to check with the LSAC to find out current charges.)

Keep the following things in mind when registering for the LSAT:

✔ **Be sure to register.** Okay, duh. But really, be sure to register. The deadlines for registration fall well ahead of test dates, so you need to be on the ball. You can find the deadlines on the LSAC Web site (www.lsac.org). (Also, test centers fill up early, so you may not get into the site you want if you don't register on time.) If you want to go to law school in September, you need to take the previous December's LSAT, which means you must register in November. Plan accordingly. And make sure you're free the day of the test!

✔ **When you register, be very careful you enter the correct code for your test center.** If you get the code wrong, you may be assigned a test center in a different state — not convenient. (The LSAC isn't checking for accuracy; the LSAS has no idea where you really want to take the test, so it won't know if you make a mistake.) Driving several hours the day before your test definitely won't calm your nerves. You can change your test center through the LSAC Web site, but you don't want to have to worry about that if you can avoid it.

✔ **Not every test center offers the LSAT on every test date.** Check to make sure that your preferred location is offering a test on your preferred date. (Occasionally you can get the LSAC to administer a test in a different location, but only if you can't travel to a regular site and if you register well in advance.) Safeguard your admission ticket when it arrives.

✔ **If something comes up — you catch the flu, you get sent overseas to war, you go into labor — and you're unable to take the LSAT, you can get a partial refund.** Granted, you only get ($40) of your registration fee back, but that's better than nothing. The LSAC Web site has deadlines for sending in a written request.

✔ **If you discover before the test date that you won't be able to make it that day, you can change your test date.** Of course, you have to pay a fee of $29. The LSAC Web site has the deadlines for sending in a written request.

If you absolutely can't afford the cost of the LSAT, you can apply for a fee waiver. The LSAC doesn't want to deny access to the legal profession solely on the basis of economic disadvantage. Be warned, though; the requirements are quite strict.

Preparing for the LSAT

Helping students prepare for the LSAT has become a multimillion-dollar (at least) industry. Test-prep companies promise huge score increases; students spend thousands on semester-long courses and tutors. Every major bookstore is full of books to help prospective lawyers on their way.

Be wary of expensive classes or snake oil salesmen that promise to reveal secrets or give you huge score increases. Usually, all that most people need is a good LSAT-prep book and a few recent LSAT tests to do their best on test day. Save your money for law school! (But be warned, many folks lack the motivation and discipline for self-study. If this describes you, either buckle down and sign a contract with yourself, form a study group, or consider enrolling in a course.)

Methods and madness

Many test-prep companies promise to teach you methods to beat the LSAT, proven techniques that make the right answers appear before your eyes like visions from the heavens. They break the test down into its component parts — 7 different kinds of logic games, 14 different types of logical reasoning questions — and expect their students to spot these types on test day, so they can approach the LSAT with the proper strategic attitude.

This book doesn't make such promises or take the complicated approach. There aren't any secrets or shortcuts to success on the LSAT. Some skills — an ability for reading rapidly, having a strong vocabulary, and being able to concentrate — certainly do help, but you acquire these skills by spending years of your life in school and reading. No book can magically endow you with these skills overnight. This book isn't going to help you analyze the test so you could do a better job writing the LSAT than the people who actually make it up; life is too short to spend much of it shuffling pieces of the LSAT into categories. And the fact is, you never know what your actual LSAT will look like. Every test is unique, and you're best off preparing to be flexible.

You can answer all the LSAT's questions by using pretty much the same approach — careful reading and calm, logical thinking. This book illustrates this approach.

What will really help

What will really help you succeed at the LSAT is exposure to the test. Exposure may mean something as simple as flipping through a sample test the night before you take the official one. More often, though, it may mean several hours of practice, or it may even mean weeks of practice.

This book, however, doesn't provide weeks of practice. It provides about 24-hours' worth, which is most profitably spent if you don't do it all at once.

If you need extra prep materials, you can't do better than the old LSATs sold by the LSAC; they're called PrepTests, and they're the actual LSATs that have been administered to willing victims over the last decade. Be warned, though; the LSAT has increased in difficulty over the years, so you'll get your most valuable practice from the most recent tests.

Staples in the central gutter hold the LSAT PrepTest booklets together. These staples aren't always flattened down to the paper, so be careful that you don't stab your finger with one as you run your hand down the page to flatten it out. (I'm speaking from personal experience.)

If you want to take a prep course, by all means do so. It can give you valuable practice. It may even improve your score. Then again, it may not. Not everyone who takes a course sees much improvement, if any. (My brother took a course that promised an LSAT score up around 180; he got a 178 on the practice test that the test center gave him, but dropped to 166 on the real thing.)

If you want to use other books that promise a foolproof "method," go right ahead. Do what you think you need to do. But if you don't think those things are necessary, don't bother. Beating the LSAT doesn't need to be the ultimate goal of your existence, and preparing for it doesn't need to take that long.

What study method works best for you?

No one wants to spend too much of her life thinking about the LSAT. Studying as efficiently as possible makes sense. Here are some possible plans for your LSAT studying.

✔ **The slow and careful approach:** You should go with this approach if you take preparing for the LSAT very seriously and are willing to spend a good deal of time on it. Start at least 2 months before you plan to take the LSAT. Go to the LSAC Web site (www.lsac.org) and order some actual LSAT PrepTests. While you wait for them to arrive, read all the chapters in this book carefully, working all the practice questions. Then take the two practice exams at the end of the book. By this time your LSAT PrepTests should have arrived for you to take. When the time comes to take the real LSAT, fear not — you'll be ready for anything it throws at you.

✔ **The quick and dirty route:** Okay, so you don't want to waste one more minute than necessary on the LSAT. Here's what you should do: Begin at least the day before the LSAT. Read Chapters 4, 8, 14, and 18. Work some of the questions in Chapters 6, 12, and 16. If you can't answer them quickly and easily, check back to the appropriate chapters to find out more about your problem areas. Outline a writing sample essay in your head to make sure you know what to do. If you have time, work one of the practice tests. Show up at the LSAT and do your best.

✔ **Riding the fence:** Most of you probably fall somewhere in the middle. That's fine; you're the one who knows what you need and how much time you can afford.

No matter how you choose to study, start sooner rather than later. The more time you spend working on the LSAT, the better you'll get at it, so you don't want to short-change yourself by procrastinating.

Practice makes perfect

Any book you consult will recommend that you prepare for the LSAT by taking a practice test or two under simulated test-day conditions. That means sitting down on a Saturday morning (or some other day when you have three or four hours unscheduled) with a test booklet, an answer sheet, a No. 2 pencil, and a timer, and working your way through the test, section by section, stopping work when the timer buzzes.

You can do that, and you should if you think it will help you. I expect, though, that you already know what test pressure is like. After all, the LSAT isn't your first standardized test. Your valuable (and presumably limited) study time may be better spent working through questions slowly and carefully, making sure that you really know how to work the analytical reasoning and read the logical reasoning questions.

A word on mood: Sometimes you just can't start studying. You're too tired, too distracted, too whatever to think clearly. Other times you fly through the problems. Try to practice when the time is right; forcing yourself to work questions when you don't feel like it won't help your skills and will certainly make you think you know less than you do.

However you decide to practice, just be sure you give yourself enough time. Try to start at least a couple of weeks before the test date. You can always slack off if you decide you don't need the preparation.

What Have You Done for Me Lately? The LSAC

Did you ever wonder who makes up the LSAT? It comes from the minds of the *Law School Admission Council,* or LSAC, a nonprofit corporation in Newton, Pennsylvania. The LSAC comprises 201 law schools in the United States and Canada; the member professors and attorneys volunteer their time to the council. The LSAC offers a number of services designed to facilitate applications to law school and improve legal education, and it also sponsors research into issues such as minority representation in the legal profession.

If you're serious about applying to law school, familiarize yourself with the LSAC and its offerings, because it's going to be part of your life for a while. You can visit the LSAC, register for the LSAT online, and do various other fun activities at the LSAC's Web site, www.lsac.org.

Creating and administering the LSAT

The LSAC administers the LSAT to more than 100,000 people every year; almost 150,000 took it in 2003. They create four complete tests every year and constantly work to develop new questions and refine the LSAT's accuracy — that's one reason why you get to take an extra, unscored section of multiple-choice questions when you take the LSAT. The LSAC compiles statistics on the number of people that take the tests and scores received, schedule test dates, field questions and complaints from test-takers, and generally make it possible for many people to apply to law school every year.

Aiding in law school applications

The LSAC also plays a major role in law school applications. When you register for the LSAT, you can also sign up to participate in the *Law School Data Assembly Service,* or LSDAS for $103.

The LSDAS streamlines the law school application process by assembling most of the information needed to apply to law schools and sending it to the schools in one package. An LSDAS report includes

- ✔ Summaries of transcripts from all your undergraduate and graduate schools
- ✔ LSAT scores and copies of the LSAT Writing Sample section
- ✔ Letters of recommendation

Your registration fee buys you one report to a law school. If you buy additional reports to law schools at the same time as you register for the LSDAS, they cost $10 each; if you buy them later, they're $12 each. (All prices are subject to change, of course.) LSDAS registration lasts five years. If you register for another LSAT during that period, your LSDAS gets extended to last for five years from your most recent registration.

Almost all the law schools approved by the ABA require that its applicants use the LSDAS, which makes your life much easier. Rather than having to assemble all that information for every school to which you apply, you just give the information to the LSAC (along with some money) and it takes care of everything. When you apply to a law school, the school requests the report from the LSAC, the LSAC sends the report, and you just sit back and wait.

You can register for the LSDAS on the LSAC Web site (www.lsac.org) at the same time as you register for the LSAT. When you do this, you authorize the LSAC to release information about you to eligible law schools, which means law schools who are interested in you may contact you.

If you don't register for the LSDAS at the same time as you register for the LSAT, you still must register for the LSDAS before you apply to law schools. Do this at least six weeks before you start applying.

Providing other goods and services

The LSAC does a number of other good deeds for the legal education system.

✔ The *Candidate Referral Service* allows law schools to search LSDAS data for students who match particular profiles (for example, LSAT scores of a certain level, minorities, women, students from a certain region, and so on) so that they can contact them and invite them to apply.

✔ Law school forums held in different states give prospective law students an opportunity to find out more about law school and the legal profession.

✔ The LSAC sells LSAT-prep materials and other information; you can buy these materials on the Web site. Buying copies of recently administered LSATs is one of the most useful tools. They come with answers, not explanations, but they're the real thing and make great practice tests. (Do focus most on the most recent tests, because they've gotten a bit harder since the late 1990s.)

✔ The LSAC also works to increase minority representation in the legal profession.

Chapter 2

Test-Taking Basics: Setting Yourself Up for Success

In This Chapter

▶ Considering guessing strategies

▶ Preparing to show up at the test site

▶ Thinking strategically about logistics

▶ Deciding what to do when the test is over

If you're contemplating law school, you're almost certainly a veteran of standardized tests. You know what to expect. Just like the SAT, ACT, and GRE, the LSAT is just another standardized test. You've been there, done that. Getting up early in the morning, walking into an unfamiliar classroom, sitting in a room of nervous strangers all twiddling their unfamiliar No. 2 pencils, and filling in circles on an answer sheet is old hat. You know this drill.

In this chapter, I review some strategies and considerations specific to the LSAT, as well as some general test-taking basics, in the hope of making your experience as painless as possible. I also discuss what to do after the test, including considering whether you need to retest (sigh).

Planning Your LSAT Test-Taking Tactics

You'll have an easier time on test day if you consider some strategic matters beforehand. The following sections provide a few simple strategies to ease your test-taking venture.

You can't "beat" the LSAT; no one can. These strategies aren't tricks to outsmart the test, but they can help you do better.

Maximizing your chances

Some people are naturally good at taking standardized tests. This strength doesn't mean they make better law students or better lawyers; they just find these tests easy. Other people have a harder time. They find tests stressful in general, and LSAT questions especially annoying. Whichever type you are, you can undertake some basic strategies to help you improve your score and give you a more pleasant test-taking experience. (Well, maybe not as pleasant as a spa visit, but more pleasant than a root canal.)

The punishing LSAT schedule

When you take the LSAT, you spend about 3½ hours actually sitting with a test booklet open in front of you. The only break you get comes after Section III, and it only lasts about 10 or 15 minutes — enough time to dash to the john and bolt an energy bar. The entire day may take five hours or so, with all the paperwork and registration business you have to do before and after the test.

The LSAT doesn't just test your ability to work its particular problems; it also tests your ability to concentrate under pressure and for a long period of time. Bring a good supply of mental fortitude and endurance.

Here are a few things you can do to maximize your chances of getting a good score:

✔ **Answer every question.** The LSAT test-makers don't penalize you for guessing, so you'd be crazy not to make sure every number on the answer sheet has a bubble filled in, even if you don't bother to read the question that goes with it.

✔ **Take your time.** You get better results by answering three quarters of the test accurately and then guessing on the last quarter than by racing through the whole thing too fast to be accurate. See the section "To Guess or Not to Guess," later in this chapter for more on guessing.

✔ **Budget your time.** You get 35 minutes for each multiple-choice section. Decide how to spend it. Allotting each question exactly 1.3 minutes may not be the most effective approach, but be careful not to get so caught up in the first Analytical Reasoning problem that you have only 5 minutes to work the last three.

✔ **Don't worry too much about your time.** If you're not going to finish, you're not going to finish. Answer as many questions correctly as you can, rather than panicking and getting everything wrong.

✔ **If you get stuck on a question, forget about it.** Move on to another question. (But be sure to circle the question in case you have time to come back to it.)

✔ **Ignore your companions.** What they do makes no difference to your score. If you have a major problem with your surroundings — the stench of cheap perfume from the woman next to you, the snuffling of the allergy sufferer behind you — speak to the proctor, but don't count on getting moved; test centers are often fully booked. If you're positive your performance has suffered, you can always cancel your test score and try again later.

✔ **Stay on target.** You may get bored, and your mind may want to wander somewhere more pleasant, but don't let it. Use visual cues to help yourself stay focused — point to questions with your pencil or finger.

Don't forget to answer every question!

Taking the straight or the winding road

Should you start with the first question and work every subsequent question until you get to the last one? Or should you jump around? It's entirely up to you.

The Analytical Reasoning and Reading Comprehension sections are both divided into four approximately equal parts, and if you want to pick the easiest part first and work your way to the hardest, by all means do so. Just be careful to match your test book and answer sheet numbers. Also, remember that initial assessments of difficulty are rarely accurate; a more productive way of choosing your first problem is to pick the Analytical Reasoning problem or Reading Comprehension passage with the largest number of questions — that way you maximize the number of questions you actually answer.

Although starting with a Reading Comprehension passage or Analytical Reasoning problem that isn't the first one in your test book is okay, after you pick one, stick with it until you're done. Don't try to jump between two or three passages or problems at the same time — that way lies madness.

Skipping around on the Logical Reasoning sections may not be such a good idea, because every question stands alone. A steady, straight-on-down-the-line approach is probably the better bet here. (Still, if you work best doing questions in your order, go for it.)

Some instructors teach their students to identify types of questions, so they can identify the easy and hard ones and work the easy ones first. This strategy can actually take more time and effort than simply working the problems. Instead, I suggest that you just do them in order and pay attention to when you're stuck so that you move on and avoid wasting time. The questions are all more or less the same level of difficulty anyway, though if you immediately spot one you prefer, go ahead and do it.

Some test-prep experts recommend that if you really can't finish an Analytical Reasoning or Reading Comprehension section, you cut your losses and just do your best on three of the four problems, tackling the scariest at the end if you have time. Sounds crazy, but this approach actually makes more sense than trying to speed through all four passages or problems; you maximize your accuracy on the parts you do instead of doing the whole section too fast and getting half of it wrong. If you do three-quarters of a section and get all those questions right, you get 75 percent, which is better than finishing the section and getting only half right. Of course you should still fill in the bubbles for the questions you haven't answered; there's no penalty for wrong answers, so you may as well. See "To Guess or Not To Guess" later, in this chapter for more info on guessing.

True confessions of a test-taker

Can you really write off an entire category of questions and still pass? Yes indeed you can. Although it's not the best strategy and I only recommend it as a last resort, it can work. After I graduated from law school, I took the Bar exam. (I hate to bring up yet another awful test, when you're already getting such great news about the LSAT, but this story can help you now, so bear with me.) One entire day of this exam was the Multistate Bar Exam, a national standardized test of six areas of law all mixed together. I had a handle on most of the types — criminal law, trusts and estates, torts, and contracts were no problem for me. But one-sixth of the exam consisted of questions on property law, and they were the most convoluted, complicated, tangled webs of property transfers and different kinds of estates that you could possibly imagine. It took five minutes just to read one, and then you had to find the answer.

Well, I discovered when I was preparing that reading the questions didn't improve my accuracy in answering them — I did as well when I just guessed without reading the questions as I did when I read the fact patterns and tried to match them with the correct (equally complicated) answers. So what was my strategy? I had to spend the entire day taking this test, and I knew my energies would be best spent answering the questions I knew I could do. So when I came to property questions, I didn't read them. I just guessed ([D] was my letter that day) and went on to the next question. I figured that one-sixth of the test was only worth 17 percent, and it made more sense to maximize my score on the other 83 percent instead of wasting a lot of effort on what I already knew was an exercise in futility. And my strategy worked — I passed. And I've never practiced property law.

Filling in the dots

The LSAT answer sheet is one of those fill-in-the-bubble things. You fill in the bubble corresponding to your answer with a No. 2 pencil. A machine then reads the dots and scores the test.

Debates rage on the best way to fill in these bubbles. Should you fill them in as you answer each question or is it preferable to concentrate on the test booklet for an entire page of questions and then transfer your answers in one block? Some people insist that saving up your bubbling to the end of a page is the only sensible way to proceed, and that any other method is insane. Other folks prefer to bubble in their circles after they answer each question.

The truth: Whether you bubble now or later doesn't really matter just as long as you fill them in before time runs out. A circle takes about the same amount of time to blacken either way. So don't spend your time worrying about this; just pick a style that works for you and go with it.

When you fill in your dots doesn't matter, but the following items are very important. Don't forget to do them before time elapses and you're stuck with a half-empty answer sheet.

- **Double-check your question numbers.** Getting off track and filling in your answer sheet incorrectly is easy; all it takes is skipping one question, and then every bubble on your answer sheet is off kilter. At every question, *look* at the question number in your booklet, say it to yourself or put your finger on it, and then fill in the right bubble.

- **Fill in every dot completely.** The machine reads completely blackened dots the best.

- **Fill in an answer for every question.** If you can't finish a section, pick a letter and use it to answer all the remaining questions. (For more on guessing, check out "To Guess or Not to Guess" later, in this chapter.)

- **Don't get caught up in the geometrical pattern formed by your dots.** Sometimes several questions in a row have the same answer. That's okay.

- **Erase mistakes completely.** The machine may misread your answer if you leave half-erased marks in the wrong bubble.

Taking the occasional break

An LSAT is a test of stamina as much as anything else. It's a long test, and it's tiring.

That's why pacing yourself is crucially important. When you finish a chunk of test — an Analytical Reasoning problem or a full page of Logical Reasoning questions — take a break. Close your eyes, twist your neck, loosen those tight muscles in your shoulders, breathe, and let your eyes focus on a distant object. Don't take more than 30 seconds or a minute, but do take the break. It helps you more than fretting about how little time you have left.

Have you ever heard the story about two guys who were cutting wood with axes? They worked side by side from morning until evening. The first man worked straight through without a break, swinging that axe from dawn 'til dusk. The second man sat down and rested for ten minutes every hour. At the end of the day, the men compared their piles of wood. The man who had rested every hour had a pile much bigger than the other man. The first man asked the second one how he had managed that feat, especially because he had spent so much of the day resting. The second man replied, "While I rested, I sharpened my axe."

Your brain is like that axe. You bring it to the test sharp, but the LSAT is designed to make it dull. Take those breaks and sharpen (and rest) your brain — the breaks really help.

To Guess or Not to Guess

When in doubt about the answer to a question, guess. Always guess. The LSAT test-makers don't penalize you for wrong answers, so guessing doesn't hurt, and you always have the chance that you may answer it right. What is certain is that you won't get it right if you don't answer it at all.

The joy of statistics

How likely is it that you'll get a question right by random guessing? Not very.

On questions where you have no idea of the correct answer, you have better luck if you pick a letter and stick to it for all your shots in the dark. Why? Each answer choice appears at more or less the same frequency. If you answer an entire test with one letter, you probably get about 20 percent right. You'd get the same results, even if the test were in a language you couldn't read — or if you didn't bother to read the questions or answers. If you jump around with your answers, you just may miss everything.

Is (B) really best?

Many people talk about which letter is statistically most likely to be the right answer. Many people recommend (B) as the best choice. I did a little survey of some recent LSATs to see how they really came out. See Table 2-1 for the results.

Table 2-1	Which Guess Is Best? Evaluating Test Answers				
LSAT Test No.	*(A)*	*(B)*	*(C)*	*(D)*	*(E)*
Test 41 (October 2003)	18%	25%	21%	18%	18%
Test 40 (June 2003)	19%	24%	21%	22%	15%
Test 38 (October 2002)	18%	17%	17%	27%	21%
Test 31 (June 2000)	21%	17%	20%	23%	20%

On a couple of these tests, if you total the percentages, you come up with 101 percent. That's because each test usually has 101 scored questions, and rounding up decimals results in a number higher that 100 percent. I analyzed the numbers even more; the percentages within different sections vary widely. For example, check out Table 2-2 to see how the letters break down within the sections of Test 41.

Table 2-2	Breaking Down Test 41's Sections				
Section No.	*(A)*	*(B)*	*(C)*	*(D)*	*(E)*
Section I	12%	28%	24%	24%	12%
Section II	26%	22%	26%	22%	4%
Section III	15%	27%	19%	12%	27%
Section IV	22%	19%	15%	30%	15%

On this particular test, (B) is the overall winner, but it only really won Section I. The habitual loser (E) actually tied for first place on Section III. (D) would be by far the best choice on Section IV.

Based on this information, I can't come up with any letter that would be better than any other, though I would probably stick with (B) or (D) if I had to choose.

Increase your odds: Eliminate the duds

A better choice than random guessing from a pool of five choices is random guessing from a pool of two or three choices. Your odds of getting a right answer improve if you can eliminate a wrong answer or two.

To increase your odds, use a process of elimination to get rid of wrong answers on every question. Take this step first, unless you get one of those rare questions where the right answer jumps out at you. Cross out the wrong answers — physically cross them off in your test booklet so they don't distract you, which makes spotting the right answer easier, or, if you're still guessing, the possible right answers.

Readying Yourself for Battle

All your preparation will be in vain if you don't get to take the test. And if you don't feel calm and collected, you may blow questions that you should get right. So keep in mind the following checklist to help you before and during test day:

- **Prepare your bag the night before.** Make sure you have your identification, several No. 2 pencils, and maybe even a pen. Pack your watch (make sure it doesn't beep) and bring a snack, drink, and some coins with you in case you want to nibble during your break. Do this the night before so you don't frantically try to find a pencil sharpener the night before! No need to add to your stress.

- **Don't stress yourself out that evening.** The night before the LSAT, if you feel compelled to study (I know, you can't help yourself), *don't* do a new test. Instead, review a section you have already done and know the answers to, which can reinforce strategies and boost your confidence.

- **Get enough sleep the night before.** Don't stay up partying, unless you find that a hangover usually improves your test scores. Definitely don't stay up studying; you're not going to discover anything extra at that point.

- **Wake up on time.** If you live far away from the test center, set your alarm extra early — or even consider spending the night at a hotel nearby. You don't need the extra stress of lack of sleep.

- **Eat breakfast.** Your brain functions better if you feed it. Drink coffee if you like to drink coffee (though not too much — it's a *diuretic,* which makes you have to pee more). Try to eat something sustaining — protein and whole grains last longer than a sugary donut. See "The test-day diet" sidebar in this chapter.

- **Make sure you know how to get to the testing site.** Don't wait until the morning of your test to try and find directions. If you don't know exactly where the site is or where to park at the site, call the test site earlier in the week for complete directions. If you have trouble parking, leave extra early. If you have to feed a parking meter, bring enough coins.

- **Get to the center early.** Doing so gives you time to get settled in, handle any last minute emergencies, and make a last bathroom stop to preempt a future bladder attack.

The test-day diet

A growling stomach and a full bladder can drive you crazy when you're trying to work out the details of an LSAT question. Are there ways to prevent these problems? Sure! Protein, fat, and salt are the keys. One of the reasons low-carb diets work is that protein and fat prevent your appetite from raring back too soon; for example, if you eat a meal heavy in protein, you don't get hungry for several hours. Try it — eat something like two eggs with cheese cooked in olive oil, and see how long it takes you to get hungry again. As for the need to pee,

you can do two things: Don't drink too much, and consume salt. Water, coffee, tea, cola, and orange juice all have a diuretic effect, which can send you running to the bathroom or wishing you could. Salty snacks can reverse this phenomenon, helping your body hold on to its fluids. Beef jerky, peanuts, and sports drinks with electrolytes can prevent your bladder from filling too fast. Hey, it may not be the healthiest diet, but desperate times call for desperate measures.

After you finish these steps, you're ready to take the test!

If your test starts at 8:30 a.m., you must present yourself at the testing center by 8 a.m. If it starts at 12:30 p.m., you must be there by 12 p.m.

What to bring

Don't sabotage your LSAT score by forgetting the essentials. The following items are essential to a smooth test experience:

- ✔ **Make sure you have your admission ticket and a photo ID.** You can't get into the test without them.

- ✔ **Bring some No. 2 pencils and functional erasers.** The erasers can be attached to the pencils or separate; just make sure they work.

- ✔ **Bring a clock of some kind.** The test center should have a clock, but don't count on it. You need to be able to time your tests yourself. It doesn't matter what sort of timer you bring as long as you know how to use it, it's reasonably accurate, and it doesn't make any noise. Oh, and it ought to be fairly small; a grandfather clock isn't a good idea.

- ✔ **Bring a sweatshirt or jacket.** Wear something with short sleeves underneath. When I was in law school, the overenthusiastic climate control system cooled the classrooms to about 50 degrees in fall and spring and warmed them up to 85 degrees in the winter. Like an explorer in the wild, you need to be prepared for any eventuality.

- ✔ **Bring a snack.** Don't eat it during the test, but if you're hungry, definitely shove it into your mouth at break time. Try to make it something sustaining — an energy bar, nuts, or a candy bar packed with peanuts. Protein helps alertness; carbohydrates make some people sleepy.

- ✔ **Bring money.** The site may have a nearby vending machine, which may save your sanity at break time.

What to leave at home

When taking the LSAT, you and your fellow test-takers want to be focused on the test. You don't want anything that could bother you (or others sitting around you). The following list includes items you can't (or shouldn't) bring into your test site:

✔ **A calculator, a dictionary, an LSAT strategy book, or any other reading material:** These items are all taboo in LSAT Land.

✔ **A wireless phone or pager:** Turn it off. The last thing any test-takers need is to have a phone or pager going off during the test.

✔ **Heavy perfume.** Other test-takers may be sensitive to it, and you really don't need to be sabotaging their efforts.

✔ **Worries, anxieties, and angst.** Worrying doesn't help now. Breathe deeply and remember everything you read in this book.

Life After the LSAT: What to Do Now?

So you've done it; you've completed an LSAT. What now? Are you happy with your performance? Great! Sit back and wait for your score. Unhappy? You don't have to accept your score; you can cancel it if you really want to. Got a score that you don't like? Try, try again, if your heart is still in it.

Yeah, that worked for me

If you liked what you did, or you're just relieved that you're finished and you just can't be bothered to worry about it now that it's done, you don't have to do anything except wait for your results. If you registered online, your score arrives by e-mail in about three weeks. Printed score reports arrive about four weeks after the test; if you have an online account with the Law School Admissions Council (LSAC), you pay a fee of $25 to get hard-copy mailings. You can also call a telephone service called TelScore to get your score over the phone about three weeks after the test; this service costs $10. The LSAC Web site (www.lsac.org) has more information.

Wait, I can do better than that!

What if you weren't happy with your performance? You may have choked on a Analytical Reasoning problem and not managed to finish the section. You may have been hung over and sleepy and not had the emotional fortitude to do your best. You may have been too sick to think straight. You may have kept a running tally of questions you thought you got wrong, and decided that this test wasn't going to give you a score that you wanted.

Canceling a score

If you decide that your life would be better if your score on this test never saw the light of day, you can cancel it. There are two ways to do this:

✔ You can cancel the score before leaving the test center; talk to the test administrators.

✔ You can send the LSAC a signed fax or overnight letter requesting that the LSAC cancel your score. You have *nine* calendar days to take this action. If you miss the deadline, your score stands.

If you cancel your score, that's the end of it. Neither you nor anyone else will ever see it.

Requesting a rescore

What if you were sure you had received a certain score, but when you receive the official report, it was much lower than you expected? You can ask the LSAC to rescore your answer sheet. An actual person reads your answer sheet, comparing your answers with the correct ones. You have 60 days to request this service, which you must do in writing. Send a letter or fax to the LSAC with your name, Social Security number or LSAT ID number, test center name and number, your reason for requesting a hand score, and payment of $34.

If you encountered a problem at the test center — for example, if you had no desk and had to hold your test on your knees — report it to the test supervisor. To make sure the problem is considered, you must also report it in writing to the LSAC; you have nine days to do this.

Repeating the LSAT

If you're disappointed with your score and you're sure you can do better, you can take the LSAT again. The LSAC's data shows that scores often improve (slightly) for repeat test takers. They also sometimes drop.

Before you commit to retaking the LSAT, look at the policy of the law schools you want to apply to. Most law schools average your LSAT scores, so even a big improvement may not make that much difference. A few schools look at the best or most recent test.

The LSAC allows you to take the LSAT three times in a two-year period, which includes any tests whose scores you cancel. That means you can't just take the LSAT every time it's offered, hoping to get the perfect test that gives you the perfect score.

Even if your score improves dramatically the second or third time you take the test, law schools still see your lower scores. The LSAC sends all LSAT scores in its reports to law schools. It also informs the law schools that the true measure of your ability is the *average* of your scores, not the highest score, especially if you took the tests during a short period of time. In the score report, your scores appear individually and averaged.

You don't have to let your scores speak for themselves. If something happened that made you score badly, tell the law schools when you send in your application. Think of this as an opportunity to practice your persuasive writing skills. If you do a good job, the law school may be so impressed with your potential as an advocate that it will accept you despite a low LSAT score.

The LSAC's score report automatically includes the scores of all the LSATs you've taken (or registered for and missed) since June 1, 1998; cancellations also appear. If you took the LSAT between June 1, 1994 and June 1, 1998, and you want law schools to see that score, you can send a written request to the LSAC. If you took the test before June 1, 1994, the LSAC won't report the score. If you decide to apply to law school but your only LSAT scores are more than ten years old, you have to take the test again. Lucky you!

Looking to the future, some (not all) state bar associations demand the law school admission records of applicants. To be safe, keep all the paperwork from your law school admission process until you've been sworn in and added that lovely "Esq." to your name.

Chapter 3

The Lowdown on Law School Admissions

*I*f you're reading a book about the LSAT, you're probably considering applying to law school, aren't you? Well, get ready for a great adventure. Applying to law school can be a rough ride, not to be attempted by the lukewarm or ambivalent. If you're truly committed to acquiring a legal education, though, the application process can be challenging and even sort of exciting. You may get to live someplace new, meet new friends, and broaden your horizons in ways you never considered.

In this chapter, I discuss the ins and outs of choosing schools and applying for admission, as well as the importance of the LSAT in this process.

Choosing a Law School

Not all law schools are created equal. You may still be able to get a fine legal education at most of them, but understand that different law schools have different characteristics. Some are extremely competitive, while others are easier to get into. Some have excellent practical legal programs, while others have a more theoretical approach to the law. Some have more financial aid than others. You need to decide what you want in a school before you let schools decide whether they want you.

Where to go for information

Sifting through the vast amount of often conflicting information about law school can be a daunting task. Finding that information in the first place, though, doesn't have to be hard. Tons of sources are available, some more subjective than others. Here are a few places to look for info:

✔ **Bookstores and libraries:** Plenty of books are available about law school, legal practice, and similar topics. (Check out *Law School For Dummies* by Rebecca Fae Greene [Wiley]!)

✔ **Career placement or guidance offices at colleges and universities:** Not only do these offices have tons of information on various schools and career options, but they also may even have real people who can give you sensible advice.

✔ **Friends and acquaintances who've gone to law school:** Don't neglect your personal network! If you know someone who's gone through this process, pump her brain.

✔ **The Internet:** If you're interested in a particular law school, check out its Web site. You can also find numerous Web sites devoted to legal issues, including law school.

✔ **Law school forums:** The Law School Admission Council (LSAC) (www.lsac.org) holds several law school forums in major cities each fall. At a forum, you can speak with real people about selecting a law school, the admissions process, whether law school is right for you, and other concerns.

Tons of information is out there, so you don't have to apply to law school in the dark. Read the next section, "Important considerations," for some of the information you want to find to help you decide which law school is right for you.

Important considerations

Keep these important considerations in mind when choosing law schools to which you want to apply:

✔ **Cost.** This is a biggie. Some law schools are expensive; others are extremely expensive. You need to decide how much money you want to spend (or are able to spend) on your education, bearing in mind that law school debts can stick with you for much of your working life. (*Note:* Cost often goes hand in hand with exclusivity and prestige, which may mean that spending more on a prestigious school results in a better payoff after graduation.)

✔ **Location.** Where do you want to live? Do you want to be near your family? Do you want to be able to drive to the beach or the mountains (when you're supposed to be in class)? Do you hate harsh winters? Do you consider yourself an East Coast, West Coast, or Midwestern person? You're going to live near your law school for nearly three years; liking the location is important. Location also plays a role in cost considerations; living in New York City is going to be more expensive than living in Baton Rouge.

✔ **Public or private.** Some law schools are affiliated with state university systems, while others are part of private universities. Some public schools are cheaper than private ones, especially for in-state residents. On the other hand, public schools tend to suffer more at the whim of state legislators, who can cut their budgets at the drop of a hat. As for prestige, some public institutions regularly appear in the top of the law school rankings, so you can't assume that a private school will be more prestigious than a public one.

✔ **Exclusivity.** Does getting into a school with a minute acceptance rate matter to you? Some schools accept a large proportion of applicants, while others skim the thin layer of cream off a giant vat of applications. This point goes with school rank (see later in this bulleted list); if exclusivity matters to you, then keep it in mind. If you have ambitions of working in the nation's top firms or climbing the judicial ladder all the way to the bench of the U.S. Supreme Court, you should attend an exclusive, highly ranked school. If you want a JD so you can make a better living in your hometown, an exclusive school may not be worth the money it would cost you.

✔ **Reputation.** Reputation is such a nebulous concept; the American Bar Association (ABA) especially hates this aspect of the *U.S. News & World Report* ranking scheme. Still, though, reputation can matter. Consider where you plan to practice law; you want to attend a school that people in that area respect.

✔ **Attrition rate.** At some law schools, if you can get in, you're virtually certain to graduate (barring extreme circumstances). Other schools let in a wider variety of applicants, but get rid of many of them before graduation by failing a number of students in their law school classes. No one wants to get weeded out. On the other hand, schools with high attrition rates can be easier to get into in the first place; if your scores are a bit low but you plan to work like crazy in law school, a law school with a high attrition rate may work well for you.

✔ **Quality of life.** Some law schools are known for being happy places to get a legal education. Students are friendly to one another, social events are at least as important as classes, and the surrounding area is bucolic. Other places aren't as pleasant, with more competition among students and crowded, ill-equipped facilities. You can get a decent education at either type, but you'll have more fun at some schools than at others.

✔ **Campus life.** You want to spend your law school years among friends, if at all possible, which often means finding a school attended by people similar to you. Some schools have a fairly wealthy student body, and most students are attending full-time within a year or two of graduation from undergraduate college. Other schools have more older students, many of whom may have day jobs and families. Some schools have more racial minorities than others. Some are more open to alternative lifestyles than others. If any aspect of campus life matters to you, take some time to research whether the schools that interest you will be congenial places to spend three years of your life.

✔ **Grading practices.** Grades are extremely important to law students; some law firms base most of their hiring decisions on law school grades. Not all schools grade alike, though. Many schools grade on a *mean,* in which the majority of students get a particular grade (such as B) with only a few getting grades above or below. Other schools grade most classes Pass-Fail. Still others don't control grading at all, and grades depend on the professors' whims.

✔ **Curriculum.** What do you want to study in law school? Do you like large lectures or small seminars? Some schools offer joint degrees, such as JD-MBA combinations. Some schools are known for specialties, such as international or environmental law. Some law schools are very liberal; others are extremely conservative. Bear that in mind when choosing your school — and your future friends — for the next three years.

✔ **Opportunities for practical experience.** Clinical programs offer students the opportunity to put their legal skills in practice early on, which can be invaluable for finding jobs and working after graduation. Some schools emphasize this more than others, providing ample opportunity for students to get hands-on practice during the school year through clinics and internships.

✔ **Bar pass rate.** You can't practice law if you can't pass the bar exam. Some schools have a higher bar pass rate than others. Don't think though that no one passes the bar from schools with low pass rates. All a lower bar pass rate means is their students overall aren't as well prepared for the bar exam. (Not that law school prepares you to pass the bar; that's what post-graduation Bar Review is for.)

✔ **Where you want to live after law school.** This point is more significant than you may realize. If you want to live on the East Coast, you'll have better luck finding a job there if you attend a nearby law school than if you go off to Washington State. If you want to practice in South Carolina, a degree from the University of South Carolina may be more useful than a degree from Michigan, even though Michigan is ranked higher.

✔ **Alumni network.** You're going to spend much more of your life as a law school graduate than as a law school student. Knowing that the friends you made in law school can help you down the road is great. A strong alumni network can be a valuable resource for the rest of your life.

Choosing a law school is a lot like choosing a college. A wide variety of choice is out there; try to find a selection of schools that really suits you.

Keeping ranking in mind

Nearly 200 law schools in the country are approved by the ABA. (Incidentally, you should go to an ABA-approved school; lots of state bars don't admit graduates of schools that aren't approved.) Naturally people have tried to rank the nation's law schools. (See the sidebar, "Law school rankings and accreditation" in this chapter for more about these organizations that rank law schools.)

In a field as competitive as law, are you really surprised to know that people are constantly trying to come up with ways to look superior to one another? Law firms like to know the relative rankings of the schools from which they recruit. Law students like to compare their school to others, usually in the hopes of bragging that their school is better than another one. Law school recruiters like to emphasize how attractive their graduates are to prospective employers.

What do you think is one of the main things *U.S. News & World Report* looks at when ranking schools? You guessed it — LSAT scores! The higher the average LSAT score of admitted students, the higher the school's ranking. Other things count, but LSAT scores are very important. These schools are best because their students' LSATs are best, which means the schools are best . . . .Wait, that's circular reasoning . . . .

The ABA and the LSAC (the folks who create and run the LSAT; see Chapter 1) disapprove of commercial rankings, which try to reduce every law school to a single numeric value, and they do have a point. There's a lot more to an individual school than a number published in *U.S. News & World Report*. They're right; rankings are random and don't reflect the true value of the education available at any given institution.

Unfortunately in the real world, rank does indeed matter. Certain law firms and other employers take their new hires from a specific group of schools, and they very rarely consider applications from anyone who didn't attend that select group, no matter how good their grades or outside experiences. The rationale behind this practice is that top law schools have already selected the "best" law students — the ones with the highest grades and LSAT scores — and these people will naturally make the best lawyers. Although in practice that doesn't always turn out to be the case, you'll have a hard time convincing those employers otherwise.

However, the law school rankings are far from perfect. Law school rankings change from year to year, sometimes dramatically. A school may be ranked seventh one year, fall to 14th the next year, and jump back to sixth the next. That fluidity alone should be a warning to you not to take rankings too seriously; there's no way a school's total quality can change that much that fast.

Are you wondering about how schools are ranked? The following list breaks down the law school rankings (which *doesn't* list specific schools):

- **Top Ten.** These are the top of the pile.
- **First Tier.** This is the top 50 schools.
- **Second Tier.** Schools ranked 50 through 100.
- **Third Tier.** Schools ranked 101 through 150
- **Fourth Tier.** Schools ranked 151 through 186 (or so).

Firms that care about these rankings restrict their recruiting to particular tiers. Other firms are more interested in the whole applicant — her grades, interests, commitment to living in a particular place, work ethic, and so on — and will interview dedicated students from any school if they seem like good prospects.

Law school rankings and accreditation

Every year, *U.S. News & World Report* publishes rankings of colleges and universities — you may remember looking at these rankings when you applied to undergrad. Law schools don't escape this ranking system. When *U.S. News* sets out to rank law schools, it concocts a numerical score based on several criteria, including the school's assessment by lawyers and peer institutions (that is, the opinion that other law schools and legal professionals hold about the school), average LSAT scores and undergraduate GPAs of the current entering class, the percentage of applicants who were accepted, student-faculty ratios, employment rate of graduates at graduation and nine months after graduation, and the school's bar passage rate in its state.

ABA accreditation is a whole different ball game. The ABA keeps tabs on law schools in an effort to make sure that all law school graduates have received a meaningful legal education; it has kept a list of accredited schools since 1921. It doesn't accredit schools where the average undergraduate GPA or LSAT score of the students is below a certain level (143 is the cutoff score for the average LSAT). After a law school applies for accreditation, the ABA evaluates it based on its admissions standards, its faculty, its facilities and library, and its program of instruction. ABA committee members actually visit the school for several days and attend classes. If a school passes the test, the ABA gives it provisional approval for three to five years, followed by full approval if it maintains its standards. (Read more about this on the ABA's Web site, www.abanet.org.) ABA accreditation is currently a touchy topic for several law schools that want accreditation but haven't yet received it, especially with the advent of online law schools in recent years.

Why do some firms rely on these rankings? Reading resumes takes a lot less time if they throw out all the ones from lower-ranking schools. They figure the law schools have already selected a good batch of future lawyers, and find it easier to limit their recruiting to those elite schools.

Rank also affects future salaries and career possibilities. Graduates of the highest-ranked law schools tend to have the highest salaries. People who eventually become law professors and major judges also come more often from higher-ranked schools.

Okay, that's depressing. So let me give you some better news. Pretty much every graduate from every law school in the country can get a legal job. That means people who barely scrape through the lowest-ranked school still get employed as lawyers, and plenty of them make good money, too. And plenty of folks who graduate from top-ten law schools don't end up practicing law at all.

What's the moral of all this? Rankings do matter, but not for everyone and not in every case. So take them seriously, but not too seriously. More importantly, look at what you want out of law school and what you want to do afterwards.

Filling Out All the Forms — Applying to Law School

Applying to law school is an art all its own. You have to choose several schools, go through the expensive and complicated application rigamarole, scrounge around for financial aid, and then decide which one of the schools that accepts you is the one you want to attend. The whole process is daunting and really not much fun, but it's the only way to get where you want to go (assuming law school *is*, in fact, where you want to go).

Pick more than one

Back when you applied for undergrad, you probably picked out several schools that interested you and applied to them all (unless you got in somewhere early). You probably knew that you couldn't count on getting into them all, but if you applied to several places, you'd most likely get into at least one and wouldn't be stuck after high school with no college to attend. (If you were fortunate, several schools accepted you and then you got to choose the one that best suited your needs.) The same principle holds true in law school.

Unless you're sure you'll get into a particular school, or there's only one place you could feasibly attend, pick several schools that you think satisfy your craving for legal education. The prevailing wisdom is to apply to at least one or two safety schools, where you're pretty sure you'll be accepted, four or five schools where you have a reasonable chance of getting in, and one or two "reaches," schools where you probably won't be accepted but still have a chance of getting in.

Applying to law schools isn't cheap. At about $65 a pop, the cost can really add up if you apply to several schools. Spend your money wisely — only send applications to schools you would seriously consider attending. If you already know that you could attend only your local law school, don't waste money applying anywhere else.

How admissions work

Law school admission offices run on a yearly cycle. In the fall, the admissions folks begin accepting applications. In the winter and spring, they read these applications and send out letters of acceptance. They spend the late spring and summer assembling the entering class — fielding letters of commitment, accepting students off the waiting list when spots open up, and getting ready for the next admission cycle. Most law schools promise to send out letters of admission by April 15, though many of them begin sending them out much sooner.

The early bird . . .

Most law schools stop accepting applications in January and give students until March to get in all their supporting materials. That doesn't necessarily mean you can wait until January with impunity. Many schools start reviewing applications in the fall, and may begin sending out acceptance letters in November. As a result, the applicants whose applications aren't complete until March are competing for fewer spaces in the entering class, which decreases their chances of acceptance.

Some law schools offer an early notification option — students who get their applications in really early — during September, October, or November of the year before they want to matriculate — receive a decision by December. This option doesn't necessarily commit a student to that particular law school, though make sure to check the rules at individual schools.

If you know you're going to apply to law school, take the LSAT in June or October of the year you want to apply. You can take it in December and still get in, but you're risking losing a space to someone who gets his or her documents in earlier. Some law schools accept February LSAT results, but don't wait that late; most of the spaces in a class are gone by the time the results come in.

A complete application

Are you wondering what comprises a complete law-school application? Don't worry. Check out this list for a complete inventory of what most law schools consider a complete application:

✔ A completed, signed application form

✔ LSAT score

✔ Transcripts of prior academic record, submitted through the Law School Data Assembly Service (LSDAS)

✔ Dean's certification forms from your prior institutions of higher education (to prove that you went there)

✔ Letters of recommendation, submitted through the LSDAS or independently

✔ A personal statement — an essay you write, usually explaining why you want to go to law school

✔ Application fee — $65 or so, though this number tends to creep upward year by year

You may also have to send in forms about your state residency, financial needs, or other relevant bits of information. Every school's admission form tells you exactly what to send.

If one single piece of your application isn't in place by the deadline (or whenever the admissions committee stops considering applications), no one will read any of it. So if the form for your dean's certification goes missing, or one of your recommenders forgets to send in his letter, your application is no good and you've wasted your money.

Review of applications

Many law schools receive far more applicants than they have spaces in an entering class. Obviously the first thing admissions committees look at is academic credentials and LSAT scores, but numbers definitely aren't everything. Every year competitive law schools admit some students with fairly low scores and grades, and reject some with stellar numbers.

Law schools are interested in more than mere academic ability. They're also hoping to create law school classes that represent a diversity of backgrounds and interests, as well as with the potential to do great things — nothing makes a law school look as good as an illustrious group of alumni. Here are a few of the factors that admissions committees consider:

✔ Geography (where students come from); schools like to get people from all over the place

✔ Ideological background

✔ Race and ethnicity

✔ Unique experiences and responses to hardships

Your personal statement is a good place to mention anything you want the admissions committee to know about you, anything that makes you unique.

Law schools take great pains to assure everyone that their admissions committees and faculty members really do read every single application, regardless of how low the applicant's numbers are. Usually at least two people review each file. Each reader makes a recommendation, whether to admit, deny, wait-list, or put on hold to reconsider later. If the two readers disagree about an application, it goes to a third reader. At the end of the admission cycle, the committee ranks everyone who is left; some get in, some don't, and some get waitlisted.

If you are waitlisted, don't despair. Every year many students receive phone calls from law schools during the summer, often as late as the week before classes begin, informing them that they have been admitted. This doesn't give you much time to prepare or find housing, but it's not a bad deal if you're flexible.

Minorities and women in the law

Lawyers in the United States are still overwhelmingly white. No minority group — African American, Latino, Asian American, Native American — comprises more than 4 percent of American lawyers. The Law School Admission Council (LSAC) wants to change this. Its Minorities Interested in Legal Education (MILE) program is designed to help minority college students find out more about the law and enter law school.

Women have entered the legal profession in record numbers; these days nearly half of all American law students are female. On the other hand, women make up very few of the partners in law firms or top general counsel in corporations. Female lawyers are much more likely than males to be dissatisfied with the legal profession and to leave it after practicing for only a few years, which is due to a variety of reasons, including long hours, lack of flexibility in scheduling, frustration with promotion opportunities, and just plain boredom. These problems also afflict men, but women seem to quit more often. Many law firms have begun offering flexible schedules and part-time partnership tracks, which does seem to be improving the situation somewhat, but attrition among female attorneys is still high. On the other hand, many female attorneys do manage to find congenial employment in settings other than large law firms; the law can be a very good field for someone who wants to work on her own, often part-time.

Don't forget the money

Law school is expensive, and seems to get pricier every year. The good news is that most people can get financial aid if they need it, from their law school or from other sources. The bad news is that the vast majority of this aid is in the form of loans, not scholarships or grants, which means you have to pay it back after you're done with law school. (The large loans are one of the factors that keep many recent and not-so-recent law school grads working outrageous hours for law firms.)

If you need financial aid, you have to fill out the correct paperwork fairly early, by March of the year in which you'll matriculate. The financial aid office at your future law school can tell you what you need to do.

Some law schools offer merit scholarships to applicants with very high LSAT scores. Some schools also waive application fees for high scorers, which is slightly less lucrative than free tuition but still pleasant.

Part II
Analytical Reasoning: Players, Rules, and Logic

The 5th Wave   By Rich Tennant

They're moving on to the Analytical Reasoning questions. That should daze and confuse them enough for us to finish changing the tire and get the heck out of here.

LSAT TEST BOOK PUBLISHERS

In this part . . .

Oh, no, not Analytical Reasoning! They're the infamous reasoning problems, sometimes called "logic games" (though not by this book), that send students scurrying for the hills. They're tough, it's true, but they're also eminently doable. In fact, Analytical Reasoning is the only section where right answers are usually immediately apparent if you work the problems correctly. A computer could do these problems, but would probably have trouble with the rest of the LSAT. So take heart; you, too, can discover how to be a computer. Just stay calm, remain focused, and let the rules be your guide.

Chapter 4

Zen and the Art of Analytical Reasoning

In This Chapter
▶ Meeting the LSAT Analytical Reasoning section
▶ Discovering the calm, cool approach to reading and thinking
▶ Diagramming the rules
▶ Making deductions based on the data given

The LSAT's Analytical Reasoning section — which some people like to call "Logic Games" — is the section that most intimidates LSAT takers. It's the bugaboo, the bête noir, the boogeyman, the nemesis of otherwise calm, cool, and collected would-be law students. No one does problems like these logic brain drainers in school, so they're a completely new experience for many people.

But I do have some good news: These problems are totally teachable. In this chapter, I show you tips that can really improve your score. After you figure out how to work these problems, you may even find that Analytical Reasoning becomes one of your best sections. See, after you crack the code of a particular fact pattern, answering every single question correctly is entirely possible. Shoot, some people even work these for fun!

In this chapter, I introduce the Analytical Reasoning section and describe the techniques to tackle the problems. I'm not really explaining a Zen approach to this section. In fact, I'm not sure the LSAT even falls in the recommended list of Zen activities, but one Zen principle is of immeasurable value in approaching Analytical Reasoning problems. Zen teaches its practitioners to always live in the present moment, mindful of their current circumstances and to not worry about the past or the future. That's the way to work these problems. Immerse yourself into each fact pattern, live it for a few minutes, and then erase it from your mind and move on to the next one. Before you know it, you'll be done.

Analyzing the Analytical Reasoning Section

The Analytical Reasoning section is a 35-minute section that contains four fact patterns, followed by five to eight questions for each problem. The fact patterns present scenarios with two or three sets of variables — people, dorm rooms, places around an office table, stuff like that — and introduce rules that govern them. The questions test your ability to apply the given rules and make deductions.

Why is this section on the LSAT?

According to the LSAC (the Law School Admissions Council and the people who make the LSAT — see Chapter 1 for more about them), "Analytical reasoning items are designed to measure your ability to understand a structure of relationships and to draw logical conclusions about the structure."

But why include logic puzzles on a test to determine who enters law school, and by extension, who gets to be a lawyer? Law students don't work logic problems. Lawyers don't work logic problems. A test like this may predict who would make, for example, an excellent restaurant manager, allocating staff to different nights, or a hospital administrator, handling the complex interlocking schedules of doctors and nurses, but most lawyers don't need to schedule the singers in a competition or determine the order of horses at a racetrack.

Lawyers do, however, need to read carefully, noting all details. When they apply what they've read to a fact pattern, they can't omit anything that's written, and they can't add anything that's not written. For example, when a lawyer reads a law to see if it affects her client, she has to read every word of it, but she can't assume it says anything that's not expressly written. Lawyers have to apply rules to given situations, and they usually have to determine themselves exactly how these rules work. The thought processes involved in applying statutory and case law to a scenario aren't very different from the thinking involved in applying rules to Analytical Reasoning problems. Furthermore, lawyers must concentrate on these arcane laws for very long periods of time, and the LSAT indicates whether you can maintain that kind of attention to detail for an extended period. So, no, lawyers don't need to work analytical reasoning problems, but yes, they do use the skills these problems test.

What skills do I need?

The skills that the Analytical Reasoning section tests are no different from those skills you need to succeed on the test's Logical Reasoning (see Chapter 8) and Reading Comprehension (see Chapter 14) sections. Basically, you need to be able to

✔ Read closely and carefully

✔ Understand what you read and be able to spot implications

✔ Maintain your concentration long enough to get through a bunch of questions accurately

Taking the Zen Approach to Analytical Reasoning Problems

Remember the Zen approach — live in the present. Each section contains four Analytical Reasoning problems. Make each problem the sole focus of your being for the time it takes you to work it. Don't think about anything else. Ignore the other problems, the rest of the test, your hopes and fears about the future, and your dinner plans for that evening. To help, pretend that you're a computer, and the fact pattern is a program. You're an old-fashioned computer, too — you can run only one problem at a time. But after you load that program into your memory, you command it completely. You understand how the rules apply to the characters, and can spot impossible situations. (What, you say a computer isn't very Zen? Tell me, what exists more in the present moment than a computer? You'll never catch a computer getting distracted by irrelevancies.)

When you walk into the room where you'll take the LSAT, leave your baggage at the door. Forget your preconceived notions about the LSAT, law, and standardized tests. Everything you need to answer all the questions on the test is contained in the test booklet. Don't read anything into the questions. Focus your whole being on the page in front of you.

Every question in every problem can be answered. Really.

Staying calm

Panic destroys some potentially brilliant LSAT scores. A student starts to work on a problem, doesn't immediately see the relationships between the characters, looks at the clock, realizes she only has five minutes left and seven questions left to answer, looks back at the problem, gets increasingly flustered, looks at the clock again, sees her future sinking into the mire, and suddenly she's blown the whole thing. It happens all the time.

Guess what? That approach doesn't help! Sure, it's nerve-racking, facing down this scary test amidst a roomful of strangers, and knowing that your professional life could be on the line. And your life may well have issues that deserve panic. But Analytical Reasoning problems don't have to be one of them.

Getting lost in the cosmos

Every Analytical Reasoning puzzle is like a little world all its own. The way to succeed is to immerse yourself in that world and become totally familiar with its rules and possibilities. In fact, while you immerse yourself into this problem's little world, you want to leave all your knowledge about the subject at home.

In order to become as familiar with that world as possible, take your time setting up your diagram (see "Setting Yourself Up for Success Step-by-Step" later in this chapter) before you start attempting the questions. Explore the rules, savoring the possibilities like a connoisseur with a mouthful of fine wine. Make sure you understand what the rules say and consider what they don't say. Draw any conclusions you can. The better you prepare yourself, the easier the questions will be.

Deciding which problem to confront first

Each Analytical Reasoning section has four problems. You don't have to work them in order. You can work the second problem first, and then the fourth, the first, and the third if you want to. No one cares — just as long as you answer them all.

How do you decide which problem to work first? Some test-prep courses suggest that you first skim all four problems and rank them in order of difficulty. Then you work them in order, from easiest to hardest. I don't recommend this. Why? Because deciphering at first glance which problems are difficult and which ones aren't isn't easy and takes away from time you could be using to solve the problems. Some problems that look hard are actually easy when you bite into them. You can waste a lot of time ranking your problems that would be better used simply working them.

My suggestion: Work the problems with the most questions first. If you have one problem that has eight questions and another one that has five, work the one with eight questions first. Each fact pattern takes about the same amount of time to figure out, so if you choose the problem with the largest number of questions, you'll maximize the payoff from your investment.

Working one problem at a time

Whatever you do, don't skip from one problem to another without finishing all that problem's questions. If you do, you're wasting time and unnecessarily addling your brain. Think about it — for every problem, you need to hold in your head a fact pattern that allows you to answer its questions. Sure, you write down notes and a diagram, but the most important information is in your brain. If you leave one problem unfinished to work on another, intending to come back to the first one, when you do come back, you have to relearn the facts. Your brain can only hold so much information at once. Given the time it takes to figure out the facts of one problem, you can get a better score by finishing three problems and skipping one than by frantically trying to hit parts of all four problems.

After you finish a problem, forget about it. It's over and done with, and you need the brain space it occupied. Be Zen — live in the present. Leave the past in the past.

After finishing a problem, take a break. Breathe, twist your head around, and look around the room. In the spirit of this whole Zen strategy, do a little meditation. Do whatever it takes to clear your mind for the next problem.

Remember, every Analytical Reasoning problem on the LSAT can be solved. The test-makers have checked to make sure. They're also trying to trip you up, though, to make you stumble under pressure. You don't have to let that happen.

Setting Yourself Up for Success Step-by-Step

Every problem can be tackled in much the same way. Differences between them are superficial; they all respond to the same thought processes. This section discusses the steps you take to successfully prepare yourself to tackle the questions.

Start by reading

When starting a new problem, read the fact pattern completely. That tip may sound obvious, but it's true. Read the facts first. Then skim the questions, and I do mean skim — reading them carefully at this stage is pointless and may even be depressing. You just want an idea of what the test-makers are asking to help you organize your information. (Actually, if you want to ignore the questions completely at this stage, that's fine, too. Everything you need to know right now is in the facts and rules.)

The fact pattern may read like this:

A boutique law firm does work in four areas of law: employment, immigration, real estate, and tax. Four attorneys share the work; their names are Burton, Duway, Cheatham, and Howard. Each attorney specializes in at least one and at most three areas of law. The areas of law are distributed among the attorneys according to the following specifications:

Duway specializes in anything that is also Cheatham's specialty.

Burton and Howard do not share any specialties with Cheatham.

One attorney specializes in tax.

Two attorneys specialize in employment.

Two attorneys specialize in real estate.

Three attorneys specialize in immigration.

Don't worry about the questions that go with this problem at the moment; this problem appears in all its glory in Chapter 6, but I'm simply using it as an illustration at the moment.

Use the following tips to help you avoid common test-taking traps:

- ✔ **Don't assume too much.** Assume only what the problem actually tells you. For example, the statement "If Mary is at work, then Oliver is, too" doesn't imply that if Oliver is at work, then Mary is, too.

- ✔ **Don't get caught up in speculation that doesn't involve the facts as stated.** The people and things in Analytical Reasoning problems aren't real, and don't actually have relationships with one another.

- ✔ **Don't try to go too fast.** Sure, you're under a time limit, but in this case, slowing down is the best way to speed up. Slow is smooth, and smooth is fast.

- ✔ **Don't lose your cool.** The LSAC-devils want you to get flustered, which absolutely doesn't help you think clearly. Just breathe deeply, ignore the room around you, and forget about the impact this test has on your future. Live in the present moment, it's just you, a pencil, and an Analytical Reasoning problem.

Close and careful reading is the ticket to success. All the information you need is right in front of you.

Diagram what you know

Don't attempt to work an Analytical Reasoning problem in your head. Doing so only leads to confusion, frustration, and wrong answers. The instructions at the beginning of the Analytical Reasoning section suggest "It may be useful to draw a rough diagram." That suggestion is both a bit of an understatement and also perfectly true. Drawing a diagram is extremely useful, but remember to keep it rough. You don't need to create a masterpiece. (You're trying to get into law school, not the Art Institute of Chicago.)

You want your diagram to incorporate all the information to solve the problem. If you organize your data correctly, you don't need to refer back to the rules at all. By organizing your data correctly, you can also add to the information provided in the rules, because you're going to include information that isn't expressly stated but that you have deduced on your own.

When taking the LSAT, you have 35 minutes to answer all the questions in an Analytical Reasoning section. If you plan to hit all four problems, you have 8 minutes and 45 seconds for each one. Your diagram is a crucial part of answering the questions, and it's worth spending some time on; three or four minutes to process the data and draw a sketch isn't unreasonable, given how much it'll help you. Just don't spend more than five minutes, or you risk running out of time. (And don't fret; slavishly watching the clock and dropping your sketch at a set time will probably just raise your stress level; if you practice enough, you'll get comfortable with the time constraints.)

Use letters, not names

You have a bunch of lawyers with names, and they all practice specialties that also have names, right? Wrong. Well, partly right — lawyers and specialties are categories. But they only exist because the LSAT test-makers needed some subjects to plug into a set of logical rules. The test-makers could have used animals and tricks, rocket ships and launch sites, or any other two categories.

What you need to do is identify your categories of subjects, and then give them your own names.

The best way to identify and name your categories is to note them by initial. The little LSAT test-devils expect you to take this step; that's why everything in the problem starts with a different letter. So you may make two lists:

Lawyers: B, C, D, H

Specialties: e, i, r, t

This easy step saves a ton of time and brainpower. Now when you read a problem or a question, you have a shorthand notation for it, and you don't waste your time fretting about irrelevancies, such as why Burton and Cheatham don't share specialties, or why this firm needs three immigration lawyers. Also, notice that the two categories have different visual styles – lawyers are in capital letters, and specialties are in lowercase. This helps you visually distinguish between the categories without having to think about what they refer to.

You're not taking an art test

Want to know a simple truth about diagrams? No one cares what the diagrams look like. What matters is that they make sense to you. You want your diagrams to include the information you need to work a problem, but nothing more than that. Seriously, the LSAT isn't a test of drawing diagrams and charts. No one will ever see them.

In addition, you don't have much space. You can't use scratch paper, so you're stuck using the bits of blank space in your test booklet, which sometimes is no more than a couple of square inches.

Keep your diagram as simple as possible. Too much detail wastes your time and doesn't help you. Use the following pointers when you're drafting your diagrams.

- ✔ You don't need a complete chart with all the lines drawn in; you just need headings and space under them or next to them.
- ✔ You don't need to worry about the names that professional logicians use for particular types of diagram; you just need something that makes sense.
- ✔ You don't need a complicated set of symbols; you need a minimal shorthand that makes sense to you for the five or ten minutes you spend on a problem.

Drawing the diagram

After you make lists of the abbreviations for your characters, you need to decide how to organize them. The first thing to do is to decide what information is permanent. That information is your *axis*, your solid foundation.

For example, if the problem involves scheduling something during days of the week, the week is part of your axis. Write the days across the page, leaving space underneath each one to plug in data.

If the problem involves two sets of data, but only one of them changes — say you have five students, each of whom must take two of three possible classes — then use the five students as an axis, perhaps listing them, initial one on top of the other.

If the problem involves some sort of shape, for example a rectangular racetrack or a round conference table, draw that shape. Mark the places where the subjects are. (See Chapter 5 for an example of this kind of diagram.)

Some problems may require you to keep track of several categories of data. In that case, you might draw a diagram with two columns, with space underneath. (See Chapter 5 for an example of such a problem.)

Consider the problem with the lawyers. This question involves matching attorneys with specialties. Because you always have only four specialties, and attorneys are going to have multiple specialties, the easiest way to organize your notes is by specialty, not by attorney. Visually, the simplest way to list the specialties is by number of attorneys, not alphabetically; that way, you always know that the specialty at the top should have one attorney and the one at the bottom three, with two for each one in the middle. Note the number of attorneys each one must hold. One way to draft your diagram is like this:

t: __

e: __ __

r: __ __

i: __ __ __

Add in details

Next, go through your rules. Write them down. If you can, incorporate them into the chart. Otherwise, jot them down in shorthand.

Here are some shorthand symbols you can use:

- ✔ < or > to mark items that are greater or less than others
- ✔ Boxes or circles to identify data that don't ever change
- ✔ Parentheses ( ) to mark data that may change
- ✔ Arrows → (or ->) to mark relationships that go in only one direction
- ✔ = or ≠ to mark positive or negative relationships
- ✔ x through a letter to indicate that it can't be someplace or do something
- ✔ Underscores _ to mark spaces that must be filled

Ultimately what matters is that you understand your own symbols. You don't need to write anything in the notation of symbolic logic; you just have to understand it for a few minutes.

In the law firm example, you know that D shares all of C's specialties. Does this mean D can only specialize in something C also specializes in? No. Does it mean C can only specialize in something D specializes in? Yes. You could note this C → D, remembering that this rule doesn't restrict D to the same specialties as C. You also know that C shares no specialties with B or H. Note this: C ≠ B or H.

Add to your diagram the following notes:

C -> D; C ≠ B or H

The idea is to get all your information summarized in the same place in a quickly readable format. You need to be able to answer all the questions from your notes, without ever referring back to the original rules.

Think it through

After you make shorthand notations of the rules, stop and think for a moment. Usually you can draw at least one or two conclusions from the rules that have already been presented.

Take the law firm. You can make a few deductions that make your thinking process easier. First, if D must share C's specialties, then C is never the sole specialist in an area. That means C can't specialize in tax. Second, if C can't share a specialty with B or H, that means the only three attorneys who can specialize in the same area must be B, H, and D. They must be the three who specialize in immigration. Third, C must be paired with D in any specialty, and only the two of them can specialize in that particular area. That means that they must practice either employment or real estate law, because those are the two areas that need exactly two attorneys. This information is valuable; note it on the chart.

t: __ (not C)

e: __ __ (C D)

r: __ __ (C D)

i: B H D

C -> D; C ≠ B or H

Could C and D practice both employment and real estate? It looks like that would be fine, as long as B or H practices tax.

 Analytical Reasoning problems are all about deductions — you answer them by applying the rules to the information you're given. You can help yourself if you spend a minute or two thinking about the implications of the rules before you start answering the questions. Doing so often reveals other data that you can add to the permanent part of your diagram. It has another advantage: The better you understand the microcosm of the fact pattern, the easier working out the questions is.

That being said, don't stress if you can't make any big deductions. If a minute or two of contemplation results in nothing, move on to the questions. You'll get more familiar with the rules as you work the problems, and often you'll discover connections that hid from you at first.

Tackling the Questions — Finally!

After you plug a fact pattern into your head, draw your diagram, plug in the rules that fit, and make notes of the ones that don't, answering the questions is your next step.

Note: This chapter doesn't go into great detail about specific questions. This chapter is just an overview. Chapters 5 through 7 go into specifics.

Picking your battles

Start with the first question and work your way to the last one. Or jump around, answering the questions that appeal to you first and postponing the more unpleasant ones. Either approach works.

No matter how you approach the questions, don't waste time trying to rate them in order of difficulty, which isn't an easy art. Often a question that looks difficult turns out to be easy. You can more effectively use your precious seconds by actually working through the possible choices and answering the questions. Anyway, you don't want to assume anything will be too difficult — that's defeatist.

All the questions can be answered on their own. They're not arranged in order of difficulty. You don't need to answer the first questions to make sense of the later ones. Starting with the first question, proceeding to the end, and getting every answer right is entirely possible. So if you like working that way, by all means do so. On the other hand, if you instantly spot a question that looks easy to you, go ahead and work it. Just be sure you answer all the questions!

What if you get stuck on a question? Skip it and move on. Exploring the fact pattern by answering the other questions may help you solve it. If you still can't figure it out, don't fret; just guess – pick a letter and fill it in – and get on with the rest of the test. (See Chapter 2 for some guidance on guessing.)

Reading the questions carefully

Work a few LSAT Analytical Reasoning problems, and they all start to look the same. The details change but the style of the fact patterns and the language of the questions don't. Here are some of the most common question types:

- ✔ "Which one of the following must be true?"
- ✔ "Which one of the following could be true?"
- ✔ "Each of the following could be true EXCEPT:"
- ✔ "Which one of the following CANNOT be true?"
- ✔ "Which one of the following could be the order, from first to last, in which the subjects are arranged?"
- ✔ "Each of the following could be an accurate and complete list of qualified subjects EXCEPT:"
- ✔ "If A is fifth, which one of the following could be true?"

You get the idea.

No matter the questions' styles, read them carefully. Misreading them is easy. You don't want to work a problem as if the question wants something that's true when, in fact, it wants something that's false.

Watch out for the words "could" and "must." If something "must" be true, there is no way it couldn't be true. If something "could" be true, there may be some possibility that it could be true but it doesn't *have* to be. Don't confuse the two.

Remembering that four wrongs make a right

Identifying wrong answers is a lot easier than searching for the right one. For some reason, violations of rules are easy to spot; answers that don't violate any rules can be harder to see. If you can eliminate four of the answers as wrong, you have your right answer.

Spot the violators

Always look for obvious rule violations first, which can sometimes help you eliminate two or three of the answer choices right off the bat.

For example, the rules say that D specializes in anything that C specializes in. That means that any answer choice that has D specializing in something that isn't also C's specialty must be wrong. You have deduced that C can't practice tax law; therefore any answer choice that makes C a taxman must be wrong.

When you identify wrong answers, use your pencil to cross out their letters. Doing so allows you to see exactly which answers are still possible, so you don't forget that you've already ruled some out.

Test the remaining possibilities

After you eliminate the obvious wrong answers, test the remaining choices. In Chapters 5 through 7, I illustrate in much more detail exactly how to do this. For the moment, just remember: Don't try to work Analytical Reasoning problems in your head. Use your notes and diagrams to plug in data and see what happens. Just think of yourself as a computer. The answer will reveal itself if you stay calm and apply the rules in an orderly and systematic fashion.

Always check all five answers, even if you think you've found the right one. You may discover that your right answer isn't so right after all, and even if you don't, you'll be that much more sure of your answer.

Zen . . . and a Bit of Practice

I know of one certain thing that can help you figure out Analytical Reasoning problems: practice. The only reason these problems are so intimidating is that no one uses these skills in daily life. Universities don't teach classes on them. Most jobs don't require them. For many of you, the LSAT is the first and last time you encounter problems in this format. But you can figure out how to do them — with just some practice.

Chapters 5 through 7 contain several Analytical Reasoning problems with detailed explanations. Remember Zen: Work your way through them, one at a time. Practice with the sample tests in the back of the book. If you want still more practice, get some LSAT PrepTests from the LSAC and concentrate on the Analytical Reasoning problems. You can also go to www. dummies.com and search for this book's title to find another set of practice questions with detailed explanations. Fear not; you, too, can figure out how to work these puppies.

Chapter 5

Analyze This: A Walk through Four Analytical Reasoning Problems

. . . .

In This Chapter

▶ Working through four Analytical Reasoning problems

▶ Figuring out how to read the rules

▶ Practicing drawing diagrams and making logical connections

▶ Blasting on through some questions

. . . .

The best way to get a handle on the Analytical Reasoning section is to walk through a few problems step by step. The first few problems you face can be a bit daunting (okay, very daunting), but remember, they can all be solved, and with practice, you can get the hang of them. The process I explain in Chapter 4 is basically the same for every problem:

✔ Read the problem and skim the questions.

✔ Make a diagram to show what you know.

✔ Fill in the details.

✔ Stop and think a moment.

✔ Answer those questions, taking each as it comes.

In this chapter, I present four Analytical Reasoning problems and walk you through their solutions. The LSAT Analytical Reasoning section always has four problems, and I wanted to give you a representative sample of what an LSAT Analytical Reasoning section might look like. The problems in this chapter are very much like those that appear on the LSAT — same style, same difficulty, same thought processes required.

Introducing . . . The College Singers!

Drum roll please . . . your first problem! Start by reading it and just skimming the questions. Remember, the facts are all in the introductory information. The questions give you an idea what to look for, but don't dwell on them at this point. They can't help you at first.

<u>Questions 1–5</u>

A college singing group has to choose four of its members to send to a competition so it decides to rank them. The members are named Emily, Frances, Georgina, Hillary, Ingrid, and Jill.

Hillary and Jill are sopranos.

Emily and Georgina are altos.

No singer ranks exactly the same as another one (for example, there can be no ties).

Four of the singers are juniors and two are seniors.

Both seniors are among the four highest-ranked singers.

One soprano is among the four highest-ranked singers. This soprano is a senior.

Hillary ranks higher than Frances and Ingrid.

Emily and Georgina rank higher than Hillary.

1. Who must be a junior?

    (A) Jill

    (B) Emily

    (C) Hillary

    (D) Georgina

    (E) Ingrid

2. If Ingrid ranks fourth, what else must be true?

    (A) Ingrid is a junior.

    (B) Frances is a senior.

    (C) Ingrid is a senior.

    (D) Frances is a junior.

    (E) Emily is a junior.

3. If Frances is a senior, which of the following could be false?

    (A) Ingrid is an alto.

    (B) Emily is a junior.

    (C) Frances is an alto.

    (D) Frances ranks fourth.

    (E) Georgina is a junior.

4. Which of the following could be false?

    (A) Emily ranks higher than Ingrid.

    (B) Georgina ranks higher than Ingrid.

    (C) Georgina ranks higher than Jill.

    (D) Hillary ranks higher than Jill.

    (E) Emily ranks higher than Georgina.

5. Which of the following is a complete list of the singers who could be altos?

    (A) Emily and Georgina

    (B) Emily, Georgina, and Frances

    (C) Emily, Georgina, and Hillary

    (D) Emily, Georgina, and Ingrid

    (E) Emily, Georgina, Frances, and Ingrid

An orderly chaos: Let the solution begin

Whoa! All these singers, and juniors and seniors, and vocal parts! What a mess!

Okay, now slow down and take a deep breath. You can solve this problem. In fact, all the Analytical Reasoning problems on the LSAT can be solved. Just take it slow and easy and do one thing at a time.

This problem gives you a lot of well-organized information. You already know a lot about these women. So write down what you know in a format that both takes little time and makes sense, with some extra room inside and around the diagram for jotting down extra notes. (For more about diagramming Analytical Reasoning problems, see Chapter 4.)

Start diagramming what you know

First, abbreviate all the singers by the first letters of their names: E, F, G, H, I, J. You're going to want to identify vocal parts, too, so use (a) for altos and (s) for sopranos. "Junior" and "senior" can be abbreviated Jr and Sr. You want all your abbreviations to look different so they help you identify categories without thinking about them.

Now, you want to put all the rules into your own shorthand, so you can answer the questions without looking back at the original rules; it's much faster to refer to your own diagram and notes. In this problem, you won't really have to use much shorthand because most of the rules can be expressed visually.

As you incorporate a rule into your diagram or write it in shorthand, cross it off in the test booklet. That will help you be sure you've covered everything.

You want to rank these singers, so pull out information that shows rank. You know that Hillary is above Frances and Ingrid but below Emily and Georgina, so plot them out like this:

$$E \qquad\qquad G$$
$$H$$
$$F \qquad\qquad I$$

At this point you don't know about relative rankings between Emily and Georgina or between Frances and Ingrid. And you know what? You don't have to worry about it yet. In fact, it may not even come up. You don't know where Jill fits yet, so put her on hold for the moment.

Fill in the details

You know something else about several of these singers: their vocal parts. So add that information to the diagram, using (a) to mark altos and (s) to mark sopranos, and jotting in Jill off to the side:

$$E\,(a) \qquad\qquad G\,(a)$$
$$H\,(s)$$
$$F \qquad\qquad I$$
$$J\,(s)$$

Stop and ponder a moment

After you consider the vocal parts, can you figure out anything else about the rankings? What about Jill?

You may be surprised to discover that you now know something about her: Jill can't be in the top four. Why not? Hillary has to be in the top four, ranked either third if only Emily and Georgina are ahead of her, or possibly fourth if Jill is ranked ahead of her. But you know only one soprano can make the cut, and Hillary is it. So Jill, who is also a soprano, must be ranked either fifth or sixth. You also know that the soprano in the top four is a senior, so that must be Hillary.

This process of deduction and making conclusions is key to solving Analytical Reasoning problems. Lots of students skip this step. Don't be one of them. Always spend a little while trying to tease more conclusions out of your rules before you start the questions. This will save you time in the long run.

After you draw your diagram, fill in the details, and think about the situation; you're ready to tackle the questions.

On to those pesky questions

You now have a pretty good foundation from which to work. You've figured out everything you can from the available information, so don't worry any more about diagramming and just start on the questions.

The diagram is your permanent information, and will be the basis for any jottings you do to answer the questions. Whether you constantly redraw it or jot down notes for each question and then erase them, you will always go back to this original at the start of every question.

1. Who must be a junior?

   (A) Jill

   (B) Emily

   (C) Hillary

   (D) Georgina

   (E) Ingrid

You know that both seniors are in the top four, but you don't know which two are the seniors, so you can't assume that anyone potentially in the top four is a junior. Emily, Hillary, and Georgina are therefore definitely out; cross off (B), (C), and (D). Ingrid has to rank either fourth or fifth, which means she could possibly make the top four and therefore possibly be a senior; cross off (E). Is there anyone you know for sure isn't in the top four? Why yes! Jill! So (A) is your answer.

This is a good example of how not to oversolve a problem. Lots of LSAT-takers make life difficult for themselves by making Analytical Reasoning problems unnecessarily difficult. Don't assume a problem is more complicated than it is; sometimes they're quite easy. If you're sure of an answer and it appears in the choices, then take it and go on.

2. If Ingrid ranks fourth, what else must be true?

   (A) Ingrid is a junior.

   (B) Frances is a senior.

   (C) Ingrid is a senior.

   (D) Frances is a junior.

   (E) Emily is a junior.

Looking at the chart, if Ingrid ranks fourth, Frances then must rank fifth or sixth (Jill will be whichever one Frances isn't), and therefore isn't in the top four. If she's not in the top four, she must be a junior because both seniors are in the top four. Determining whether Emily or Ingrid is a junior or senior is impossible; (A), (B), (C), and (E) all could be true but don't have to be. So the answer to Question 2 is (D).

3. If Frances is a senior, which one of the following could be false?

   (A) Ingrid is an alto.

   (B) Emily is a junior.

   (C) Frances is an alto.

   (D) Frances ranks fourth.

   (E) Georgina is a junior.

Question 3 requires a bit more work. First, consider the possibilities.

If Frances is a senior, then she is in the top four and must rank fourth, so (D) is out. She also must be an alto, because Hillary is a soprano and only one soprano is allowed, so (C) is out.

You know that Hillary is a senior, and only two seniors can be in the top four, so if Frances is also a senior, then Emily and Georgina must be juniors, which nixes (B) and (E), leaving (A) as the answer.

$$E \ (a) \ Jr \qquad\qquad G \ (a) \ Jr$$
$$H \ (s) \ Sr$$
$$F \ (a) \ Sr$$
$$I \qquad\qquad J \ (s)$$

So could Ingrid be an alto? Sure. She could also be a soprano; the group must have the three altos in the top four, but no rule states that the total number of altos must be either three or four, so she could be an alto or soprano.

4. Which one of the following could be false?

   (A) Emily ranks higher than Ingrid.

   (B) Georgina ranks higher than Ingrid.

   (C) Georgina ranks higher than Jill.

   (D) Hillary ranks higher than Jill.

   (E) Emily ranks higher than Georgina.

Question 4 is easy. Just look at the chart of the singers you know have to be in the top four: Emily, Georgina, and Hillary. Four of the questions involve the relative rankings of one person known to be in the top four and one person definitely or possibly excluded from it. You know Emily ranks higher than Ingrid, so (A) is out. You know the same thing about Georgina, so (B) is out. Georgina definitely ranks higher than poor Jill, so (C) is out. And you know Hillary ranks higher than Jill, eliminating (D). But you have no way of knowing whether Emily ranks higher than Georgina, so (E) is your answer.

If the wording of this question stumped you, you aren't alone. Take a look at the question: "Which one of the following could be false?" Be sure to keep in mind what the right and wrong choices will look like. The wrong choices are those that MUST be true. That means you can eliminate every answer choice that you know must be true. You should knock (A) and (B) out of the running immediately.

5. Which one of the following is a complete list of the singers who could be altos?

   (A) Emily and Georgina

   (B) Emily, Georgina, and Frances

   (C) Emily, Georgina, and Hillary

   (D) Emily, Georgina, and Ingrid

   (E) Emily, Georgina, Frances, and Ingrid

You already know that Emily and Georgina are altos. You know Hillary is a soprano, so you nix (C). Could Frances be an alto? Sure; nothing says she can't be. Eliminate (A) and (D). What about Ingrid? Well, in the absence of other information, she's identical to Frances (at least as far as these computations go), so she could be an alto, too. So that gives you (E) as the answer.

The Contractor's Workers

If you came up with the right answers with the first problem, give yourself a quick pat on the back. Take a couple of deep breaths. Look out the window or twiddle your pencil for a moment or two. Feel relaxed? Good.

If you had trouble following the logic, please read or reread Chapter 4 before you proceed to the next problem.

Now forget all about the little doo-wap group. Empty your mind of the details concerning junior altos and senior sopranos, and tackle the conundrum of which workers to assign to the work site.

Questions 6–11

A building contractor must send six workers to work on a construction site. His workers include three electricians: Harry, Ingrid, and Jésus; three carpenters: Mary, Nick, and Oliver; and three bricklayers: Andrew, Bert, and Ernie. He must observe the following conditions:

Oliver and Andrew absolutely refuse to work together.

Jésus and Harry always fight, so they can't be put on the job together.

Jésus refuses to work unless Mary is there too.

Mary refuses to work unless Oliver is also on the job.

6. Which one of the following is an acceptable roster of workers?

    (A) Ingrid, Jésus, Mary, Oliver, Bert, Ernie

    (B) Ingrid, Jésus, Nick, Oliver, Bert, Ernie

    (C) Ingrid, Jésus, Mary, Nick, Bert, Ernie

    (D) Harry, Jésus, Mary, Oliver, Andrew, Bert

    (E) Harry, Ingrid, Mary, Nick, Bert, Ernie

7. If the contractor sends all three bricklayers to the site, what else must be true?

    (A) He sends exactly two carpenters.

    (B) He sends all three electricians.

    (C) He sends exactly one electrician.

    (D) He sends Mary.

    (E) He sends Nick.

8. The six-person crew must include

    (A) Exactly two electricians

    (B) Exactly three electricians

    (C) Exactly two bricklayers

    (D) At least one of every kind of worker

    (E) At least two carpenters

9. Each of the following pairs of workers could be sent to the job EXCEPT

    (A) Ingrid and Jésus

    (B) Mary and Oliver

    (C) Jésus and Andrew

    (D) Bert and Ernie

    (E) Mary and Ernie

10. If the contractor includes Andrew in the crew, which of the following pairs of workers must he also include?

    (A) Harry and Jésus

    (B) Harry and Ingrid

    (C) Ingrid and Oliver

    (D) Mary and Ernie

    (E) Nick and Oliver

11. If the contractor selects Jésus and Nick, which one of the following could be true?

    (A) The contractor selects exactly one carpenter.

    (B) The contractor selects exactly two carpenters.

    (C) The contractor selects Harry.

    (D) The contractor selects Andrew.

    (E) The contractor selects Ernie.

Making sense of the rules

Well, this problem looks pretty complicated. What's up with all these workers who can't get along with each other? What kind of building contractor would let his employees get away with this? (Sounds like a few people need some interpersonal-skills counseling!)

Ah, but this problem isn't really about construction workers (and their childish problems). It's only an occasion for you to show off your ability at analytical thinking. So if you're worried about the apparent love triangle among Jésus, Mary, and Oliver, or if you spent a summer working construction and you know that no contractor would ever send more bricklayers to a project than electricians, forget about it. Check your preconceived notions at the door, and focus on the underlying logic.

Start a basic diagram

Forget the names; list the workers by letter. Put the letters under headings so you can visualize which letter goes with which job:

Electricians	Carpenters	Bricklayers
H	M	A
I	N	B
J	O	E

Fill in the details

You know that anything that pairs O and A is no good; same with anything that pairs J and H. So note this: O x A; J x H. In this case, the *x* means that O and A or J and H can't be together. See Chapter 4 for more on shorthand; this is a flexible art, and you can really use whatever notations make sense to you.

You also know that if J is at work, M must be too, and if M is at work, O must be too. So if J is at work, M and O are both there too. If M is at work, so is O, although J doesn't necessarily have to be. Note this: If J, -> M + O; M -> O. That means that JMO will move as a unit when they go to work; if one of them is at work, the other two are. JM move as a unit when they're not at work; O can go to work without them.

Make some deductions

Think a little more. You know that if O is working, A isn't. That effectively means that if M is working, A isn't, because M won't work without O. So: M x A. And because JMO is a unit at work, JMO x A.

What about M and H? Not a problem; J won't work with H and he won't work without M, but M doesn't mind if H is there, so they can be together. That doesn't matter in this case, though, because M is always with J; so JM x H.

Now combine the rules that you can. Remember six workers must go to the site, and three must stay home. You can make a diagram with nine spaces, six at work and three at home, and you can note each worker's specialty in parentheses; you can refer back to your occupations diagram for quick reference if you need to. Because JMO must be together at work, one of the diagrams will have all three of them together on the work side. If JMO go to work, then H and A stay home; you don't know for sure who else does what, but that's a good start. Make another diagram with JMO at home; if those three stay home, then everyone else must go to work. There's one more possibility; JM stay home and O goes to work. If O works, A doesn't, which leaves the other five workers to go to work.

Your complete diagram could look like this:

Electricians	Carpenters	Bricklayers
H	M	A
I	N	B
J	O	E

Work: J(e) M(c) O(c) __ __ __ Home: H(e) A(b)

Work: H(e) A(b) I(e) N(c) B(b) E(b) Home: J(e) M(c) O(c)

Work: H(e) O(c) I(e) N(c) B(b) E(b) Home: J(e) M(c) A(b)

Wow! Now, that's a diagram! That tells you a whole lot. Now you're ready to confront those questions.

As you can see, this diagram summarizes the information pretty well, and should make working the problems much easier. Analytical Reasoning problems often lend themselves to this type of diagram; it might seem like this is a really easy question, but combining the rules like this certainly is part of that ease. You could work it without creating this diagram, but it might take a little longer. The more conclusions you can draw before you start the questions, the easier your job will be when you try to answer them.

Confronting the questions

Okay, time to plunge in. Remember to use your trusty diagram, and keep your cool.

6. Which one of the following is an acceptable roster of workers?

   (A) Ingrid, Jésus, Mary, Oliver, Bert, Ernie

   (B) Ingrid, Jésus, Nick, Oliver, Bert, Ernie

   (C) Harry, Jésus, Mary, Nick, Bert, Ernie

   (D) Harry, Jésus, Mary, Oliver, Andrew, Bert

   (E) Harry, Ingrid, Mary, Nick, Bert, Ernie

Make your life easy by eliminating the obviously wrong answers first. Pick a rule and start eliminating; keep going until only one answer is left. Anything with O and A is wrong — eliminate (D). Anything with J and H is wrong — eliminate (C). Anything with J but without M is wrong — eliminate (B). Anything with M but without O is wrong — eliminate (E). That leaves (A). (A) violates no rules, so it's the correct answer.

7. If the contractor sends all three bricklayers to the site, what else must be true?

   (A) He sends exactly two carpenters.

   (B) He sends all three electricians.

   (C) He sends exactly one electrician.

   (D) He sends Mary.

   (E) He sends Nick.

If all three bricklayers (A, B, and E) go, your diagram would be this one:

Work: H(e) A(b) I(e) N(c) B(b) E(b) Home: J(e) M(c) O(c)

Skimming the answers, you see that (E) looks good; the contractor must send Nick. That's your answer, but if you want to check the others, here goes. J is an electrician, so all three electricians can't go; (B) is out. You know M doesn't go, so (D) is out. He's only sending one carpenter, N, so (A) is out, and he's sending two electricians, I and H, so (C) is out. (E) it is.

8. The six-person crew must include

    (A) Exactly two electricians

    (B) Exactly three electricians

    (C) Exactly two bricklayers

    (D) At least one of every kind of worker

    (E) At least two carpenters

Remember, when you answer this question, you're looking for an answer that MUST be true, not one that might be true but doesn't have to be. Okay, remember your two possible scenarios

Work: J(e) M(c) O(c) _ _ _ Home: H(e) A(b)

Work: H(e) A(b) I(e) N(c) B(b) E(b) Home: J(e) M(c) O(c)

You already know from Question 7 that sending all three bricklayers is possible, so (C) is out. You know that H and J can't go out together, so the contractor can't send three electricians; (B) is out. In Question 7, the crew would have only one carpenter, so (E) is out. Is it possible to have a crew of all bricklayers and all carpenters? No. O and A don't work together, so you can never have all three bricklayers and all three carpenters at the same site. The contractor must have one of each worker, which makes (D) look like the answer. To double-check (A), does a crew have to have exactly two electricians? If the contractor sends only J to do electrics, he could make a crew like this:

Work: J(e) M(c) O(c) N(c) B(b) E(b) _ _ _ Home: H(e) A(b) I(e)

So sending only one electrician is possible. (D) is correct.

9. Each of the following pairs of workers could be sent to the job EXCEPT

    (A) Ingrid and Jésus

    (B) Mary and Oliver

    (C) Jésus and Andrew

    (D) Bert and Ernie

    (E) Mary and Ernie

Look at your diagrams, and try to find an answer with a pair that is always on opposite sides of the pattern. According to the diagram, the answer should be (C). J and A can never be on the same crew. It's visually obvious, but here's the full explanation anyway. You know that I and J are okay, so (A) is out. M and O are okay, so (B) is out. B and E are okay, so (D) is out, and M and E are okay, so (E) is out. That leaves (C). Why can't J and A be on the same crew? Well, J doesn't work without M, and M doesn't work without O, but O doesn't work with A, so J and A effectively can't work together, although they bear no obvious animosity toward one another. (C) it is.

10. If the contractor includes Andrew in the crew, which of the following pairs of workers must he also include?

    (A) Harry and Jésus

    (B) Harry and Ingrid

    (C) Ingrid and Oliver

    (D) Mary and Ernie

    (E) Nick and Oliver

Look at your diagrams. If A is on a crew, J, M, and O can't be on it. So any answer that includes one of them must be wrong — eliminate (A), (C), (D), and (E), which leaves (B). Any problem with H or I working with A? No. (B) is correct.

11. If the contractor selects Jésus and Nick, which one of the following could be true?

    (A) The contractor selects exactly one carpenter.

    (B) The contractor selects exactly two carpenters.

    (C) The contractor selects Harry.

    (D) The contractor selects Andrew.

    (E) The contractor selects Ernie.

If J and N go, then the diagram will look like this:

Work: J(e) M(c) O(c) N(c) __ __ __ Home: H(e) A(b)

You have established that J can't work with A, so (D) is out. You know H and J fight, so (C) is out. If J is working, so are M and O; with N, that makes three carpenters, so (A) and (B) are out. Any problem with E? No. (E) is correct.

Pizza Anyone?

If you've stuck with me so far, congratulations. If all those explanations make sense to you, congratulations again. If you worked the problems before reading the answers and got them all right, then terrific, you can stop studying now if you want (but I don't recommend it — the problems in this chapter are about to get harder). If you think you need some more, then keep going. Lots more Analytical Reasoning problems await you in this and the following chapters.

You probably have a good idea of how these questions work by now. This section contains the third of four Analytical Reasoning problems with explanations. This problem and the next are a bit harder than the first two in the chapter, but you can still solve them by using the same techniques.

Now take the time to help some college students solve their pizza dilemma before they all starve.

Questions 12–18

Eight college students order a custom-made pizza; the pizza has eight slices with a single topping on each slice. The toppings are anchovies, black olives, Canadian bacon, green olives, hamburger, onion, pepperoni, and sausage. Each slice is of equal size, so four slices make exactly half the pizza; a slice is opposite the slice separated from it by three slices. The students are very picky about how their pizza is arranged, so they have set the following conditions:

Each slice contains exactly one topping; each topping is used exactly once.

When counting from one slice to another, always move clockwise.

The green olive slice must be adjacent to and clockwise from the pepperoni slice.

The black olive slice is directly across from the anchovies slice.

The anchovies slice can't be adjacent to the Canadian bacon slice.

The Canadian bacon slice can't be adjacent to the hamburger slice.

12. If the hamburger slice is directly opposite the green olive slice, then which of the following slices CANNOT be adjacent to the pepperoni slice?

(A) Anchovies

(B) Black olives

(C) Canadian bacon

(D) Onion

(E) Sausage

13. If the Canadian bacon slice isn't adjacent to the black olive slice, which two slices could be adjacent to the onion slice?

(A) Anchovies and sausage

(B) Canadian bacon and anchovies

(C) Canadian bacon and sausage

(D) Hamburger and black olives

(E) Sausage and black olives

14. Which one of the following could be a series of four adjacent slices, moving clockwise?

(A) Anchovies, sausage, hamburger, black olives

(B) Black olives, Canadian bacon, hamburger, pepperoni

(C) Black olives, green olives, pepperoni, hamburger

(D) Hamburger, anchovies, Canadian bacon, sausage

(E) Onion, black olives, pepperoni, green olives

15. If the Canadian bacon slice is opposite the hamburger slice, what is the minimum possible number of slices that could fit between the hamburger slice and the black olive slice?

    (A) Zero

    (B) One

    (C) Two

    (D) Three

    (E) Four

16. If the pepperoni slice is adjacent to the onion slice, which slice must be adjacent to the anchovies slice?

    (A) Black olives

    (B) Canadian bacon

    (C) Green olives

    (D) Hamburger

    (E) Sausage

17. If the black olives slice is between the pepperoni and Canadian bacon, which two slices could be adjacent to the sausage slice?

    (A) Anchovies and green olives

    (B) Anchovies and pepperoni

    (C) Canadian bacon and anchovies

    (D) Canadian bacon and green olives

    (E) Hamburger and onion

18. What is the minimum possible number of slices between the green olives slice and the onion slice?

    (A) Zero

    (B) One

    (C) Two

    (D) Three

    (E) Four

Solving the pizza problem

Yikes! This is a tough one! How in the world do you figure this out? (Is it lunchtime yet?)

Organize, organize

Okay, first step. Forget that this problem is about pizza. Forget the names of the toppings. Make an alphabetical list of starting letters: A, B, C, G, H, O, P, S, and work from that list.

Start a diagram

You're basically looking at a clock face with this problem. The easiest way to visualize this problem is to draw it — just make a simple line drawing, noting 8 positions. You know B is opposite A, so draw them in; they're like the north and south poles, and there will be three slices of pizza separating them in each direction. You know that C can't be next to A, so mark it out in both positions. This drawing is your permanent diagram, the basis for all your calculations.

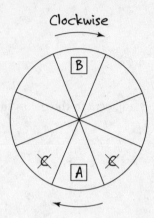

Add details

You know a few other things as well. You know that G must always come after P, so write them down as a unit: P-G. You know C can't be next to H, so note that C x H.

Think and deduce

What else can you determine? Well, because P and G operate as a unit, and they're going to have to occupy two of three consecutive spaces (because there will never be more than three consecutive spaces between the poles, B and A), nothing can come between them. Whichever side of the diagram they occupy, the slice that shares it with them has to be next to either A or B.

This information never changes. Use this information as the foundation to answer all the questions.

Slicing into the questions

This is a challenging problem. You're going to have to use your diagram to solve this one, but don't worry; it all makes sense once you work it out.

12. If the hamburger slice is directly opposite the green olive slice, then which of the following slices CANNOT be adjacent to the pepperoni slice?

   (A) Anchovies

   (B) Black olives

   (C) Canadian bacon

   (D) Onion

   (E) Sausage

Maybe some people can answer these questions quickly in their heads, but I don't know them. So try each possibility; sketch it out on the diagram. If you put P clockwise from A, and G clockwise from P, and H opposite G, then you have to put C between G and B because the only other slots are next to H. O and S can go there with no problem. So (A) is okay, and therefore wrong. Now try (B). If you put P clockwise from B and G clockwise from P, and H opposite G, you run into a problem. C can't fit into any of the three remaining slots. It looks like (B) is the answer. Just to check the other choices, you can fit in C-P-G if C is clockwise from B; O-H-S or S-H-O would work on the other side, so (C) is wrong. If you put O clockwise from A, and P-G clockwise from that, you get B-C-S-H, which works, so (D) is wrong. If you put S clockwise from A, and P-G clockwise from that, you get B-C-S-H, which also works, so (E) is wrong. (B) is correct.

13. If the Canadian bacon slice isn't adjacent to the black olive slice, which two slices could be adjacent to the onion slice?

   (A) Anchovies and sausage

   (B) Canadian bacon and anchovies

   (C) Canadian bacon and sausage

   (D) Hamburger and black olives

   (E) Sausage and black olives

Are you getting hungry? Oh well. Going back to your trusty diagram, note the added rule that C can't be on either side of B. That leaves two slots for C, the two positions at 90 degrees from A and B (like the east and west poles, if there is such a thing); assume for the moment it doesn't matter what side you put it on. P and G have to go together, so they have to be on the opposite side of whichever side C is on; so does H, because it can't go next to C. O can either be between C and B, or between C and A. C and B isn't a choice, but C and A is. The correct answer is (B). The order of slices could go: A, P, G, H, B, S, C, O. If you want to check the other answers, you'll see you can't fit exactly one slice between any of them.

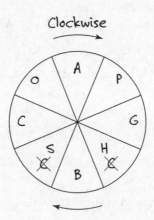

14. Which one of the following could be a series of four adjacent slices, moving clockwise?

   (A) Anchovies, sausage, hamburger, black olives

   (B) Black olives, Canadian bacon, hamburger, pepperoni

   (C) Black olives, green olives, pepperoni, hamburger

   (D) Hamburger, anchovies, Canadian bacon, sausage

   (E) Onion, black olives, pepperoni, green olives

You can answer this question fairly quickly if you look for rule violations. (A) has A and B separated by two slices, which is impossible if they're opposite one another. Cross it off. (B) starts with B, which means the slice that follows P is A; but P must always be followed by G, so that doesn't work. (C) has G and P in the wrong order. (D) has A and C next to each other, which is forbidden. Looks like (E); no violations there, so that's the answer.

15. If the Canadian bacon slice is opposite the hamburger slice, what is the minimum possible number of slices that could fit between the hamburger slice and the black olive slice?

   (A) Zero

   (B) One

   (C) Two

   (D) Three

   (E) Four

Well, where can C go? You have to leave room for P-G, so C and H can't be equidistant from B and A on either side (meaning, they can't occupy the positions at 90 degrees to A and B, the east and west poles). The only places you can put C are adjacent to B, which puts H adjacent to A. If you put H clockwise from A, then two slices separate it from B. There's no way to move it closer, so (C) is the answer. The order of slices could go: A, H, P, G, B, C, S, O. (Sketch it out if you're stumped! And remember you can eliminate (E) and (D) right away because with A opposite B, you can never have three or four slices separating a slice from either one of them.)

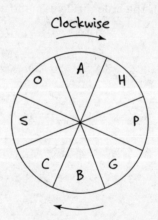

Clockwise

16. If the pepperoni slice is adjacent to the onion slice, which slice must be adjacent to the anchovies slice?

   (A) Black olives

   (B) Canadian bacon

   (C) Green olives

   (D) Hamburger

   (E) Sausage

The only way to have P next to O is if O is counterclockwise of P-G. So try putting O-P-G clockwise from B. In order to keep C from being next to either H or A, C has to be adjacent to B, and H has to be adjacent to A, with S separating C and A. That would give you the following order: A, H, S, C, B, O, P, G. (Sketch that out, and it'll be clear.) If you try it the other way, with O-P-G running clockwise from A, it works the same way; H must be next to A in order to keep C from touching either A or H. (But because you're supposed to move clockwise, putting H clockwise from A is the better choice, not that it makes any real difference.) So the answer is (D).

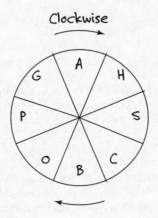

17. If the black olives slice is between the pepperoni and Canadian bacon, which two slices could be adjacent to the sausage slice?

    (A) Anchovies and green olives

    (B) Anchovies and pepperoni

    (C) Canadian bacon and anchovies

    (D) Canadian bacon and green olives

    (E) Hamburger and onion

From this information, you know where four slices must be: P-G must be clockwise from B, and C must be counterclockwise; A is in its usual place. That leaves three slots for O, H, and S. H must be adjacent to A, on either side; O and S can each occupy any of the three slots, with the understanding that they can't both be adjacent to A. That means S could conceivably be between A and G, so (A) looks good. There are two slices between A and P, so (B) is out. There are two slices between C and A, so (C) is out. B and P are between C and G, so (D) is out. H and O are either adjacent to one another, or have A between them, so (E) is out. (A) is correct.

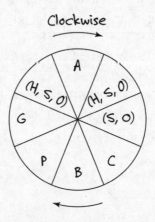

18. What is the minimum possible number of slices between the green olives slice and the onion slice?

    (A) Zero

    (B) One

    (C) Two

    (D) Three

    (E) Four

Lucky you! You already worked this out in the previous question. Let your work on other questions help you out! Looking back at the notes you took for 17, recall that G and O could be adjacent to one another — zero slices between them. That makes the answer (A).

You're probably getting a bit tired right about now, after singers and workers and then that pizza. Fatigue is natural. So take a break. Take 30 seconds or so to look around, relax your neck, adjust your position in your chair, wiggle your toes. Pretend you're deliberately NOT staring at anyone else's paper. You're not done yet, and you need to pace yourself. You don't want to take a very long break — definitely no more than a minute — but a short one will make your brain sharper.

The Photography Museum

You figured out the pizza problem, and college students worldwide will love you. And hey, if you don't get into the law school of your dreams, you can always open up a pizza parlor. Take a moment to reflect on your place in the universe, allowing all thoughts of pizza to trickle out of your head. Then move on to the next problem — and help a museum with its photography dilemma.

Questions 19–25

A museum keeps a collection of five kinds of photographs: abstract, landscapes, portraits, sports, and underwater. The collection includes both color and black and white (B&W) prints of each kind of photograph. The museum doesn't have space to display all ten types of photograph at once. (And no, asking the museum to add on isn't an option.) When deciding what to display, the museum must apply the following conditions:

If neither color nor B&W sports photographs are displayed, then color portraits are.

If both color and B&W sports photographs are displayed, then neither color nor B&W abstract photographs are displayed.

If both color and B&W portraits are displayed, then both color and B&W underwater photographs are displayed.

If any abstract photographs are displayed, then no underwater photographs are.

Color landscapes are not displayed.

B&W portraits are displayed.

19. Which of the following could be a complete and accurate list of the photographs on display?

    (A) Color abstract, color landscapes, B&W portraits, color sports, B&W sports

    (B) B&W abstract, B&W portraits, color sports, color underwater

    (C) B&W portraits, B&W sports, B&W underwater, color underwater

    (D) Color abstract, B&W abstract, B&W landscape, B&W portraits

    (E) B&W landscapes, color portraits, B&W portraits, color underwater

20. If the museum does not display color underwater photographs, which of the following must be true?

    (A) At least one kind of portrait is not displayed.

    (B) At least one kind of sports photograph is not displayed.

    (C) Color abstract photographs are not displayed.

    (D) Color abstract photographs are displayed.

    (E) B&W landscapes are not displayed.

21. If the museum displays only four kinds of B&W photographs, each of the following must be false EXCEPT:

    (A) No sports photographs are displayed.

    (B) No landscapes are displayed and no underwater photographs are displayed.

    (C) B&W landscapes are not displayed.

    (D) B&W sports photographs are not displayed.

    (E) B&W underwater photographs are not displayed.

22. If the museum displays neither color nor B&W sports photographs, then which of the following could be false?

    (A) B&W landscapes are displayed.

    (B) Color abstract photographs are not displayed.

    (C) Neither kind of abstract photograph is displayed.

    (D) B&W underwater photographs are displayed.

    (E) Both kinds of underwater photographs are displayed.

23. If the museum displays both B&W and color sports photographs, what is the minimum number of types of color photographs that the museum could display?

    (A) One

    (B) Two

    (C) Three

    (D) Four

    (E) Five

24. If color underwater photographs are the only color photographs on display, which of the following CANNOT be true?

    (A) B&W abstract photographs are not displayed.

    (B) B&W landscapes are not displayed.

    (C) B&W sports photographs are not displayed.

    (D) B&W underwater photographs are displayed.

    (E) B&W underwater photographs are not displayed.

25. Which of the following CANNOT be true?

    (A) Neither type of abstract and neither type of sports photograph is displayed.

    (B) Neither type of abstract and neither type of landscape is displayed.

    (C) Neither type of sports photograph and neither type of underwater photograph is displayed.

    (D) Neither type of landscape and neither type of sports photograph is displayed.

    (E) Neither type of landscape and neither type of underwater photograph is displayed.

Developing the photos

Hmm. Complicated. This question is tough because you have to keep track of three different categories of information – color vs. B&W, displayed vs. not displayed, and the five types of photograph. That makes for a dizzying array of permutations. Not to worry, though; you can sort this one out!

Organize your thoughts

First step: Identify everything by initials. You actually have ten kinds of photographs, because you have color and B&W versions of all five types. If you use capital letters to identify types of photograph, and lowercase letters to identify color or B&W, you could list them like this: cA, bA, cL, bL, cP, bP, cS, bS, cU, bU.

Start a diagram

You have three different categories here: color versus B&W, displayed versus not displayed, and the five types of photograph. All the rules and questions deal with which photographs are displayed and not displayed, so that probably makes the best way to organize the information. Make two headings, one called "D" (for "displayed") and one called "ND" (for "not displayed"). You know that color landscapes aren't displayed, so put cL under ND. You know B&W portraits are displayed, so note that under D.

$$\frac{D}{bP} \qquad \frac{ND}{cL}$$

Rules and details

Now, write the rules in a shorthand format to make reading them easier. Use an *x* to mark photos that aren't displayed, and nothing to mark photos that are displayed. In this case *x* means "not." (It may not be formal logical notation, but it doesn't have to be; it just has to make sense to you.) See Chapter 4 for more discussion of ways to note rules in shorthand.

Every problem has different rules, which is why every problem will use a different diagram and a different set of shorthand notes. This is the first problem in this chapter to use positive and negative categories such as "displayed" and "not displayed." Adapt your notes to the circumstances.

> If xcS & xbS -> cP
>
> If cS & bS -> xcA & xbA
>
> If cP & bP -> cU & bU
>
> If cA or bA -> xcU & xbU

Keep thinking

What deductions can you make from these rules? Well, the presence of either cA or bA prevents the display of both bU and cU; but if both bP and cP are displayed, then both bU and cU must be. That means you can't have either kind of abstract photograph displayed if color portraits are, because you would then run into an impossible situation with regard to the underwater photographs. So you can write "If cP & bP -> xcA & xbA". This also prevents color portraits from being displayed if either kind of abstract is; write that "If cA or bA -> xcP".

You can come with more deductions as you answer the questions. This problem is fairly complicated, and you have to work the rules in both directions. So, for example, adding cP to the list of displayed photos affects cS and bS. Adding cU or bU affects cA and bA. It's a bit like algebra, in that you need each side of the equation to balance. You could ponder this one for a long time, but it's time to start working.

"If-then" rules can be tricky. Here's one way to make deductions from them: Switch places of the "if" and "then," and make both sides negative. For example, "If it's rainy, then it must be cloudy" turns into the valid deduction "If it's not cloudy, then it's not rainy." This works for any if-then statement.

Picturing the answers to these questions

This problem is complicated, but it's solvable; the rules are the key to everything.

19. Which of the following could be a complete and accurate list of the photographs on display?

    (A) Color abstract, color landscapes, B&W portraits, color sports, B&W sports

    (B) B&W abstract, B&W portraits, color sports, color underwater

    (C) B&W portraits, B&W sports, B&W underwater, color underwater

    (D) Color abstract, B&W abstract, B&W landscape, B&W portraits

    (E) B&W landscapes, color portraits, B&W portraits, color underwater

Look for rule violations. You know the museum doesn't display color landscapes; (A) includes them, so (A) is out. (B) has both abstract and underwater photos; you can't have underwater if you have any abstract, so (B) is out. (C) doesn't appear to violate any rules, so it could be the answer, but check the next two letters to make sure. (D) is a bit tricky; look at what it doesn't include. It doesn't have either kind of sports photo, and if that is the case, it needs to have color portraits. They're not in the list, so (D) is out. (E) has both kinds of portrait, and if you have both portraits, you need both kinds of underwater photo; they aren't there, so (E) is out. To double-check (C), you have both underwaters so you can't have abstracts, and you don't. You have one kind of sports photo, so you don't need color portraits. Looks good. (C) is correct.

The rules don't work backwards. Including both kinds of underwater photo doesn't mean you need both kinds of portrait.

20. If the museum doesn't display color underwater photographs, which of the following must be true?

   (A) At least one kind of portrait isn't displayed.

   (B) At least one kind of sports photograph isn't displayed.

   (C) Color abstract photographs aren't displayed.

   (D) Color abstract photographs are displayed.

   (E) B&W landscapes aren't displayed.

Record cU under the ND heading. Now try the choices. Start with (A). You know bP is displayed. If you also display cP, then you must display both kinds of underwater photo, which is impossible; so in order for cU to be not displayed, cP can't be either. It looks like (A) is correct, but you still need to test the other options. Try (B); if you don't display either kind of sports photo, it has no effect on underwater photos. Try (C); if you don't display an abstract photo, it has no effect on underwater; same with (D). As for (E), no rules mention landscapes, so their display status has no effect on underwater. (A) is correct.

21. If the museum only displays four kinds of B&W photographs, each of the following must be false EXCEPT:

   (A) No sports photographs are displayed.

   (B) No landscapes are displayed and no underwater photographs are displayed.

   (C) B&W landscapes aren't displayed.

   (D) B&W sports photographs aren't displayed.

   (E) B&W underwater photographs aren't displayed.

Here's the quick way to answer this one: You know from the question that four kinds of B&W photo will be displayed, and that means one won't be. You know from the rules that either bA or bU will be displayed, but both can't be. If you skim the answer choices, you see that only one of those two types appears as not displayed: (E) says that bU isn't displayed. That must be the answer.

Here's the fuller explanation of all the answer choices. Test each proposition. First (A): If the museum doesn't display any sports photographs, then the museum must display color portraits. Because this exhibit includes only B&Ws, (A) doesn't work. (B) can be dismissed out of hand; you need four types of B&Ws, and you would have only three if you got rid of both landscapes and underwater photos. Try (C). If you try to display B&W portraits, sports, underwater, and abstract, you run into a problem: If you display either type of abstract photo, you can't display underwater photos. So (C) doesn't work. Try (D). You run into the same problem with abstract nixing underwater, so (D) doesn't work either. Try (E). If you take underwater photos out of the mix, then the presence of abstract photos doesn't cause a problem. (E) is the answer.

22. If the museum displays neither color nor B&W sports photographs, then which of the following could be false?

    (A) B&W landscapes are displayed.

    (B) Color abstract photographs aren't displayed.

    (C) Neither kind of abstract photograph is displayed.

    (D) B&W underwater photographs are displayed.

    (E) Both kinds of underwater photographs are displayed.

The best approach with this question is to fill in your chart with the photos that you know are and aren't displayed. If the museum doesn't display either kind of sports, then color portraits are. Because the museum is displaying both color portraits, both kinds of underwater photograph must be displayed. If the museum displays either kind of underwater photograph, neither kind of abstract photograph can be. Now, look at the choices. (A) mentions landscapes, and you don't know where they fit in the chart; could be true, but could be false. Save that one. (B) and (C) are both true, because you know the museum isn't displaying abstract photos. (D) and (E) are both true, because you know both kinds of underwater photos are displayed. So (A) is correct.

23. If the museum displays both B&W and color sports photographs, what is the minimum number of types of color photographs that the museum could display?

    (A) One

    (B) Two

    (C) Three

    (D) Four

    (E) Five

If you have both kinds of sports photograph, you can't have color abstracts. You already know you can't have color landscapes, so you're down to three possibilities. Is there any rule requiring you to include color portraits or color underwater photos? No, color sports photographs could legitimately be the only color on the walls. So the answer is one, (A).

24. If color underwater photographs are the only color photographs on display, which of the following CAN'T be true?

    (A) B&W abstract photographs aren't displayed.

    (B) B&W landscapes aren't displayed.

    (C) B&W sports photographs aren't displayed.

    (D) B&W underwater photographs are displayed.

    (E) B&W underwater photographs aren't displayed.

If you draw out the diagram, it'll look like this:

D	ND
bP	cL
cU	cA
	cP
	cS

Now you can apply the rules to the answer choices. If the museum displays either type of underwater photo, you can't have any abstracts, so (A) is true. (B) is fine; nothing requires the museum to display B&W landscapes. If you don't display either color or B&W sports photos, you have to display color portraits; (C) can't be true, but check the others anyway. No rule requires the museum to display B&W underwater photos, but no rule forbids it either, so (D) and (E) could be true. The answer is (C).

25. Which one of the following CANNOT be true?

   (A) Neither type of abstract and neither type of sports photograph is displayed.

   (B) Neither type of abstract and neither type of landscape is displayed.

   (C) Neither type of sports photograph and neither type of underwater photograph is displayed.

   (D) Neither type of landscape and neither type of sports photograph is displayed.

   (E) Neither type of landscape and neither type of underwater photograph is displayed.

Once again, apply the rules and look for violations. Having a display with no abstract or sports photographs is possible, so (A) could be true. Likewise, no rule requires abstract landscape photographs, so (B) could be true. Look at (C). If you don't display either kind of sports photograph, you have to display color portraits, which means that both kinds of portrait are displayed and in that case you must display both kinds of underwater photograph. (C) can't be true, but look at (D) and (E). These both involve landscape photographs, and no rules require involving landscapes, except for the requirement that color landscapes not be displayed. (D) and (E) could both be true. The answer is (C).

Whew! Congratulations! You survived and figured out these problems. How did you do? Did you find yourself tripping up on a few steps? If your brain isn't too fried and you want a quick refresher on answering Analytical Reasoning problems, go back to Chapter 4.

Chapter 6

Give It a Try: An LSAT Analytical Reasoning Section

In This Chapter
▶ Working another LSAT Analytical Reasoning Section
▶ Dealing with even harder questions

*T*his chapter provides some practice for the LSAT Analytical Reasoning section. The questions are a bit harder than the ones in Chapter 5, but they're still totally representative of the types of questions that have appeared on recent LSATs. The answers and explanations are in Chapter 7.

Who's Teaching What at the Yoga Studio?

Questions 1–6

A yoga studio offers classes in three kinds of yoga: ashtanga, bikram, and iyengar. It has five instructors — Caroline, Janice, Marty, Suzanne, and Virginia — each of whom teaches at least one of and as many as three of these kinds of yoga. The following conditions apply:

> Exactly two of the instructors teach classes in the same kind or kinds of yoga.
>
> Marty and Suzanne both teach iyengar.
>
> Caroline and Marty each teach fewer kinds of yoga than Janice.
>
> Caroline does not teach any kind of yoga taught by Virginia.
>
> Virginia does not teach any kind of yoga taught by Janice.

1. Which one of the following must be true?

   (A) Caroline teaches fewer kinds of yoga than Virginia does.

   (B) Marty teaches fewer kinds of yoga than Suzanne does.

   (C) Suzanne teaches fewer kinds of yoga than Janice does.

   (D) Virginia teaches fewer kinds of yoga than Janice does.

   (E) Virginia teaches fewer kinds of yoga than Suzanne does.

2. If Virginia does not teach iyengar, then which one of the following must be true?

   (A) Janice teaches bikram.

   (B) Janice teaches iyengar.

   (C) Marty teaches ashtanga.

   (D) Suzanne teaches ashtanga.

   (E) Virginia teaches bikram.

3. Which one of the following could be a complete and accurate list of the instructors who teach only bikram?

   (A) Caroline

   (B) Janice

   (C) Caroline, Virginia

   (D) Marty, Suzanne

   (E) Caroline, Suzanne, Virginia

4. Which one of the following could be a complete and accurate list of the instructors who teach iyengar?

   (A) Marty, Suzanne

   (B) Janice, Suzanne

   (C) Caroline, Janice, Suzanne

   (D) Caroline, Marty, Suzanne

   (E) Janice, Marty, Suzanne

5. How many instructors must teach only one kind of yoga?

   (A) one

   (B) two

   (C) three

   (D) four

   (E) five

6. If exactly three instructors teach ashtanga, which one of the following could be true?

   (A) Caroline teaches iyengar.

   (B) Janice does not teach ashtanga.

   (C) Marty teaches ashtanga.

   (D) Suzanne teaches bikram.

   (E) Suzanne doesn't teach ashtanga.

The End of the Roman Republic

<u>Questions 7–12</u>

Toward the end of the Roman Republic, seven Roman noblemen — Antonius, Brutus, Cassius, Deciumus, Octavius, Servilius, and Vipsanius — had to decide whether they supported or hated the rule of dictator Julius Caesar. Those who supported Caesar called themselves Patriots; those who hated Caesar and wanted to overthrow him called themselves Liberators. Due more to personality conflicts amongst themselves than any real political convictions, they sorted themselves according to the following principles:

Octavius and Cassius hated each other and would never join the same group.

Antonius and Decimus, likewise, hated each other and would not join the same group.

If Decimus decided to be a Patriot, so did Servilius.

If Brutus decided to be a Patriot, then both Cassius and Vipsanius would be Liberators.

If Octavius decided to be a Patriot, Servilius would be a Liberator.

7. If Octavius joined the Liberators, which of the following must be true?

(A) Antonius joined the Liberators.

(B) Brutus joined the Liberators.

(C) Decimus joined the Patriots.

(D) Servilius joined the Patriots.

(E) Vipsanius joined the Patriots.

8. If Cassius and Vipsanius both joined the Liberators, then which of the following must be false?

(A) Antonius joined the Patriots.

(B) Brutus joined the Liberators.

(C) Decimus joined the Liberators.

(D) Octavius joined the Patriots.

(E) Servilius joined the Patriots.

9. If Antonius and Vipsanius both joined the Patriots, then which one of the following could be true?

(A) Brutus and Cassius both joined the Liberators.

(B) Brutus and Octavius both joined the Patriots.

(C) Cassius and Decimus both joined the Patriots.

(D) Cassius and Octavius both joined the Liberators.

(E) Decimus and Servilius both joined the Patriots.

10. Which one of the following pairs of men could not both be Liberators?

(A) Antonius and Octavius

(B) Antonius and Servilius

(C) Antonius and Vipsanius

(D) Cassius and Vipsanius

(E) Octavius and Servilius

11. What is the maximum number of Patriots?

    (A) one

    (B) two

    (C) three

    (D) four

    (E) five

12. Which one of the following could be an accurate and complete list of the Patriots?

    (A) Antonius, Cassius, Vipsanius

    (B) Antonius, Cassius, Decimus, Servilius

    (C) Antonius, Octavius, Servilius, Vipsanius

    (D) Brutus, Decimus, Octavius

    (E) Decimus, Servilius, Vipsanius

Planning the Theater Festival

<u>Questions 13–18</u>

Six plays are scheduled to be performed at the Dionysia, the annual theater festival in Athens. They are: *Antigone, Clouds, Electra, Frogs, Helen,* and *Orestes*. In order to mix up comedy and tragedy, give the actors an occasional break, and accommodate the desires of the town fathers, the organizers must observe the following rules when arranging the schedule:

> The plays will be performed on six consecutive days, beginning on Tuesday.
>
> The ethnarch of Sparta can only attend on Thursday; *Helen* is his favorite play, so it must be scheduled for that day.
>
> *Antigone* must be performed after *Orestes*.
>
> *Antigone* and *Frogs* cannot be scheduled consecutively; there must be a break of at least one day between them.
>
> The same actors are performing both *Clouds* and *Frogs,* and they must have a break of exactly one day between performances.

13. Which play CANNOT be performed on Sunday?

    (A) *Antigone*

    (B) *Clouds*

    (C) *Electra*

    (D) *Frogs*

    (E) *Orestes*

14. Which one of the following must be true?

    (A) Either *Antigone* or *Orestes* is performed on Wednesday.

    (B) Either *Antigone* or *Orestes* is performed on Friday.

    (C) Either *Clouds* or *Frogs* is performed on Wednesday.

    (D) Either the *Clouds* or *Frogs* is performed on Friday.

    (E) Either *Electra* or the *Orestes* is performed on Saturday.

15. Which one of the following is an acceptable schedule for the festival, starting with the play performed on Tuesday?

    (A) *Antigone, Electra, Helen, Frogs, Orestes, Clouds*

    (B) *Electra, Orestes, Helen, Clouds, Antigone, Frogs*

    (C) *Frogs, Clouds, Helen, Orestes, Antigone, Electra*

    (D) *Orestes, Frogs, Helen, Clouds, Antigone, Electra*

    (E) *Orestes, Antigone, Frogs, Helen, Clouds, Electra*

16. Which one of the following must be false?

    (A) *Antigone* and *Clouds* are performed on consecutive days, with no other play between them.

    (B) Exactly one play is performed between *Antigone* and *Clouds*.

    (C) *Electra* and *Orestes* are performed on consecutive days, with no other play between them.

    (D) *Frogs* and *Orestes* are performed on consecutive days, with no other play between them.

    (E) Exactly one play is performed between *Helen* and *Orestes*.

17. Which one of the following is a complete and accurate list of the days on which the *Frogs* could be performed?

    (A) Tuesday, Wednesday, Friday

    (B) Wednesday, Thursday, Saturday

    (C) Wednesday, Friday

    (D) Wednesday, Friday, Sunday

    (E) Wednesday, Friday, Saturday, Sunday

18. Which one of the following CANNOT be true?

    (A) *Clouds* is performed on Wednesday.

    (B) *Electra* is performed on Wednesday.

    (C) The *Frogs* is performed on Wednesday.

    (D) *Orestes* is performed on Tuesday.

    (E) *Orestes* is performed on Saturday.

Working in a Law Firm

Questions 19–25

A boutique law firm does work in four areas of law: employment, immigration, real estate, and tax. Four attorneys share the work; their names are Burton, Duway, Cheatham, and Howard. Each attorney specializes in at least one and at most three areas of law. The areas of law are distributed among the attorneys according to the following specifications:

Duway specializes in anything that is also Cheatham's specialty.

Burton and Howard do not share any specialties with Cheatham.

One attorney specializes in tax.

Two attorneys specialize in employment.

Two attorneys specialize in real estate.

Three attorneys specialize in immigration.

19. If Duway specializes in two and only two areas of law, which one of the following must be true?

   (A) Burton doesn't specialize in tax.

   (B) Cheatham doesn't specialize in employment.

   (C) Duway doesn't specialize in tax.

   (D) Howard doesn't specialize in employment.

   (E) Howard doesn't specialize in tax.

20. Which one of the following must be true?

   (A) Burton specializes in more areas of law than Cheatham.

   (B) Howard specializes in more areas of law than Duway.

   (C) Duway specializes in more areas of law than Howard.

   (D) Duway specializes in more areas of law than Cheatham.

   (E) Burton specializes in more areas of law than Howard.

21. Each of the following could be a complete and accurate list of the attorneys who specialize in both employment and immigration EXCEPT:

   (A) Duway

   (B) Burton

   (C) Burton and Howard

   (D) Duway and Burton

   (E) Duway and Howard

22. If Cheatham specializes in exactly two areas of law, then each of the following must be false EXCEPT:

   (A) Duway specializes in tax.

   (B) Duway specializes in exactly two areas of law.

   (C) Howard specializes in employment.

   (D) Howard specializes in tax.

   (E) Howard specializes in exactly three areas of law.

23. If Burton specializes in exactly three areas of law, which one of the following must be true?

    (A) Burton specializes in employment.

    (B) Burton specializes in real estate.

    (C) Burton specializes in tax.

    (D) Howard specializes in employment.

    (E) Howard specializes in tax.

24. Which one of the following statements CANNOT be true of the attorney who specializes in tax?

    (A) The attorney also specializes in immigration but does not specialize in real estate.

    (B) The attorney also specializes in both immigration and real estate.

    (C) The attorney also specializes in real estate but not in immigration.

    (D) The attorney also specializes in employment but not in real estate.

    (E) The attorney specializes in neither employment nor real estate.

25. Each of the following must be false EXCEPT:

    (A) Burton specializes in three areas: employment, immigration, and real estate.

    (B) Burton specializes in three areas: employment, real estate, and tax.

    (C) Duway specializes in three areas: employment, immigration, and real estate.

    (D) Duway specializes in three areas: employment, real estate, and tax.

    (E) Howard specializes in three areas: employment, real estate, and tax.

Chapter 7

The Mysteries of Chapter 6 Solved

In This Chapter

▶ Drawing effective diagrams

▶ Breaking down the problems

▶ Getting answers and explanations

Here are the answers and explanations to the problems in Chapter 6. In this chapter, I show you how your diagrams could look and explain how to arrive at the correct answers.

Figuring Out the Yoga Studio

The answers to the questions in this section are: 1.(D); 2.(B); 3.(A); 4.(E); 5.(C); 6.(D).

Organizing the information

You have two categories: instructors and types of yoga. The instructors will be the unchanging information, so organize the information that way. Abbreviate the instructors by initials: C, J, M, S, and V. The kinds of yoga will be a, b, and i. For now, just write the instructors' initials from top to bottom on your diagram, and save room to write their classes to the right of them.

Write the rules in shorthand. The first rule doesn't really go into a short notation, so just write "2 instructors identical." Doing so helps you remember that two and only two instructors must teach the same class or classes. M and S both teach iyengar, so write "i" next to each of them; draw a square around it to mark it as permanent information. For the next rule, write C<J and M<J. For the last two rules, write C≠V and V≠J. At this point the diagram could look like this:

C<J	C
M<J	J
C≠V	M [i]
V≠J	S [i]
2 instructors identical	V

Now think about this situation. If C and M both teach fewer classes than J, then they must teach either one or two classes, and J must teach either two or three. But you know that J doesn't teach any classes that V teaches, which means J can't teach three classes, and must teach two. Therefore, C and M must each teach one class. You already know that M teaches iyengar, which must be M's only class. You also know that V can teach only one class, because she doesn't overlap with J's two classes. What about S? Well, at this point it looks like she could teach one, two, or three classes; you can't decide. Mark these numbers on the diagram, using either blank spaces, numbers, or both:

$$
\begin{array}{lll}
C & \_\,(1) & C<J \\
J & \_\_\,(2) & M<J \\
M\,[i]\,(1) & & C\neq V \\
S\,[i]\,\_\_\,(1\text{-}3) & & V\neq J \\
V & \_\,(1) & 2\ \text{instructors identical}
\end{array}
$$

Drawing conclusions

Here are the answers and explanations for each of the yoga questions. Don't hurt yourself stretching to reach for the truth.

1. You can answer this question by looking at the diagram. You know Caroline and Virginia each teach one kind of yoga, so (A) is wrong. You don't know how many kinds of yoga Suzanne teaches, so (B) doesn't have to be true, though it could be. Suzanne might teach fewer kinds of yoga than Janice, but she doesn't have to, so (C) is wrong. You know that Virginia can teach only one kind of yoga, and Janice teaches two, so (D) looks right. Double-checking (E), Virginia may or may not teach fewer kinds of yoga than Suzanne, so (E) is wrong. (D) it is.

2. If Virginia doesn't teach iyengar, she must teach either ashtanga or bikram. You know that Janice teaches the classes Virginia doesn't teach, which means Janice must teach iyengar. It looks like (B) should be the answer. Just to check the other answers: Janice will teach either bikram or ashtanga, whichever one Virginia doesn't teach, but you can't know which one from the given information; that knocks out both (A) and (E). Marty can teach only iyengar, which eliminates (C). Suzanne might be able to teach ashtanga, but she doesn't have to, which knocks out (D). (B) is correct.

3. Can you eliminate any choices? You know Janice teaches two classes, so any choice including her can't be right; cross off (B). You know Caroline and Virginia can't teach the same class, so cross off (C) and (E). You know Marty teaches only iyengar, so cross off (D). Could Caroline teach only bikram? Yes, she can teach only one kind of yoga, and it could be bikram. So the answer must be (A).

4. You know Marty and Suzanne must teach iyengar, so you can eliminate any choice that doesn't include both of them; cross off (B) and (C). Consider (A) a possible right answer, but test the other choices to see if the list could be expanded; remember, you want a complete list. Could Caroline teach iyengar? No, if Caroline teaches iyengar, Virginia

can't teach iyengar, but if Virginia can't teach iyengar, then Janice must teach iyengar. (D) doesn't include Janice, so it's not a complete list. How about (E)? Sure; if Janice teaches iyengar, she can also teach ashtanga, Caroline could teach ashtanga, too, which would leave bikram for Virginia. The answer is (E).

5. Look at your diagram. You already figured out this one. Caroline, Marty, and Virginia can all teach only one kind of yoga. Janice must teach two kinds, and you don't know about Suzanne; she could teach only one, but could also teach two or three, so you can't say she must teach only one kind. The answer is three, (C).

Pay attention to "must," "can" and "could," and "all/except" questions. Underline these words and think about what the right and wrong answers will mean *before* you begin working out the question. In this case, if only one "must" be true, all the other choices are merely possible or false. By thinking this beforehand, you're less likely to jump at the first possible choice.

6. If three instructors teach ashtanga, who must they be? Marty can't teach ashtanga, because she teaches only iyengar. Virginia can't share classes with either Caroline or Janice, so she can't teach ashtanga because only Suzanne could share it with her. So the three instructors must be C, J, and S. That eliminates (A) because Caroline is teaching only ashtanga, (B) because Janice must teach ashtanga, (C) because Marty can't teach ashtanga, and (E) because Suzanne must teach ashtanga. Can Suzanne teach bikram? No reason she can't. The answer is (D).

Ending the Roman Republic

Here are the answers to this set of questions: 7.(B); 8.(B); 9.(A); 10.(B); 11.(D); 12.(A).

Contemplating the rules

The good news: This problem is chock-full of rules. The bad news: The facts and the rules don't fit into a particularly neat format. Never fear, though; just grab your pencil and start scribbling.

Those of you with a passing acquaintance of Roman history know that several of these characters acted in ways that don't correspond with the rules proposed in this problem. Don't let that interfere with your analysis. (Remember when in Rome, do as the Romans do, or more appropriately for this book, when in LSAT Land, do as the LSAT-writers do.)

Your first step, as always, is to abbreviate all names as initials, So you have A, B, C, D, O, S, and V. Use lowercase letters to mark Patriots and Liberators (p and l). You're going to be sorting these people into two categories, so probably the easiest way is to write two headings — Patriots and Liberators — and record members under them. Don't get too hasty about doing that, though, because you don't have much permanent information, and in many cases you don't have to resort to plugging data into categories. You'll be able to answer lots of questions just by spotting rule violations.

The most important step is to explore the rules. Write them down in shorthand:

$$O \neq C$$

$$A \neq D$$

$$\text{If } Dp \rightarrow Sp$$

$$\text{If } Bp \rightarrow Cl \text{ \& } Vl$$

$$\text{If } Op \rightarrow Sl$$

Now, think about this. If O ≠ C, you can conclude that if Op -> Cl and if Ol -> Cp. Same with A and D; if Ap -> Dl, and if Al -> Dp. Those equations both work in reverse, too. What that means is any time you put A or O under one heading, you must put C or D under the other; it also means that you always have at least two men on each side. Furthermore, you can expand some of the rules. For example, you now know that if D is a Patriot, then S is a Patriot and A is a liberator. If O is a Patriot, then S is a Liberator and C is a Liberator, too. Add those notes to your shorthand rules: If Dp -> Sp & Al; If Op -> Sl & Cl.

Consider other implications. Don't run into the trap of imagining the rules work backwards. For example, the statement "If Dp -> Sp" doesn't mean that "If Sp -> Dp." But you can make some conclusions. What if S is a Liberator? In that case, D must be a Liberator, too, to avoid breaking the rule requiring S to be a Patriot if D is a Patriot. You could write that "If Sl -> Dl." If either C or V is a Patriot, then B must be a Liberator, because if B is a Patriot, then C and V must both be Liberators; write that "If Cp or Vp -> Bl." Make sense? If S is a Patriot, then O must be a Liberator, because otherwise they would violate the rule requiring S to be a Liberator when O is a Patriot; write that "Sp -> Ol." Incorporate all this info into your notes (except for the O ≠ C and A ≠ D, which are fairly obvious).

$$O \neq C$$

$$A \neq D$$

$$\text{If } Dp \rightarrow Sp \text{ \& } Al; \text{ if } Sl \rightarrow Dl$$

$$\text{If } Bp \rightarrow Cl \text{ \& } Vl; \text{ if } Cp \text{ or } Vp \rightarrow Bl$$

$$\text{If } Op \rightarrow Sl \text{ \& } Cl; \text{ if } Sp \rightarrow Ol$$

Conquering the questions

7. Now is a good time to start jotting down initials under your two headings, Liberator and Patriot. Doing so can help you visualize who is going where and prevent your trying to hold it in your head. Jot O down under the Liberators. That automatically puts C under the Patriots. Look at your list of rules; if Cp -> Bl, so put B under the Liberators, like this:

Liberators	Patriots
O	C
B	

The answer is (B). Can you determine anything about the other four choices? No. The factoid of Octavius joining the Liberators tells you nothing about Antonius, Decimus, Servilius, or Vipsanius. They could join either side (subject, of course, to the rules governing them). The answer is (B).

8. Plug the initials into your categories. If Cassius is a Liberator, then Octavius is a Patriot. If Octavius is a Patriot, then Servilius is a Liberator. If Servilius is a Liberator, Decimus is a Liberator. That leaves Brutus undecided; he could go either way. Skimming the choices, the only one that doesn't match up is (E); Servilius must be a Liberator, so that's the only false statement.

Liberators	Patriots
C	O
V	A
S	
D	

9. Okay, make a new set of headings or erase your notes from the last problems. Jot down A and V under Patriots. Place other men — D goes under Liberators, and so does B because V is under Patriots. Now consider your options, eliminating violators first. (B) can go because Brutus isn't a Patriot. (C) and (E) can go because Decimus can't be a Patriot. (D) is definitely wrong because Cassius and Octavius can't be on the same side, which leaves (A). Try Cassius as a liberator; that makes Octavius a Patriot, which makes Servilius a Liberator. (A) looks good.

Sometimes I suggest working off old diagrams, and sometimes I suggest erasing your notes and starting over for each question. Which is better? It depends; in particular, it depends on how much space you have, which usually isn't much. It depends on whether or not your notes might help you in another problem; sometimes they do, though every question can be answered independently of the others. It also depends on personal preference. Some teachers always counsel students to keep their old notes. My own preference is to get rid of them so that they don't confuse me later. I would say, if you have lots of space, keep your notes; if you don't, consider erasing. Experiment to find what works best for you.

10. Create new headings or erase your notes. Apply the rules one at a time, until you've placed everyone. Try Antonius and Octavius as Liberators. If Antonius is a Liberator, then Decimus is a Patriot. If Decimus is a Patriot, then Servilius is a Patriot. If Octavius is a Liberator, then Cassius is a Patriot. If Cassius is a Patriot, then Brutus is a Liberator, and Vipsanius could go either way. That works, so (A) is possible. Your notes could look like this:

Liberators	Patriots
A	D
O	S
B	C

Try (B), Antonius and Servilius. If Antonius is a Liberator, then Decimus must be a Patriot, which means Servilius must be a Patriot, so Antonius and Servilius can't both be Liberators. (B) is the answer. If you're confident, go ahead and leave it at that; I'm going to work through the rest of the possibilities anyway.

(C) gives you a roster of Liberators: Antonius, Vipsanius, Octavius, and Brutus; and Patriots: Decimus, Servilius, and Cassius. How? If Antonius is a Liberator, Decimus must be a Patriot, which makes Servilius a Patriot, which makes Octavius a Liberator, which makes Cassius a Patriot, which makes Brutus a Liberator. (D) gives you Liberators: Cassius, Vipsanius, Servilius, and Decimus; and Patriots: Octavius, Antonius, and Brutus. How? If Cassius is a Liberator, then Octavius is a Patriot, which makes Servilius a Liberator, Decimus a Liberator, and Antonius a Patriot. Cassius and Vipsanius are both Liberators, which makes Brutus a Patriot, too. (E) gives you a roster of Liberators: Octavius, Servilius, Decimus, and Brutus; and Patriots: Cassius and Antonius. Note that leaves out Vipsanius. If Octavius is a Liberator, Cassius is a Patriot, which makes Brutus a Liberator. If Servilius is a Liberator, Decimus must be a Liberator. Where does Vipsanius fall in all this? Amazingly, you can't tell. He could go on either side.

11. Based on work in the previous question, you can immediately eliminate (A) and (B); you already know you can have at least three Patriots. See if you can concoct a roster with five Patriots (five because you're looking for a maximum and it's the largest number offered to you). Try making Decimus and Servilius Patriots, which forces Antonius to be a Liberator. Brutus isn't a good choice for a Patriot, because he forces Cassius and Vipsanius over to the Liberators, so instead make Cassius and Vipsanius Patriots and let Brutus be a Liberator. That makes Octavius a Liberator, too, because he doesn't play on the same team as Cassius. There doesn't seem any way to get five guys onto the Patriots, but you know you can do four. That makes the answer (D).

12. Look for obvious rule violations first. Antonius and Decimus can't be on the same side, which nixes (B). Making Servilius a Patriot makes Octavius a Liberator, which nixes (C). Now try the others. Try (A). If Antonius is a Patriot, then Decimus is a Liberator. If Cassius is a Patriot, then Octavius and Brutus are both Liberators. You can make Servilius a Liberator without violating any rules, so (A) is a good choice. Now try (D). If Decimus is a Patriot, then Servilius must also be a Patriot; Servilius isn't in that list, so (D) is wrong. Now (E): If Decimus is a Patriot, then Antonius must be a Liberator. If Servilius is a Patriot, then Octavius must be a Liberator. If Vipsanius is a Patriot, then Brutus must be a Liberator. Cassius can't be on Octavius' side, so Cassius must be a Patriot, so the list in (E) isn't complete. The answer is (A).

Question 12 is a particularly notes-intensive problem. When I worked it, I ended up with scribbles all over the page, from plugging various combinations into the Liberator and Patriot categories, as well as a ton of eraser dirt all over my desk. (One of the reasons I suggest erasing your notes between questions on this problem is simply the sheer amount of note-taking you must do; it's unlikely that a mass of scribbles is going to be terribly useful from one problem to the next.) That's okay. Scribble away if that's what it takes to solve the questions.

Performing at the Theater Festival

The answers to Questions 13–18 are: 13.(E); 14.(D); 15.(D); 16.(C); 17.(D); 18.(B).

Diagramming the data

This problem is pretty straightforward — put the items in order, with no real twists or turns. As always, abbreviate your participants: A, C, E, F, H, and O. The plays will be put in order by days of the week, so make that the foundation of the diagram: write T, W, R, F, Sa, Su across the page, leaving space underneath to fill in information. You know H must be performed on Thursday, so write that under Thursday's heading; put a box around it to mark it as permanent information.

Now consider the other rules. Write them in shorthand.

A comes after O, so write O -> A. Note the break between A and F: A x F; you don't know how many days must come between them, but it must be at least one.

The rules don't tell you that A must come before F. F could come before A, but there will still be at least a one-day break between them. The same thing goes for C and F, although here you know the break is exactly one day; write that C [ ] F.

Think about the situation with C and F. A confirmed one-day break tells you a lot. Because H is scheduled for Thursday, you know neither C nor F can be performed on Tuesday or Saturday. That leaves Wednesday, Friday, and Sunday as possible dates for C and F. Note that on the diagram:

$$T \quad W \quad R \quad F \quad Sa \quad Su$$
$$[C,F] \quad [H] \quad [C,F] \qquad [C,F]$$

Obviously A and F need only two days to be performed, and one of the other plays will be performed on Wednesday, Friday, or Sunday, but for the moment knowing that those are the only possible days for A and F is useful.

Can you come up with any more conclusions? Probably. However, this information is enough to get you started, and time's a-wasting.

Reveling in the answers

Here's how to work these questions. Several of them are quite straightforward; schedule problems like this are nice because you only have one level of data to work with, instead of having to combine two or three factors.

13. This question is easy. What play must be performed before another play? *Orestes* must come before *Antigone,* which means *Orestes* can never be performed on Sunday. The answer is (E).

14. You could consider all the answer choices, but that wouldn't be the fastest way to work this problem. Instead, think about what you know about the schedule. *Clouds* and *Frogs* can be performed on Wednesday, Friday, or Sunday. There must be one and only one day between the two of them. The only way to accomplish that is to perform *Clouds* and *Frogs* either on Wednesday and Friday, or on Friday and Sunday. Either way, you have to perform either *Clouds* or *Frogs* on Friday. That makes the answer (D).

15. Every choice but one here violates some rule. Eliminate the easy one first. Which choice has *Helen* on a day other than Thursday? (E), so you can cross it off. Does any choice fail to separate *Clouds* and *Frogs* by exactly one day? (C) does, so cross it off. Does any choice put *Antigone* and *Frogs* next to each other? (B) does so eliminate it. Does any choice place *Orestes* after *Antigone*? (A) does, so it's wrong. That leaves (D), which observes all rules and is therefore correct.

16. Sketch out the possibilities on your chart. Try (A). If you do *Clouds* on Friday, and *Antigone* on Saturday, that gives you a schedule of *Orestes, Frogs, Helen, Clouds, Antigone,* and *Electra,* which works. Try (B). If you do *Clouds* on Friday and *Antigone* on Sunday (that's the only possibility here), you must put *Frogs* on Wednesday, which leaves

Tuesday and Saturday for *Orestes* and *Electra,* which works. Try (C). Friday is reserved for *Clouds* or *Frogs,* so it's off limits, as is Thursday. You could perform *Electra* and *Orestes* on Tuesday and Wednesday, *Frogs* on Friday, and *Clouds* on Sunday, but that would force *Antigone* to be next to *Frogs,* which is forbidden. Or you could perform *Electra* and *Orestes* on Saturday and Sunday, but that would place *Orestes* after *Antigone,* which is also forbidden. (C) must be false. Just to consider the other possibilities, try (D). Actually, you already worked that one out; look at the schedule for choice (A). So (D) is possible. What about (E)? The same schedule works there, so (E) is also possible. The answer is (C).

17. You know from your chart that *Frogs'* possible performance dates are Wednesday, Friday, and Sunday, so you can eliminate any choice that has a day other than those three: (A), (B), and (E). Double-check Sunday to make sure it really can work for *Frogs.* If you do *Frogs* on Sunday, *Clouds* falls on Friday. In order to avoid scheduling *Antigone* next to *Frogs,* it must be performed on Monday or Tuesday; but *Orestes* must come before *Antigone,* so *Orestes* must be on Monday and *Antigone* on Tuesday. That leaves *Electra* for Saturday, with the lineup: *Orestes, Antigone, Helen, Clouds, Electra,* and *Frogs,* which works. The answer is (D).

18. You've already established that *Frogs* can be performed on Wednesday, so cross off (B). *Clouds* can be performed on Wednesday if *Antigone* is performed on Sunday, so cross off (A). Try (B). If *Electra* is performed on Tuesday, then *Clouds* and *Frogs* must be performed on Friday and Sunday. But you run into a problem there, because in order for *Antigone* to be performed after *Orestes,* it must fall on Saturday, but it can't because that would put it next to *Frogs.* (C) is your answer. Just to try the other possibilities, put *Orestes* on Tuesday; there are several acceptable schedules, such as *Orestes, Frogs, Helen, Clouds, Antigone,* and *Electra,* or *Orestes, Antigone, Helen, Clouds, Electra,* and *Frogs,* both of which you have already worked out for other problems, so (D) is wrong. What about performing *Orestes* on Saturday? Sure, you could have the schedule: *Electra, Clouds, Helen, Frogs, Orestes,* and *Antigone,* which is fine. The answer is (B).

Working in a Law Firm

The answers to questions 19-25 are as follows: 19.(C); 20.(D); 21.(B); 22.(D); 23.(C); 24.(C); 25.(C).

Sketching it out

Okay, this question is going to involve matching attorneys with specialties. Because there will always be only four specialties, and attorneys are going to have multiple specialties, the easiest way to organize your notes is by specialty, not by attorney. Visually, the simplest way to list the specialties is by number of attorneys, not alphabetically; that way, you always know that the specialty at the top should have one attorney and the one at the bottom three, with two for each one in the middle. Note the number of attorneys each one must hold. Your list could look like this:

t: __

e: __ __

v: __ __

i: __ __ __

List your attorneys by first initial: B, C, D, and H. Now, think about what you already know. You know that D shares C's specialties. Does this mean D can only specialize in something C also specializes in? No. Does it mean C can only specializes in something D specializes in? Yes. Note this C -> D, remembering not to restrict D to the same specialties as C.

You also know that C shares no specialties with B or H. Note this:

$$C \neq B \text{ or } H.$$

Think a bit more before embarking on the questions. You can make a couple of deductions that can make your thinking process easier. First, if D must share C's specialties, then C is never the sole specialist in an area. That means C can't specialize in tax. Second, if C can't share a specialty with B or H, that means the only three attorneys who can specialize in the same area must be B, H, and D. They must be the three who specialize in immigration. Third, C must be paired with D in any specialty, and only the two of them can specialize in that particular area, which means that they must practice either employment or real estate law, because those areas need exactly two attorneys. This information is valuable; note it on the chart.

$$t: \underline{} \text{ (not C)}$$

$$e: \underline{} \underline{} \text{ (C D)}$$

$$r: \underline{} \underline{} \text{ (C D)}$$

$$i: B H D$$

The jury's out: Defending the answers

And now the solutions to this ultra-fun problem.

19. You know Duway has to specialize in immigration. You also know Duway must specialize in either employment or real estate, but it doesn't matter which one. That puts Burton or Howard in tax, and Burton and Howard in either employment or real estate. Looking at the choices, (B) is wrong because Burton can specialize in tax. (B) is wrong, because Cheatham can specialize in employment. (C) must be right because Duway can't specialize in tax. To double-check, (D) is wrong because Howard can specialize in employment, and (E) is wrong because Howard, like Burton, can specialize in tax. So (C) is correct.

20. You already know one attorney who must specialize in more areas than another: Duway must specialize in more areas than Cheatham, because Duway must specialize in immigration. It looks like the answer must be (D). If you want to check the other possibilities, Burton can in fact specialize in more areas of law than Cheatham, but doesn't have to, so (A) is wrong. Howard can in fact specialize in more areas of law than Duway, but doesn't have to, so (B) is wrong. Duway can specialize in more areas than Howard, but doesn't have to, so (C) is wrong. Burton can specialize in more areas than Howard, but then Howard can also specialize in more areas than Burton, so (E) is wrong. (D) it is.

21. You know Duway specializes in immigration, so the correct answer doesn't include Duway. That eliminates (A), (D), and (E). You also know that immigration could include Burton and Howard. You have four possible pairs of attorneys who can specialize in

employment: Cheatham and Duway, Burton and Howard, Duway and Burton, or Duway and Howard. If Burton and Howard specialize in employment, they're the only attorneys who specialize in both employment and immigration, so (C) is wrong. Can Burton do it alone? No, Burton must be paired with Howard or Duway, so Burton alone can't be a complete list of the attorneys specializing in both employment and immigration. (B) is the answer.

22. The only two areas of law that Cheatham can specialize in are employment and real estate. If Cheatham occupies those areas, so does Duway. Those two with immigration give Duway the maximum three specialties, so Burton or Howard must specialize in tax. The chart would look like this:

$$t: B \text{ or } H$$

$$e: C \ D$$

$$r: C \ D$$

$$i: B \ H \ D$$

Now read the choices and see which answer may be true. (A) is false because Duway can't specialize in tax; (B) is false because Duway must specialize in three areas; (C) is false because Howard can't specialize in employment; (D) may be true because Howard can specialize in tax; (E) is false because Howard can't specialize in three areas of law. (D) is the only one that can be true, and it's your answer.

23. If Burton is to specialize in three fields, you already know one of them is immigration. You know Cheatham and Duway specialize in either employment or real estate, so Burton can specialize in one of those but not both, which excludes (A) and (B). Burton must specialize in tax to get a third specialty. It looks like (C) is the answer. (E) is wrong because Howard can't specialize in tax. (D) is wrong, too, because you don't know anything about Howard aside from the fact that he must specialize in immigration. Howard could possibly specialize in employment along with Burton, but doesn't have to. (C) is correct.

24. You know that the only attorneys who can specialize in tax are Burton, Duway, and Howard; these three also happen to be the attorneys who must specialize in immigration. Any answer choice that doesn't have the attorney specifically specializing in immigration must be false, and because you're looking for something that *can't* be true, that would be the right answer. Are there any choices that include that the attorney who doesn't specialize in immigration? Yes, (C). That's the answer, but if you want to test the other propositions, you can use Burton as a hypothetical. Can Burton specialize in immigration but not in real estate? Yes, if Cheatham and Duway take real estate, so (A) is wrong. Can Burton specialize in both immigration and real estate? Yes, if Cheatham and Duway take employment, so (B) is wrong. Can Burton specialize in employment but not real estate? Yes, if Cheatham and Duway take real estate, so (D) is wrong. Can Burton specialize in neither employment nor real estate? Yes, Cheatham and Duway can possibly take both of these specialties. (C) is the only good answer.

25. Look for rule violations. You know Burton can't share specialties with Cheatham, and you know that Cheatham must specialize in either employment or real estate. (A) and (B) have Burton specializing in both of those specialties, which is impossible. Can Duway specialize in employment, immigration, and real estate? Yes, consider (C) a good prospect. Duway can't specialize in employment, real estate, and tax, because he also specializes in immigration, and that gives him four specialties — against the rules — so (D) is out. The same reasoning nixes (E). (C) is correct.

Part III
Logical Reasoning: Arguing Well

In this part . . .

So you think you can think like a lawyer? Logical
Reasoning is designed to help you and the Law School
Admissions Council (LSAC) figure out whether you're right
about that. Lawyers don't actually spend their time working
Logical Reasoning problems, but law students and lawyers
do need to have the skills Logical Reasoning tests. This
section consists of short paragraphs — called arguments —
followed by single questions about those arguments that
test your understanding of how the arguments are constructed and how that construction might be wrong.
Questions ask you to strengthen or weaken the argument,
find flaws in the reasoning, spot assumptions, make infer-
ences, and perform other pleasurable activities along
those lines.

Don't skip prep for this section — Logical Reasoning
makes up half your total LSAT score!

Chapter 8

Stay on Your Toes: The Basics of Logical Reasoning

In This Chapter
▶ Meeting the LSAT Logical Reasoning section
▶ Looking at the facts
▶ Creating a systematic approach to Logical Reasoning questions
▶ Exploring essential Logical Reasoning vocabulary

The LSAT Logical Reasoning section, popularly called "arguments," tests your ability to deconstruct statements. This section, like the rest of the LSAT, measures your ability to read carefully and quickly. Unlike the other sections (Analytical Reasoning and Reading Comprehension), though, Logical Reasoning doesn't want you to immerse yourself in one text or one problem for several minutes and come to a deeper understanding of it. Logical Reasoning rewards speed and flexibility.

To add to the fun, every LSAT has two Logical Reasoning sections. The LSAT-makers think Logical Reasoning is really important and valuable in predicting law-school success, so on test day you spend at least 70 minutes answering these lovely little questions. I can't over-state the importance of preparing for this section; it's half your score, which is a big deal. Logical Reasoning is also particularly exhausting. Instead of getting to spend several minutes absorbing the details of a long reading passage or Analytical Reasoning problem, you have to switch gears constantly, spending a minute pondering the principle behind some statement about new doctors, and the next minute coming up with evidence to support a proposal to start school later. It's tough out there in the field.

In this chapter, I describe the basics of Logical Reasoning — how the chapters are set up, what the questions look like, why this section is on the test. This chapter is a general overview of Logical Reasoning; Chapters 9 through 11 go into detail about specific Logical Reasoning question types.

What You Can Expect in the Logical Reasoning Sections

Here's the bare-bones info you need to know about the test's Logical Reasoning sections:

✓ **A section of Logical Reasoning contains about 25 or 26 questions. Every question consists of a short statement called an *argument* — usually 3 or 4 sentences — followed by a question about that argument.**

The LSAT-makers design questions to see how well you understand the structure of arguments, or more basically to test your understanding of how someone else thinks. The questions may ask you to strengthen or weaken a statement; they may ask you to identify the argument's conclusion; they may ask you to duplicate the argument's pattern of reasoning.

✓ **Every question stands alone.**

For the 35 minutes of a Logical Reasoning section, you need to switch gears every minute or so. You may spend a moment pondering the implications of the shape of sickles found at different archaeological sites, and the next minute analyzing the reasoning in a claim about the profits earned by movies.

Don't immerse yourself into any one problem. Instead, read and answer as fast as you can without sacrificing accuracy.

Chapters 9 through 11 discuss the nitty-gritty of particular kinds of Logical Reasoning questions in greater detail. Chapter 12 contains an entire section of Logical Reasoning questions, and Chapter 13 contains detailed explanations of those questions.

Just the Facts, Ma'am: Arguing for Logic

What do lawyers do? They argue. They make statements and support them with evidence in order to convince a judge or jury that they're right or that their opponents are wrong. They read statutes and cases and briefs looking for tidbits of information that they can use to prove that their side is right or the other side is wrong — all under an intense time crunch.

What don't lawyers do? They don't argue from personal conviction or emotion. They don't structure their arguments based on their own feelings, but on the facts and the laws. They don't always get to choose the side they represent, which occasionally results in a lawyer supporting a side that she personally believes should lose a case.

The LSAT Logical Reasoning section is designed to test your ability to do many of these lawyerly tasks.

Starting off with an argument

In every Logical Reasoning argument the author states some conclusion and attempts to support it with evidence. Your job is to identify this conclusion, figure out how the author is supporting it, and then determine why it's successful or not.

Here's an example: "My house is full of bees. I need to call an exterminator." What's the conclusion of this argument? I need to call an exterminator. What evidence is used to justify this conclusion? My house is full of bees.

This basic statement, simple though it is, could become the basis for a variety of Logical Reasoning–style questions. For example, what assumptions does this statement make? It assumes that an exterminator can eradicate bees in a house. What information could strengthen the conclusion? Maybe something like "exterminators are specialists in ridding houses of insect pests." What information could weaken the conclusion? How about a statement such as "Ordinary exterminators don't handle bee swarms, and recommend that customers call animal control specialists to take care of them."

Logical Reasoning questions, like all LSAT questions, include all the information you need to answer them correctly. That means you don't have to be an expert in any esoteric topic — say, bees or exterminators — to answer them. That doesn't mean, however, that you don't have to understand what they're talking about. Logical Reasoning questions presume a fairly high level of reading proficiency and vocabulary; you have to be a skilled reader in order to understand the arguments well enough to work with them. So you should still leave your preconceived notions about a subject at home, but you should definitely keep thinking actively and put your vocabulary and reading skills to work.

Most Logical Reasoning questions are a bit longer than this example, and they're usually not as straightforward. At heart, though, they're not that different. Every one offers a proposition and supports it with evidence. The proposition may be right or wrong, and the evidence may or may not support it, but the basic structure doesn't change.

Here's an actual Logical Reasoning question from Chapter 12:

Prosecutor: I have furnished evidence that the accused committed the crime in question. The defense agrees that the crime did occur; they say that the accused did not commit the crime, but they have not proven that someone else did. Therefore, the jury should find that the defendant is guilty.

The reasoning in the prosecutor's argument is flawed because the argument

(A) ignores evidence that the accused might be innocent

(B) criticizes the arguments by the defense without addressing their flaws

(C) confuses the defense's failure to prove that someone else committed with proof that the accused is guilty

(D) implies that because the defense has admitted that the crime did occur, the defendant must be guilty

(E) fails to consider the possibility that someone else committed the crime

Note the structure: A paragraph that states the proposition — the argument — followed by a question asking something about the argument. Some Logical Reasoning questions are considerably longer than this one; few are shorter. (I'm not going to answer it here; try it in Chapter 12, and then see Chapter 13 for the answer.)

Every argument has a speaker or an author, someone who is making the point in question. Some arguments identify their speaker, while others don't. If an argument doesn't name a speaker, though, don't assume that one doesn't exist. When discussing arguments without identified speakers, I sometimes refer to the speaker as the "author." I do that because some active individual is responsible for whatever claims are made, even if you have no idea who that individual is.

Some Logical Reasoning questions follow one argument with two questions. Most recent LSATs, though, haven't included many (or any) of these two-question arguments. Maybe people worked those questions too fast. Be prepared for Logical Reasoning sections that give one question for every argument, but if you come across an argument with two questions, don't fret about it; just answer it and enjoy the small reprieve. Think of it as a bonus — two questions for the price of one argument!

Questioning the argument

Following are some of the main types of Logical Reasoning questions you may encounter on the LSAT:

- **Assumptions:** Which one of the following is an assumption required by the argument above?

- **Flaws:** A reasoning flaw in the argument is that the argument . . .

- **Logical conclusions:** Which one of the following most accurately expresses the main conclusion of the argument?

- **Strengthen:** Which one of the following, if true, most strengthens the argument?

- **Weaken:** Which one of the following, if true, most seriously weakens the argument above?

- **Support:** Each of the following, if true, supports the claim above EXCEPT:

- **Role played by a claim:** The claim that attorneys sometimes serve as their own secretaries plays which one of the following roles in the argument?

- **Resolving discrepancies or paradoxes:** Which one of the following, if true, most helps to resolve the apparent paradox described above?

- **Patterns of reasoning:** Which one of the following exhibits a pattern of reasoning most similar to that exhibited by the argument above?

- **Principles:** Which one of the following conforms most closely to the principle illustrated by the statements above?

- **Structure of argument:** In responding to Larry, Stephen . . . (criticizes, accuses, explains, challenges, assumes)

Chapters 9, 10, and 11 go into much greater detail about the specific types of questions.

Elementary, My Dear Watson: Reasoning Logically

Every Logical Reasoning question follows the same basic structure: argument followed by question followed by five pesky answers. To maximize your efficiency in answering them, follow the same approach with each question. I don't know of any tricks you can use; just think systematically and stay flexible.

Thinking quickly

An entire Logical Reasoning section contains about 25 or 26 questions. You have 35 minutes to answer them, which gives you slightly more than a minute per question. Some questions are short. Others are quite long; sometimes you'll see a question that, with all five choices, takes up an entire column of the page.

If you see such a long question, just know that the LSAT-writers are testing your ability to read and think quickly.

The best way to improve your reading speed is to read a lot. Obviously you won't be able to get in extra reading practice if you're taking the LSAT in one month, but if your test date is months away, you may have the time. Turn off the television and read books and magazines — even "frivolous" reading material, like romance novels or motorcycle magazines, can help. That reading practice will help in law school, too, where all you do is read.

For the moment, don't worry about speed. You have all the time pressure you need when you take the LSAT for real. Right now, just concentrate on the questions and the reasoning required to answer them.

Taking a systematic approach

Try out this basic approach that works for all Logical Reasoning questions:

1. **Read the question before you read the argument.**

2. **Read the argument.**

3. **Try to answer the question in your head before you read the answer choices.**

4. **Choose an answer.**

   Read all the answers and eliminate wrong ones. Pick your answer. Then forget about that question and move on to the next one.

You don't have much time to devote to each question. If you follow an orderly plan of attack for every question, you can move much faster than if you concoct your strategy on the fly.

Reading the question first

The structure of Logical Reasoning questions doesn't change: They're all arguments followed by questions followed by answer choices. No rule, though, says you have to read them in this order.

Read the question before jumping into the argument. Then you can read the argument with the specific question in mind. For example, if a question asks you to reconcile an apparent discrepancy, you can read the argument looking for a discrepancy. If a question asks you for an assumption, you can read the argument looking for an assumption. Reading the argument before the question doesn't hurt, but most arguments lend themselves to several different question types, and if you read the argument first and only then read the question, you may have to backtrack through the argument.

Underlining the key words in the question may help. For example, if you get a question that asks you to resolve a discrepancy, underline the word "discrepancy." If it asks you for the author's conclusion, underline the word "conclusion."

It's okay to write in the test booklet. In fact, I recommend it. Notes and diagrams play a big role in a successful LSAT experience.

Reading the argument

After you know what you're looking for, actively read the argument. You're a reader on a mission. Look for whatever the question asks for. If it asks for an assumption, look for an assumption — you know one is in there. If it asks for a flaw, find a flaw.

Again, if it helps you to underline key words, underline them. Be careful, though, because you don't want to underline too much, which won't help you. If you're a chronic underliner, or if you find the exercise of underlining to be distracting, forget about it and just read carefully.

LSAT arguments seem like fairly scholarly or specialized statements, but they're really just made-up paragraphs. So if their facts seem wrong, or if an argument makes a point that you disagree with, don't let it bother you. You need to find the argument structure. That's all. Forget about the facts. They don't matter.

Formulating an answer

Now try to answer the question in your head before you read the answer choices. If you have an answer in your head before you read the answer choices, the correct answer should just jump right out at you. The wrong answers will be glaringly wrong, and crossing them off should take no time.

Of course, you can't always concoct the exact right answer. For example, if a question asks what information would strengthen the author's conclusion, you can't always hope to imagine the exact factoid that'll be in the right answer; but you probably can come up with something in the ballpark. My point: You need to actively approach the answers, already armed with an idea of what you want to find.

Many students overlook this step, not realizing what a valuable tool anticipating the answer can be. Don't make this mistake yourself. Always try to concoct an answer before you check out the choices. Paraphrasing the right answer in your head saves time in the long run. The answer choices are meant to confuse you. But if you have a solid idea of what you're looking for, the right answer will appear more obvious, and you won't be lead astray by wrong choices.

One kind of question can't be answered beforehand: a question that asks you which of the five answer choices is most similar to the pattern of reasoning in the argument. You can, however, break down the pattern of reasoning in the argument before you confront the choices, so really you're still coming up with an answer first. See Chapter 10 for more information.

Reading the answers and eliminating the wrong ones

Now read the answers. Having one obviously correct choice and four obviously wrong ones would be nice, but of course the LSAT doesn't work that way. All five choices seem plausible. The LSAT-makers want you to spend your time agonizing over the answer choices, fretting because two of them look right, and you just can't figure out which is which. Remember, though, there are never two right answers. Four answers are always wrong, one answer is always right, and the test-makers have to be very clear about which is which. Choices that seem ambiguous really aren't.

The winding or the straight road?

Do you work Logical Reasoning sections straight through, from first to last question? Or does it make more sense to jump around, answering the questions you like first and saving the ugly ones for later?

I don't think it matters. There's no reason not to begin on the first question and work your way to the last, filling in the dots on your answer sheet as you go. Then again, if you find jumping around easier, go for it. And if you get stuck on a question, it makes sense to skip it and move on, coming back later if you have time. Just be sure not

to mess up your answer sheet. Use your finger or pencil to point to the answer you want to bubble in, or some other technique that keeps your answers matched up. (See Chapter 2 for more on this topic.)

If you do jump around, realize that rating questions for difficulty uses up some of your valuable test time. There's not all that much variation in difficulty from problem to problem, so you may get better results just tackling each question without categorizing it first.

Even when you know which answer you want to find, reading through all the choices can take a little time. Logical Reasoning answer choices can sometimes be nearly as long and complicated as the actual arguments.

You know what to do, though: Read each answer quickly but carefully. Cross it off if you know for sure that it's wrong; leave it alone if you think it might be right.

Don't get too caught up in the quest for speed. If you feel like you need to read an argument twice to find the answer, go ahead and do it and don't fret because you had to backtrack. You've already put the time into reading the argument, so you may as well give it a fair shake.

Choosing an answer

After reading all the answer choices, pick an answer. If you cross off four obviously wrong answers and find one obviously correct one, great. If you can't decide between two answers, think about them for a little while, no more than 30 seconds or so. If you still can't decide which one is right, pick one and move on. You have other fish to fry.

Forgetting about that question and moving on

After you answer a question, forget about it. Erase it from your mind. It has absolutely no bearing on the rest of your life, which at this point includes the rest of the LSAT. You need that brainpower to tackle more questions. (And, presumably, you want to use your brain for non-LSAT pursuits someday, too.)

Take a break after each page. Your brain gets tired after several straight minutes of logical reasoning. These questions are tiring because there are so many of them and because you're constantly stuffing new information into your already overstuffed mind. So every time you finish a page of questions, take a break. Not a long break — just a few seconds is enough. Close your eyes, roll your head around, stare out the window, and let your brain recharge. Then forge ahead.

While you look around the room or out the window, be sure you *don't* look at anyone else's test, or even seem like you might be. LSAT proctors don't tolerate even a suspicion of cheating. If you cherish hopes of a legal career, you won't ever cheat or look like you're cheating on the LSAT.

Logical, Reasonable Vocabulary

If you don't already know, you'll discover that lawyers use words in specific ways; they have a particular vocabulary all their own. The LSAT-makers do the same thing. One key to success with logical reasoning is to understand how the LSAT uses certain words.

The Big 7

You may be able to get away without studying too much logical reasoning, but you absolutely must master these words and their nuances. The LSAT uses these terms in a near-mathematical sense. Certain questions depend on the way the test-makers use these terms.

- ✔ **None:** This one is easy. *None* means none, absolutely none, not even one.

- ✔ **One:** *One* means one. Enough said.

- ✔ **Some:** Well, what does *some* mean? Some is more than one but less than all. If you encounter a question that uses both *some* and *most,* assume that they may mean the same thing.

- ✔ **Most:** *Most* means more than half.

- ✔ **Many:** This one is another vague term, like *some. Many* means quite a bit more than one, but still not all.

- ✔ **All:** *All* refers to every group member.

- ✔ **Every:** *Every* means what it says; a question that uses the term *every* means every member of a group, just like *all.*

The main thing to remember with these terms: They're always used relative to one another. Therefore, a question that mixes the terms *some, most,* and *all* wants you to compare the three, which can be confusing. *All* is the only term that has a definite meaning here. *Some* and *most* could potentially be the same amount. For example:

Mountain laurels thrive in a cool environment. Butterfly bushes bloom best in full sun. In most of South Carolina, gardens contain either mountain laurels or butterfly bushes.

If the statements above are true, which one of the following must be false?

(A) Most of South Carolina is cool.

(B) Most of South Carolina is sunny.

(C) Half of South Carolina is both sunny and cool.

(D) Some parts of South Carolina are neither sunny nor cool.

(E) No mountain laurels grow in South Carolina.

Okay, if most of South Carolina gardens have EITHER mountain laurels OR butterfly bushes — which means they don't contain both — then most of South Carolina — more than half — is EITHER sunny OR cool, but not both. (A) is wrong because it's possible that most of South Carolina is cool; same with (B). The information doesn't tell you about relative proportions, and it's possible that most of South Carolina is cool and none of it is sunny, or most of it is sunny and none of it is cool. Look at (C). If most of South Carolina contains either mountain laurels or butterfly bushes, then most of South Carolina is cool or sunny, *not* cool and sunny; because "most" means more than half, the portion of South Carolina that doesn't have either mountain laurels or butterfly bushes must be less than half, so even if that other portion is both cool and sunny, it can't comprise half of South Carolina. (C) must be false. What about (D) and (E)? The plants grow in most of the state, not all of it, so it's possible for some parts to be neither sunny nor cool. Likewise it's possible that no mountain laurels grow in South Carolina. So (D) and (E) could be true. That leaves (C).

Other special words

Look over these other words that you may encounter in the Logical Reasoning section:

- ✔ **Assume:** To take for granted that something is true, without proof; the noun form is *assumption.*

- ✔ **Conclude:** To reason one's way to a judgment or decision; the noun form is *conclusion.*

- ✔ **Deduce:** To draw a logical conclusion by reasoning from available facts; the noun form is *deduction.*

- ✔ **Discrepancy:** A difference, incompatibility, or lack of agreement between two or more statements.

- ✔ **Explain:** To describe an idea and its facts in such a way as to make it clear; to provide reasons or justifications for some phenomenon; the noun form is *explanation.*

- ✔ **Flaw:** An error or mistake; a fault or weakness.

- ✔ **Imply:** To suggest a conclusion without stating it directly; a conclusion that can be drawn from something not directly stated can be called an *implication*.

- ✔ **Infer:** To use evidence and reasoning to reach a conclusion that isn't directly stated; the noun form is *inference*.

- ✔ **Paradox:** A statement that leads to a conclusion that is senseless or logically impossible.

- ✔ **Parallel:** Corresponding; running side-by-side; a similarity; something that is analogous to something else.

- ✔ **Premise:** An assertion or statement that is used as the basis for a conclusion; to base a conclusion on a particular claim or statement.

- ✔ **Presume:** To assume; to suppose that something is true based on available evidence, but not necessarily direct proof; the noun form is *presumption*. Lawyers and judges often talk about *presumptions,* which are basically the same thing as assumptions but sound fancier.

- ✔ **Reconcile:** To make two things consistent with one another; to restore harmony; the noun form is *reconciliation*.

- ✔ **Support:** To furnish evidence or reasons that make a conclusion seem more likely.

- ✔ **Vulnerable:** Weak; open to attack.

Don't confuse "deduce" and "deduct." *To deduct* is to subtract something from something else. Its noun form is also *deduction*.

A word on "big words"

The LSAT uses lots of tough words. People who go to law school have college degrees, and the LSAT-makers assume that test-takers can read English at a high level. So, for instance, a question may use the word *carcinogen* without explanation, because a college graduate ought to know that a carcinogen is something that causes cancer. Actual LSAT questions have used words such as "libelous," "bilirubin," "stringent," "quintile," "macaque," and other million-dollar words. The bad news: A book like this or any other standard LSAT-prep program can't prepare you for texts with hard words. The good news: If you're a good reader and if you've spent your time in college doing your reading assignments and flipping through the newspaper on occasion, you've probably encountered most of the words on the LSAT. In addition, your college reading may have trained you to decipher the meaning of words from the context in which they are used. Not getting tripped up because you don't know a word is a valuable skill to have both on the LSAT and in law school!

Chapter 9

Conclusions, Assumptions, and Flaws in Logical Reasoning Questions

. . . .

In This Chapter

▶ Identifying conclusions

▶ Spotting assumptions

▶ Naming the role played by a claim

▶ Rooting out logical flaws

. . . .

At its most basic level, an argument is a statement of opinion — an opinion that favors whatever side the speaker is supporting. The first thing you have to do when you meet an argument is to figure out what it's all about — what's the author's point?

The next thing you have to do is figure out how the author gets to the conclusion from the evidence she uses. Sometimes the process is straight and sensible, but sometimes it isn't. Believe it or not, not every conclusion in every argument is valid. Uh huh, it's true, both in the LSAT Logical Reasoning section and real life, including the study and practice of law. The ugly fact: Many arguments are based on assumptions, mistakes, and logical flaws. The even uglier fact: People often get away with making invalid conclusions. They base their claims on erroneous information and faulty logic, and no one stops them.

The most basic task involved in Logical Reasoning questions is identifying the argument's conclusion. In order to answer most questions, you first have to spot the conclusion, and then figure out how and why the author reached that conclusion. For some questions, though, all you have to do is identify the conclusion. Look at those questions as a gift. (That is, if you find them easy; otherwise, look at them as just another kind of question.) Other Logical Reasoning questions are a bit more complicated; not only must you spot the conclusion, you must also figure out how the author uses her evidence to support the conclusion. Did the author make a leap of logic that she shouldn't have? Did she make an invalid assumption? Did she just plain make a mistake?

In this chapter, I focus on questions that ask you to spot conclusions and then to figure out how the authors reached those conclusions. The most basic "conclusion" type questions simply require you to spot the conclusion. The more complicated "assumption" and "logical flaw" type questions ask a bit more of you — you have to first spot the conclusion, and then figure out what facts the author assumed in order to reach that conclusion, or perhaps spot a mistake the author made in applying the evidence.

Jumping to Logical Conclusions

Some Logical Reasoning questions ask you to identify an argument's conclusion. The *conclusion* is the point the argument tries to make. When you find a conclusion question, read the argument asking yourself why that argument exists. What is the author trying to say? Why did someone bother putting these sentences together in this order? What is the opinion the author is trying to persuade you about?

A great way to spot the conclusion is to look for words that signal that a conclusion is coming. *Therefore, thus, so, consequently,* and *hence* are transition words that connect evidence to a conclusion. In other arguments, you'll have a string of evidence and you'll be asked to formulate the conclusion. If so, after you read the argument, predict the conclusion by beginning your prediction with, "therefore . . . "

Eyeing conclusive questions

Many of these questions use the word *conclusion,* which makes your job in identifying the question type easier. They may, however, ask what you can *infer* from the argument, which is another way of asking for the argument's conclusion. Or the question may ask which one of the answers is most supported by the evidence, or which of the answers must be true if the argument's statements are true.

Check out the following examples of questions that ask you to identify the argument's conclusion:

- ✔ Which one of the following most accurately expresses the main conclusion of the argument?
- ✔ Which one of the following most accurately expresses the conclusion of the editorialist's argument?
- ✔ Which one of the following most logically completes the argument?
- ✔ Which one of the following is most strongly supported by the information above?
- ✔ The statements above, if true, most strongly support which one of the following?
- ✔ If all the statements above are true, which one of the following must also be true?
- ✔ If the statements above are true, which one of the following must be false?
- ✔ If the statements above are true, each of the following could be true EXCEPT:
- ✔ The statements above, if true, most strongly support which one of the following?
- ✔ The dialog above lends the most support to the claim that Sam and Fred disagree with each other about which one of the following statements?
- ✔ The statements above, if true, most strongly support which one of the following conclusions about the global warming and its effects in North America?
- ✔ Which one of the following can be inferred from the statements above?
- ✔ From the statements above, which one of the following can be properly inferred?
- ✔ From the zoologist's statements, which one of the following can be properly inferred about the specimen of animal X in the zoologist's laboratory?

No matter how the LSAT-writers word the question, you have to decide what the author is saying and why he has assembled these particular bits of evidence in such a way as to support some statement or other.

Some test-prep books refer to conclusion questions as "main point" questions, and have tons of examples in which the question asks, "What is the main point of the argument?" I haven't seen that wording in any of the most recent LSATs, so I don't include it in the previous listing. However, just because I don't include it doesn't mean it may not appear on the LSAT when you take it. So if you see the words "main point," know they mean "conclusion."

Looking at some conclusion questions and explanations

Check out the following example that asks for the argument's conclusion. I also give you the correct answer and explain how to reach that answer.

Pediatrician: Some parents have decided not to have their children receive the MMR vaccine because they fear that it may cause autism; they cite a study that found a possible link between the vaccine and the disease. Two other much larger studies, however, have found no link between the MMR vaccine and autism. These parents have, therefore, willfully put their own children and many others at risk of catching measles, mumps, and rubella, while failing to do anything to prevent their children from becoming autistic.

Which one of the following most accurately expresses the main conclusion of the pediatrician's argument?

(A) Parents should not pay attention to medical studies because they can't understand them; they should instead get medical advice from their pediatricians.

(B) The study that found a link between autism and the MMR vaccine was unsound because the doctor who conducted it was being paid by a group who wanted him to find a connection.

(C) Public health concerns demand that parents have their children vaccinated regardless of their own reservations about the procedure.

(D) Parents' refusal to have their children receive the MMR vaccine is both medically unjustifiable and dangerous, because the vaccine has known disease-preventing benefits and refusing it will have no effect on whether or not their children become autistic.

(E) Despite the results of the two large studies, there is still some possibility that the MMR vaccine might cause autism.

Always follow the same basic steps when approaching a Logical Reasoning question.

1. **Read the question.**

   See what the LSAT-writers are asking and then keep that in mind when you read the argument.

2. **Read the argument and identify the conclusion.**

   Look for keywords like *therefore, hence, consequently,* and so on to recognize the conclusion.

3. **Make up an answer in your own head *before* going to the answer choices.**

   Creating a vision of the right answer cuts down on time in the long run because you'll be less confused by wrong answer choices. Do yourself a favor and make up your answer before entering the land mine of choices! Many students think this is the single-most beneficial tip for Logical Reasoning questions.

4. **Read the answer choices and pick your answer.**

   Finally, go to the choices, with your prediction in mind. Eliminate choices that are far from what you're looking for.

(A) isn't the pediatrician's conclusion. Nothing in the argument suggests that parents shouldn't pay attention to medical studies. (B) isn't the conclusion, though the doctor could use it as evidence to support the conclusion, as further proof that the parents who don't vaccinate their kids are basing their decision on bad information. (C) isn't the conclusion, though the pediatrician probably would agree with the statement; the doctor says that parents who don't vaccinate their kids are endangering others but he doesn't specifically say that parents should put aside their own reservations. (D) restates the pediatrician's conclusion; that's your answer. (E) most definitely isn't the pediatrician's conclusion; he uses the two large studies as conclusive evidence of the contention that the MMR vaccine doesn't cause autism. (D) is correct.

Here's another conclusion-type question. This one asks what you can *infer* from the information in the argument, which is another way of asking you to draw a conclusion from the evidence given.

Most competitive cyclists lift weights, and most competitive cyclists watch their diets carefully. Furthermore, all cyclists who watch their diets carefully also monitor their body fat.

Which one of the following can be properly inferred from the statements above?

(A) Some cyclists who don't lift weights watch their diets carefully.

(B) All competitive cyclists monitor their body fat.

(C) Some cyclists who lift weights also monitor their body fat.

(D) All cyclists who monitor their body fat are competitive cyclists.

(E) Most cyclists who monitor their body fat are cyclists who lift weights.

The question asks you to infer something from the argument, which means you're looking for something that's not expressly stated but that you can logically conclude based on what has been said. This argument doesn't offer evidence in proof of a conclusion, but rather a series of factual statements that fit together. The first sentence makes claims about "most competitive cyclists." The second sentence makes claims about "all cyclists." Note that "competitive cyclists" are a subset of "cyclists."

The argument doesn't give you enough information to concoct the answer before looking at the choices, though you can make some guesses. For example, it logically follows that all competitive cyclists who watch their diets carefully also monitor their body fat. Wouldn't it be easy if that were an answer choice? But the LSAT-writers want you to use your brainpower. All you can do in this case is read the answer choices and see which one you could infer from the argument.

Don't add anything to the equation; don't assume anything the argument doesn't tell you.

(A) could be true, but you can't infer it from the argument. The argument tells you nothing about cyclists who don't lift weights. (B) assumes too much; most competitive cyclists do monitor their body fat, but you can't prove that they all do. (C) is definitely true. If most competitive cyclists monitor their body fat, and most competitive cyclists lift weights, there has to be some overlap between those two groups, because "most" implies more than half. It may be a small group, but some cyclists who lift weights definitely must monitor their body fat. (D) doesn't work. You know that all cyclists who watch their diets also monitor their body fat, but that doesn't tell you anything about whether or not they're all competitive cyclists; some may be mere amateurs. (E) makes a claim that you can't infer from the facts. Although there is bound to be some overlap between cyclists who lift weights and cyclists who monitor body fat, nothing in the argument justifies the conclusion here. So (C) is your answer.

Making Assumptions

Making an argument without assuming at least one or two points is nearly impossible. If you back up everything you say, it can take forever, and sometimes you have to assume something just for the sake of argument. Assumptions aren't necessarily bad, but you do need to recognize them when they occur.

When you assume . . .

Most Logical Reasoning sections have a number of questions asking you to identify assumptions in arguments. The questions can look like this:

✔ Which one of the following is an assumption required by the argument above?

✔ The professor's conclusion follows logically if which one of the following is assumed?

✔ Which one of the following is an assumption on which the scholar's argument depends?

✔ The politician's argument depends on assuming which one of the following?

✔ On which one of the following assumptions does the argument rely?

✔ Which one of the following, if assumed, would allow the conclusion to be properly drawn?

✔ Which one of the following, if assumed, enables the argument's conclusion to be properly inferred?

✔ The argument requires the assumption that . . .

✔ The argument's reasoning is vulnerable to criticism on the grounds that the argument presumes, without giving warrant, that . . . (I could also have put this question in the "Finding Flaws in an Argument" section, but it's asking for a presumption, which is pretty similar to an assumption.)

When you see a question with the word *assume* or *assumption* (or occasionally *presume* or *presumption*), read the argument looking for something that the author doesn't state outright, but that she must believe is true in order for the argument to hold together. Identify both the conclusion and the evidence used to support the conclusion. Then figure out what's missing between the two — that's the assumption.

For example, if the argument says "My house is full of bees, so I need to call an exterminator," the author must assume that the exterminator can do something about the bees, though the argument doesn't explicitly state this fact.

Walking through an assumption question

Here's an assumption-type question about fad diets:

Melissa: Many people are eager to lose weight and keep it off. However, instead of improving the nutritional content of their diets, restricting calories, and exercising, they often opt for fad diets that promise rapid weight loss. Because people who follow a balanced diet and exercise have changed their habits for the better, they have very good long-term success at maintaining a healthy weight. Therefore, fad diets are unlikely to result in meaningful weight loss.

Which one of the following is an assumption on which Melissa's argument depends?

(A) The fad diets she mentions do not provide the same weight loss benefits as a balanced diet combined with exercise.

(B) People who use fad diets do not understand basic principles of nutrition.

(C) Some people who follow fad diets do lose weight and keep it off.

(D) It is very difficult to maintain a balanced diet and a regular program of exercise.

(E) Some fad diets were created by doctors who have years of experience counseling overweight patients.

Read the question. You know the argument contains an assumption, and without that assumption, the argument falls apart. Melissa's conclusion is that fad diets don't result in meaningful weight loss. She says that people who lose weight on balanced diets with exercise keep weight off because they change their habits. She doesn't say anything about the changed habits of people who follow fad diets, but presumably she would say that they haven't changed their habits in such a way as to keep weight off. So she's assuming that fad diets don't really work at keeping weight off in the long run.

(A) looks like a good choice; Melissa clearly believes that fad diets don't have the same weight-loss benefits as balanced diets. Melissa may believe (B), but her argument doesn't depend on the assumption that people on fad diets don't understand nutrition, simply that fad diets don't work. (C) definitely isn't Melissa's assumption; quite the contrary, she assumes that fad diets usually don't work. (D) isn't part of the argument, though it may be true. (E) is irrelevant to Melissa's argument; the involvement of doctors in the development of fad diets has nothing to do with her conclusion that fad diets don't work. (A) is the correct answer.

Knowing the Role Played by a Claim

If you make a statement in an argument, you have a reason for doing it. You may want to provide an example to illustrate your point, you may want to respond to your opponent's conclusion, or you may want to provide evidence to back up your conclusion. Law students not only have to be able to form arguments, but they also have to analyze their opponents' arguments. A large part of that analysis lies in understanding why their opponents say particular things.

Spotting role-playing questions

Some Logical Reasoning questions test your ability to determine why a certain sentence or claim is in an argument. Almost all these questions use the term *role*, as in "what role does this statement play in the argument?" Glance at some of the following examples:

- ✔ The claim that people have positive or negative responses to many nonsense words plays which one of the following roles in the argument?

- ✔ Which one of the following most accurately describes the role played in the teacher's argument by the assertion that participating in organized competitive athletics may increase a child's strength and coordination?

- ✔ Which one of the following most accurately describes the role played in the psychologist's argument by the claim that the obligation to express gratitude cannot be fulfilled anonymously?

- ✔ The claim that humans are still biologically adapted to a diet of wild foods plays which one of the following roles in the nutritionist's argument?

- ✔ Which one of the following most accurately describes the role played in the scientist's argument by the claim that recent scientific research can often be described only in language that seems esoteric to most contemporary readers?

- ✔ The claim that inventors sometimes serve as their own engineers plays which one of the following roles in the argument?

When you encounter one of these questions, ask yourself why the argument includes the information or claim. Is it evidence? Is it an attack on someone else's argument? Whatever it is, try to answer the question before you scan the answer choices; it may make the right answer jump right out at you.

Playing around with a role-playing example question

Look at this example of a role-played-by-a-claim question:

When selecting a horseback-riding vacation, it is important to be honest about your actual riding ability. Some vacations require riders to handle spirited horses in open terrain, or to spend six hours a day in the saddle, which for a beginner would be uncomfortable at best and dangerous at worst. Even for novice-level vacations, you should be able to post a trot, control a slow canter, and care for your horse's tack. Almost anyone can learn to ride a horse well, provided they are willing to put in the effort, but it is never wise to overestimate your ability.

The claim that some vacations require riders to handle spirited horses in open terrain plays which one of the following roles in the argument?

(A) It is the main conclusion of the argument.

(B) It undermines the argument's main conclusion.

(C) It is evidence that supports the argument's conclusion.

(D) It summarizes the evidence in support of the conclusion.

(E) It is an assumption on which the argument's conclusion depends.

Read the question first. Note the words "plays which one of the following roles." That means you have to figure out why the author included the point about handling spirited horses in rough terrain.

Now read the argument, looking for where the author mentions the spirited horses. If you find underlining helpful, underline those words when you see them. You can find this tidbit in the second sentence. Now, what is this argument trying to do? The author's conclusion, stated at the beginning and the end of the paragraph, is that anyone going on a horseback-riding vacation should evaluate his or her riding ability honestly. Why? Because taking a riding vacation may require more skill than a rider has and could inevitably be dangerous or unpleasant.

So why does the author mention the need to handle spirited horses in open terrain? In this case, she's using this information as an example of something a rider on a horseback-riding vacation may have to do, and telling you that it's something a beginner shouldn't attempt. In effect, the "handling spirited horses" statement is evidence that the author uses to support the conclusion.

Now go through the answer choices and look for a response that matches this. (A) is wrong because the argument's conclusion is that people shouldn't overestimate their riding ability. (B) is wrong because that factoid doesn't undermine the conclusion; instead it supports it. (C) looks good; the author is using the fact that riders must be able to handle spirited horses in open terrain as an example of something that beginners shouldn't attempt, which supports her conclusion. (D) is wrong because that fact doesn't summarize the evidence at all. (E) is wrong because it's not an assumption but a stated fact. (C) is the only answer that works.

Finding Flaws in an Argument

Not every argument is good. In fact, many (if not most) arguments have something wrong with them. As a lawyer, you'll have to spot bad arguments from your opponents — so you can attack them, and in your own work — so you can fix them.

I see your flaw . . .

Many Logical Reasoning questions have flaws. The LSAT-makers place the flaws there to test your ability to spot them. These questions ask you to identify flaws, reason flaws, or catch arguments vulnerable to criticism.

These problems are a bit more complicated than questions that simply ask you to identify a conclusion. First you have to find the conclusion, then you have to figure out how the author reached it, and then you have to figure out what's wrong with that reasoning process.

Take a look at some examples of spot-the-flaw questions:

- ✔ Which one of the following most accurately describes a flaw in the argument?

- ✔ A reasoning flaw in the argument is that the argument . . .

- ✔ The reasoning in the astronomer's argument is flawed because this argument . . .

- ✔ The reasoning above is flawed because it fails to recognize that . . .

- ✔ The argument is vulnerable to criticism on which one of the following grounds?

- ✔ The reasoning in the argument is most vulnerable to criticism on the ground that the argument . . .

- ✔ Which one of the following, if true, would most call into question the economist's explanation of the stock price increase?

- ✔ The reasoning in the argument is most vulnerable to criticism on the grounds that the argument . . .

- ✔ The reasoning in the argument is most vulnerable to criticism because the argument fails to consider the possibility that . . .

- ✔ The reasoning in the argument is flawed because the argument fails to take into account that . . .

- ✔ A questionable aspect of the reasoning above is that it . . .

- ✔ The argument is questionable because it fails to consider . . .

- ✔ Otis's reply suggests that he misinterprets Chari's use of the term . . .

- ✔ Which one of the following most accurately describes a flaw in the reasoning in Sarah's response to Becky's statements?

When you see a question with the word *flaw, criticism, questionable, fails to consider,* or anything else like that, you automatically know that the argument contains a flaw. Read the argument with that in mind.

A flawless example of a flaw-finding question

Study this example of a question that asks you to spot the flaw in the argument's reasoning:

Some Southern towns have quaint downtown areas, and some Southern towns have small colleges. Therefore, some towns with small colleges also have quaint downtown areas.

The reasoning in the argument is flawed because the argument

(A) infers a definite causal relationship from a coincidence that could be explained in other ways.

(B) contains a premise that could not be true unless the conclusion is known to be true.

(C) employs the term "quaint" to mean two different things.

(D) fails to acknowledge that one group could have members in common with each of two other groups without those other two groups sharing any members in common.

(E) mistakes towns that have quaint downtown areas for towns that have small colleges.

As always, your first step is to read the question. It asks you to figure out what's wrong with the argument's reasoning. Now read the argument. It concludes that because some Southern towns have quaint downtowns and some have small colleges, some have both. If you recall from Chapter 8, the word *some* means something more than *none* or *one,* and something less than *all.* (If you don't recall or haven't read Chapter 8 yet, flip back and give it a gander.) It may be synonymous with *most,* but you don't know that. So the problem with the argument's conclusion is that it assumes overlap between two sets that don't necessarily have to overlap; it's entirely possible that the two sets of towns don't overlap at all.

Now read through the answers, looking for a choice that says something about the possibility that the two sets of towns don't necessarily overlap at all. (A) is wrong because no causal relationship is implied. (B) is wrong because no premise of the argument depends on the conclusion; in other words, the first statement can stand on its own without the conclusion. (C) is wrong because the word "quaint" is used the same way both times to describe downtown areas. (D) looks correct; the argument does suppose that one group (Southern towns) could have members in common with two other groups (towns with quaint downtown areas and towns with small colleges), without those two other groups sharing any members. (E) is wrong because the argument doesn't confuse the two types of towns with one another; it keeps them distinct while reaching the erroneous conclusion. (D) is the best answer.

If the argument had used the word *most* instead of *some,* you could assume overlap. The statement "Most towns have quaint downtowns and most towns have small colleges; therefore some towns have both" would be perfectly acceptable.

Chapter 10

Strengthening, Weakening, and Supporting Arguments

··

In This Chapter

▶ Analyzing Logical Reasoning questions

▶ Strengthening arguments

▶ Weakening arguments

▶ Finding the EXCEPTions

··

*W*hen a lawyer argues a point, she must support it with evidence. Her opponent argues the opposite point, and she must find evidence that can weaken his argument. Law students take an entire class on evidence where they explore how to use evidence to support their cases or to destroy the other side's evidence, and using evidence to support arguments is a constant requirement in all their other classes. In order to succeed as a law student and a lawyer, you absolutely must have a good understanding of how evidence can strengthen or weaken a conclusion.

The LSAT-writers design Logical Reasoning questions to test your ability to strengthen or weaken arguments. These questions present an argument and then ask you to strengthen it, weaken it, support it, criticize it, or some other similar exercise.

In this chapter, I show you how to identify strengthen/weaken questions and provide strategies for working them.

How These Questions Work

In order to answer strengthen/weaken questions, you have to take two steps:

1. **Identify the author's conclusion.**

2. **Figure out what evidence strengthens it, weakens it, or whatever.**

That sounds simple enough, doesn't it? Not so fast though. The LSAT-writers like to keep you on your toes, so continue reading this chapter for specific tips and tactics you can use to work your way through these types of questions.

 Strengthen/weaken questions lend themselves quite well to the technique of trying to answer the question before reading the answers. If you can identify the conclusion, take a moment to think about how you would answer the question if you didn't have an array of answers to choose from. Consider what the author is claiming, and then consider how you would strengthen it, weaken it, support it, or whatever the question wants you to do.

Take a look at this example and see how it works.

Letter to the editor: The school superintendent has proposed changing school start times, starting high schools earlier and elementary schools later, claiming that this would benefit the majority of students. This is a good idea and should be implemented. It would allow all students to take advantage of free school breakfasts and it would solve school bus scheduling problems. Letting younger students sleep later would help them perform better. Finally, releasing high school students earlier would give them more time for homework or part-time jobs.

Each of the following, if true, would weaken the letter-writer's argument EXCEPT:

(A) High school students don't perform well early in the morning, and usually do better with later school start times.

(B) Under the current schedule, it is impossible to transport all students to school in buses, forcing their parents to make other arrangements for them.

(C) Parents have arranged their work and carpool schedules with the current school start times in mind, and changing them would be extremely disruptive.

(D) Sending teenagers home earlier would give them too much unsupervised time in the afternoon, increasing the risk that they will get involved in drugs, drinking, and other dangerous behavior.

(E) All the students who qualify for free school breakfast already arrive at school in time to eat it.

What does the question want? It wants the one answer that doesn't weaken the argument. That means four choices do weaken it. Use the process of elimination to cross off any choice that weakens the argument.

You may notice that this question ends in the word "EXCEPT." I devote a whole section to "EXCEPT questions later in this chapter (see "A Twist: EXCEPT Questions"), but don't worry about the distinction at the moment. Strengthen/weaken/support questions all require you to find the answer or answers that strengthen/weaken/support the conclusion. In this case, you know four answers weaken the conclusion. I put this question first in the chapter simply to provide one example of how strengthen/weaken/support questions work. For more detailed explanations of the specific types, keep reading this chapter!

What's the conclusion? The letter writer thinks that the school district should change school start times. As evidence, she cites several benefits.

To weaken her argument, you need to supply evidence showing that the students don't in fact benefit from different start times, and that keeping the current start time is better. What you are in effect doing is weakening the link between the conclusion and its support. The correct answer, therefore, is the choice that doesn't show students being harmed (or at least failing to benefit) from different start times.

✔ (A) weakens the argument. The letter writer wants to have high schools starting earlier, and (A) suggests that earlier start times hurt them.

✔ (B) looks good; it actually strengthens the letter-writer's argument, because it provides an example of a drawback of the current schedule.

✔ (C) weakens the argument, because throwing everyone's schedule into turmoil isn't good.

✔ (D) weakens the argument because it shows how teenagers suffer if they go home earlier.

✔ (E) weakens the argument because it suggests that changing start times doesn't result in more students getting free breakfast.

(B) is the only choice that doesn't weaken the argument, so it's the correct answer.

Don't try to answer strengthen/weaken questions without identifying the conclusion first. Why is this important? Well, in order to weaken an argument, you need to know the author's conclusion. In other words, you need to know what the author is trying to persuade you to think. After you identify the conclusion, you can go about strengthening or weakening it. But if you don't know what the author is trying to persuade you of, then you may be missing the point.

Hints to identify the conclusion: Look for key words like *therefore, thus, so, hence,* and my favorite, *in conclusion.* Sometimes, however, the author isn't so obvious. So, try to spot other "opinion-triggers" like *we should* or *I think.* If you still can't spot the conclusion, paraphrase the argument in your own words. Start with the conclusion: "Based on the evidence, we should . . . " And then back it up with the key support: " . . . because . . . " Paraphrasing is an especially useful tactic when you've come across a long, convoluted argument and are a bit confused about the conclusion.

Build It Up: Strengthen/Support Questions

Sometimes lawyers want to bolster their arguments. They look for evidence, court decisions, and laws that support the claims they're making. Spotting evidence that can support an argument is a real skill; law schools teach it, but they want their students to arrive already understanding the basic concept. That's why the LSAT includes Logical Reasoning on the test.

Spotting supportive questions

The Logical Reasoning section often includes some questions that ask you to pick answers that can strengthen the argument. The questions may use the word *strengthen,* but they may also ask you to support a position or justify reasoning. No matter how they're phrased, they're all asking you to do the same thing — to spot the answer that can make the argument's conclusion stronger and more likely to be accepted.

Check out some examples of strengthen/support questions:

- ✔ Which one of the following, if true, most strengthens the argument?
- ✔ Which one of the following, if true, most strongly supports the statement above?
- ✔ Which one of the following, if true, would provide the most support for the teacher's assertion?
- ✔ Which one of the following, if true, most helps to support the position of the second group of economists?
- ✔ Which one of the following discoveries, if it were made, would most support the hypothesis stated above?
- ✔ Which one of the following, if true, most supports Martin's counter to Jessica?
- ✔ Which one of the following principles most helps to justify the reasoning above?
- ✔ Which one of the following principles, if established, most helps to justify Susan's position?
- ✔ Which one of the following principles, if valid, most helps to justify the bookstore owner's argumentation?
- ✔ Which one of the following principles, if valid, most justifies the physicist's conclusion?

You may notice that most of these questions include the phrase "if true." This phrasing is very common in LSAT questions. The LSAT-makers just want to be sure you understand what they mean. Assume for the purposes of the question that the answer is in fact true, and not to worry about whether or not an answer may not be entirely accurate.

The approach to answering all these strengthen/support questions is the same: Figure out what the conclusion is, and then figure out what would make it stronger and more believable. Try to come up with your own answer before you consider the choices.

A supportive example

Here's an example of a strengthen question:

Agriculture Secretary: The United States will increase the testing of cattle for mad cow disease, testing about 220,000 "downer" cows (cows that cannot walk) and 20,000 outwardly healthy cows older than 30 months. This testing will reassure consumers all over the world that American beef is safe to eat.

Which one of the following, if true, most strengthens the Agriculture Secretary's argument?

(A) The Japanese system requires the testing of all beef cattle after slaughter, not just a selected few animals.

(B) Testing this many animals will allow investigators to focus their attention on the animals most likely to carry the disease, effectively spotting all identifiable cases of mad cow disease before the meat goes to market.

(C) An infected cow recently identified in the United States was neither a downer cow nor an older cow, and she would not have been identified under this testing scheme.

(D) If farmers know of this testing scheme, they will kill downer cows themselves and destroy the corpses before investigators arrive, thereby endangering other cows.

(E) The testing period is scheduled to run for 18 months, after which it will end.

Before you read the argument, read the question; it wants you to strengthen the Agriculture Secretary's argument. What is the Secretary's conclusion? That consumers all over the world will be reassured that American beef is safe. What is the evidence for this conclusion? The United States is increasing testing for mad cow disease. What strengthens the conclusion? If testing reassures people that beef is safe, then anything indicating that this testing program is effective at catching mad cows before people eat them can help convince people that America's testing program is successful and its beef is safe. Anything that allows consumers to suspect that mad cows are slipping through the cracks is a wrong answer. Look for a choice that makes the testing program seem effective, and that could be used to convince the public of its effectiveness. Avoid choices that make it look as if the testing program doesn't actually catch mad cows.

✔ (A) doesn't look good. If the Japanese think testing all cows is important, then testing just a selected population won't reassure them.

✔ (B) emphasizes the efficiency of this testing program, because testing a selected population ought to catch all cases of the disease without wasting time testing obviously healthy animals; it looks good.

✔ (C) certainly doesn't help; the proposed testing scheme would have missed this cow, which is bad publicity.

✔ (D) shows how farmers will try to get around testing requirements, possibly spreading mad cow through healthy-looking cows, which doesn't strengthen the argument.

✔ (E) tells you that the testing program isn't meant to last very long; surely people will worry about what would happen afterward.

(B) is the only choice that could help the Agriculture Secretary convince people that the testing program will be effective and that American beef is likely to be mad-cow-free. The answer is (B).

Strengthen your own claim

Your claim is that you would make a good law student. The evidence you can muster in support of this conclusion is your GPA, your roster of extracurricular activities, your glowing recommendations, and (soon) your stellar LSAT score. You already know how to think in terms of supporting arguments. The same process works here. Remember, always find the conclusion, figure out how the author got there, and then figure out what can help keep the conclusion in place or tear it down.

Tear It Down: Weakening Questions

Almost as important as strengthening your own arguments is tearing down your opponent's. Lawyers spend at least as much time attacking their opponent's arguments as they do bolstering their own. No matter how strong your case is, your opponent is going to have a tough case in response. Even if the opposing case is flimsy as gauze, you still have to go through the necessary steps of taking it apart. That's why the LSAT tests for this skill.

Knowing when to attack your opponent

The Logical Reasoning section contains several questions asking you to weaken an argument. These questions may use the word *weaken*. They also may ask you to criticize the argument or undermine it, or perhaps attack it.

Here are some weaken questions:

- ✔ Which one of the following, if true, most weakens the argument?
- ✔ Which one of the following, if true, most seriously weakens the argument?
- ✔ Which one of the following statements, if true, most seriously weakens the argument above?
- ✔ The reasoning above is most vulnerable to criticism on the grounds that it . . .
- ✔ Which one of the following, if true, most undermines the doctor's argument?
- ✔ Which one of the following, if true, most undermines George's objection to Marisol's analysis?

The approach to these questions is exactly like the approach to strengthen questions, except that you want to hurt the argument, not help it. Find the conclusion, figure out what evidence and reasoning the author used to get there, and come up with something that makes that reasoning and evidence seem wrong.

A strong example of a weakening question

Here's an example of a weaken question:

The Japanese people have three systems of writing. They use a combination of Chinese characters, called *kanji,* and a set of phonetic characters, called *hiragana,* for most words. They use a third set of characters called *katakana* to write words of foreign origin. Even the names of people of Japanese origin who no longer live in Japan are written in katakana, marking the holders of the names as "not really Japanese." This is evidence of Japan's mistrust of anything foreign, including people.

Which one of the following, if true, most seriously weakens the argument above?

(A) For the last ten years, the Japanese government has run a program that places young foreigners as teachers in public schools, specifically to increase Japanese exposure to people from other countries.

(B) Japanese parents are prohibited by law from giving their children names that have not been approved by the government as being properly Japanese.

(C) Japanese children who have lived in other countries and then return to school in Japan are often teased and bullied by their classmates, who call them "foreigners."

(D) Japanese residents with Korean ancestors are not considered Japanese even if their families have lived in Japan for several generations.

(E) Japanese people prefer to eat rice grown in Japan, claiming that rice grown in other countries is difficult for them to digest.

First read the question, which informs you that you want to weaken the argument. What is the argument's conclusion? The writer suggests that the Japanese don't trust anything foreign. What evidence does the writer use to support this statement? He suggests that the use of a special alphabet only for foreign words means that the Japanese want to make sure everyone knows which words and people aren't Japanese. The first two sentences, describing the three kinds of writing, are just background information leading up to the key evidence and the author's conclusion.

How do you weaken this argument? The author wants you to believe that the Japanese don't trust foreigners, so any evidence to the contrary, showing that the Japanese do trust and even welcome foreign things and people weakens the argument. When you read the answer choices, look for anything that indicates openness to foreign things.

 Spot the conclusion to most effectively tackle strengthen/weaken questions (and all other Logical Reasoning questions, for that matter). Many test-takers mistakenly identify a piece of evidence as the conclusion. For example, a hapless test-taker who mistakenly believes that the fact that Japan has three different writing systems is the conclusion of the argument may then be attracted to the wrong answer introducing another writing system. The conclusion *isn't* that Japan has three different writing systems. This information is a fact, and you take it at face value.

✔ (A) looks good. If the Japanese government is specifically trying to increase Japanese children's exposure to foreign nationals, that statement weakens the argument. See if you can eliminate the other choices.

✔ (B) doesn't work, because it shows the Japanese people's reluctance to allow non-Japanese names for Japanese people.

✔ (C) certainly doesn't show any openness to foreign cultures.

✔ (D) only strengthens the author's argument.

✔ (E) is evidence of Japanese unwillingness to eat foreign foods, so that's no good.

That leaves (A) as the only choice that weakens the argument instead of strengthening it, so (A) is the correct answer.

A Twist: EXCEPT Questions

Many strengthen/weaken/support questions don't ask for the choice that best strengthens (or weakens, or supports, or undermines) the argument, but instead for the one choice that doesn't do one of those things. These questions end in the extremely important word "EXCEPT." It's always capitalized, so you can't miss it.

They're like the other questions EXCEPT...

These questions look like this:

- ✔ Each of the following, if true, supports the claim above EXCEPT:
- ✔ Each of the following, if true, would weaken the commentator's argument EXCEPT:
- ✔ Each of the following, if true, supports the physicist's hypothesis EXCEPT:
- ✔ Each of the following, if true, weakens the argument EXCEPT:
- ✔ Each of the following, if true, strengthens the argument EXCEPT:

They can also look like this:

- ✔ Which one of the following, if all of them are true, is LEAST helpful in establishing that the conclusion above is properly drawn?
- ✔ Which one of the following, if all of them are true, is LEAST effective at undermining the politician's claim?

They're still strengthen/weaken questions, but instead of finding one answer to strengthen/weaken/support/undermine, you want to find four.

As always, first read the question *carefully*. These questions aren't your standard strengthen/weaken questions. Instead, they offer four choices that do strengthen or weaken the conclusion, and one that doesn't. You don't necessarily have to find an answer that strengthens or weakens the conclusion; you just want an answer that doesn't do what the other four do. For example, if the question reads "Each of the following, if true, weakens the argument EXCEPT:," the correct answer doesn't necessarily strengthen the argument, but it definitely doesn't weaken it.

An exceptional example: Finding the strong among the weak

Here's an example of a question that has four answers that weaken the argument and one that doesn't:

Some workers in microwave popcorn factories have contracted a rare lung disease. Experts have linked this disease to a chemical used in the process of mixing popcorn and flavorings. Consumers should, therefore, stop buying and eating all types of microwave popcorn to avoid the risk of contracting this lung disease.

Each of the following, if true, weakens the argument EXCEPT:

(A) The lung disease is caused by being exposed to the chemical for many hours at a time over a period of years.

(B) The chemical only becomes toxic when it is held at a high temperature (much higher than popcorn in a microwave reaches) for several hours.

(C) The lung disease has only been found in workers who handled the Cajun Spice flavor of popcorn.

(D) In twenty years of widespread microwave popcorn consumption, no consumer has ever contracted this rare lung disease.

(E) The EPA has not yet done any research to determine whether the chemical that causes the lung disease is present in the steam and air that come out of a bag of popcorn when it is opened.

From reading the question first, you know you want an answer that doesn't weaken the argument's conclusion. The conclusion is that consumers should stop eating all types of microwave popcorn in order to avoid catching a disease. The evidence for this conclusion is that a chemical in microwave popcorn caused this disease in popcorn factory employees.

What weakens the conclusion? Any evidence that makes consumers seem safe. If you can prove that the disease is somehow restricted to the factory workers, you can reassure consumers that they can eat microwave popcorn with impunity. What doesn't weaken the conclusion? Any evidence indicating that consumers can catch the disease from eating microwave popcorn. Look for an answer showing increased danger to consumers.

   ✔ (A) weakens the argument because most consumers aren't exposed to the chemical in question for long periods of time.

   ✔ (B) weakens the argument because consumers aren't keeping their popcorn super-hot for hours.

   ✔ (C) weakens the suggestion that consumers should avoid all kinds of microwave popcorn, though possibly not the suggestion that they avoid Cajun Spice flavor.

   ✔ (D) weakens the suggestion because it makes the risk to consumers appear very small.

   ✔ (E) doesn't weaken the argument; if the EPA hasn't yet done any research into the chemical's presence in popcorn steam, then the chemical could well be lurking in there, ready to sicken hapless consumers.

(E) doesn't especially strengthen the argument, but it doesn't weaken it, either. (E) is the correct answer.

Chapter 11

Patterns of Reasoning, Explanations, and Resolving Discrepancies

*L*awyers are artists of a sort, or maybe craftsmen is a better word. They build arguments. Lawyers use as much craft in drafting a brief or presenting a closing argument as craftsmen do in building a fine cabinet. The LSAT tests to see if you have the natural aptitude for this craft, to see if you understand how arguments hold together, and to see why an author uses particular words.

The questions I discuss in this chapter are all concerned with the way arguments are put together — with the thought processes that underlie the statements. Law schools want people who can do more than simply understand the words in an argument. They want people who understand why the words are there, what words haven't been said but are implied, and how the argument has been put together. To succeed with these questions, you can't just ask "what." You must also ask "why" and "how." Think like a craftsman, an artisan of arguments, and you'll be fine.

Demanding an Explanation

Making an argument without skipping some steps and including some assumptions is nearly impossible. Limited space makes this problem especially evident; a lawyer who has only three minutes or ten pages to argue a case must often leave something out. As a result, the argument may be open for attack; but a good lawyer, given the opportunity, can refute those attacks. Explaining what you mean is a crucial skill for anyone in the legal profession, so the LSAT looks for people who can do it.

Identifying explanation questions

Some Logical Reasoning questions ask you to explain results. The argument usually presents some facts about a topic that don't tell the whole story; someone who wanted to poke holes in the argument could find places where the argument's explanation is incomplete. You get a list of answer choices that you could use to fill in the gaps in the argument. Picking the one that goes the furthest toward making the argument complete is your job.

Explanation questions can look like this:

- ✔ Which one of the following, if true, most helps to explain the relative amounts of cholesterol found in the three groups?

- ✔ Which one of the following, if true, contributes most to an explanation of the behavior of chimpanzees describe above?

- ✔ Which one of the following, if true, most helps to explain the ability of newborn monkeys described above?

- ✔ Which one of the following, if true, does most to explain why the water of Lake Erie currently contains high levels of mercury?

- ✔ Each of the following, if true, could contribute to an explanation of the doubling described above EXCEPT:

The last question in the list ends in the word "EXCEPT." It's still an explanation question; the word "EXCEPT" just means that four of the answers will be good explanations and one won't be, instead of one good explanation and four bad ones.

You can't concoct a full answer to an explanation question before you look at the answers because usually they involve information that you haven't seen. (And definitely don't try to fill them in based on your own expertise in a subject area — restrict your speculation to the information in front of you.) What you can do, though, is consider the argument's failings and guess what *kind* of information may help explain the result.

Examining an explanation example

Here's an example of an explanation question:

In their natural habitat of the salt marshes of South and Central America, Chilean flamingos have brilliant pink plumage. In North American zoos, however, their feathers are a dull buff color.

Which one of the following, if true, contributes most to an explanation of the difference in color between wild and captive flamingoes?

(A) When wild flamingoes are placed in zoos, the color of their feathers gradually fades to match that of the other captive birds.

(B) Captive flamingoes are subject to carefully engineered breeding programs designed to enhance genetic diversity.

(C) The color of flamingoes' feathers serves no camouflage purpose, and in fact makes the birds more conspicuous.

(D) Zoos attempt to replicate the natural habitats of flamingoes as closely as possible.

(E) Flamingoes' feathers are colored by the pigments they ingest with their food; wild flamingoes become pink from eating shrimp and other crustaceans that are not available in North American zoos.

Always follow the same basic steps when approaching a Logical Reasoning question. 1. Read the question. 2. Read the argument and identify the conclusion. 3. Make up an answer in your own head. 4. Read the answer choices and pick your answer.

Read the question. It wants you to explain the reason for the difference in color between wild and zoo flamingoes. What sort of explanation works here? Based on the information contained in the argument, the same flamingoes in different environments have different colored feathers; perhaps some difference in the environments explains the difference in coloration. See if you can find an answer choice that mentions something that is different between zoos and the wild.

✔ (A) may be a true statement, but it doesn't explain why the zoo flamingoes' feathers change.

✔ (B) doesn't address coloration at all; perhaps this breeding program accounts for different-colored feathers, but you can't assume that based on what this choice says.

✔ (C) does nothing to explain why zoo birds have different colored feathers than wild bird.

✔ (D) offers no explanation for why zoo flamingoes' pink feathers fade; it mentions zoos' efforts to replicate the birds' wild habitat, which may be confusing because you're looking for an answer that has an environmental explanation, but because it doesn't address the color issue it's wrong.

✔ (E) contains a very good explanation for the difference in color. The food that wild birds eat isn't available in the zoo environment, and if diet accounts for feather color, then the lack of shrimp in the zoo diet explains why zoo flamingoes don't have pink feathers.

(E) is the correct answer.

Reconciling Discrepancies and Paradoxes

Sometimes an argument just doesn't seem to hold together. The pieces seem to contradict one another. If everything the argument says is true, then the conclusion looks like it can't possibly make sense. But often it does. A statement may look like a paradox, but in fact it makes perfect sense — if, that is, you know something that hasn't been said.

Looking for paradox questions

The Logical Reasoning sections include a number of questions designed to test your ability to resolve paradoxes or discrepancies. They almost always contain the word *resolve*, followed by a word like *paradox, discrepancy,* or *conflict.* To answer these questions, you have to figure out what piece of information would help you explain why any apparent conflict is not in fact a conflict at all.

The following list includes some examples of paradox and discrepancy questions:

✔ Which one of the following, if true, most helps to resolve the apparent paradox?

✔ Which one of the following, if true, would most effectively resolve the apparent paradox above?

✔ Which one of the following, if true, most helps to resolve the apparent discrepancy in the passage above?

✔ Which one of the following, if true, most helps to resolve the apparent discrepancy described by the representative?

✔ Which one of the following, if true, most helps to resolve the apparent conflict described above?

✔ Which one of the following, if true, most helps to reconcile the specialists' two claims?

✔ Which one of the following, if true, most helps to reconcile the experts' belief with the apparently contrary evidence described above?

You answer these questions the same way you answer explanation questions (see "Demanding an Explanation" earlier in this chapter for more information). Read the argument, and figure out what piece of information is missing. Then try to come up with an idea to explain the whole thing and make the paradox disappear. You probably won't be able to envision the exact answer before reading the choices, but you can come up with something in the ballpark.

Perusing a paradox example

Here's an example of a paradox question:

Skydiving experts expect improvements in gear and training techniques to lead to fewer fatalities than occurred in the earlier years of the sport. Yearly surveys by the U.S. Parachute Association, however, indicate that fatalities have been holding steady for the last 12 years. Ironically, most of these fatalities have occurred among very experienced skydivers using the most modern gear equipped with a device that automatically opens the reserve parachute if the skydiver has not opened the main parachute by a certain altitude; this means that most of these fatalities occurred among skydivers who landed with open parachutes.

Which one of the following, if true, most helps to resolve the apparent paradox in the passage above?

(A) Most skydivers prefer not to buy improved gear as it appears because it costs too much.

(B) Experienced skydivers favor tiny parachutes that fly at high velocities and that must be landed precisely, which makes them more likely to hit the ground at an uncontrolled high speed even under an open parachute.

(C) Not all jumpers choose to use the device that automatically opens their reserve parachute for them.

(D) The U.S. Parachute Association recommends minimum opening altitudes but has no way of ensuring that skydivers follow them.

(E) Most inexperienced skydivers rent gear from drop zones instead of owning their own gear.

Read the question. The argument contains an apparent paradox, but it has an explanation. What's the paradox? Most skydiving fatalities occur among experienced skydivers with open parachutes, which isn't at all what you would expect. Most people think that once a parachute is open, then the skydiver is home free. What could account for the fact that this is not true, and evidently skydivers can die after their parachutes open? If experienced skydivers are dying under open parachutes, something must be killing them after their parachutes open. Snipers are unlikely picking them off from the ground, so they must be dying on landing. Perhaps experienced skydivers land differently from novices. See what the answer choices have to offer.

✔ (A) doesn't explain anything you want to know; the argument says that most fatalities occur among skydivers using the most modern gear, so these skydivers must have acquired the gear despite the cost.

✔ (B) does explain the results; experienced skydivers land differently and more dangerously than novices do.

✔ (C) might explain parachutes that fail to open, but the argument says that most fatalities occur under open parachutes.

✔ (D) likewise accounts for skydivers failing to open their parachutes, but not for them dying under open parachutes.

✔ (E) doesn't explain anything about fatalities. It may explain why inexperienced and experienced skydivers use different gear, but not why experienced skydivers die despite having good, high-tech, perfectly functioning equipment.

So, it looks as though (B) is the correct answer.

Reasoning by Pattern

A well-structured argument is a beautiful thing. A reader can follow the steps of the reasoning from start to finish with no effort at all, and the conclusion should seem self-evident if the author has done her job right. Structuring an argument well isn't that easy, though. Lawyers spend years perfecting the art of putting arguments together and taking apart their opponents' arguments. The first step toward doing both is understanding how existing arguments work. The LSAT exists partly to test your ability to do this.

Finding pattern-of-reasoning questions

Some Logical Reasoning questions ask you to match the pattern of reasoning in the argument with the pattern of reasoning in one of the answers. Look over these examples of pattern-of-reasoning questions:

- Which one of the following exhibits a pattern of reasoning most similar to that exhibited by the argument above?

- Which one of the following arguments is most similar in its pattern of reasoning to the argument above?

- The reasoning in which one of the following arguments is most similar to that in the argument above?

- Which one of the following most closely parallels the newscaster's argument in its reasoning?

- Which one of the following is most closely parallel in its flawed reasoning to the flawed reasoning in the argument above?

- Which one of the following employs a flawed argumentative strategy that is most closely parallel to the flawed argumentative strategy in the letter above?

- Which one of the following uses flawed reasoning most similar to that used in the argument above?

- The flawed reasoning in the argument above is most similar to that in which one of the following?

These questions are kind of hard, if only because you can't answer them before you read the answer choices. But you can do something — you can break down the argument into its component parts. You can even try to make it into something as close to a mathematical formula as possible. Then breaking down all the answer choices into their component parts and spotting the one that matches your argument is easier. These questions can be time-consuming, but usually there aren't too many of them on any given section, and if you know how to work them, you have a good chance of getting the answer right.

You may have noticed that most of the questions mentioned the *flawed reasoning* or the *flawed argumentative strategy* in the arguments. You know what that means — something is wrong with the argument. For your purposes, knowing that the argument is flawed actually isn't that important. Pattern-of-reasoning questions work the same way whether the reasoning is flawed or not.

Patterning a reasonable example

Here's an example of a pattern-of-reasoning question:

Formaldehyde is a known carcinogen. Many nail polishes contain formaldehyde. Therefore anyone who wears nail polish will get cancer.

Which one of the following is most closely parallel in its flawed reasoning to the flawed reasoning in the argument above?

(A) Hot dogs can contain insect parts. Insects are dirty and carry disease. Therefore people should not eat hot dogs.

(B) Ultraviolet rays can cause skin cancer. Sunscreen can prevent damage from ultraviolet rays. Therefore people who wear sunscreen will not get cancer.

(C) Sodium can cause high blood pressure. Potato chips contain sodium. Therefore anyone who eats potato chips will get high blood pressure.

(D) Beans contain a large amount of dietary fiber. Dietary fiber might be able to prevent some kinds of cancer. Therefore people who do not eat beans will get cancer.

(E) Alcohol consumed during pregnancy can cause fetal brain damage. Wine contains alcohol. Therefore pregnant women should not drink wine.

Read the question. You need to find the answer that uses the same process of reasoning as the argument. You know that this process of reasoning is flawed because the question tells you so. So, how is it flawed? The flaw is in the conclusion, which makes an unjustified assumption that the presence of a known carcinogen in nail polish means that everyone who wears nail polish will get cancer.

The problem with the conclusion is that it assumes that a carcinogen automatically causes cancer in everyone who encounters it, which isn't justified by the evidence presented in the argument. The argument doesn't say that formaldehyde always causes cancer, or that nail polish causes cancer; all it says is that formaldehyde can cause cancer, and that nail polishes contain formaldehyde. You can't assume based on that information that nail polishes inevitably cause cancer.

Truthfully, though, the flaw isn't the important thing here. The reasoning process is all you really care about. You want to find the answer choice that uses the same process of reasoning as the argument. For the purposes of finding the answer with parallel reasoning, break down the argument's structure. You could rewrite it in a formula like this: F causes C; NP contains F; therefore NP always causes C.

In questions like this, it can be helpful to abbreviate players just as you do in Analytical Reasoning questions. When writing equations, single letters are faster and easier to use than full words and can make the pattern of reasoning clearer.

Which answer choice makes this same kind of logical leap?

✔ (A) says that H can contain I; I causes disease; therefore don't eat H. That's not the same as the argument.

✔ (B) says that U causes C; S prevents damage by U; therefore S prevents cancer. That's not the same as the argument.

✔ (C) says that S cause H; P contains S; therefore P always causes H. That looks identical to the reasoning in the argument.

    ✔ (D) says that B contains F; F can prevent C; therefore B prevents C. That's not the same as the argument.

    ✔ (E) says that A during P causes BD; W contains A; therefore P shouldn't drink W. That's not the same as the argument.

(C) is the correct answer because it exactly parallels the argument's reasoning.

Arguments Based on Principles

Lawyers often base their arguments on particular principles or propositions. These propositions sound like statements of truths, especially universal truths — "we hold these truths to be self-evident" sort of statements. The thing about statements like this is that the person making them utters them as if the statements were inarguable, but they aren't necessarily true. They're statements of opinion and require as much proof as any other utterance.

Pinpointing principles questions

Some Logical Reasoning questions test your ability to identify principles stated in arguments and then pick the answer that conforms most closely to that principle or that most accurately expresses the principle. These questions can look like this:

    ✔ Which one of the following most closely conforms to the principle above?

    ✔ Which one of the following judgments best illustrates the principle illustrated by the argument above?

    ✔ Which one of the following judgments conforms most closely to the principle stated by Laila?

    ✔ To which one of the following principles does the critic's commentary most closely conform?

    ✔ Which one of the following conforms most closely to the principle illustrated by the statements above?

    ✔ Which one of the following most accurately expresses the principle underlying the argumentation above?

    ✔ Which one of the following best illustrates the proposition above?

    ✔ Which one of the following most accurately expresses the point at issue between Tia and Melinda?

    ✔ Which one of the following most accurately represents what is at issue between Jurgen and Rutgar?

When you see the word *principle,* or occasionally *proposition* or *point at issue,* read the argument looking for some statement of a truth that is really an opinion. These arguments often start with the words "it is," as in "it is crucial," or "it is essential."

A principle is a kind of abstract rule or concept that applies to all situations. For example, people fight war over "principles," or refuse to back down from a silly fight because of the "principle" involved. When you see a "principle" question, try to come up with an abstract rule that governs the situation.

Read the argument looking for a principle. The argument may even state it explicitly, or it may just imply it. Definitely try to answer principle questions before you tackle the answers. Stating the principle in your own words usually isn't that difficult, and it can save you tons of time spotting the right answer.

An example with principles

Here's an example of a principle question:

It is important that new doctors swear the Hippocratic oath, in which they promise to remember that their patients are human beings and that medicine is an art as much as a science. Doctors who take this oath seriously constantly remember the humanity of their patients and this makes them better doctors than those who do not truly espouse the Hippocratic principles.

Which one of the following most closely conforms to the principle above?

(A) The best doctors are those who empathize with their patients; many people go to doctors for emotional comfort as much as physical treatment, and a cold, clinical demeanor on the part of the physician can be as detrimental to medical care as failing to diagnose the proper ailment.

(B) Law schools traditionally teach civil procedure to first-year students and let students study professional responsibility in their last semester. This should be reversed, because first-year students are more idealistic and more likely to benefit from the study of legal ethics, while third-years are better able to understand civil procedure.

(C) A couple who are marrying should pay close attention to the words of the marital vow, because this will be the guide for the rest of their married life; a couple who follow their vows will have a better marriage than a couple who do not.

(D) It is important to have witnesses in a trial swear to tell the truth in their testimony. In addition, it is important to inform them of the possible penalties for perjury. This will encourage them to tell the truth.

(E) Young children cannot tell the difference between truth and falsehood because to them the world has not yet settled into the real and the imaginary. Parents must therefore teach their children that telling imaginary stories is the same as lying.

Read the question. It wants you to find the answer that conforms to the principle stated in the argument. What is that principle? The argument suggests that swearing the Hippocratic oath makes doctors better doctors. The act of swearing helps the doctors remember that their patients are people, which makes the doctors better able to treat their patients. The connection is between the oath (some principle that doctors espouse) and their improved performance.

✔ (A) looks like a possible answer because it's about doctors and medical care and empathy. But look closely; it says nothing about doctors working from a particular principle, only that empathetic people can make better doctors.

✔ (B) discusses professional ethics, but it doesn't suggest that law students should be taught a principle that would then make them better lawyers.

✔ (C) does conform to the principle stated in the argument; it suggests that couples who espouse the principles contained in their marital vows have better marriages.

✔ (D) begins with the same words as the argument, but that's a red herring meant to tempt you away from the right answer. It does suggest that swearing an oath helps witnesses remember to tell the truth, but it also includes a threat of penalties for perjury, which changes the equation; the argument mentions nothing about penalties.

✔ (E) is nothing like the argument; it says that parents must teach young children the difference between truth and falsehood.

As you can see, then, (C) is the correct answer. It suggests that couples who follow marital vows have better marriages, which is based on the principle that following the words of an oath produces better results than ignoring the oath.

Some Logical Reasoning questions are hard just because they're long, and it takes a long time to read them. Spending a little more time on longer questions is okay. Just don't let the time pressure get to you. If you find that you get stressed when you work these longer questions, skip them and do them last.

Figuring Out an Argument's Structure

Arguments are like wars; individuals who argue use a variety of tactics to make their points and disarm their opponents. They may deny something the other person says, challenge their opponent's evidence, explain what they mean, or use analogies to illustrate their points. Lawyers, being in the business of argument, use these tactics all the time. Law schools want to pick students who already understand the rudiments of this art.

Spotting structure questions

A number of Logical Reasoning questions focus on the structure of arguments. These questions usually involve two speakers who disagree with one another in some way. The question usually asks you to explain how the second speaker responds to the first. These questions can look like this:

- Yolanda responds to Javier by . . . (arguing, denying, using analogy, challenging, showing evidence)
- In responding to Penelope, Odysseus . . . (accuses, criticizes, challenges, explains, assumes)
- Carter counters Yvette's argument by . . . (questioning, suggesting, denying, pointing out, calling into question)
- This advertisement proceeds by . . . (using analogy, proving, understating the role, demonstrating, asserting)
- Seth challenges Arne's reasoning by . . .
- Kelsey's criticism suggests that he interpreted Mac to be . . .
- Landrieu and Blanco disagree about whether . . .
- Marquis responds to Theodora's argument in which one of the following ways?
- Rinn responds to Julio's criticism by . . .

Your goal is to figure out how the second speaker's argument relates to the first. The second speaker is addressing the first speaker in some way; you have to figure out how.

Tackling a structure-of-argument example

Here's an example of a structure-of-argument question.

Gabrielle: The man who invented the shopping mall in the United States envisioned it as the heart of a pedestrian community much like the centers of European towns, with their side-walk cafes, boutiques, and pleasant boulevards. Malls now provide a safe environment in which people can walk from shop to shop and meet with their friends.

Antonia: Although people walk within a mall, the very existence of the shopping mall has killed pedestrian culture. American town centers are now wastelands where no one goes, and malls themselves exist in the center of massive parking lots. People isolated in their cars drive to suburban malls and then wander around the mall ignoring and avoiding their fellow shoppers.

Antonia responds to Gabrielle by

(A) arguing that the invention of the mall has led to consequences that are exactly opposite what the mall's inventor intended.

(B) proposing that sensible urban planning could result in the shopping mall becoming a positive force in communities.

(C) using an analogy to illustrate the detrimental effects of malls.

(D) pointing out that European cities now have shopping malls in their suburbs.

(E) explaining why American cities have developed in such a way that private automobiles are the only practical form of transportation.

Read the question first. It asks how the second speaker responds to the first. The answers to this sort of question always start with verbs, such as *criticize, argue, point out,* and things like that. You want to decide for yourself how Antonia responds before you start reading the answer choices.

Gabrielle suggests that the shopping mall has evolved as its creator envisioned, as a safe, enclosed, walkable community. Antonia disagrees with her, contending that malls have ended pedestrian culture and community spirit. So you want to find an answer that disagrees with Gabrielle's argument and claims that the mall isn't the institution its creator imagined.

✔ (A) looks like exactly the answer you want; Antonia does argue that the mall's consequences are opposite those intended by its creator.

✔ (B) is wrong because Antonia doesn't mention sensible urban planning.

✔ (C) is wrong because Antonia doesn't use an analogy.

✔ (D) is wrong because Antonia doesn't mention Europe.

✔ (E) is wrong because Antonia doesn't mention automobiles.

(B) through (E) all bring up points that Antonia might use if she were to continue her argument, but they're not relevant here. (A) is the correct answer.

Chapter 12

Be Reasonable! — Logical Reasoning Practice Questions

In This Chapter

▶ Working an entire Logical Reasoning section

▶ Trying your hand at strengthening, weakening, and spotting patterns of reasoning

▶ Eliminating wrong answers and choosing correct ones

*E*very Logical Reasoning section on the LSAT has 25 or 26 questions. You have 35 minutes to answer them all. A section includes a mix of any or all of the question types I discuss in Chapters 9 through 11. This chapter contains 26 Logical Reasoning questions. The mix of question types is similar to that in recent LSATs. You can find the answers and explanations to these questions in Chapter 13.

Don't worry too much about timing yourself at this point; just get through the questions and do your best.

If you get done with this chapter and want more practice, you're in luck! Each of the practice tests in Part VI contain not one, but *two* Logical Reasoning sections — just like an actual LSAT — which gives you about 100 more questions to play with. Have fun!

1. Manufacturer: Our child car seat is the safest on the market. We know it's safe because the most conscientious parents have bought it. We're sure they're the most conscientious customers because they bought the car seat that claimed to be the safest on the market, which proves that our seat is the safest.

   Which one of the following uses a pattern of reasoning that is most closely parallel to the flawed reasoning in the manufacturer's statement?

   (A) This soft drink is the best-tasting soft drink on the market. We know it's the best-tasting because 8 out of 10 people who participated in taste-tests said it was best.

   (B) Children who attend high-quality preschools tend to perform well when they enter elementary school. They perform well in elementary school because they attended high-quality preschools.

   (C) These soccer shoes must be the best because all the best soccer players use them, and the best players wear only the best shoes.

   (D) This Web browser is the best on the market. The most technologically savvy people use this browser, and they can choose any browser they want.

   (E) This curl-enhancing lotion is the best styling product available. People with curly hair find that this lotion enhances their curls better than any similar product.

2. A cosmetics company did a study of hair colors involving 100 women, all of whom dyed their hair with the same product. Half of them then washed their hair with special shampoo made for color-treated hair, and half of them washed their hair with ordinary shampoo. After two months, there was no difference in color fading between the two groups. Therefore, shampoo for color-treated hair is valueless.

Which one of the following statements, if true, most seriously weakens the argument?

(A) Most shampoos contain the same basic ingredients, such as sodium lauryl sulfate or sodium laureth sulfate.

(B) Most hair experts recommend touching up hair color every four to six weeks.

(C) Both groups had equal numbers of women in their 30s, 40s, and 50s, with comparable natural hair colors.

(D) The women who had used shampoo for color-treated hair had softer and shinier hair than the women who used ordinary shampoo.

(E) Hair color technology has improved tremendously in the last ten years, making it possible for all women to successfully color their hair at home.

3. Prosecutor: I have furnished evidence that the accused committed the crime in question. The defense agrees that the crime did occur; they say that the accused did not commit the crime, but they have not proven that someone else did. Therefore, the jury should find that the defendant is guilty.

The reasoning in the prosecutor's argument is flawed because the argument

(A) ignores evidence that the accused might be innocent

(B) criticizes the arguments by the defense without addressing their flaws

(C) confuses the defense's failure to prove that someone else committed the crime with proof that the accused is guilty

(D) implies that because the defense has admitted that the crime did occur, the defendant must be guilty

(E) fails to consider the possibility that someone else committed the crime

4. Dermatologist: Many people believe that they can prevent acne by using clay masks to draw impurities from pores, and applying toner, which they think will close pores and prevent dirt from getting into them. If this were true, then acne would be very easy to treat with topical measures. In fact, acne blemishes develop within the skin itself, and are affected by internal factors such as hormones and sebum. Therefore, using external measures such as masks and toners is useless.

The dermatologist's conclusion follows logically if which one of the following is assumed?

(A) Clay masks can dry out the skin.

(B) Some people like the sensation of toners on their skin.

(C) Dirt on the skin doesn't cause acne.

(D) Doctors have successfully treated acne with oral antibiotics.

(E) Most dermatologists recommend that patients clean their faces with gentle soap instead of harsh cleansers.

5. American citizens believe that they live in a democracy. In presidential elections, though, citizens don't get to vote for president. They can only choose electors who cast votes for president on behalf of entire states. Therefore, Americans don't actually live in a democracy.

Which one of the following exhibits a pattern of reasoning most similar to that in the argument above?

(A) Most colleges have student government. All students are allowed to vote in student government elections. In fact, though, very few students vote or take any interest in student government affairs. Therefore, student government serves no useful purpose.

(B) All cities have local law enforcement programs. Usually the police handle crime in the city, the sheriff's department handles county matters, and the state police handle matters that affect the entire state. Therefore, most cities have too much duplication of law enforcement jobs.

(C) The U.S. is said to have a free market economy. In fact, though, the U.S. economy is heavily regulated by the government, which gives many advantages to large businesses and punishes small companies and the self-employed. Therefore, the U.S. doesn't really have a free market economy.

(D) Most teachers believe that education courses are valuable. Many colleges and universities, on the other hand, look down on education degrees. Therefore, future teachers shouldn't major in education.

(E) Most health insurers claim to offer their customers a variety of choices in health care. Doctors, however, don't post a menu of prices for customers to peruse before accepting treatment, and patients in hospitals don't get to choose the doctors who treat them. Therefore, health insurers are dishonest.

6. People usually meet expectations. Thus, if Person A informs Person B that he or she is expected to perform a particular duty and Person B accepts that duty, generally Person B will perform the duty as expected.

Which one of the following best illustrates the proposition above?

(A) A teacher informs a girl that she is responsible for feeding the class hamster every morning, and the girl agrees to do this. After this, the girl feeds the hamster every morning without the teacher telling her to.

(B) A partner asks an associate to write a memo on a legal issue. Because the associate is inexperienced, the partner supervises his work closely and helps him write several drafts of the memo.

(C) Country A has agreed to be Country B's military ally. Country A then elects a new president who disagrees with Country B's policies, and when Country B goes to war, Country A refuses to help.

(D) A coach teaches his players a particular strategy. The first time they use it in a game, they win. Thereafter, go on to win the league championship.

(E) A psychologist tells a patient that behavior modification will help her quit smoking. The patient follows the program designed by the psychologist and quits smoking successfully.

7. Since the late 19th century, German schools use a series of aptitude tests to shunt students into various tracks, some leading to the university, some to two-year clerical colleges, and some straight to technical jobs. The German educational system is currently plagued with discipline problems and students who fail to learn anything. Therefore, aptitude tests are valueless for sorting students.

All of the following weaken the argument above EXCEPT:

(A) Disciplinary and other problems are most profound at technical schools with large immigrant populations, where students feel that society will not give them opportunities to improve themselves.

(B) Schools that attempt to teach the same subjects to students of all abilities are the most likely to suffer from discipline problems and failure, because the work is too easy for bright students and too hard for slower ones.

(C) Sorting students by ability allows schools to gear curricula to individual needs, which results in better overall results.

(D) Until the early 1990s, the German school system was one of the best in the world, with excellent test results and virtually no disciplinary problems.

(E) Students who graduate from German technical schools are usually prepared to perform highly skilled jobs that pay them well, and many parents work hard to have their children placed in these schools.

8. Individual worker bees have no sense of themselves as individuals. They instead live to further the welfare of the queen and her hive as a whole, helping her to lay eggs and raising her offspring. This means that workers spend their lives helping the queen to pass on her genetic traits and fail to pass on their own genes to offspring.

Which one of the following statements most seriously weakens the argument above?

(A) All the bees in a hive are related to one another; the workers are all sisters and the queen is their mother. There is no need for workers to pass their own genes on because they are furthering their mother's line.

(B) When a hive loses its queen, some workers develop the ability to lay eggs; these unfertilized eggs can hatch only into male drones.

(C) A bee colony has only one queen at a time. When a new queen hatches in a hive, she immediately seeks out all other queens and tries to kill them or drive them out.

(D) If a beekeeper can catch the queen from a swarm, he can install her in a beehive and the entire swarm of worker bees will immediately move into the hive with her.

(E) Queen bees mate once in their lives, and store sperm from this mating to fertilize all their worker eggs. Male drones hatch from unfertilized eggs.

9. Some scholars of mythology claim that myths exist to explain natural phenomena; for example, the myth of Zeus casting lightning bolts from heaven helped the ancient Greeks explain an otherwise unexplainable event. Other scholars argue that myths are a way in which people explore psychological phenomena, such as a son's feelings toward his mother. These two interpretations of myth need not be mutually exclusive; all myths can work both as explanations of natural events and explorations of psychology.

The argument is most vulnerable to criticism on the grounds that it

(A) draws a conclusion about myths that has already been discounted by experts in the field

(B) takes for granted that the myths of ancient people are relevant today

(C) imposes a modern, western sensibility on the myths of pre-modern people from a variety of cultures

(D) criticizes scholars who insist that one or the other interpretation of myths must be correct

(E) assumes without giving proof that all myths contain both natural and psychological phenomena

10. Identifying the sex of parrotfish can be difficult. Juveniles of both sexes look alike. Sexually mature males are large and brightly colored, with brilliantly colored scales that resemble those of colorful tropical parrots. Mature females, on the other hand, are smaller than males and have more subdued coloration. In some species, immature males pass through a phase in which they look identical to females before maturing into their full adult size and coloration.

If the above statements are true, which one of the following would also have to be true?

(A) In some species of parrotfish, males grow straight from their juvenile form to their large, colorful adult male form without passing through a stage in which they look exactly like females.

(B) All male parrotfish are large and brightly colored.

(C) Female parrotfish use the bright colors of male parrotfish to judge which males are good mating prospects.

(D) Smaller size and subdued coloring help female parrotfish escape predators, to which mature male parrotfish are especially vulnerable.

(E) In all species of parrotfish, all males spend a part of their lives looking exactly like adult females.

11. Schools today have decreased funding and time for art, music, and drama classes, citing lack of money and a need to spend more time on academic subjects. This is tragic. The next generation of citizens will be a mass of automatons with head stuffed full of facts and no appreciation of or talent for the more beautiful and enjoyable parts of life.

The conclusion drawn in the argument above follows logically if which one of the following is assumed?

(A) In the absence of school arts programs, many parents sign their children up for extracurricular classes in art and music.

(B) Schools with strong arts programs tend to produce students who also excel in academic subjects.

(C) Many people who never studied art, music, or drama in school nevertheless have gone on to become famous artists.

(D) If people are not exposed to the arts at school, they will not ever learn about them.

(E) The primary purpose of schools is to teach students the academic subjects they will need to flourish in the business world.

12. Columnist: Our town has lost its minor-league baseball team. Another town in a different state offered to build a large, modern baseball stadium if the team would move there; our town has refused to update the stadium for years. This is a catastrophic loss to our town and will be very detrimental to the local economy.

Which one of the following, if true, most strongly supports the statement above?

(A) Building a new baseball stadium would have cost the town several million dollars that it would be unlikely to recoup through revenues generated by the baseball team.

(B) The baseball team's presence generated millions of dollars of revenue for the town every year by attracting out-of-town visitors who spent money on hotels, restaurants, and other goods and services.

(C) The current baseball stadium was already larger than necessary, and the bleachers were never more than half-full during home games.

(D) The baseball team would have gone to any city that was willing to grant its frankly unreasonable demands for new facilities, and it had no real loyalty to the town that had been its home for twenty years.

(E) In a local referendum, only a small minority of town citizens voted to spend the money necessary to build a new baseball stadium.

13. The President has proposed an initiative to help people stay married by teaching them skills needed to maintain relationships and raise healthy children. This initiative would focus on low-income unmarried people, who studies have shown are not likely ever to marry even after they have children. We should support this initiative because it would be very beneficial to our most vulnerable citizens: the children of poor, unmarried women.

Which one of the following is an assumption required by the argument above?

(A) If more poor people were married, society would be plagued by less drug dependency, crime, and teen pregnancy.

(B) People with higher incomes do not need as much help in maintaining their marriage and raising their children.

(C) Children raised by a mother and father who are married to one another are better off than children raised by a mother alone.

(D) The majority of welfare payments go to unmarried parents; encouraging marriage would reduce the number of people on welfare.

(E) Other governmental programs designed to assist the family have been successful, so this one would be too.

14. Isabel: The popular novels depicting the end of the world and the violent annihilation of all people who do not espouse a particular religion are dangerous. They encourage members of that religion to see all nonbelievers as evil people who deserve a horrific fate.

Ferdinand: I think you are overstating the significance of popular fiction. People read these books solely for entertainment purposes, and do not allow them to affect their beliefs or actions.

Which one of the following is most strongly supported by the conversation above?

(A) Ferdinand and Isabel disagree about the religious nature of these popular novels.

(B) Isabel believes that the end of the world is not a suitable topic for a popular novel.

(C) Ferdinand disagrees with Isabel that the books are popular.

(D) Isabel believes that popular fiction can affect people's beliefs and actions and that novels therefore can be a dangerous influence on mass behavior.

(E) Isabel and Ferdinand disagree about the amount of violence that is appropriate in a work of popular fiction.

15. Tia: Scientists and doctors have found that obesity is increasing rapidly in this country. Obesity causes many significant health problems. The government should therefore step in to regulate food manufacturing and advertising, which would help people consume fewer calories.

Muriel: It's true that obesity is increasing. People have made a personal choice to eat too much. Their weight is entirely in their control. Therefore, the government should not step in except perhaps to encourage people to eat more healthily and exercise occasionally.

The dialog above lends the most support to the claim that Tia and Muriel disagree with each other about which one of the following statements?

(A) Diet and exercise have proven effective at curing and preventing obesity in a large number of people.

(B) Governmental regulation is never the appropriate method for dealing with public health problems.

(C) Public schools can play an important role in teaching children the value of fruits, vegetables, and a balanced diet; therefore, the government should invest in public school nutrition programs.

(D) A primary cause of obesity is modern food, which is heavily advertised, full of calories and unhealthy ingredients, packaged in large portions, and priced to encourage consumption of large amounts; regulating these practices would help prevent obesity.

(E) Private-sector approaches are always more successful than governmental programs; therefore, the government should provide tax credits to companies that want to sell weight-loss products and programs.

16. Politician: Environmentalists claim that pollution is leading to global warming, which supposedly will raise the earth's temperatures and lead to the melting of the polar ice caps, higher overall sea levels, and various other catastrophes. They must not have been paying attention to the winters lately; the last five years have seen record low temperatures in January and February. Therefore, global warming can't be happening.

The reasoning in the politician's argument is most vulnerable to criticism on the grounds that the argument

(A) attacks environmentalists for frightening people with doomsday scenarios

(B) uses an emotional appeal instead of arguing based on facts

(C) reassures listeners that even if global warming is happening, the effects will not be severe

(D) confuses isolated instances of low temperatures with proof that the world as a whole is not getting hotter

(E) suggests that environmentalists are politically biased

17. People should not focus just on immediate payoffs when deciding on a course of action; many acts bring few immediate payoffs, but result in much larger payoffs in the future.

    Which one of the following most closely conforms to the principle above?

    (A) A college graduate with a lucrative job offer decides to decline it and instead borrow several thousand dollars to attend medical school, in the hopes of receiving a much larger future income as a physician.

    (B) Investing in the stock market is a wise choice for anyone with enough excess cash; the stock market has historically outperformed other forms of saving, though occasionally investors have lost all their money.

    (C) Parents should encourage their children to attend religious services every week because people with strong religious faith tend to be more successful than those without faith.

    (D) Building houses for Habitat for Humanity is a good activity, allowing poor people to become homeowners with all the pride of ownership and responsibility for paying for their own property.

    (E) It makes sense to buy the best furniture one can afford; good pieces will last a long time, whereas cheaper furniture breaks quickly and must be replaced.

18. Studies have shown that women make at least half of all car-purchasing decisions. Women notice details that men don't; for example, women especially appreciate drink holders and a back seat that makes it easier for them to reach children in child seats. Women are also more likely than men to choose cars based on environmental friendliness. Only a few car models have been designed with women's tastes in mind, but these vehicles outsell all others by a huge margin.

    Which one of the following is most strongly supported by the information above?

    (A) More car manufacturers should work to reduce emissions from their vehicles; customers claim to like environmentally friendly automobiles, but car manufacturers instead have concentrated their energies on building large, gas-guzzling truck-like vehicles.

    (B) Most purchasers of minivans are women. Women drive their children to school and extracurricular activities, and they appreciate the size, safety, and convenience of minivans.

    (C) All car manufacturers should conduct market research; otherwise they have no way of knowing what their customers want in vehicles.

    (D) Cars that are designed according to female tastes are very attractive to female customers; car manufacturers that pay attention to the female market can earn huge profits with cars designed to please women.

    (E) Station wagons were very popular in the 1970s and 1980s. It is now difficult to find a station wagon, but many women choose sport-utility vehicles that closely resemble stations wagons; therefore car manufacturers should make more station wagons.

19. Carter: A new study has shown that the more young children watch television, the more likely they are to develop attention deficit disorder. Television, for its part, has nothing to offer children. Because television offers no benefits and bears significant risks to development, children should never watch television.

    Neri: The experts who ran that study believe that attention deficit disorder results from the extremely fast pace and disjointed nature of commercial television, not from the actual content of programs. Educational programs can actually stimulate brain development in young children; programs made by experts in child development can help them learn valuable lessons.

Carter and Neri disagree about whether

(A) Violent programs on television teach children to behave more violently than they would if they didn't watch such programs.

(B) There is a difference in risk between children who watch less than one hour of television per day and those who watch more than three hours.

(C) Children can ever benefit from watching television.

(D) The generation of people who grew up with educational programming have shown evidence of having benefited from their youthful television watching.

(E) Children who watch movies on videotape or DVD without commercials are as much at risk as children who watch commercial television.

20. Park ranger: The National Park Service should pay close attention to naming its parks and monuments. Parks and monuments with attractive names bring in many more tourists than facilities with less inspiring names.

Which one of the following, if true, would provide the most support for the park ranger's assertion?

(A) Civil War buffs especially love Civil War battlefields, monuments, and state parks; they especially enjoy reenacting historic battles on actual battlegrounds.

(B) National parks in the western United States attract far more visitors than national parks in the east; this is because the scenery in the west is more dramatic and impressive.

(C) The Sand Creek Massacre National Historic Site has a much catchier name than the Martin Van Buren National Historic Site; the word "massacre" catches peoples' attention.

(D) South Carolina's Congaree Swamp National Monument received very few visitors; as soon as its name was changed to Congaree National Park, tourists began driving hundreds of miles to visit it.

(E) Yellowstone National Park attracts many visitors because it has wonderful attractions such as the geyser Old Faithful, petrified trees, and a profusion of wildlife.

21. It's outrageous that the government has outlawed smoking in so many public places. This is a question of civil liberties. Smokers know that smoking can make them sick, and if they choose to poison themselves that should be their business. The government doesn't have the right to stop people from doing an activity that can only hurt the person engaging in it.

Which one of the following, if true, most weakens the argument?

(A) An irony of politics is that many people who believe that government should not interfere with people's economic lives and property rights also believe that the government has every right to regulate morality and private behavior.

(B) Smokers who quit smoking quickly regain their health; five years after quitting smoking, a former smoker's lungs are difficult to distinguish from the lungs of someone who has never smoked.

(C) Lung cancer continues to be one of the most deadly cancers. Most people who are diagnosed with lung cancer die within five years of the diagnosis.

(D) Smoking rates in the United States have decreased dramatically in the last two decades. Experts attribute this change to better education about the effects of smoking, the Surgeon General's warning on packs of cigarettes, and laws limiting the advertising of cigarettes.

(E) Recent studies have shown that nonsmokers who are exposed to secondhand smoke suffer more heart attacks, slower-healing wounds, and in general higher mortality than people who breathe smoke-free air.

22. Actors tend to be extroverts who are perfectly comfortable appearing and speaking before a crowd of people. People who want to become more extroverted should therefore study drama and perform in plays.

   The reasoning in the argument is most vulnerable to criticism on the ground that the argument

   (A) assumes that it is better to be extroverted than introverted

   (B) supposes that actors become extroverted because they study drama, not that they choose to study drama because they are extroverted

   (C) attributes a characteristic to actors without providing evidence to support the claim

   (D) fails to define the term "extrovert"

   (E) ignores the other ways that people can improve their confidence in situations such as public speaking

23. Mathematician: In 1590, Sir Walter Raleigh discovered that the best way to store spherical objects such as cannonballs was stacked in a pyramid. Grocers who stock oranges also know intuitively that this principle makes sense, because it allows the top objects to sink into the spaces between the lower ones, maximizing the number of objects that can fit into a given space. Raleigh created an equation to express this principle and the famous scientist Johannes Kepler agreed with him, but it was not until 2004 that mathematicians using computers came up with an acceptable proof of the concept. The proof requires far too many calculations to do by hand, and mathematicians have not double-checked them all; nevertheless, computers are extremely accurate at calculations and all portions of the proof that have been checked are correct, so the mathematical community can feel confident that the computer-created proof is valid.

   Which of the following most accurately expresses the main conclusion of the statistician's argument?

   (A) Although a computer-created proof might be too complex to check by hand in the traditional manner, computers are reliable enough today that mathematicians should be willing to admit proofs done by computers into the body of accepted mathematical knowledge.

   (B) Although stacking spheres in a pyramid is one of the most efficient ways of storing them, there is another method that is as efficient: arranging them in a honeycomb shape. Because the proof doesn't acknowledge this, it should not be accepted as valid.

   (C) Mathematicians have done proofs by hand for centuries. This is the accepted method for proving mathematical hypotheses. Computers have no place in the world of theoretical mathematics.

   (D) The mathematical journal that published this proof noted that scholars have not checked the entire proof, although the portions they have checked have all been proven accurate. This level of accuracy is not high enough to justify publication of the proof.

   (E) A rigorous mathematical proof follows a chain of logic that begins with stated assumptions and leads inexorably to an inescapable conclusion. It should include every step along the way. The sphere-stacking problem has far too many steps to prove by hand.

24. In 1995, the federal government gave states the right to set their own speed limits; several states immediately increased their speed limits to 70 miles per hour, and some even abolished limits entirely. In most cases, this has not been a problem; the overall percentage of accidents per drivers has not increased since the speed limits were raised. At the same time, however, highway accident fatalities have increased 6 percent.

Which one of the following, if true, most helps to reconcile the apparent discrepancy between highway accidents holding steady and the increase in fatalities?

(A) Teenage drivers are the most likely to exceed speed limits, and their driving skill is not yet equal to the task of avoiding high speed accidents.

(B) Accidents that occur at a higher speed are much more likely to be fatal than those at lower speeds.

(C) State governments are not as concerned with highway safety as the federal government was in the days of a federally mandated speed limit.

(D) In the 1970s, more people drove smaller, compact cars that got good gas mileage; these cars were not capable of maintaining a high speed.

(E) Drivers today are often distracted by compact disc players, radios, cell phones, and other gadgets, which makes them more likely to get into accidents.

25. Consultant: It's always a good idea to start off a speech with a little joke. This relaxes the audience and makes them more willing to listen to what you have to say. Humor is a universal concept, so you should still start your speech with a joke even when speaking in a foreign country.

All of the following weaken the argument above EXCEPT?

(A) It is very difficult to translate a joke into another language, and American jokes can be deeply offensive to people from other countries.

(B) In some societies, it is terribly offensive for women to tell jokes.

(C) Many interpreters refuse to interpret jokes; instead, they will simply inform the audience that the speaker has told a joke and request that the audience laugh.

(D) Studies have shown that audiences appreciate the opportunity to laugh while listening to a speech.

(E) Humor is a sign of aggression or dominance in some countries, and can make an audience feel that the speaker is trying to exert power over them.

26. Activist: New laws limiting telemarketing have not limited unwelcome phone calls at all. Instead, they have legalized many phone calls that before the law were of dubious legality. Now that companies know exactly which numbers they can call, they have stepped up their calls to those numbers. My own telephone has received many more telephone calls since the law went into effect; some evenings, telemarketers call me ten times in as many minutes, much more often than before the law was passed. It seems clear that the new telemarketing laws have increased rather than decreased the practice of making unsolicited telephone calls in an effort to sell goods and services.

The claim that the activist has received more telemarketing calls since the law went into effect plays which one of the following roles in the argument?

(A) It is a complaint designed to illustrate the activist's disgust with companies that choose to advertise their products through unsolicited telephone calls.

(B) It points out the way in which the government obviously favors the interests of businesses over those of private citizens.

(C) It illustrates the difficulty of trying to have a pleasant family dinner while the telephone rings constantly.

(D) It expresses the activist's idiosyncratic tendency to blame the government for all inconvenient aspects of life in this country.

(E) It serves as a concrete example of the way in which the law has increased rather than decreased unwelcome calls from telemarketers.

Chapter 13

Check Yourself! — Answers and Explanations for Chapter 12

. . . .

In This Chapter

▶ Discovering the answers to the Logical Reasoning questions in Chapter 12

▶ Exploring the explanations to those answers

. . . .

So you worked your way through the Logical Reasoning questions in Chapter 12. Congratulations!

This chapter has the answers to all those questions, along with detailed explanations of them. Read through them. See if they make sense to you. If they do, great! If not, review Chapters 8 through 11 again, and then try them again.

The Beloved Answer Key

If the questions in Chapter 14 stumped you, or you just want to check your answers, you've come to the right place! (It's too bad you can't peek at an answer key if you get stumped during the real test, huh?)

1. (C)	10. (A)	19. (C)
2. (D)	11. (D)	20. (D)
3. (C)	12. (B)	21. (E)
4. (C)	13. (C)	22. (B)
5. (C)	14. (D)	23. (A)
6. (A)	15. (D)	24. (B)
7. (A)	16. (D)	25. (D)
8. (B)	17. (A)	26. (E)
9. (E)	18. (D)	

Methods to the Madness: The Explanations

1. The question asks you to identify the argument's pattern of reasoning. You know that the reasoning is flawed because the question tells you so. So what's the flaw? This argument's reasoning is totally circular: The car seat is safest because the most conscientious parents bought it; they're most conscientious because they bought the car seat that claims to be safest. No external evidence is available; each half of the argument depends on the other half to support it. So look for an answer that has two conclusions, each of which depends on the other conclusion for support.

   (A) is wrong. A taste-test is perfectly good evidence of a soft drink's good taste, so this reasoning isn't flawed. (B) is wrong, though it may look a bit like the argument. The difference is that attending a good preschool could help kids do better in elementary school, so the conclusion in the second statement isn't circular. (C) does duplicate the reasoning in the argument. The writer bases the claim that the soccer shoes are the best on the fact that the best soccer players use them, and justifies the claim that those players are the best with the evidence that the best players wear only the best shoes. That's completely circular, so (C) looks like a good answer. (D) is wrong because it makes sense; the fact that technologically savvy people buy a particular browser is good evidence that a browser is good, and the argument doesn't use the fact that these people buy this browser to prove that they're technologically savvy. (E) is also wrong; if the curl enhancing lotion really works for curly-haired people, then maybe it is the best. (C) is the right answer.

2. The question wants you to weaken the argument. The argument concludes that shampoo for color-treated hair is valueless. The evidence for this claim is that colored hair washed with shampoo for color-treated hair faded as much as colored hair washed with normal shampoo. What weakens the claim that special color shampoo is valueless? Evidence of its value does the trick, so look for an answer that shows that this kind of shampoo does do something desirable that ordinary shampoo doesn't do.

   (A) is irrelevant to the argument; it's just a statement of ingredients, but doesn't address the quality or performance of either kind of shampoo. (B), (C), and (E) also have nothing to do with the performance of shampoos. (D) is the only answer choice that addresses the possible value of shampoo for color-treated hair. If it makes hair softer and shinier than ordinary shampoo, then it does have some value, even if it doesn't preserve hair dye any better than ordinary shampoo. All you have to do is weaken the argument; you don't have to prove that it's wrong. (D) is the best choice for that.

3. The question asks you to spot the flaw in the argument's reasoning. What is that flaw? The prosecutor says that the defense hasn't proven that someone else committed the crime, which proves that the accused did commit it. That's wrong. Even if you don't know about the principle of "innocent until proven guilty," failing to show who did commit a crime isn't the same as proof that the accused did commit it. Look for an answer that shows the prosecutor's confusion of the defense's inability to furnish the proper criminal with evidence of the accused's guilt.

   (A) is wrong, because the argument doesn't mention any evidence of the accused's innocence. Some evidence may exist, and the prosecutor may be ignoring it, but if it's not in the argument, you can't put it in an answer. (B) is wrong because the prosecutor does name a flaw in the defense's arguments: The defense has failed to prove that someone else committed the crime. Whether or not that is a valid criticism is beside the point. (C) is exactly what you're looking for; it looks like the right answer. (D) is a bit tricky, because the defense has agreed that the crime did occur, but the prosecutor isn't trying to use this admission as proof that the defendant committed the crime. (E) is wrong. Whether or not the prosecutor has considered that someone else may have committed the crime isn't really the point. The prosecutor is trying to prove that the accused is guilty, and the possibility that someone else committed the crime is irrelevant. (C) is the correct answer.

4. The question asks you to find the assumption that the dermatologist must make in order to make the conclusion follow logically. The conclusion is that external treatments have no effect on acne. The evidence for this conclusion is that acne develops within the skin. The unstated assumption must be that acne isn't caused by anything on or outside the skin's surface; see if that's one of the answers.

(A) is wrong because the dermatologist isn't critiquing the effects of external acne treatments. (B) is wrong because the sensation caused by toners has nothing to do with the causes of acne or the effectiveness of toners as a treatment. (C) looks like the answer you want. If dirt on the skin doesn't cause acne, and it's only caused by internal sources, then (C) justifies the doctor's claim that toners and masks don't work. (D) supports the doctor's conclusion that acne is an internal problem, but the dermatologist doesn't need to assume that oral antibiotics work to make the conclusion. (E) may be true, but the dermatologist doesn't need to assume it to reach the conclusion. In fact, you could conceivably use (E) as evidence against the conclusion. So the answer is (C).

5. The question asks you to identify the pattern of reasoning and match it with an answer. The argument's pattern of reasoning goes like this: Although people think the United States is a democracy, citizens don't actually vote for president, so it's not a democracy. You can further simplify the pattern thus: People think A, but here's an example of something that runs counter to A, so A isn't the case.

Questions like this can be a bit time-consuming because you have to work out the thought pattern in all the answers. So forge ahead! You could summarize (A) like this: Most colleges have A, but few students participate, so A is useless; that's wrong. (B) goes: All cities have A, but so do counties and states, and that means A is needlessly duplicated. That's wrong. (C) goes: The United States is said to be A, but here's an example of something that's not A, so A isn't really the case. That looks pretty close to the argument's reasoning, so (C) could be the answer. (D) says: Most teachers think A, but colleges disagree, so teachers shouldn't do A. That's wrong. (E) goes like this: Most insurers claim A, but doctors and hospitals don't, so insurers are dishonest. That's wrong. (C) is by far the best choice, so it's your answer.

If you're running low on time, you can try to quickly whittle down the possible answers by looking at the last sentence of each choice and comparing it with the conclusions of the argument. What conclusion looks most like, "Therefore, Americans don't actually live in a democracy"? That conclusion says that because a democracy isn't pure or direct, it's not a democracy at all. So you should be looking for an answer choice with the conclusion that mirrors the idea that "it is not ____ at all." A quick look at the answer choices may highlight a few choices that are most attractive. A) "no useful purpose" B) "too much duplication" C) "doesn't really have a free market economy" (this one looks the best so far!) D) "shouldn't major" E) "health insurers are dishonest" (maybe). At this point, take a look at the entire sentences of the two choices that seem attractive. If one of them hits the nail on the head, that's your answer

6. The question wants you to find an example that illustrates the proposition stated in the argument. That proposition is that people meet expectations. Look for an answer that shows someone receiving a task and performing it as expected. (A) looks like a perfect choice: The teacher presents the girl with a task and expects her to do it, and the girl does. (B) is wrong. In this case, the partner assigns the associate a duty, but obviously doesn't expect the associate to be able to perform it and therefore supervises him closely. (C) is an example of someone failing to meet expectations, so it's wrong. (D) seems close to the proposition but doesn't fit it exactly. The players do learn the coach's strategy, but the result is that they win; for this answer to fit the proposition, they should instead merely execute the strategy as expected. (E) doesn't involve anyone's expectations. The psychologist tells the patient something that may help her, and the patient follows his suggestion and succeeds, but the psychologist never tells the patient that behavior modification is her duty. (A) is the best answer.

7. The question informs you that four of the answer choices weaken the argument, but one doesn't. The argument's conclusion is that aptitude tests have no value in sorting students. As evidence, it cites the problems that currently plague German schools, which have used these tests for more than a century. What weakens this argument? Well, if the argument blames aptitude-test–based sorting for the problems in German schools, anything that shows that the problems aren't due to the sorting or the tests weakens it. When you read the answers, look for four choices that do this. The correct answer doesn't; it doesn't necessarily strengthen the argument, but it doesn't weaken it.

   (A) doesn't obviously weaken the argument. If disciplinary problems are worst at technical schools, and the cause is that students fear they won't ever receive the opportunity to improve, perhaps the sorting system is the root of the problem. You could argue that aptitude-test–sorting schemes are explicitly designed to restrict opportunities. The sorting can have benefits, but perhaps in this case it also causes problems, such as resentment on the part of those students who get sorted into the lower echelons. (B) weakens the argument by showing a reason why sorting students by ability is important, citing the problems that occur when students of mixed abilities end up in the same classroom. (C) weakens the argument by claiming that schools that sort students by ability get better results. (D) weakens the argument by claiming that the sorting system worked fine for more than 90 years. If the problems have only arisen in the last decade, perhaps some other cause is to blame. (E) weakens the argument by stating that technical schools are actually very good and desirable; if parents want their children to attend what appears to be the lowest level of school, then something must be working in the educational system. (A) is the only choice that doesn't weaken the argument, so it's the answer.

8. The question asks for a statement that weakens the argument. The argument's conclusion is that worker bees aren't individuals, at least as far as genetics are concerned. The evidence is that instead of reproducing themselves, they put all their energy into nurturing the queen and her offspring. To weaken this argument, you want to find a statement that shows workers acting in a way that advances their own reproductive interests.

   (A) looks like the answer, because it suggests that workers are in fact furthering their genetic line by caring for the queen, who is after all related to them. But it doesn't quite work because it doesn't contradict the argument, which says that workers fail to pass on their own genes to offspring. See if a better choice is available. (B) does in fact contradict the argument's conclusion. If workers can in fact lay eggs, they do occasionally pass their genetic traits on to offspring, even if their offspring are strictly male. (C) doesn't weaken the argument. It doesn't strengthen it, either; it's merely a statement of fact about queens. (D) doesn't weaken the argument either; if anything, it shows how workers subordinate their interests to the queens. (E) is just more information about queens (and drones); it neither strengthens nor weakens the argument. (B) is the best answer.

   Beware of assuming you know something about a topic. Maybe you know all about bee biology. Maybe you disagree about worker bees ever acting in their own interests; certainly, even egg-laying workers are still laying eggs on behalf of the hive, not themselves. That doesn't matter. Forget about it. Just read what's in front of you and work strictly from that.

9. The question asks you to find the argument's weak point. The argument concludes that all myths can fit into both categories (explanations of natural phenomena and explorations of psychological phenomena). But what if they can't? All you need to disprove this argument is one example of a myth that explained a natural event but contained no psychological elements, or one myth illustrating a psychological principle without delving into the natural world. See if you can find an answer that questions the statement that all myths can be interpreted both ways.

(A) is wrong. You don't know if experts in the field have already discounted this conclusion because the argument doesn't say anything about them. (B) is wrong because the argument says nothing about the relevance of myths in today's world. (C) is wrong because the argument doesn't impose any sort of modern sensibility on myths; it doesn't mention pre-modern people or the difference between them and people today. (D) is wrong because the argument doesn't criticize anyone. (E) matches with the answer you hoped to find; the argument does indeed assume that all myths contain both natural and psychological phenomena and doesn't offer any proof. Perhaps the author could furnish proof, but at this point the assumption without proof is the weakest part of the argument, and therefore most vulnerable to criticism. (E) is the answer.

10. The question asks you to find a statement that must be true if everything in the argument is true. The argument's conclusion is that identifying the sex of parrotfish can be difficult, and as evidence it cites the various color patterns that male and female parrotfish display at different stages in their lives. You know enough information is available for you to infer more facts, but at this point you don't know what, so why try speculating? You can't predict what the answer will be, so just read the argument carefully and get your head around the parrotfish facts. Then just read the answer choices one by one and see if one fits what you now know about these colorful fish.

    Right off the bat, (A) looks like a good choice. The argument says that in some species of parrotfish, males spend some time looking like females before they grow into their adult coloration, which implies that in some species, they don't. If they don't spend time looking like females, they must mature straight into the adult male form. Check the other answers to make sure this one is the best. (B) can't be right, because the argument tells you that some male parrotfish spend part of their lives looking like the smaller and more subdued females; sexually mature males are the ones who are large and brightly colored. (Well, the argument doesn't mention the appearance of juvenile parrotfish, so for all you know, males and females both could be gigantic and colorful, though it seems more likely that they're small, but that doesn't matter here.) (C) may be true, but nothing in the argument implies that it must be. (D) may also be true, but the argument says nothing about the importance of camouflage in avoiding predators. (E) is just plain wrong; the argument said that in *some* species, males spend time looking like females; *some* definitely isn't *all*. (A) is your answer.

    This sort of question invites you to let your own background intrude. You've probably taken biology, and you may know about coloration and camouflage and baby fish and all that good stuff, but as always, forget it. It's not relevant here.

11. The question wants you to spot the assumption that the author makes in developing the conclusion. The argument concludes that because schools have decreased arts teaching, the next generation of citizens won't appreciate art. Now, the only way that could be the case is if they don't learn about the arts outside of school. The author must assume that schools are the only place where children get any arts education.

    (A) is wrong. If the author assumed that, then she couldn't conclude that everyone would grow up ignorant of the arts. The author doesn't assume (B), though she could possibly cite it as evidence in favor of keeping arts programs in schools. (C) is wrong; the author certainly isn't assuming that people become great artists independent of art education in school. (D) is right. The author definitely assumes that if people don't learn art in school, they'll never learn it. (E) is wrong; it serves as an argument in favor of ending arts programs in schools. (D) is the right answer.

12. The question wants you to find an answer that supports the argument's conclusion. The conclusion is that the loss of the baseball team will hurt the town, especially economically. To support this, look for an answer that shows how much money the team brought to the town.

    (A) doesn't support the conclusion. In fact, it supports the opposite conclusion, that keeping the team would actually cost the town money instead of bringing in income. (B) does support the conclusion; it shows how the team's presence brought in money by bringing visitors to the town. (B) looks like a good answer. (C) provides another reason why losing the team wouldn't hurt the town; no one attended the games anyway. (D) criticizes the baseball team's loyalty and its demands, which does nothing to support the argument that the town would benefit by keeping it. (E) is evidence of the town's apathy toward the team, not support for an argument that says losing the team would hurt the town. (B) is the only answer that actually supports the conclusion, so it's the best one.

13. The question informs you that the argument makes an assumption, and asks you to identify it. The argument concludes that the president's initiative is worth supporting because it will help the children of poor, unmarried women by helping these women get married and stay that way. Clearly the writer assumes that married mothers benefit these children; if kids don't benefit, then the argument falls apart. Look for an answer that says something about the benefits kids get from having married parents, perhaps mentioning the presence of fathers.

    (A) is wrong because the author says nothing about drug dependency, crime, or teen pregnancy. This argument sticks to statements about relationships and healthy children. A reader might assume that drugs and crime are part of the equation, but the author of this argument doesn't (at least, not here). (B) doesn't work. The author doesn't need to involve people with higher incomes in the conclusion about marriage and low-income people. (C) is exactly what you want. If children raised by married moms and dads are better off than those raised by single mothers, it justifies the author's conclusion. (D) may be another reason to encourage marriage, but the author is talking about children, not welfare. (E) is irrelevant; the author makes no mention of other governmental programs, successful or otherwise, and doesn't need this statement to make the argument hold together. (C) is the correct answer.

14. The question asks you to find a statement that the argument supports. (Note that it doesn't ask you to support the argument; that would be hard to do with a conversation like this, which doesn't really have a conclusion.) Think for a moment about what's going on in the conversation. Isabel says that the novels in question are dangerous and explains why she thinks that. Ferdinand says he thinks she's wrong because she's exaggerating the influence the books have. So clearly they disagree about the impact these books have on their readers. See if one of the answers says this.

    (A) is wrong. Ferdinand and Isabel don't argue about the religious nature of the books; Isabel mentions religion, but Ferdinand doesn't address that part of her contention. (B) is definitely wrong. Isabel says nothing about the appropriateness of the end of the world as a topic for a novel. (C) is clearly wrong. Isabel and Ferdinand aren't arguing about whether the books are popular or not. (D) looks like a good choice. Isabel certainly does believe that popular fiction can affect people's behavior and can therefore be a dangerous influence. This answer choice doesn't mention Ferdinand, but that doesn't necessarily mean that it's wrong. (E) is another wrong answer. Ferdinand and Isabel don't argue about the amount of violence that is appropriate in fiction. That leaves (D) as your best choice.

    The right answer to this question doesn't exactly match up with the answer I earlier suggest you look for. That's okay. This sort of question is open-ended and guessing exactly what the right answer will be is nearly impossible. Just be sure you understand what the argument says, and you'll be fine.

15. This question wants you to identify the source of Tia and Muriel's disagreement. Why are they arguing? Tia thinks the government should regulate food manufacturing and advertising, and Muriel thinks it shouldn't, not necessarily because that regulation wouldn't work but because she thinks individuals are in control of their own weight. They also disagree about the causes of obesity; Tia seems to place the blame squarely on modern food manufacturers and advertisers, while Muriel blames the obese individuals for their bad habits.

    (A) is wrong because Tia and Muriel aren't debating the effectiveness of diet and exercise in weight control; they may well agree with the statement. (B) is tricky. Tia obviously thinks the government should intervene in public health problems, while Muriel seems to disapprove of such intervention. I'd hesitate, though, because (B) is a pretty extreme statement, and Muriel did say that the government could take some limited action in encouraging diet and exercise. See if you can find something better. (C) is wrong; neither speaker has mentioned public schools, so there's no telling what they think about school nutrition programs. (D) looks pretty good. Tia obviously thinks that a lot of obesity comes from modern food, but Muriel thinks it comes from overeating. (E) doesn't work because neither Muriel nor Tia has mentioned the difference between public- and private-sector efforts. (D) is the best answer here.

16. The question asks you to find the point where the politician's argument is most vulnerable. The politician suggests that global warming isn't happening. As evidence, he mentions that recent winters have set record low temperatures, which is great evidence if it indeed indicated a trend of colder weather, or at least an absence of overall warming. See if one of the answers refutes its validity as evidence.

    (A) is wrong; the politician doesn't claim that environmentalists are frightening people with doomsday scenarios, merely that they say that pollution causes global warming, which might have unpleasant consequences. (B) is wrong. The politician isn't appealing to emotions at all. (C) is wrong because the politician doesn't debate the potential effects of global warming. (D) is right because the politician assumes that a few low temperatures can refute the claim that overall temperatures worldwide are increasing. (E) is wrong because the politician doesn't mention the political leanings of environmentalists. (D) is your best answer.

17. The question asks you to identify the answer that conforms to the principle stated in the argument. What is that principle? Basically, the argument suggests that investing for the future is better than taking immediate profits, because the long-term profits from the investment will ultimately be larger. Look for an answer that shows someone postponing gratification or payoff in exchange for higher future profit. (This principle is familiar to anyone contemplating law school.)

    (A) looks like a great choice. The student who turns down a job offer to pursue higher studies definitely exemplifies the principle in the argument. (B) doesn't exactly fit the principle. It discusses the benefits of investing for the future, but it's not about postponing immediate gratification for future rewards. (C) is wrong. It recommends a particular action because there's a correlation between that action and future success, but attending church and postponing immediate gratification to invest in the future aren't the same thing. (D) is wrong because although Habitat for Humanity offers a great opportunity for poor people who want to own homes, neither the volunteer builders nor the new homeowners are declining a current opportunity in order to invest more heavily in a future one. (E) may be sound advice, but it doesn't duplicate the argument's principle. In fact, if you buy good furniture now, you're not delaying anything. (A) is the best answer.

18. You want to find the answer best supported by the argument, which probably means spotting the answer that's closest to the argument's conclusion. The argument's conclusion is that women like to buy vehicles designed just for them. It would probably go on to suggest that car manufacturers would profit from putting more effort into designing cars with women's tastes in mind. You're not going to be able to concoct the exact answer to this question without reading the choices, so just bear in mind the argument's points: Plenty of women buy cars, women notice certain details, and cars designed with those details outsell cars that aren't designed with those details.

    (A) is wrong. True, women don't like polluting cars, but that's not the main point of the argument; you'll almost certainly find a better choice than this. (B) is wrong because it focuses on a particular kind of car that women especially like, not the overall issue of designing vehicles for women. This answer is here to distract you with irrelevance. (C) may be true, but it's not really the point of the argument. (D) looks great. It's exactly what you would expect the author of the argument to say, so it's a very good answer. (E) is also wrong. Although many people lament the passing of the station wagon, and it's entirely possible that car manufacturers may find that they still have a huge market for these vehicles, the argument isn't concerned with particular types of cars. (D) is your answer.

19. The question wants you to identify the source of Carter and Neri's disagreement. Carter says that kids shouldn't watch television because it gives them ADD. Neri says that a blanket prohibition on children's television watching isn't necessary because the disorder comes from watching a particular kind of program, and some programs are actually beneficial. Both speakers agree that television can cause ADD; they disagree on whether television can ever benefit children.

    (A) is wrong; Carter and Neri haven't mentioned violence on television, so you can't possibly know what they think about it. (B) is wrong. Although Carter does mention the time factor, Neri doesn't address it, so you don't know if they disagree about that or not. (C) looks right; they definitely disagree about whether children can ever benefit from watching television. (D) is wrong. Neri does mention educational programs, but Carter doesn't specifically address them, and neither speaker discusses the past generation of TV watchers. (E) is wrong because neither speaker addresses this issue. (C) is correct.

20. The question asks you to support the park ranger's assertion, which means you have to find an answer that provides evidence showing that the assertion is correct. The park ranger claims that parks and monuments with good names get the most visitors, so the National Park Service should give its parks and monuments appealing names. Look for an answer that shows how giving a park a good name attracted lots of tourists; a good example may compare a park with a good name to a park with a lousy one.

    (A) is totally wrong; it doesn't mention park names at all. (B) is wrong because it attributes attractiveness of parks to location and scenery instead of name. (C) may work, because it does compare two parks with different names, but it doesn't say anything about how many people visit either park, so it's not the best choice. (D) looks perfect; if a park had more visitors after changing its name, then that's evidence to support the ranger's conclusion. (E) is wrong, too. It claims that Yellowstone attracts visitors because people want to see the sights there, not because they like the name "Yellowstone." (D) is correct.

21. You want to find evidence that weakens the argument. The argument concludes that the government shouldn't pass laws outlawing public smoking; the reason for this conclusion is that smoking hurts no one but the smoker, and the smoker has the right to choose whether or not to hurt himself or herself. What weakens this argument? If the argument is wrong about the effects of smoking on innocent bystanders, then it weakens the contention that smokers hurt only themselves. Look for an answer that mentions the effects of smoke on nonsmokers.

(A) is incorrect; complaints about political inconsistency don't hurt the argument. (B) doesn't weaken the argument at all; you want to find evidence of smoking hurting people, not evidence that its effects are minimal. (C) is wrong. It does emphasize the damage that smoking does to smokers, but the argument already admitted that, and claimed that smokers should be allowed to take on the risk of giving themselves lung cancer. (D) doesn't affect the argument either way; whether or not smoking is decreasing doesn't affect the claim that smokers aren't hurting anyone but themselves. (E) is a perfect answer. The argument bases its conclusion on the claim that smoking doesn't hurt nonsmokers, but this answer completely refutes that claim. If smoking does indeed hurt nonsmokers, the government has a clear interest in protecting them by limiting smoking. (E) is your answer.

22. The question asks you to determine where the argument is vulnerable. The argument claims that studying drama and performing can make a person more extroverted; the evidence for this conclusion is that actors are extroverted. The problem with this claim is that you don't know for sure that actors are extroverted because they studied drama, or that people who are extroverted to begin with choose drama as a profession. If the latter is true, then studying drama won't make an introvert into an extrovert.

    (A) is incorrect because the argument makes no judgments about the benefits of extroversion or introversion. (B) looks correct; the argument does confuse effect with cause. (C) isn't right. The argument doesn't supply much evidence of extroversion, but it does supply a little. However, a lack of evidence isn't the problem. (D) is wrong; the argument does define extrovert somewhat, as someone who is comfortable before a crowd of people, and even if it didn't define the term, that's not really the argument's chief weakness. (E) is wrong. It doesn't matter whether or not there are other ways for people to improve their self-confidence, because that's not why the argument fails. (B) is right.

23. The question asks you to identify the statistician's conclusion. This is a long and complex argument on an esoteric topic, but don't let that bug you. Essentially, the statistician is suggesting that the mathematical community should accept the computer-created proof of the orange-stacking concept; the statistician's reason is that computers are very accurate and all the parts that have been hand-checked so far have been correct. So look for an answer that says this. The validity of the proof is the key.

    (A) seems to be exactly what you want; the argument does conclude that computers are reliable enough to create acceptable mathematical proofs. (B) is wrong because the statistician isn't concerned with alternate methods of stacking oranges. He doesn't mention them at all, so they can't be part of his conclusion. (C) is wrong because it's the exact opposite of the statistician's conclusion; he thinks computers *do* have a place in the world of theoretical mathematics. (E) is wrong because it describes the process of proving a mathematical theorem, not the statistician's actual conclusion. (A) is correct.

24. The question asks you to resolve a discrepancy. What's the discrepancy? The overall percentage of accidents per drivers hasn't increased since states raised their speed limits, but total accident fatalities have increased. So even though accidents haven't increased, they have become more deadly, which is entirely possible. Look for an answer that connects cause — higher speeds — with effect — more fatalities.

    (A) is wrong; the argument doesn't mention illegal speeding, just higher legal speeds. (B) looks correct. If higher speeds make accidents more deadly, then it makes sense for fatalities to rise even if total accident numbers don't. (C) is wrong because state regulation of speed limits doesn't affect accident fatalities. (D) is wrong because it doesn't connect speed with fatality; perhaps these slower cars caused fewer deaths, but the answer doesn't say that. (E) is wrong because it attributes accidents to distractions, not to speed. (B) is the best answer.

25. You need to find the answer that doesn't weaken the argument; that means four answers do weaken it. Remember, you don't have to find an answer that actually strengthens the argument; you just have to find one that doesn't hurt it. Spotting the statements that *do* weaken the argument may be easier; if you can find four of those, the fifth choice is probably your answer. The argument's conclusion is that speakers should always start their speeches with a joke, even in foreign countries, because audiences like jokes. What would weaken this claim? Well, what if audiences don't actually like jokes? What if jokes don't translate well? Anything that disproves the contention that audiences like jokes weakens the argument.

    (A) definitely weakens it; speakers shouldn't tell jokes if they'll offend their audiences. (B) weakens the argument, at least as far as female speakers are concerned. (C) weakens the argument; the last thing a speaker needs is for an interpreter to refuse to translate the speech. (D) actually doesn't weaken the argument; if audiences like to relax by laughing, then telling a joke is a good idea. (E) once again weakens the argument; no speaker wants to inadvertently commit an act of aggression. (D) is the best answer.

26. The question asks you to identify the role a claim plays in the argument. The argument says that telemarketing calls have increased since the enactment of a law that was supposed to limit such calls. As evidence, the activist cites her own experience. She has received more calls since the law went into effect. So the claim in question functions as evidence, as an illustrative example of the conclusion.

    (A) is incorrect. Though the activist is complaining, the claim that she's received more calls since the passage of the law doesn't function specifically to express her disgust with telemarketing companies, but instead to illustrate her point. (B) is wrong because the activist doesn't claim that government favors businesses over individuals. (C) is wrong because the activist doesn't mention dinner. (D) is wrong because the activist isn't blaming the government for all her problems; she's blaming one specific law for one specific problem. (E) is correct. The claim that the activist has been getting more calls since the law was passed does illustrate the way in which the law has increased unwelcome calls. (E) is the answer.

Part IV

Reading Comprehension: Read 'Em But Don't Weep

The 5th Wave — By Rich Tennant

In this part . . .

Lawyers (and law students) have to read a lot. Most of what they read is arcane, complicated, and even boring. Despite these inherent flaws in the reading material, lawyers and law students have to understand and apply what they read. The Reading Comprehension section tests your skill in this area. You get four passages on different subjects, and you have to answer several questions after each passage. The questions determine how well you understand what you read — whether you can identify the passage's main point, whether you can determine how the passage is organized, and whether you can spot the author's biases and intentions. Don't fret if you lose interest while reading or answering these questions; just stay on target and work your way through.

Chapter 14

Everybody's Got an Axe to Grind: Reading Comprehension

One of the four scored sections on the LSAT is Reading Comprehension. Like the other multiple-choice sections, it contains between 24 and 28 questions and lasts 35 minutes. You may think this section sounds fairly straightforward — after all, you've been reading and understanding what you read for years. But LSAT Reading Comprehension questions aren't designed just to test your ability to pick information out of a text. They're meant to determine whether you can figure out *why* the author wrote the text, not just what the words say.

Reading carefully is an extremely important skill for a lawyer. Lawyers have to be able to understand what they read and apply that information to facts; for example, a lawyer must be able to read and understand the rules of court in order to pursue a lawsuit. Lawyers have to spot biases and positions in their opponents' arguments. They have to identify pieces of evidence. They have to understand why documents are constructed as they are. (They also have to concentrate on extremely boring and often badly written documents for hours on end.)

The Reading Comprehension section tests all these skills. It forces you to read rather dense passages on subjects that probably don't interest you, and it asks you various questions about what you've read. To succeed on this section, you first must read carefully and grasp what you read. But more than that, you have to understand why the author wrote the text in the first place.

Grinding That Axe

The whole objective of the Reading Comprehension section is to test your comprehension of what you read. (Well, duh!) Okay, but how can a test-maker determine if someone understands a passage? By asking questions about it, of course! But LSAT Reading Comprehension questions go way beyond basic queries that require you to regurgitate verbatim what you've read.

Little biases everywhere

Every LSAT Reading Comprehension passage has an agenda. No one sits down to write something for no reason — writing is hard work! Why does an author write a text? Who does she expect to read it? Why does she organize it in a particular way? To succeed, you have to get into the author's head and answer those questions.

For example, why did I write this chapter? Who do I envision reading it? Well, I wrote it to introduce the LSAT Reading Comprehension section to an audience who is considering applying to law school, and have therefore decided to take the LSAT. That's why I say things like "To succeed, you have to get into the author's head and answer those questions."

If I were writing for a different audience, such as an audience of test-prep teachers, I would have organized this chapter quite differently. Test-prep teachers aren't planning to take the test, so I wouldn't give them direct advice. Instead I'd mention things they could tell their students; you'd see sentences like "Tell your students to take nothing for granted."

No text on any subject is a foregone conclusion. Someone always decides what to say and why. Give the same topic to two different writers and you get two completely different editorials; this can happen whether one editorialist is ultra-liberal and the other is ultra-conservative, or they both work in the same political party for the same candidate. Different writers organize their information differently and emphasize different points.

Every text has some bias. Even the most outwardly objective of books or articles has an author who chose what to include and what to leave out.

The passages in the Reading Comprehension section represent a variety of viewpoints. Some explicitly argue one point or another. Some don't have as obvious an agenda. In either case, you have to ask yourself what the passage is all about and why the author chose to organize it in a particular way.

Question types

Here are some of the types of questions the LSAT-makers use to test your reading comprehension. Some of them simply ask you to apply what you've read, but most of them require much more.

Main idea/main point

Main-idea questions look like this:

- ✔ Which one of the following most accurately summarizes the main point of the passage?
- ✔ Which one of the following most accurately states the central idea of the passage?
- ✔ Which one of the following most accurately states the main idea of the passage?
- ✔ Which one of the following titles most accurately describes the contents of the passage?
- ✔ Which of the following would be the most appropriate title for the passage?

The first question to most passages is a main-point question, which is good, because it helps you get your thoughts in order right away. To answer these questions, you have to digest the entire passage's contents and summarize them. It helps if the passage has a clear statement of *thesis* (main idea), but most of them don't. Don't despair, though. Concentrate on the first and last paragraphs and ask yourself how the author got from one to the other; doing so can give you an idea of what the main point is.

Another way to think about this is to create a title for the passage that accurately describes the big picture or what the passage is about. When creating a title for the passage, make sure you include the big title and the subtitle (what might come after a colon). For example, a title might be, The Big Bang: Proposing a Hybrid Theory.

Primary purpose

These questions ask you why the author wrote the passage. They can look like this:

- ✔ The primary purpose of the passage is to
- ✔ The primary purpose of the passage is most likely to
- ✔ Which one of the following is most likely the author's overall purpose in the passage?
- ✔ The passage provides the most support for which one of the following statements?

Purpose questions are subtly different from main-point questions. Main-point questions are slightly more related to content, whereas purpose questions are more interested in why the author wrote the text. To answer these questions, try to figure out who the author imagines reading the passage and what exactly he wants them to take from it.

Author's attitude

These questions test your understanding of the author's attitudes or opinions toward the passage's subject. They can look like this:

- ✔ The author's attitude toward traditional teaching methods can most accurately be described as
- ✔ Which one of the following best captures the author's attitude toward Warhol's work?

Or they can ask you to extrapolate the author's opinion on other subjects:

- ✔ The author of the passage would be most likely to agree with which one of the following statements?
- ✔ From the passage it can be most reasonably inferred that the author would agree with which one of the following statements?
- ✔ Given the information in the passage, the author is LEAST likely to believe which one of the following?

If you already figured out the passage's main point and purpose, you probably have some idea of the author's opinions and attitudes. To answer these, think about what the author says and how he says it. What words does she use to describe things? Are they extreme or ordinary? What sort of transitions does she use, such as "nevertheless" or "despite"? Has she made any explicit statements of opinion, or is her opinion hidden in the information she chooses to convey?

Another way to think about this is to ask yourself if the author is smiling, being neutral, or frowning. The answer choices are almost always gradations of "approving," "objective," or "critical."

The passage's structure

Some questions ask you to determine why the author has constructed the passage in a particular way, or why the author has included certain paragraphs or pieces of evidence. They can look like this:

- ✔ The function of the third paragraph is to
- ✔ Which one of the following most accurately describes two main functions of the first sentence of the passage?

- ✔ Which one of the following most accurately describes the organization of the passage?

- ✔ The discussion in the third paragraph is intended primarily to explain which one of the following?

To answer these questions, you must first understand the author's main point and purpose. Then look at how the passage is organized. See if you can spot an outline. (That's not always easy to do; Reading Comprehension passages aren't always organized very clearly.) After you understand the passage's structure, then figuring out why the author has included a particular sentence or paragraph is easier.

A great way to do this is to jot down notes next to each paragraph about what the point is of that paragraph. You'll end up with the central "nuggets" of information of each paragraph, and when you connect the dots, you'll have created a useful outline of the passage. Jotting down notes about the main point of each paragraph also helps make sure you understand what each paragraph is about, thereby also increasing your general comprehension of the passage.

Use of evidence

Some questions ask you to figure out why the author has chosen to include particular pieces of evidence. These questions may look like this:

- ✔ The author most likely lists some of the themes and figures that appear in Warhol's paintings in order to

- ✔ Which one of the following most accurately represents the primary function of the reference to maximization of economic gains?

- ✔ Which one of the following does the author use to illustrate the difference between the two techniques?

To answer these questions, first figure out the author's point. If you know that, then ask yourself what the items in question have to do with that point. Do they support it? Do they attack an opponent? Do they describe something in greater detail?

The passage's application

Some questions require you to apply information you discover from the passage to new situations. There's a huge variety of questions in this category, but here are a few examples:

- ✔ Which one of the following does the passage identify as a prime influence on Warhol's work?

- ✔ With regard to religious freedom, the passage explicitly states each of the following EXCEPT:

- ✔ Based on the passage, which one of the following would be an example of art most in keeping with Warhol's philosophy?

- ✔ Based on the passage, which one of the following can most reasonably be inferred about modern art?

- ✔ Which one of the following can most clearly be inferred from the description of molecular physics in the second paragraph?

- ✔ Which one of the following is most analogous to the ideal described in the passage?

Some of these questions are fairly straightforward, simply asking you to find the answer right in the text. Most of them are harder, though, and require you to read between the lines to find deeper meaning. Inference questions are extremely common. These questions once again go back to the question of why the author wrote the passage in the first place.

Reading Incomprehensible "Gibberish"

Reading Comprehension passages are usually pretty dense and, dare I say it, boring. That's intentional. The test-makers want to see if you can force yourself to consume and digest the text despite a total lack of pleasure or interest in the material. After all, lawyers (and law school students!) have to do that every day.

About the reading passages

The LSAT test-makers adapt the Reading Comprehension passages from previously published texts — you can see the acknowledgements at the end of the test, on the page that precedes the sample. They take good articles of a decent length and condense them into about 450 words, thereby turning what may originally have been a good read into a work of moderate banality and difficulty.

That's not to say that some of the passages aren't interesting. Occasionally you do find one that's quite informative, or that appeals to some personal interest. That's great if it happens, but don't take it too seriously; the passages you enjoy don't deserve any more of your time than the ones you hate, because they're all worth about the same number of points.

Every question on the LSAT is worth exactly one point. You're not penalized for wrong answers, so guess away. See Chapter 1 for more on scoring.

Passages come from articles on law, science, the humanities, and the social sciences — usually you get one of each. You don't have to know anything about any of these subjects. All the information you need to answer the questions is contained in the text. *Don't* contribute anything from your own background. So if you especially detest quantum physics and the first passage is all about that, plunge on in; the water's fine. Likewise, if you love Mexican art and it just happens to be the subject of the third reading passage, you're not gaining an advantage over anyone else because you have to restrict yourself to what's written on the page in front of you.

Obscuring what was clear

One reason LSAT Reading Comprehension passages are so hard to read is simply the way they're formatted — they're in a small font and a narrow column with no breaks between paragraphs. They're visually dense, and crucial bits of information tend to get buried. The same passage printed in a more user-friendly format — say, a *For Dummies* format — would be much more accessible. So if you find these passages hard to read on the real LSAT, it's not really your fault.

The LSAT complicates these passages even more by using long sentences. The vocabulary is advanced, but it's the length of the sentences that makes them tough to break down. Simply dividing most sentences in two would make the passages considerably easier to grasp. Does this mean the writing in LSAT reading passages isn't that great? Well . . .

Don't expect a sensible structure to these reading passages. For example, you may expect to find a passage's thesis in the first paragraph. Forget about that. The thesis can be anywhere, say, buried in the middle of the third paragraph or at the very end of the passage, or even not explicitly stated anywhere. You have to figure out what the point is.

Talking Technique

Reading a passage of 450 words ordinarily wouldn't take you long, and you'd probably come away understanding every bit of it after one read. That doesn't happen with LSAT Reading Comprehension passages. These little buggers are hard to get through, so you need to attack them with concentration and a plan.

Deciding whether to work in or out of order

No one says you have to work the Reading Comprehension section in order. If you want to spend half a minute or so at the beginning of the section flipping pages and ranking the passages from your favorite to your most detested, go right ahead. If you prefer to save that half a minute and work the section from start to finish, that's great, too.

As with Analytical Reasoning, if you choose to work the passages out of order, your best criterion for ranking them is the number of answers attached to them. If you anticipate running out of time, concentrate on the passages with a large number of questions first — so if one passage has eight questions and another only six, choose the one with eight questions first.

Although hopping around within the Reading Comprehension section if you want is fine, working two or more passages at once isn't a good idea. It takes time to load the information in a passage into your brain, and you don't want to interfere with your concentration by hopping around. When you pick a passage, stick with it until you've answered all the questions, and then move on.

Reading aggressively

Reading can be a fun passive activity, but when you take the LSAT, you need to take charge of the reading situation. Getting bogged down in Reading Comprehension passages is easy. To prevent that, you need to hit them with a systematic plan of attack.

1. **Skim the questions first.**

   Before you dive into the passage, make sure you know why you're reading it. Read through the questions. You'll nearly always have one that asks you what the passage's main point is. Often you'll have to explain why the author included one of the paragraphs, or what the author's attitude toward the subject is. Don't bother reading the answers at this point, but do get an idea of what information you should be looking for.

   Use your pencil here. Underline or circle the key words in the questions, which can help you focus on finding that information when you read the passage.

2. **Read the passage slowly.**

   Take your time. Speed-reading doesn't help, and may actually waste your time if you have to go back and reread something you missed. Savor the passage like a fine wine, appreciating all its nuances.

   That being said, don't take too much time. You don't want to memorize the passage, and you can always refer back to it to check details. A general rule: Spend no more than four minutes or so reading the passage, which gives you the other four minutes to answer the questions that go with it.

3. Read with an active pencil.

When you start reading, start marking stuff. Circle important words. Underline key statements, especially ones that look like the passage's main point. Mark any obvious statements of opinion and clear transitions. If you notice any kind of obvious structure, mark it so you can see it clearly. Doing so helps you spot necessary words when you need them. Jot little notes off to the side that identify bits of info. You want to transform this undifferentiated block of text into something with noticeable breaks and pauses.

Here are some things you're trying to find:

- The author's main idea
- The author's purpose
- The author's attitudes and opinions
- The passage's structure
- Transition words, such as *for example, nevertheless,* or *in sum*
- Pieces of evidence that the author uses
- Anything that stands out as an answer to one of the questions

Spotting transition words can really help you identify the passage's structure. These words serve as kind of a road map for the passage; if you underline them and ignore the rest of the content, you should still have a good idea of the passage's direction. Look for transitions such as *moreover, for example, in contrast, furthermore,* and *therefore.* If you spot any of these, you know where the author has been and where he plans to go.

Whatever you do, don't underline or circle too much! Many students highlight or underline nearly every word in their textbooks or notes, which has the virtue of canceling out anything they've underlined and making plain text stand out. If you don't know how much is too much, aim to put pencil to paper no more than 20 times, which includes circled words and phrases and underlined sentences.

4. Contemplate the passage for a moment.

After you read the passage, think about it for a moment. Ask yourself what it's all about. Try to come up with a main idea, a statement that summarizes the content. Ask yourself why the author wrote it, and who would most likely read it. Note any obvious biases. Don't spend more than a minute or so on this step, but do put your thoughts in order before you plunge into the questions.

5. Don't worry about getting it all!

You *will* refer back to the passage to answer the questions. Don't try to memorize the text and all its information. You can look back at it whenever you want to. Read it to get an idea of what the passage says and how it's organized so that you know where to look to find the answers to the questions. So read it once and then get on to the questions.

6. After you finish the questions, forget the passage.

You have more passages to read and questions to answer. Don't get bogged down by one passage, no matter how troublesome. After you finish it, let it go. You're done with it; move on.

Skimming a little off the top

Should you skim the passage first? Probably not; it takes up time and it's not especially useful for understanding the passage. If Reading Comprehension passages were clearly written and well-organized texts, skimming might help, but LSAT reading passages are so dense (verbally and visually) and hard to take apart that often nothing stands out to catch your eye during a skim.

Tackling the questions

After you read the passage and underline the bits you hope will help you, start to answer the questions.

In or out of order?

You can answer the questions from first to last, or you can jump around on the page. It doesn't really matter, as long as you transfer your answers to the answer sheet correctly. If you spot a question that you like, go ahead and do it first. Each question can stand alone, and they're not intentionally organized by difficulty. The first question very often is a main-point question that requires you to understand why the author wrote the passage.

Answering the question yourself

After you read a question but before you read the five answer choices, try to come up with an answer in your own words. Doing so helps you spot the right answer when you see it.

This step is crucial. The wrong answer choices are *meant* to be attractive and distract you. But if you have a clear idea of what you're looking for, you'll be more able to spot the right answer choice. I can't tell you how many students have improved their scores just by applying this one crucial step!

Eliminating the duds

Four answer choices are wrong. It's always that way. Knocking off wrong answers is just as valuable as spotting right answers (well, almost as valuable; you don't get points for spotting the wrong choices). When you find an answer that's obviously wrong, cross it off so you aren't tempted to consider it again. If you can't decide whether an answer is wrong or not, leave it; chances are you'll be able to resolve that conflict by the time you've read all the choices.

Typically any question has at least two and usually three obviously wrong answers. Normally you should have no more than two, or possibly three, answers that look plausible. The LSAT-makers deliberately create some answers that are very close to the correct answers, but there's always something wrong with them that makes them less than best.

Picking an answer and moving on

If you find an answer that you know is right, good for you! Mark it and move on. If, after careful scrutiny and contemplation, you're still stuck between (A) and (C), fret not; pick one of them and move on to the next question. Spending too much time on any one question doesn't help the answer magically materialize before your eyes, but it does use up time you could employ answering more promising questions.

If you're one of those readers who loses concentration, you may want to use your pencil or finger to keep your eyes focused on the page. You may think that makes you look like a first-grader just learning to read, but it helps you keep focused.

Chapter 15

Getting Acquainted with Reading Comprehension Passages and Questions

● ●

In This Chapter

▶ Working through two Reading Comprehension passages and questions

▶ Figuring out a successful Reading Comprehension strategy

● ●

*I*n this chapter, I walk through two Reading Comprehension passages and how to tackle them. This chapter shows you how to skim the questions, some things you may want to mark in a passage, and how to approach and conquer the questions. Because this chapter is the first one to introduce Reading Comprehension passages, it's a bit easier than a real LSAT Reading Comprehension section, which would contain four passages, not two. Read Chapter 16 for more extensive practice!

Giving Passage 1 a Shot: Influenza Vaccination

In this section you find a typical Reading Comprehension passage followed by questions about the passage. However, because the point of this chapter is to show you how to tackle Reading Comprehension, I also provide you with tips and tricks for doing just that all along the way. Enjoy!

Skimming the questions first

If you follow the steps I outline in Chapter 16, when you first tackle a Reading Comprehension passage, skim the questions before actually reading it. Why? Skimming the questions tells you what information you need to find as you read the passage.

You can find the questions for this first passage under the section, "Knocking down the questions." Based on these questions, keep these considerations in mind:

✔ The main idea (that's what the first question wants)

✔ The author's attitude toward influenza vaccination

✔ Discussion of current techniques of producing flu vaccine

✔ The author's opinion of the lawsuits brought by people claiming to have contracted Guillan-Barré syndrome from flu vaccine

    ✔ The passage's primary purpose

    ✔ Who should make the greatest effort to receive vaccination against influenza?

    ✔ The author's opinion of the government's role in public health matters

As you skim these questions, underline key words. (Don't underline the entire questions!)

Reading and underlining

After skimming the questions, read the passage. Underline or otherwise mark anything that looks important, which can help you answer a question. (Don't underline the whole passage!)

Okay, here's Passage 1. For your convenience and learning pleasure, I already marked various words and phrases that may be important to answering the questions:

Line   Every winter, public health officials warn people that a major influenza outbreak could occur and encourage all <u>vulnerable</u> people to get vaccinated. They have <u>good reason</u> to do this; <u>the flu is a major inconvenience at best, and deadly at worst</u>. The Spanish Flu epidemic of 1918 killed more than 20 million people worldwide. More

(05)   Americans died from this flu than were killed during all the wars of the 20th century; a disproportionate number of the dead were young adults in the prime of life.

      The name influenza is an Italian word meaning "influence"; Italians in the mid-18th century called the illness "influenza di freddo," which means "influence of the cold." The disease is usually not fatal — it kills about one tenth of one percent of the people who

(10)   catch it — but it can be extremely dangerous in <u>vulnerable</u> groups, such as the <u>elderly, young children, pregnant women, and anyone with a compromised immune system, diabetes, or heart or lung disease</u>. The precise strain of the disease changes every year as new viruses arise. The flu virus originates in birds, usually in southeast China. The birds give the virus to pigs, who then pass it on to humans, although scientists are now con-

(15)   cerned that some strains of the virus can jump straight from birds to humans, bypassing the pig vector.

      Because influenza is caused by a virus, there is no way to treat it. <u>The best approach to flu is to prevent it by vaccination</u>. Public health officials in the U.S. developed a vaccine for the flu in 1944, which they produced by <u>cutting a hole in the shell of a</u>

(20)   <u>fertilized hen's egg, injecting the virus into the amniotic fluid, and allowing the chick embryo to breathe in the virus</u>. The virus would multiply inside the chick, and then be exhaled back into the amniotic fluid, which gradually became cloudy with viruses. Scientists <u>still use this technique today</u>, which <u>why it takes so long for pharmaceutical manufacturers to make flu vaccines</u> each year.

(25)   Vaccines have been extremely effective at reducing the severity of flu outbreaks. Unfortunately, the Swine Flu vaccination fiasco of 1976 gave many people a <u>mistaken view of the vaccine's dangers</u>. That year the Centers for Disease Control and Prevention feared a devastating flu epidemic and urged the government to implement a nationwide vaccination campaign, which President Ford agreed to do. People were vaccinated in droves, but then two bad things happened: The swine flu epidemic never materialized,

(30)   and some people claimed the vaccine gave them a nerve disease, Guillan-Barré syndrome, and nearly 4,000 of them filed lawsuits against the government. There has been <u>no scientifically proven link between the flu vaccine and Guillan-Barré syndrome</u>. Some people still fear vaccinations and the <u>federal government has become more hesitant</u> to recommend mass vaccination schemes, but <u>there is no need for this</u>; the flu vaccine is a

(35)   <u>tremendously successful product with few detrimental side effects</u> and <u>people should get their flu shots every year with confidence</u>.

You can also make little notations in the margins, draw circles around words, draw arrows from one place to another — anything that makes finding what you need easier. Don't sweat this process too much; you don't have to mark everything, and you'll have access to the passage while you answer the questions.

Thinking about the passage

Before you start on the questions, think a bit about the passage you just read. What's the main point? Well, the author obviously thinks flu vaccine is a good thing; he includes a bit of information about influenza and its virus, a bit of history of the flu vaccine, and a lamentation about the unfortunate lawsuits surrounding the 1976 vaccination program. The piece is mostly informative but also expresses a definite opinion. All that information is relevant to the questions.

Knocking down the questions

Now tackle the questions. Try to answer them yourself first. Use a blank sheet of paper to cover the answer and explanation, and then see if you answered it correctly. Don't peek.

Regardless of whether you can answer the question on your own or not, make sure you read the explanation of how to come to the correct answer. You may find this information helpful later when working on other Reading Comprehension passages, whether practice or real.

1. The passage is primarily concerned with discussing which one of the following?

   (A) The symptoms of the flu and the effects of the 1918 influenza pandemic

   (B) The 1976 Swine flu vaccination fiasco and its detrimental effects on subsequent vaccination drives

   (C) The constant mutation of the flu virus in birds and pigs

   (D) The efforts of the scientists who first identified the cause of influenza

   (E) The effects of the flu and the history and benefits of the influenza vaccine

This question is pretty much the same thing as a main-idea or main-point question; all you have to do is understand what the passage — the *whole* passage — is about. In this case, the passage is primarily concerned with providing some information about the flu, the virus that causes it, and the history of the vaccine, arguing that the vaccine is beneficial and not at all dangerous.

Now consider the answer choices: (A) is wrong because the author doesn't actually describe the symptoms of the flu anywhere. (B) would be correct if the question asked about the third paragraph, but not in the case of the entire passage. The author mentions (C), but as part of his discussion of the flu virus; it's not the passage's main topic. (D) isn't right; the author doesn't really say anything about the scientists' efforts, beyond describing the egg-injection process. (E) looks correct; it's an overall theme, not restricted to a particular paragraph, and pretty well sums up the passage. (E) is the correct answer.

2. Which one of the following best describes the author's attitude toward influenza vaccination?

   (A) conviction that the vaccine is the best way to prevent a flu epidemic and that people should not fear it

   (B) skepticism as to whether the vaccine's benefits outweigh the risks

   (C) annoyance that the government has tried to interfere with people's lives by encouraging them to get vaccinated

   (D) admiration for the heroic efforts of the scientists who developed the flu vaccine in the 1940s

   (E) disgust at the attorneys who took advantage of the government's vulnerability in the Guillan-Barré lawsuits

The author quite clearly thinks the flu vaccine is a good thing; he calls it a "tremendously successful product with few detrimental side effects," claims that "the best approach to flu is to prevent it by vaccination," and says that "people should get their flu shots every year with confidence."

Skim the first words of the answers and knock out anything that is obviously wrong: (A) looks promising, summing up the author's attitude toward the vaccine. (B) should go, because there's no skepticism here. (C) is likewise wrong, because the author isn't at all annoyed at the government's efforts. (D) is also probably true of the author's attitudes, but he doesn't really get into this topic in the passage. (E) describes an attitude that the author probably has, but it doesn't answer this question. (A) is the correct answer.

3. The passage suggests which one of the following about current techniques of producing flu vaccine?

   (A) Scientists have taken advantage of technological developments in the second half of the 20th century to make the process more efficient and precisely tailored to specific strains of the influenza virus.

   (B) Because scientists use chicken embryos in eggs to incubate the virus, they can only create vaccines that are effective against flu transmitted by chickens.

   (C) Because the technique has not changed appreciably since it was developed in the 1940s, it is a fairly inefficient process with some major limitations.

   (D) It is unfortunate that scientists use fertilized hens' eggs to create the flu vaccine because this means that the developing chicken embryos will die before they hatch.

   (E) There are many better ways of creating vaccines, but scientists are unable to put them into practice because of economic restrictions.

What does the author says about current techniques? "Scientists still use this technique today, which why it takes so long for pharmaceutical manufacturers to make flu vaccines each year." That sounds like he thinks the process is slow and possibly inefficient. Be careful about assuming that he thinks the process is outdated, because he doesn't suggest that scientists should use a different, more efficient method.

Now, consider which choice is the right answer: (A) is wrong because scientists haven't in fact updated the flu vaccine creation process. (B) is wrong; the author says nothing about this. (C) restates the author's words but with a little more judgment; this works as an answer because the author does note that it takes pharmaceutical companies a long time to generate vaccines, which is limiting. (D) doesn't work; the author says nothing about the sad implications to the chick embryos. (E) is wrong; the author doesn't mention newer and better techniques of producing vaccines; perhaps there aren't any, and the egg method is still the best way. (C) is the best answer.

4. Which one of the following best describes the author's opinion of the lawsuits brought by people claiming to have contracted Guillan-Barré syndrome from flu vaccine?

    (A) They were justified because the flu vaccine had caused people to contract Guillan-Barré syndrome.

    (B) They were frivolous lawsuits that did not prove a connection between the vaccine and Guillan-Barré syndrome and did major damage to the public health drive to vaccinate people against influenza.

    (C) They were an important cautionary lesson for the government in the dangers of getting involved in public health matters.

    (D) They are an example of unscrupulous lawyers and runaway juries taking advantage of a defendant with deep pockets and a cause of action that is too complicated for a typical juror to understand.

    (E) They illustrate the necessity of government indemnification of pharmaceutical companies that manufacture necessary but potentially dangerous substances such as vaccines.

A couple of things should give you a clue about the author's attitude: the use of the word "unfortunately" to describe the events following the 1976 vaccination program, and the statement that there has been no link proven between the vaccine and Guillan-Barré syndrome. You know that this author believes strongly in the value of the flu vaccine and thinks everyone should get it, and he thinks that the damage done by the 1976 lawsuits is unfortunate.

Look for an answer that says something like that: (A) is definitely wrong because the author doesn't think the lawsuits were justified, and he notes the lack of a proven connection between vaccine and disease. (B) looks very good. The author mentions the lack of a connection, and goes on to describe the aftereffects, including government reluctance to try another vaccination program and unfounded public fears of the vaccine. (C) may well be true, but the author doesn't seem to think the government should use the 1976 story as a cautionary tale. In fact, he says there is "no need" for the government to hesitate to vaccinate people. The author may secretly believe (D), but he never mentions either unscrupulous lawyers or runaway juries in this passage, so you can't assume anything about his opinions of them. (E) doesn't work because the author never mentions the fact that the government indemnified the pharmaceutical companies in these cases. (B) is the correct answer.

5. What is the primary purpose of the passage?

    (A) To encourage all American citizens to receive the flu vaccine every year

    (B) To criticize the government's drive to vaccinate all Americans against the 1976 Swine Flu, which was a premature action that led to unfortunate products liability lawsuits and large damage awards

    (C) To discredit any claims of a link between the influenza vaccine and nerve diseases such as Guillan-Barré syndrome

    (D) To suggest that vaccinating people against influenza is the best way to respond to the threat of a major global epidemic, several of which have already occurred with devastating consequences

    (E) To argue against allowing products liability lawsuits against the manufacturers of vaccines

The author has a definite axe to grind. He wants to convince people that the flu vaccine is safe and effective, along with providing a little information about the process of creating the vaccine and the devastating consequences of the disease.

See which answer choice best fits this agenda: (A) isn't exactly right; the author isn't addressing this piece specifically to the government, and he's not really suggesting that the government take this exact action, though he probably does think a yearly vaccination program would be a good idea. See if there's a better answer. (B) is totally wrong, the complete opposite of what the author thinks. (C) isn't the primary purpose of the passage. The author mentions this lack of a link once, in the last paragraph, but it would have to appear more often than that to be the primary purpose. (D) looks pretty good. The author does emphasize the benefits of vaccination and mentions the devastating consequences of a previous flu epidemic, the 1918 pandemic. (E) is just plain wrong; the author doesn't say anything about products liability at any point in the passage. Though he certainly thinks the lawsuits were wrong, you can't assume anything he doesn't state explicitly or implicitly. (D) is the best answer.

6. What is the primary purpose of paragraph 2?

 (A) To provide some background information about influenza, such as the origin of the name and the way the virus mutates

 (B) To suggest that pregnant women in particular should receive the flu vaccine

 (C) To describe the method scientists use to replicate the flu virus inside fertilized hen's eggs

 (D) To speculate on possibly unverified ways in which the flu virus can jump from animals to humans

 (E) To criticize the way influenza received its name because the Italian version of the name gives the mistaken impression that influenza is caused by cold temperatures

Paragraph 2 describes the origin of the name "influenza," lists the people most at risk from the disease, and briefly describes the way the virus develops.

Look for an answer that hits those points: (A) actually looks good; keep that in mind as a good possible answer. Though the author mentions that pregnant women should get vaccinated, that isn't the only thing he says in this paragraph, so (B) doesn't work. (C) is simply wrong; that information is in the third paragraph. (D) is wrong, too, because the author doesn't speculate about virus transfers. Likewise, (E) is wrong. The author simply states that the word "influenza" comes from an Italian phrase, but doesn't suggest that this is in any way misleading to English speakers. (A) is by far the best answer.

7. According to the passage, who should make the greatest effort to receive vaccination against influenza?

 (A) medical workers such as nurses and doctors, who are most likely to be exposed to the flu on a daily basis and then transmit the virus to their own patients

 (B) young children and people who work around children, such as daycare workers and elementary school teachers

 (C) people who are most vulnerable to dying from the flu, such as the elderly, young children, pregnant women, and people with compromised immune systems, diabetes, or heart or lung disease

 (D) scientists who work with flu viruses

 (E) people who are planning to travel to Asia, particularly southeastern China, at the time of year when the flu virus tends to jump from birds to pigs to humans

In the first paragraph the author mentions that vulnerable groups in particular should get vaccinated against flu. In the second paragraph, he writes that flu "can be extremely dangerous in vulnerable groups, such as the elderly, young children, pregnant women, and anyone with a compromised immune system, diabetes, or heart or lung disease."

Skimming the first words of the answers results in the following: (C) jumps out as a near-perfect answer. Double-check the others to be sure, though. The author doesn't mention medical workers or kids at all, so (A) and (B) are wrong. He doesn't mention scientists or travelers, so (D) and (E) are wrong. (C) is the only answer that works here.

8. Which one of the following best describes the author's opinion of the role the government should take in public health matters?

   (A) The government should take an active role informing people of the dangers of diseases such as influenza and encouraging people to receive vaccines to prevent national or international epidemics

   (B) The government should avoid taking any extreme stands on public health matters because of the danger of lawsuits, frivolous or otherwise

   (C) The government should subsidize research into better vaccines for dangerous illnesses such as influenza

   (D) The government should quarantine people who contract dangerously communicable diseases such as influenza in order to prevent the diseases from spreading rapidly throughout the population

   (E) The government should increase the budget of the Centers for Disease Control and Prevention because the CDC is the organization most capable of preventing a major outbreak of influenza.

You're pretty familiar with the author's attitudes by now; he certainly thinks the government can have a role in preventing influenza epidemics.

So which answer choice works best here? (A) looks like a good answer. (B) isn't right because the author actually says that there's no reason for the government to hesitate to recommend vaccination. (C) is wrong because nowhere does the author address funding for research. (D) is also wrong because quarantine isn't a topic in this passage. The author may agree with (E) but he doesn't mention funding for any group, including the CDC, so that can't be right. (A) still looks best.

Conquering Passage 2: Manifest Destiny

Great, you've plowed your way through a Reading Comprehension passage and questions! Wasn't that fun? (Play along, please.) Good job.

Now forget all about the flu and vaccines and weird procedures involving cutting holes in eggshells. You have to clear your brain for this next passage.

You can tackle this reading passage just as you did the last one. Start by skimming the questions, reading and underlining the passage, and then pondering its meaning for a moment or two before answering the questions.

Skimming the questions

The questions for Passage 2 are in the section, "Answering the questions — full speed ahead." Based on these questions, look out for the following in this passage:

   ✔ The main point
   ✔ The concept of manifest destiny
   ✔ Consequences of the Mexican-American War

✔ 19th-century American views of movement toward the Rio Grande

✔ The phrase "fearing to anger America's southern neighbor"

✔ Polk's attitude toward expansion

✔ The passage's organization

As you skim the questions, underline key words.

Reading and underlining

Now you're ready to tackle this second passage. Here's how you could mark up this passage to help you answer the questions:

Line   During the <u>middle of the 19th century</u>, the United States <u>increased its geographi-</u> <u>cal area</u> by 1.2 million square miles. Many Americans <u>justified</u> this tremendous expansion, which inevitably came at the cost of the lives and way of life of Native Americans and other colonists, with the self-righteous claim <u>that the United States was divinely</u>

(05) <u>ordained to spread democracy over the world</u>. They summed up this belief in the phrase "<u>manifest destiny</u>," a term invented in 1845 by writer John O'Sullivan, in an editorial defending the U.S.'s claim to Texas; in this editorial, O'Sullivan argued that the U.S. was destined to be the great nation of the future because of its <u>superiority in individual</u> <u>freedom, equality, and progress, and therefore had a divinely granted right to expand its</u>

(10) <u>government everywhere</u>. Americans of that time, at the height of the American Romantic movement, sincerely believed that it was their country's duty to spread the American way of life as far as possible, and therefore willingly supported the federal government's expansionist policies. At the same time, many citizens <u>disliked the</u> <u>German and Irish immigrants</u> crowding into Northeastern cities and wanted to force

(15) these newcomers to move elsewhere.

     James K. Polk campaigned for the 1844 presidential election on a wildly popular <u>expansionist</u> platform and won handily. He immediately set about adding to U.S. territory and in the process <u>precipitated a major war with Mexico</u>. The <u>territory of Texas</u> <u>was hotly contested</u> at that time; Mexico considered it Mexican territory, but American

(20) settlers in the area had declared Texas an independent republic in 1836. The previous U.S. administrations had hesitated to annex Texas as a state, fearing to anger America's southern neighbor, but Polk had no such qualms. He <u>admitted Texas to statehood in</u> <u>1845</u>, and, as expected, Mexico ended diplomatic relations with the U.S. Soon afterward, Polk sent his envoy to Mexico to discuss the purchase of California, but the Mexican

(25) minister refused to receive the man, and Polk used this as <u>an excuse to send American</u> <u>troops to the Rio Grande</u>, which the American residents of Texas considered their southern boundary.

     Mexico disagreed, and Mexican troops crossed the river to attack American troops. Polk <u>bullied</u> a reluctant Congress into declaring war on Mexico, assuring them that the conflict would resolve itself after a few minor skirmishes. Instead, the Mexican-

(30) American War lasted from <u>1846 until 1848</u> and cost a multitude of <u>lives</u>, to say nothing of the vast monetary <u>expense</u>. Ultimately, the investment paid off as Polk had hoped it would. Mexico surrendered and relinquished the land from Texas to California, effectively ceding half its territory to the U.S. The war also functioned as a <u>training ground</u> for several army officers, including Robert E. Lee and Ulysses S. Grant, who became key

(35) figures in the next major conflict fought by Americans, the Civil War.

You could also make notes, such as noting next to the second paragraph that it's about Texas, or circling words, or anything else that helps you keep this information in order.

Thinking about the passage

What do you think is the main point? Probably something about how the philosophy of manifest destiny led to Americans electing an expansionist president who proceeded to go to war and take half of Mexico's territory for the United States. It may help you to try to come up with a suitable title for the passage, perhaps with a subtitle that further refines the title (the subtitle would be the part that follows the colon in a two-part title). You also know you have a question about the passage's organization, noting the topic of each paragraph probably doesn't hurt — manifest destiny, Texas, and the Mexican-American War and its payoff to the United States — or something similar. Don't make an elaborate outline, but do consider organization for a moment.

Answering the questions — full speed ahead

After you skim the questions once and read the passage, hunker down and answer the questions.

Try to answer the questions on your own first before peeking at the answer. Read the answer explanation regardless — it's good practice. The explanations help you think more about the passage and about the way LSAT questions are constructed, and may give you some insights when you take the test for real.

1. Which one of the following most accurately states the main point of the passage?

   (A) Without the Mexican-American War as a training ground for military officers, the outcome of the American Civil War might have been quite different.

   (B) A belief in manifest destiny, a desire for more land, and the election of an aggressive president led the United States into a war with Mexico and generated tremendous territorial expansion in the mid-19th century.

   (C) Manifest destiny, a belief that the United States was destined to be the great nation of the future because of its superiority in individual freedom, equality, and progress, was the predominant philosophy of Americans in the 1840s.

   (D) Polk was a strong president who managed to force his ideas about war through Congress despite the fact that most of America was ambivalent about the republic of Texas and aggression against Mexico.

   (E) The Mexican-American War was a worthwhile investment of time, money, and lives because it added a huge chunk of territory to the United States, including land on the Pacific Coast.

You've already thought about the main point, so see if one of the answers matches your thinking: (A) doesn't look right. This passage mentions the Civil War only in the very last sentence, so the Mexican-American War's effects on the Civil War can't be the main point. (B) looks pretty good; it hits all the passage's highlights. (C) looks like it could be the answer, except that it stops with manifest destiny and ignores the two-thirds of the passage concerned with the Mexican-American War, so it's not right. (D) also seems plausible, but Polk's aggression toward Congress really isn't the main point, only part of the passage's point. (E) makes a claim about the value of the Mexican-American War that the author really doesn't make; she expresses no opinion as to whether that endeavor was worthwhile or not (though she does make some negative comments about manifest destiny in the first paragraph). (B) is the best answer.

2. Given the information in the passage, which one of the following best summarizes the concept of manifest destiny?

    (A) It was a concept created by a newspaper writer who used the phrase in an editorial supporting the United States' claim to Texas

    (B) It was a religious belief cherished by many American Protestants, particularly those who settled in the western and southwestern territories, that God had given them the entire North American continent for their own purposes

    (C) It was the political platform on which James K. Polk based his 1844 presidential election campaign

    (D) It was a racist sentiment that American citizens used to justify their hatred of new immigrants

    (E) It was an idea born of 19th-century romanticism that claimed that the United States had divinely ordained duty to spread its ideas about government and social equality as far as possible, even if that meant conquering other lands and people.

First, make sure you know what the question is asking; underline the word "summarize" so you remember your mission. Here's what the author says: "Many Americans justified this tremendous expansion with the self-righteous claim that the United States was divinely ordained to spread democracy over the world. They summed up this belief in the phrase 'manifest destiny,' a term invented in 1845 by writer John O'Sullivan; O'Sullivan argued that the U.S. was destined to be the great nation of the future because of its superiority in individual freedom, equality, and progress, and therefore had a divinely granted right to expand its government everywhere."

Consider which answer choice works best: (A) isn't right because it doesn't address the concept of manifest destiny, just the phrase's origin. (B) isn't right; manifest destiny wasn't explicitly a religious or Protestant belief, though it did have a religious component to it. (And the author never mentions Christianity or Protestants anywhere in the passage.) (C) doesn't summarize the concept, though Polk did campaign on an expansionist platform; note, too, that Polk ran for president in 1844 and O'Sullivan coined the phrase in 1845. (D) isn't right; the passage doesn't say that manifest destiny was an explicitly racist philosophy. (E) looks good because it focuses on the American sense of having a divinely ordained mission to spread democracy, which is exactly what the passage says. (E) is correct.

3. Which one of the following is NOT identified by the author of the passage as a consequence of the U.S.'s war with Mexico?

    (A) The U.S. Congress came to resent Polk's imperious attitude.

    (B) Many soldiers died in the conflict.

    (C) Officers who later became major figures in the Civil War had their first combat training.

    (D) The United States added the entire southwest, from Texas to California, to its territory.

    (E) Mexico lost approximately half its territory.

Skim the answers and cross off the ones that you can find in the passage; the last one standing is your answer: The only fact that the author doesn't mention is Congress's growing resentment of Polk's attitude, so (A) looks right. Many soldiers died in the war with Mexico, so (B) is out. The last sentence of the passage mentions (C). (D) is mentioned in the last paragraph, as is (E). (A) is indeed the correct answer.

4. Based on the passage, the American people of the early 19th century would be most likely to hold which one of the following views of America's movement toward the Rio Grande?

(A) It was a mistake because it ran the chance of alienating Mexico.

(B) It was economically sound because it would provide territory for new immigrants to settle far away from the cities of the eastern seaboard.

(C) It was an excellent means of spreading Protestant Christianity among the predominantly Catholic Mexicans.

(D) It was a dangerous maneuver likely to spark a war with Mexico.

(E) It was the right thing to do because the United States had been created by God to spread democracy and equality throughout as much of the world as possible.

You know what 19th century Americans thought of expansion — they liked it and thought it was their country's duty; that's what the whole manifest destiny business is about. (A) is wrong; the passage gives you no reason to believe that ordinary Americans worried about alienating Mexico by settling Texas. The same reasoning invalidates (D). (B) is wrong; the passage suggests that American citizens wanted more territory for immigrants, but doesn't specifically state that they thought Texas was the place for these newcomers. This is a tricky answer, though, because it could plausibly seem right. (C) is wrong; the passage doesn't suggest that Americans wanted to proselytize the Catholic Mexicans. (E) sums up the prevailing philosophy nicely. (E) is correct.

5. The phrase "fearing to anger America's southern neighbor" in the second paragraph (line 18) is most likely intended to

(A) justify Polk's agreeing to annex Texas as a state

(B) argue that the annexation of Texas was precipitous and done out of anger at Mexico

(C) suggest that Mexico had plans to go to war with the United States in order to reclaim the Texas territory

(D) describe the effect that Polk's predecessors believed annexing Texas as a state would have on Mexico's government

(E) condemn the actions of the American residents of Texas who declared the territory an independent republic without Mexico's permission

"America's southern neighbor" in this sentence is, of course, Mexico. (The LSAT will assume a bit of rudimentary geography — you do, of course, know that Mexico is south of the United States.) Presidents before Polk hadn't wanted to annex Texas as a state because they were afraid Mexico would get angry if they did.

(A) doesn't work because the phrase doesn't justify Polk's actions. (B) is wrong because it has nothing to do with fearing to anger Mexico, but in fact suggests that the United States didn't care if it did anger Mexico. (C) is the opposite of the answer. Polk's predecessors didn't want to anger Mexico, fearing that would spark a war, but didn't think Mexico would start a war unprovoked. (D) is the best answer to this question. Polk's predecessors didn't take action on Texas because they were afraid Mexico would get angry and go to war. (E) totally doesn't work; it's not condemning Texans, who certainly weren't concerned about angering Mexico. (D) is correct.

6. The passage suggests which one of the following about Polk's attitude toward expansion?

   (A) Polk believed that, as president, he was justified in bullying Congress into approving troops and funding for the Mexican-American War, even if most legislators disagreed with him.

   (B) Until his envoy was turned away at Mexico City, Polk thought he would be able to purchase California from Mexico without recourse to violence.

   (C) Polk was determined to expand U.S. territory and power, but he did not want to jeopardize good diplomatic relations with other countries.

   (D) Polk disapproved of the residents of Texas taking matters into their own hands by declaring Texas an independent republic.

   (E) Polk wanted to continue the policies of previous administrations with regard to Texas and Mexico.

According to the passage, Polk wanted to expand the United States regardless of whom he had to alienate, whether it be Congress or Mexico. (A) looks like a good answer. (B) doesn't look so good. If Polk used Mexico's refusal to receive his envoy as "an excuse to send American troops to the Rio Grande," he probably didn't expect his offer to buy California to go over well in the first place. (C) is obviously wrong; the passage provides no evidence that Polk cared about good diplomatic relations with other countries. (D) doesn't work, either; Polk had no problem with independent Texans and was quite willing to annex them as a state, even when he knew Mexico wouldn't like it. (E) is also explicitly wrong; Polk most definitely didn't continue the previous administrations' policies. So (A) is correct.

7. Which one of the following most accurately describes the organization of the passage?

   (A) A description of American philosophy and prevailing opinions in the early to mid-19th century, followed by an account of the start of the Mexican-American War and its effects on the United States

   (B) A description of the philosophy called manifest destiny, introduced as justification for the war against Mexico

   (C) A description of a newspaper editorial that introduced a phrase that became very popular in 19th century American literary circles, followed by a condemnation of the expansionist policies of Polk and an account of the injustices forced on Mexico

   (D) A detailed account of U.S. territorial expansion in the 19th century, beginning with the war against Mexico and ending with the Civil War

   (E) An analysis of the philosophy of manifest destiny, followed by a description of Congressional action to expand U.S. territory, followed by an account of the Mexican-American War, and concluding with the years preceding the Civil War

Make a quick mental outline of the passage (or look at your notes if you've jotted down main points of each paragraph). It starts with a description of manifest destiny, followed by a paragraph on Polk's expansionist tendencies and the start of the Mexican-American War, and concludes with a paragraph on the results of that war.

Look for an answer choice that echoes this organization. (A) looks like a good answer. (B) is wrong because the passage doesn't just address manifest destiny. (C) is wrong because the passage doesn't condemn Polk or describe injustices inflicted on Mexico. (D) is wrong, too, because it skips the paragraph on manifest destiny and includes material that's not in the passage; the only territorial expansion that appears is what resulted from the war with Mexico, and you can't assume that's all the expansion that occurred in the 19th century. (E) starts well, with the analysis of manifest destiny, but the passage doesn't actually discuss Congressional action, nor does it address the years preceding the Civil War. (A) is correct.

Chapter 16

Comprehending the Incomprehensible: Practice Passages and Questions

....

In This Chapter

▶ Working through four Reading Comprehension passages and questions

▶ Focusing on Reading Comprehension practice questions

....

This chapter contains four Reading Comprehension passages each followed by several questions. It's basically the same format you'll encounter on a real LSAT; when you take an actual LSAT, you get 35 minutes to work the entire section. Take as much time here as you need, though. (You can worry about timing yourself when you take the full-length practice exams in Chapters 20 and 22.)

The answers and explanations to these questions are in Chapter 17. Try working on them first before checking the answers.

Passage 1: Pondering a Japanese Poet

Line

Junzaburou Nishiwaki, a 20th-century Japanese poet, scholar, and translator, spent his career working to introduce Japanese readers to European and American writing and to break his country out of its literary insularity. He was interested in European culture all of his life. Born to a wealthy family in rural Niigata prefecture in 1894,

(05) Nishiwaki spent his youth aspiring to be a painter, and traveled to Tokyo in 1911 to study the "White Horse" school of painting with the artist Seiki Kuroda; this painting style fused Japanese and European artistic traditions. After his father died in 1913, Nishiwaki studied economics at Keio University, but his real love was English literature. After graduating, he worked for several years as a reporter at the English-language

(10) *Japan Times* and as a teacher at Keio University.

Nishiwaki finally received the opportunity to concentrate on English literature in 1922, when Keio University sent him to Oxford University for three years. He spent this time reading literature in Old and Middle English and classical Greek and Latin. He became fluent in English, French, German, Latin, and Greek. While he was in England,

(15) Roaring Twenties modernism caught his eye, and the works of writers such as James Joyce, Ezra Pound, and T.S. Eliot were crucially important to his literary development. In 1925, Nishiwaki published his first book, *Spectrum,* a volume of poems written in English; he explained that English offered him much more freedom of expression than traditional Japanese poetic language.

(20) Nishiwaki returned to Keio University in 1925 and became a professor of English literature, teaching linguistics, Old and Middle English, and the history of English literature. He remained active in modernist and avant-garde literary circles. In 1933 he published *Ambarvalia,* his first volume of poetry written in Japanese; this collection of surrealist verse ranged far and wide through European geography and history, and

(25) included Japanese translations of Catullus, Sophocles, and Shakespeare. Angered by the Japanese government's fascist policies, Nishiwaki refused to write poetry during the second world war. He spent the war years writing a dissertation on ancient Germanic literature.

After the war, Nishiwaki resumed his poetic pursuits and in 1947 published *Tabibito kaerazu,* in which he abandoned modernist language and returned to a classical Japanese (30) poetic style, but with his own postmodernist touch, incorporating both Eastern and Western literary traditions. In 1953 Nishiwaki published *Kindai no guuwa,* which critics consider his most poetically mature work. He spent his last years producing works of criticism of English literature and Japanese translations of the work of such writers as D.H. Lawrence, James Joyce, T.S. Eliot, Stéphane Mallarmé, Shakespeare, and Chaucer. (35) Nishiwaki retired from Keio University in 1962, though he continued to teach and write poetry. Before his death in 1982, he received numerous honors and awards; he was appointed to the Japanese Academy of Arts and Sciences, named a Person of Cultural Merit, and nominated for the Nobel Prize by Ezra Pound. Critics today consider Nishiwaki to have exercised more influence on younger poets than any other Japanese poet (40) since 1945.

1. Which one of the following most accurately states the main idea of the passage?

    (A) Nishiwaki was a Japanese poet who rebelled against the strictures of his country's government and protested its policies toward Europe during World War II.

    (B) Nishiwaki was a Japanese poet and literary critic who embraced European literature as a way of rebelling against the constraints of his family and traditional Japanese culture.

    (C) Nishiwaki was a Japanese poet and professor who spent his life trying to convince young Japanese students that European literary forms were superior to Japanese poetic styles.

    (D) Nishiwaki was a Japanese poet and linguist who throughout his life chose to write in English rather than Japanese.

    (E) Nishiwaki was a Japanese poet and scholar who spent his life specializing in European literature, which proved tremendously influential to his own work.

2. The author's attitude toward Nishiwaki's life and career can be best described as

    (A) scholarly interest in the life and works of a significant literary figure

    (B) mild surprise at Nishiwaki's choosing to write poetry in a language foreign to him

    (C) open admiration for Nishiwaki's ability to function in several languages

    (D) skepticism toward Nishiwaki's motives in refusing to write poetry during the second world war

    (E) envy of Nishiwaki's success in publishing and academia

3. The primary function of the first paragraph is to

    (A) describe Nishiwaki's brief study of painting

    (B) introduce Nishiwaki and his lifelong interest in European culture

    (C) summarize Nishiwaki's contribution to Japanese literature

    (D) explain why a Japanese man chose to specialize in English literature

    (E) analyze European contributions to Japanese culture at the start of the 20th century

4. According to the passage, why did Nishiwaki stop writing poetry during World War II?

    (A) He was too busy with his contributions to the Japanese war effort.

    (B) The Japanese government rationed paper and ink, which made it impossible for him to write.

    (C) He disapproved of the Japanese government's policies and in protest refused to write poetry.

    (D) The Japanese government, fearing sedition, ordered him to stop writing poetry.

    (E) Work on his dissertation on German literature took up all his time.

5. The passage is primarily concerned with

    (A) comparing Nishiwaki's poetry to that of other Japanese poets of the 20th century

    (B) discussing the role of the avant-garde movement in Nishiwaki's writing

    (C) providing a brief biography of Nishiwaki that explains the significance of his work

    (D) explaining why writers can benefit from studying literature from other countries

    (E) describing the transformation in Japanese poetic style during the post-war period

6. According to the passage, which one of the following types of literature did NOT greatly interest Nishiwaki?

    (A) Old English literature such as _Beowulf_

    (B) modernist English verse such as _The Waste Land_

    (C) Middle English literature such as _The Canterbury Tales_

    (D) classical Greek works such as _Antigone_

    (E) classical Japanese literature such as _The Tale of Genji_

7. Based on the passage, why did Nishiwaki choose to write his first published poems in English?

    (A) He found that English allowed him to express a wider variety of thoughts and emotions than Japanese.

    (B) He published the poems in London, and believed that English readers would buy them if they were written in English.

    (C) The poems were translations of Japanese poems into English.

    (D) He believed that writing poetry in English would be a good way to improve his English language skills.

    (E) The English literature department at Keio University required him to publish work in English before he could become a professor there.

Passage 2: Saluting the Sea Urchin

Line

Biologists often fail to recognize the importance of a species to an ecosystem until that species is no longer present in the ecosystem. A case in point is that of the long-spined sea urchin, *Diadema antillarum*. Scientists and fishermen long considered the sea urchin a spiky pest that served no useful purpose; recreational divers would even feed
(05) sea urchins to fish just for fun. The last 20 years, however, have proven that the sea urchin does indeed play a valuable role in the marine environment.

Sea urchins are members of the phylum Echinodermata, the category of invertebrate animals with spiny exterior shells, which also includes starfish, brittle stars, and sand dollars. Sea urchins have a spherical body contained in a hard shell that is covered
(10) with long sharp spines. They walk around on shorter spines located on the underside of their bodies. A sea urchin's mouth is also located on its underside; this mouth is a five-toothed structure called Aristotle's Lantern, adapted to scraping algae and organic matter from rocks and corals. Sea urchins eat a vast amount of algae.

Exactly how much algae they consume has become clearer in the past two decades
(15) because urchins have virtually disappeared from many Atlantic environments. In 1983 a barge traveled from the Pacific to the Atlantic through the Panama Canal carrying a bacterium that proved devastating to the sea urchin population. Nearly all long-spined urchins in the tropical western Atlantic died as a result of this exposure. Without sea urchins to eat the algae, aquatic greenery grows out of control. It has completely cov-
(20) ered some coral reefs — in Jamaica, before the sea urchins died off, algae covered just 1 percent of shallow reefs, but two years after the plague it covered nearly 95 percent of shallow coral. Many reefs in the Bahamas have abruptly transformed from multicolored undersea wonderlands into monochromatic mossy-looking hillocks. Coral that is covered by algae quickly dies, unable to receive necessary sunlight and nutrients from the
(25) water. The algae cover also makes it difficult for both corals and sea urchins to breed, because their larvae cannot find a clean surface on which to anchor.

Scientists have completely changed their views of sea urchins from that of the early 1980s. Sea urchins are one of the first organisms to show signs of stress when water quality is bad, so the Environmental Protection Agency has begun monitoring sea urchins as an indicator of water conditions. Other scientists have taken on the
(30) task of redistributing the remaining sea urchins to endangered coral reefs. They hope that the sea urchins will clean off the reefs and make it possible for both coral and sea urchins to breed successfully and restore the marine environment to its healthy state.

8. Which one of the following most accurately expresses the main point of the passage?

(A) Events of the last two decades have shown that sea urchins play a vital role in the maintenance of the ecosystems in which they live, contrary to what many scientists formerly assumed.

(B) It is the duty of responsible scientists to manipulate environments to ensure that they remain in ecological balance, such as by transporting sea urchins to reefs that have become overgrown with algae.

(C) Members of the phylum Echinodermata are often underappreciated but are extremely important to the health of coral reefs.

(D) Excessive algae growth is a severe problem in the tropical western Atlantic, and if governments fail to take action in the very near future, all the coral reefs in that area could die.

(E) Governments should educate their citizenry on the importance of keeping ecosystems in balance because this will help prevent people from abusing natural resources or introducing foreign substances that might be dangerous to local plants and animals.

9. The primary purpose of the second paragraph is to

   (A) support the claim that sea urchins are important to their ecosystems

   (B) describe the appearance and eating habits of sea urchins

   (C) argue that the loss of sea urchins is devastating to the overall ecosystem

   (D) illustrate the attitude of scientists toward invertebrates

   (E) suggest that other members of the phylum Echinodermata might also eat algae

10. Based on the passage, which one of the following best describes the relationship between sea urchins, starfish, brittle stars, and sand dollars?

   (A) They are all invertebrates that eat algae.

   (B) They were all devastated by the bacterium that entered the Atlantic in 1983.

   (C) They are all members of the same phylum.

   (D) They are all covered with long, sharp spines.

   (E) They can all be divided into five segments that radiate out from a center point.

11. According to the passage, what happened to the sea urchin population in the tropical western Atlantic in the mid-1980s?

   (A) Fishermen and water sports enthusiasts systematically killed them off, hoping to eradicate what they believed was a pest.

   (B) A plague killed the coral, which became so covered with algae that sea urchins could no longer reproduce.

   (C) A sudden increase in triggerfish, one of the main predators of sea urchins, resulted in most juvenile sea urchins being eaten before they could reach breeding age.

   (D) A virus spread by other echinoderms caused sea urchins from the Bahamas to Jamaica to sicken and die.

   (E) A bacterium carried by a ship entering the Atlantic from the Pacific spread throughout the population and killed nearly all sea urchins.

12. Which one of the following, if true, best supports the author's claim that sea urchins are the key to removal of algae from coral reefs?

   (A) Other animals, such as damselfish, also eat algae growing on coral reefs.

   (B) The population of parrotfish, which eat coral, has increased in the years since the sea urchin population dropped.

   (C) Coral reefs in regions that still have healthy sea urchin populations have almost no algae growing on them.

   (D) Several different kinds of algae have grown on reefs in Jamaica and the Bahamas.

   (E) New types of coral are beginning to predominate in areas that have lost sea urchin populations.

13. The author mentions the Environmental Protection Agency in the last paragraph primarily to

   (A) suggest a way in which the government could get involved in the preservation of coral reefs

   (B) argue that the government should prevent shipping companies from transporting microbes from one marine environment to another

   (C) provide an example of an organization that finds sea urchins to be of great value in the overall health of marine ecosystems

   (D) illustrate how scientists have failed to recognize the significance of sea urchins

   (E) encourage voters to take a greater interest in environmental issues

14. Based on the passage, with which one of the following statements would the author be likely to agree?

   (A) Humans can take an active role in assisting the recovery of ecosystems that have been harmed by human actions.

   (B) It is a bad idea to remove sea urchins from successful breeding populations and introduce them into environments that might be hostile to them.

   (C) Eradicating pests from the marine environment will make the waters of the tropical western Atlantic more pleasant for scuba divers and snorkelers.

   (D) The Environmental Protection Agency should have fined the owner and pilot of the ship that carried the bacterium into the Atlantic in 1983.

   (E) Animals other than sea urchins can adapt themselves to the ecological niche that sea urchins formerly occupied.

Passage 3: Fun with the FMLA

Line

   The Family and Medical Leave Act (FMLA), signed by President Clinton in 1993, was enacted to help employees balance workplace needs with the demands of their families. Congress hoped to prevent workers, especially women, from being forced to choose between work and family. Employers must now take care not to violate the FMLA

(05) and various corresponding state laws that guarantee employees other types of leave.

   The FMLA applies to employers who employ at least 50 employees at the same workplace or within a 75-mile radius. It guarantees employees 12 weeks (consecutive or intermittent) of unpaid leave during any 12-month period for childbirth and caring for a newborn, for adoption of a child, to care for a spouse, child, or parent with a serious

(10) health condition, or for their own serious health conditions. To be eligible for leave under the FMLA, an employee must have worked for the same employer for at least 12 months and at least 1,250 hours within the previous 12 months. Employers must post information about the FMLA in the workplace and include it in employee handbooks. Employees who want to take leave must notify their employers as soon as they can, and,

(15) if possible, schedule treatments so as to disrupt work as little as possible. Employers may require employees to provide certification of health problems from a healthcare provider, and may insist that employees get second medical opinions. Employers must maintain employee health benefits during leave periods. Once leave is over, an employee is entitled to the same position he or she had before leave began or to an

(20) equivalent position with equivalent benefits.

   Some states have also passed family leave statutes that supplement the FMLA. A number of states allow family or medical leave for people who work in companies with fewer than 50 employees. Others guarantee leave periods longer than 12 weeks under specific circumstances, such as a complicated pregnancy, or guarantee leave for parents

(25) who want to participate in their children's school activities. Employers who are affected by both the FMLA and state law must always grant employees the most generous leave allowed by either law, and often must grant leave under both.

   Employers who violate the FMLA can be forced to pay back wages, including bonuses and stock options. Courts can also award damages for violations of state leave statutes. Some employees have increased their damages by combining claims for viola-

(30) tions of the FMLA with tort claims under state law. An Illinois man recently won $11.65 million in damages by combining a claim of violation of the FMLA and a state claim for intentional infliction of emotional distress. Employers should take note; when in doubt about family leave, it is best to err on the side of generosity.

15. Which one of the following most accurately expresses the main idea of the passage?

   (A) The FMLA and state family leave statutes are an excellent way of helping workers, especially women, balance work and family obligations.

   (B) The FMLA and state family leave statutes place a number of unreasonable expectations on employers, who are likely to suffer because they must grant leave to so many workers and will suffer penalties if they fail to comply.

   (C) The FMLA applies to employers with more than 50 workers at the same work site, and guarantees most of those workers the right to 12 weeks of unpaid leave for family purposes every year.

   (D) Employers must learn what their obligations are under federal and state family leave statutes and must allow employees to take time off from work under certain circumstances.

   (E) Most employers know their obligations under the FMLA, but few are aware that individual states have also passed a number of laws that guarantee family leave in specific cases.

16. The passage provides information that answers each of the following questions EXCEPT:

   (A) how long an employee must have worked for an employer before qualifying for leave under the FMLA

   (B) where an employer can find more information on the FMLA and state family leave statutes

   (C) which situations make an employee eligible for leave under the FMLA

   (D) what kind of job an employer must provide for an employee who returns to work after FMLA leave

   (E) what sort of penalties exist for employers who violate the FMLA

17. Which of the following is the most accurate description of the author's attitude toward the FMLA?

   (A) unemotional respect for a law that employers must observe if they want to avoid punishment

   (B) grudging admiration for a law that makes it easier for Americans to work and have families

   (C) open contempt for an unfair law that interferes with ordinary business practices

   (D) undisguised boredom with a law that has so many specific details and requirements

   (E) scholarly interest in a law that might have far-reaching implications for family life

18. The most likely intended audience for this passage is

   (A) law students

   (B) employment lawyers

   (C) owners of businesses with fewer than 20 employees

   (D) owners of businesses with more than 50 employees

   (E) factory workers

19. According to the passage, which one of the following employers would NOT be subject to the FMLA?

    (A) a law firm that employs 29 attorneys, 14 paralegals, 20 secretaries, a business manager, and three runners

    (B) a university with several hundred employees and comprehensive health benefits

    (C) a data collection service that employs 500 college students full-time during the summer months

    (D) a dry cleaning company with six different locations within one city, each of which has 12 full-time employees

    (E) a national corporation with offices in several states, each of which employs at least 200 people

20. The primary purpose of the second paragraph is to

    (A) list some of the main requirements and guarantees of the FMLA

    (B) provide a checklist for human resources departments to follow

    (C) inform employers that they must post information about the FMLA in the workplace

    (D) argue that employers should not be forced to observe the FMLA

    (E) describe the interaction between the FMLA and corresponding state laws

21. Why does the author mention the amount of damages awarded to an Illinois man who won a lawsuit against his employer?

    (A) to provoke outrage against employees who take their employers to court in the hopes of enriching themselves with large damage awards

    (B) to illustrate the unfairness of allowing plaintiffs to combine tort claims with claims under federal law

    (C) to encourage employees to speak to their employers about their right to leave under the FMLA and state law

    (D) to provide a sobering example of an employer who suffered severe consequences as a result of violating the FMLA

    (E) to commiserate with employers who must observe the requirements of federal and state laws, regardless of the costs to their businesses

Passage 4: Considering Cloning

Line   Since Dolly the cloned sheep arrived on the scene in 1997, and the Clinton administration banned cloning research that same year, cloning has spawned an ethical debate that is out of proportion to the procedure's reality. Cloning produces a plant or animal that is genetically identical to its "parent." To make a clone, scientists remove the

(05)   DNA from an embryo and replace it with the DNA from another individual, presumably but not necessarily of the same species. Then they watch and wait for it to develop, either into a more mature embryo in a petri dish or a full-grown creature gestated in a female's womb.

      Cloning could be used for many positive purposes. It could help in research on

(10)   cancer, organ donation, contraception, and brain damage. Parents at risk of passing on genetic defects could have children without fear. Infertile couples wouldn't have to use the services of a sperm or egg donor; same-sex couples could reproduce together. The parents of a dead child could have a genetic copy of it made.

(15) Critics of cloning raise issues that are more part of the debate on genetic engineering and science fiction, suggesting that nefarious scientists might use cloning to create a master race, presumably to carry out their abominable purposes. Some critics dislike the idea of manipulating human reproduction, preferring to believe that all humans are the result of entirely natural processes, and ignoring the many cases of genetic engineering and assisted reproduction among humans, from in vitro fertilization

(20) to choosing to have children in an attempt to get offspring of a particular sex. Cloning does carry some legitimate risks — clones seem to age faster than normally conceived offspring, and carry a large number of genetic defects — but these are practical concerns outside the ethical points that cloning critics raise.

What many critics of cloning don't seem to realize is that creatures who are genet-
(25) ically identical to other creatures arise in nature all the time — identical twins are genetically identical to one another. A human being is only partly the product of his or her genes. A clone looks like the individual that donated its genes, but in all other ways it is unique. Critics worry that cloned children won't be treated naturally; but what does that mean? Parents might have unreasonable expectations of a cloned child, but that happens all the time with children conceived the usual way. Every child born enters the

(30) world to expectations and burdens, and no one says that the parents were therefore wrong to reproduce. Cloning is no more bizarre or artificial than other techniques of assisted reproduction. Every family has odd relationships; surely a cloned child could fit in as well as anyone. Reproduction is an intensely personal issue, and for that reason the government doesn't interfere in most reproductive choices, including adoption and

(35) surrogacy. The creation of a family is always a fertile ground for dysfunction, unjustified expectations, and hurtful behavior. A cloned child, though conceived in an unusual way, would ultimately be just a child, and its parents just parents.

22. Which one of the following titles would best suit the contents of the passage?

(A) Cloning and the death of the family

(B) Dolly, Dr. Frankenstein, and DNA: The dangers of cloning

(C) The mechanics of cloning

(D) Cloning: Just another way of making just another baby

(E) The government's role in preventing unethical scientific research

23. The author of the passage would most probably agree with which one of the following statements about critics of cloning?

(A) People who criticize cloning are deeply devoted to religion and use their faith to justify obstructing scientific research that could have many benefits.

(B) Critics of cloning are correct to worry about the potentially destructive aspects of cloning, such as the creation of a master race or the manipulation of children to meet the specific needs of their parents.

(C) Those who worry about human cloning also object to techniques commonly used today in assisted reproduction, such as in vitro fertilization or the use of surrogate mothers.

(D) Most critics of cloning are worried about aspects of cloning that are not substantially different from the potential problems associated with methods of reproduction already in common use.

(E) Critics of cloning are most concerned about the practical drawbacks of cloning, such as the fact that clones seem to age faster than individuals conceived the normal way, and that they contain a larger than usual number of defective genes.

24. The primary purpose of the passage is to

    (A) argue that most critics of cloning are focusing on drawbacks that are either outlandish or no different from the drawbacks of normal reproduction, and that ethically cloning is not very different from normal reproduction

    (B) explain the process of cloning and compare it to other techniques of genetic engineering and assisted reproduction, such as in vitro fertilization

    (C) recommend that scientists and medical ethicists carefully consider the implications of allowing or banning research into cloning

    (D) extol the many benefits of cloning, such as allowing same-sex couples to reproduce without having recourse to an external egg or sperm donor or allowing parents to make a clone of a dead child

    (E) warn readers of the dangers of cloning, including both the ethical dilemmas of the odd family relationships cloning could create and the physical problems involved in the process of cloning

25. The author uses the words "nefarious" and "abominable" in the second paragraph in order to

    (A) indicate that scientists who work with clones are morally bankrupt

    (B) defend the Clinton administration's ban on research into human cloning

    (C) describe the personalities of people who oppose cloning research

    (D) criticize parents who want to use cloning to create particular children

    (E) show that the worries of cloning critics are exaggerated and based more in fantasy than fact

26. The author would most probably agree with which one of the following statements about assisted reproduction?

    (A) Children who are born as the result of fertility treatments tend to have emotional and health problems that aren't as common in children conceived the traditional way.

    (B) Governments should regulate scientific procedures and research according to what the citizen body believes is ethical and proper.

    (C) Parents tend to treat children born through assisted reproduction differently from children conceived naturally because they value them more highly.

    (D) In vitro fertilization is a sensible and positive use of technology to help people accomplish a natural human goal.

    (E) Older parents and same-sex couples shouldn't be allowed to use assisted reproduction to have children because that would violate the natural order.

27. The author mentions all the following risks of cloning EXCEPT:

    (A) Clones appear to age faster than individuals conceived by normal means.

    (B) Clones are more prone to genetic defects than individuals conceived normally.

    (C) Parents of cloned children might not treat their clones naturally.

    (D) People might have unreasonable expectations of cloned children.

    (E) Cloned embryos have a high risk of dying during gestation and before birth.

Chapter 17

Answers and Explanations for Chapter 16

In This Chapter
▶ Checking your answers
▶ Figuring out why the right answers are right

*I*f you're reading this, you've probably just worked some or all of the questions in Chapter 16. Good job! This chapter provides the answers to those questions in a quick list, and follows with detailed explanations to all the questions.

Your Handy-Dandy Answer Key

Here are the answers to the questions in Chapter 18:

1. (E)	10. (C)	19. (C)
2. (A)	11. (E)	20. (A)
3. (B)	12. (C)	21. (D)
4. (C)	13. (C)	22. (D)
5. (C)	14. (A)	23. (D)
6. (E)	15. (D)	24. (A)
7. (A)	16. (B)	25. (E)
8. (A)	17. (A)	26. (D)
9. (B)	18. (D)	27. (E)

Read on for explanations.

Explaining the Answers

If you answered any of the questions incorrectly, you may be wondering how you were supposed to come up with the correct answer. Or maybe you answered a question correctly but you don't know why. Well, you've come to the right place. Following are explanations of why the correct answers are correct and why the wrong ones are wrong.

Passage 1

1. This passage is biographical, telling the life story and listing significant contributions of a major Japanese literary figure. The author is fairly objective and doesn't seem to have much of an agenda beyond emphasizing Nishiwaki's embrace of European literature and culture. (Note, though, that this *is* an agenda; the author had to choose what details of Nishiwaki's life most interested him, and chose to focus on Nishiwaki's interest in Europe. He didn't have to do this; for example, he could have emphasized Nishiwaki's participation in the avant-garde circles of the time, or spent more time describing Nishiwaki's work and less on his life story. No text is a foregone conclusion before the author begins to write it.)

   (A) is wrong. Nishiwaki did protest his government's policies, but rebellion against the government certainly isn't the passage's main point; the author mentions it in only one place. (B) isn't exactly the main idea. Nowhere does the author suggest that Nishiwaki's family disapproved of his studying European literature; in fact, his father was still alive when he went to study a European-influenced style of painting, and you have no reason to assume he objected. He did choose to write in English to give himself more freedom than Japanese allowed, but that wasn't explicitly rebellion. (C) isn't right, either; nowhere does the author say that Nishiwaki tried to convince his students that European literature was better than Japanese literature. (D) is wrong, too; as far as you know, Nishiwaki only chose to write his first work in English, and then wrote many others in Japanese. (E) is correct, pretty well summing up the passage.

2. Skim the first words of the answers, which can help you eliminate a few right away. (D) and (E) are certainly wrong; the passage doesn't include any skepticism or envy. (B) is wrong, too. The author doesn't express surprise at Nishiwaki's use of a foreign language; nor does he seem particularly admiring, which eliminates (C). (A) looks like the best choice, because this passage is objective, and it's definitely scholarly, with all the author's emphasis on literary movements and descriptions of literary works.

3. The first paragraph informs you that Nishiwaki was a major literary figure who was deeply interested in European culture, and it describes Nishiwaki's early years and education. So look for an answer that says something like that. (A) isn't right. Although the author does mention Nishiwaki's brief study of painting, that's not the paragraph's main point. (B) looks like the right answer; the first paragraph does introduce Nishiwaki and sets up the reader to expect him to have more contact with European literature. (C) is wrong. Aside from the first sentence, the paragraph doesn't actually say much about Nishiwaki's contribution to Japanese literature. (D) isn't right, and in fact nowhere in the passage does the author attempt to explain Nishiwaki's choice, beyond noting that Nishiwaki found European literature interesting. (E) is clearly wrong; this paragraph has nothing to do with European contributions to Japanese culture. (B) is correct.

4. The relevant sentence reads, "Angered by the Japanese government's fascist policies, Nishiwaki refused to write poetry during the second world war." That makes (A), (B), and (D) obviously wrong. (C) rephrases that sentence, which makes it look like a good answer. (E) may confuse you, because the following sentence does tell you that Nishiwaki spent the war years writing a dissertation on German literature, but the way the two sentences are phrased makes it clear that the dissertation was simply how Nishiwaki chose to fill his time because he had already made the decision not to write poetry. So (C) is correct.

5. This is similar to a "main idea" question. You already figured out what the author meant to do with this passage: Provide a biography of a Japanese writer that explained why his work is important. Skim the answer choices and see if one of them uses the word "biography." Sure enough, (C) looks like a good answer. Check the others just in case. (A) is wrong because the author doesn't mention the work of other Japanese poets. (B) is wrong because although the avant-garde movement did influence Nishiwaki's writing, the author's discussion of it takes up only a small part of the entire

passage. (D) is wrong because the author doesn't mention the benefits of studying foreign literature. (E) is wrong because the passage doesn't discuss changes in overall Japanese poetic style after the war. (C) is the best answer.

6. You know what Nishiwaki studied Old and Middle English, classical Greek and Latin, and a smattering of modernist English works at Oxford. That covers (A) through (D) and leaves (E). You also know that Nishiwaki didn't especially love traditional Japanese poetic forms, of which *The Tale of Genji* is an example. That makes (E) the best answer. (Yes, Nishiwaki did have *some* interest in Japanese literature, and he may well have appreciated *The Tale of Genji,* but it didn't interest him "greatly" as the question states.)

7. Here's the relevant sentence: "In 1925, Nishiwaki published his first book, *Spectrum,* a volume of poems written in English; he explained that English offered him much more freedom of expression than traditional Japanese poetic language." That makes (A) the only sensible answer. The rest of them are just plain wrong.

Passage 2

8. This passage is about the importance of sea urchins to the marine environment, which has come as a surprise to many people who formerly discounted the significance of the spiny creatures. (A) sums this up pretty well; it looks like a good answer. (B) isn't really the main point; the author mentions a project to relocate sea urchins in the last paragraph, but that doesn't play a major role in the passage as a whole. (C) isn't the main point, though it might be true; anyway, the passage is about sea urchins, not all echinoderms. (D) is also true, but it's not the main point either. The author uses information about excessive algae growth to prove her point that sea urchins are important to the ecosystem. (E) is just plain wrong; nowhere does the author mention the government's duty to educate people about the environment. (A) is the correct answer.

9. The second paragraph is a concise description of urchins and their activities. Skim the first words of the answer choices to see if one of them uses a word like "describe." (B) does, and it looks like a good answer. Quickly check the others to make sure (B) is best. (A) is wrong because the second paragraph doesn't claim that urchins are important to the ecosystem; that claim is elsewhere. (C) is wrong because that also is in another part of the passage, not in the second paragraph. (D) is wrong because that information is in the first and last paragraphs. (E) is wrong because the author doesn't mention the diets of other echinoderms. So (B) really is the best answer.

10. Here's what the passage says: "Sea urchins are members of the phylum Echinodermata, the category of invertebrate animals with spiny exterior shells, which also includes starfish, brittle stars, and sand dollars." So they're members of the same phylum. Is there an answer that says that? Yes — (C) looks like your answer. (A) is wrong because the passage doesn't say that all echinoderms eat algae (starfish eat clams), though they're all invertebrates. As far as you know, only sea urchins were devastated by the bacterium in 1983, so (B) is wrong. (D) is a bit tricky because that sentence does say that all echinoderms have spiny shells, but it doesn't say that all the spines are long and sharp. (And they aren't; even some sea urchins have spines that are kind of thick and stumpy and not especially sharp.) (E) happens to be true of echinoderms, but the passage doesn't tell you that. So (C) is the best answer.

This passage doesn't really require you to know much about invertebrate taxonomy, but the LSAT-makers do assume that you remember some rudiments from your science classes, such as the meaning of the word *phylum*. (You don't have to know a very specific meaning, but you should remember that it's a kind of category into which scientists sort animals and plants based on their physical characteristics.)

11. Refer to this quotation: "In 1983 a barge traveled from the Pacific to the Atlantic through the Panama Canal carrying a bacterium that proved devastating to the sea urchin population. Nearly all long-spined urchins in the tropical western Atlantic died as a result of this exposure." (E) is the only answer that sums up this tragedy. The other answers are simply wrong. The author does mention people killing sea urchins, but doesn't connect this with their near eradication, so (A) is wrong. (B) is wrong because the passage says that coral is dying because it's covered with algae, not that it was killed by a plague. Nowhere does the author mention triggerfish, so (C) is wrong. (D) isn't right either, because a bacterium killed the urchins, not a virus (they're very different), and it didn't come from other echinoderms. That makes (E) the answer.

12. What would support the claim? Well, if someone had examined reefs with and without sea urchins on them and the reefs with sea urchins had much less algae on them, all other conditions being equal, that would tend to prove this hypothesis. (C) looks like the best answer. (A) doesn't work and really is a bit irrelevant; evidence that other animals also eat algae doesn't do anything to prove or disprove the claim that urchins eat algae. (B) is also irrelevant and tells you nothing about what sea urchins eat. (D) is beside the point, and the article never mentions different types of algae in relation to urchins. (E) is interesting, but doesn't tell you that urchins eat algae. (C) is by far the best answer.

13. Refer to that sentence: "Sea urchins are one of the first organisms to show signs of stress when water quality is bad, so the Environmental Protection Agency has begun monitoring sea urchins as an indicator of water conditions." So the EPA finds that sea urchins are useful for something, in this case monitoring water quality. Look for an answer that says something like that. (A) is wrong because the author isn't suggesting anything the government should do; in fact, the government has already embraced urchins as useful creatures. (B) is wrong; nowhere does the author mention any relationship between government and shipping. (C) looks like a potential right answer. (D) is wrong and is in fact backwards, because EPA scientists *have* recognized the significance of sea urchins. (E) is also wrong, because nowhere does the author mention voters. (C) is the correct answer.

14. The correct answer is probably a statement that recaps the author's main point or one of her items of evidence. (A) looks like something the author would say. In the last paragraph, she writes approvingly of the scientists who are currently relocating sea urchins to algae-covered reefs. (B) contradicts (A); if the author likes the statement in (A), she won't agree with the one in (B). (C) seems just plain wrong; in the first paragraph, the author writes of the ignorant folks who used to kill sea urchins for sports, not realizing the importance of their victims. (D) might well be true, but you can't really tell because the author never mentions punishment for the shipping company that introduced the deadly bacterium; (A) still looks better. (E) is almost certainly not something the author would say. Based on her evidence, no creature has yet adapted itself to the sea urchins' niche, and that's why corals are now covered with algae. (A) is the best answer.

Passage 3

15. First try to answer the question yourself. What is the passage's main idea? This passage is a fairly straightforward discussion of the FMLA and related state laws, intended to inform interested people — probably employers — of the laws' requirements, and to recommend that they take care to comply with them — that's why the author mentions the huge damage award in the last paragraph. See if you can find an answer that says something like that.

    (A) isn't right; the author mentions that Congress wanted to help workers balance work and family in the first paragraph, but then abandons that topic forever. (B) is wrong; the author doesn't express any opinion as to whether the FMLA is unduly burdensome to employers. (C) is true, because the passage does communicate these facts about the FMLA, but that's not the passage's main idea, just some information that the author gives along the way. (D) looks like it could be correct; this passage is all about the requirements the FMLA and state statutes impose on employers, and it does recommend that employers allow employees to take time off when they're entitled to it. (E) isn't right; the author does mention that state laws impose requirements that supplement the FMLA, but doesn't mention anything about widespread employer ignorance of those laws. (D) is the best answer.

16. You can't really come up with an answer to this one on your own, so plunge right into the answer choices. The wrong answer is something that the passage doesn't mention. You can find the answer to (A): 12 months. The author doesn't address (B). From this passage, you wouldn't know where to look for more information, so (B) looks like a good answer. (C) is in there; employees can take leave for childbirth, caring for a newborn or parent, adoption, and so on. You also know the answer to (D): the same job or an equivalent one. And the answer to (E) appears in the last paragraph. Employers who violate the FMLA must pay back wages and possible other damages. (B) is the only choice not answered in the passage, so it's correct.

This question is a little bit tricky; the passage tells you that employers are required to post information about family leave, which might give you the impression that (B) does have an answer — to get information about the FMLA, all you have to do is look at the postings in the workplace and inside the employee handbook. But look at the answer — it specifically mentions employers. The information employers must post is for the benefit of their employees, not for the employers who should actually know more about the subject of family leave than their workers. In order for them to discover what they need to know, particularly if they haven't already created an employee handbook or family leave posters, they'll need to look someplace else, and the passage doesn't tell you where.

17. What is the author's attitude toward the FMLA? Nothing very extreme or emotional, certainly. The author doesn't express any opinions about the law's merits or the law's effects on employers and workers. In this author's view, the law is what it is and employers have to follow it or suffer the consequences.

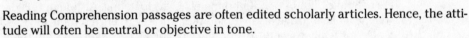

Reading Comprehension passages are often edited scholarly articles. Hence, the attitude will often be neutral or objective in tone.

You can skim the first two words of these answers and immediately knock off two of them, (C) and (D), because the author definitely is neither contemptuous of nor blatantly bored by the FMLA (privately bored, maybe, but that's not the answer). (B) looks wrong, too, because the author doesn't say anything to give the impression that he admires the law, and he certainly doesn't dwell on the law's impact on families. That leaves (A) and (E). (A) looks like a good answer; the author must respect the law, at least in the sense that he urges employers to obey it, and he doesn't express any particular emotion about it. (E) isn't as likely. This passage isn't at all theoretical or speculative, which you would expect in a scholarly article, and nowhere does the author mention the law's future effects on families. (A) is your best choice.

18. Who did the author envision reading this piece? Probably not any kind of legal professional — the tone is much too educational and informative, and doesn't contain any clues such as references to "your clients," which you may expect to see in that kind of article. So you can eliminate (B), and really (A), too, because law students are almost lawyers themselves. The piece probably isn't meant for factory workers, either, because they probably don't have any interest in what happens to them if they violate family leave laws, so that knocks off (E). The author really seems to have employers in mind as an audience — the several references to what employers must do or suffer the consequences is a clue. The article tells you which employers must observe the FMLA: employers with at least 50 employees. Smaller employers could certainly read this article, and different state laws may well apply to them. However, this piece is primarily concerned with the FMLA, which doesn't apply to small businesses. That makes (D) your best answer.

19. This question wants you to apply knowledge you've gained from the passage to hypothetical situations, much as lawyers have to apply case law or statutes to particular situations. Look at the information in paragraph two, which explains the law's details. You're going to want to find an employer with fewer than 50 workers in the same area, or a similar situation that invalidates the FMLA.

    The FMLA applies to (A), because the law firm has more than 50 employees and, in the absence of information to the contrary, you can assume they work full-time. (You should also assume that the 29 attorneys all fall under the heading "employee." Why? Because the answer uses the word "employs." Don't second-guess yourself with concerns about whether some of the attorneys may be partners and thus technically employers, thereby dropping the total employee count below 50.) It definitely applies to (B) and (E), and (D) is covered, too, because six locations in a city with 12 employees each results in more than 50 employees in a 75-mile radius (unless the city is unreasonably large). The FMLA doesn't apply to (C). Why? The data collection service only employs its college workers in the summer months, and that isn't enough time for anyone to work 1,250 hours for the same employer. (C) is the answer.

20. Take a look at the second paragraph. What does it talk about? It's all about the FMLA — who it applies to, what rights it guarantees, and what employers and employees must do to comply with it. (A) looks like a good answer because it sums up this paragraph's content. (B) isn't as good a choice as (A) because this paragraph doesn't include anything resembling a checklist; someone could possibly use it that way, but that's not how it's designed. (C) is true, because the paragraph does inform employers that they must post information about the FMLA at work, but it's not the paragraph's primary purpose. (D) is totally wrong; the author doesn't argue any point, pro or con. (E) is wrong, too, because state law doesn't appear in paragraph 2; it's in paragraph 3, but that's not relevant here. (A) is your answer.

21. The last paragraph discusses penalties for violating family leave laws and concludes on a cautionary note, warning employers that they had better follow the law or else. The mention of that humongous damage award serves to emphasize this point — employers will take note of that if nothing else. (A) is wrong. Although this damage award may well provoke outrage against plaintiffs who try to enrich themselves with lawsuits, that's not really the author's primary purpose. He never says anything to blame the plaintiff or suggest that this award is unfair. (B) is likewise wrong, for the same reasons. (C) doesn't work because the author really doesn't address employees at any point in this article. For (C) to be correct, he should say something like "Employees can feel justified in taking their concerns about family leave to their employers; the law is on their side." (D) looks like a good answer. A multimillion-dollar damage award is certainly sobering, if not terrifying, and would get the attention of many employers who live in fear of such an event. (E) is no good because the author doesn't commiserate or otherwise make the reader feel as if he thinks the employers are getting a raw deal and deserve sympathy. (D) is correct.

    Don't get thrown if you don't know a word in the passage or answer choices. The word "tort" may have thrown you off balance. Don't let it. Focus on the big picture of the sentence, or, if all else fails, just cover up the word and read on.

Passage 4

22. A "title" question is similar to a "main idea" or "main point" question. To come up with an accurate title, you have to understand what the whole passage is about. In this case, what is the author's point? She's arguing that the ethical debates about cloning, particularly the ones that suggest that clones won't be treated as normal children, don't make sense because all children face expectations and plenty of children are born into odd circumstances. (Incidentally, there are lots of valid criticisms of research into human cloning, which seems increasingly unlikely to work, but that's not what this passage is about. The author is focusing on a particular category of arguments against cloning that seem to be the ones predominating in the debate.)

(A) doesn't make a very good title. The author is explicitly arguing that cloning would *not* harm families. (B) is wrong because this article isn't about the dangers of cloning. Although it does mention several dangers that people have suggested, both ethical and physical, they're not the point. (C) isn't right; the author briefly discusses the mechanics of cloning in the first paragraph, but by way of introducing the subject, not as a thesis. (D) makes a perfect title; this is exactly the author's point, that cloning is just another way of conceiving a child. (E) doesn't work because the passage isn't about the government's role in the debate. Aside from a quick reference to the Clinton administration in the first paragraph, the government doesn't appear at all in this passage. (D) looks like the right answer.

23. The author's point is that the criticisms of cloning are aimed at fanciful concerns and fantasies about "natural" relationships between parents and children. She would probably think that the people who have criticized cloning based on these concerns are arguing from emotion, not fact, and that their arguments are flawed because they could potentially apply to normal reproduction as well.

    (A) doesn't work; the author doesn't ever suggest that cloning critics are religious fanatics. (B) is definitely wrong; the author raises the point about creating a master race as an illustration of an outrageous fear, so unlikely as to be laughable. (C) is wrong; though the author doesn't state this explicitly, she implies that foes of cloning don't object to other techniques of assisted reproduction. (D) does match up with the author's point; she would argue that children already enter the world in difficult and unpredictable circumstances and that parents already treat children differently depending on their expectations, even when they conceive their kids the usual way. (E) is clearly wrong; the author says that cloning critics tend to ignore these practical considerations in favor of fanciful ones. (D) is correct.

24. You've already considered the passage's main point in the previous two questions. Based on that, (A) looks like a very good answer. The author is arguing that cloning critics have seized on concerns that aren't really valid, and that cloning shouldn't be all that different from other techniques of conception. (B) isn't right, because most of the passage isn't concerned with the mechanics of cloning or other genetic engineering processes. (C) doesn't work; the author doesn't address scientists particularly, and makes no explicit recommendations. (D) looks like it might work because the author does list some potential benefits of cloning, but it's really not her main purpose; (A) still looks like the best answer. (E) is definitely wrong; if anything, the author is doing the opposite, suggesting that many so-called dangers of cloning are nothing of the kind. (A) is the best choice.

To save time, just glance at each answer choice. Notice that they all start with verbs. First predict the answer in your own words. It seems as if the author is making a point, arguing, persuading to some degree. So, you can do some quick elimination — is the author mainly (A) arguing? (B) explaining? (C) recommending? (D) extolling? (E) warning? You can eliminate (C), (D), and (E) pretty much right off the bat. Now read the remaining choices. You've just saved yourself some valuable time on the LSAT.

25. "Nefarious" and "abominable" are very strong words, commonly used to describe only the most evil of people and deeds. They're definitely too strong to describe the personalities and intentions of most scientists. The author uses them here in a tongue-in-cheek fashion to emphasize the fantastic nature of many criticisms of cloning and to suggest that these fears are probably derived from science fiction instead of real information. Note, too, that those words are an aberration from the writer's usual vocabulary, which is generally down-to-earth.

When a question refers back to a specific detail in the passage, it's worth your time to reread that sentence and the area around it to give it context.

Predict the answer whenever possible. Your prediction will help you spot the right answer and be less distracted by the "attractive" wrong answer choices meant to trap you.

(A) is wrong because the author isn't in fact suggesting that cloning researchers are morally bankrupt, but that the people who fear them are deluding themselves. (B) isn't right; the author definitely doesn't defend the ban on cloning, and those adjectives don't describe the ban anyway. (C) is wrong because "nefarious" and "abominable" describe scientists and deeds, not cloning foes. (D) is wrong for the same reason. (E) is correct because that is indeed why the author uses those particular words.

26. Based on her comments, the author seems to believe assisted reproduction is a perfectly acceptable way to have children. She wouldn't agree with (A); her statements in the last paragraphs show that she doesn't find that much difference in the results of various reproductive techniques. (B) is definitely wrong. Though the author doesn't explicitly state this, she implies that the benefits of cloning outweigh the risks, and that the governmental ban on cloning research is misplaced, and she would almost certainly extend this opinion to regulation of other types of reproductive technology. (C) is wrong because the author's point is that kids are just kids, regardless of how they get created. (D) looks good; the author obviously thinks reproductive techniques should be allowed, and that they're not all that different from normal conception. The author wouldn't agree with (E); among the benefits of cloning, she includes helping same-sex or infertile couples reproduce, and if she would allow it for cloning, she would allow it for other forms of assisted reproduction. (D) is the best answer.

27. To answer this question you have to look back at the passage and find sentences that mention the various risks of cloning. (A) and (B) appear at the end of paragraph 3. (C) and (D) both appear too, in the last paragraph. The author mentions these as risks that she doesn't think really are risks, but they do appear in the passage so they count. (E) is the only risk that the author doesn't mention, so (E) is correct.

Part V
The Writing Sample: No Score but Can Count

The 5th Wave   By Rich Tennant

YOUNG STEPHEN KING SUBMITS HIS LSAT WRITING SAMPLE.

©RICHTENNANT

"I finished my essay early, so I wrote essays on all the other questions, and then I had some time so I wrote a few more essays on some spooky stuff I've been thinking about..."

In this part . . .

As a special treat, after you finish the four multiple-choice sections, plus the extra "testing" multiple-choice section, you get to spend 30 minutes writing an essay on some refreshing topic. The topic is always something that involves a choice between two alternatives. Your job is to choose a side and write a convincing argument — just like what lawyers do every day.

The Writing Sample doesn't count toward your score, but don't be tempted to blow it off — every law school that receives a copy of your LSAT score also receives a copy of your LSAT Writing Sample.

Chapter 18

No Right or Wrong Answers Here: Just Pick a Side

In This Chapter

▶ Trying out two LSAT Writing Sample topics

▶ Helping a widow choose between a German Shepherd and a Pekingese

▶ Contemplating essay practice time

The last thing you get to do on LSAT day is write a little essay. This essay doesn't count toward your score. The people at the Law School Admission Council (LSAC) don't read it. For these reasons, many people don't take this part of the LSAT very seriously. They should, though. Do you want to know what happens to your Writing Sample? The good folks at the LSAC photocopy it and send a copy of it with your score report to every law school that receives your LSAT score.

The people who decide whether or not to admit you to law school are the only ones who get an opportunity to read your LSAT-inspired prose. Now, chances are they're not going to read it very carefully — after all, they have plenty of other stuff to read, and a short essay written in 30 minutes by hand isn't very informative. But your essay may make a difference; an admissions official may see some egregious mistake in your writing and decide not to admit you. (Alas, the converse is unlikely — having a law-school admissions official actually admit a student simply because his or her LSAT Writing Sample is so glorious is hard to imagine.)

No matter what happens to your Writing Sample, you still need to spend a little time thinking about the exercise and polishing your writing skills. During the LSAT won't be the last time you have to write a quick essay, especially if you go to law school and then practice law. Besides, good writing is a valuable skill regardless of what you end up doing.

Pick a Side — No Ridin' the Fence

The Writing Sample is a 30-minute exercise in written advocacy. The test gives you a situation in which someone has to choose between two alternatives, each of which has advantages and disadvantages. You have to write your answer by hand in the block provided to you, which is about two-thirds of a page long. You only have that space to write your essay, so you have to budget your available space accordingly. To get an idea of exactly how much space you have, check out the practice exams in Chapters 20 and 22.

Some recent topics have included the following:

✔ Picking a travel package for a tour of South America on behalf of a travel club

✔ Deciding which archaeological dig would most benefit the career of a young scholar

✔ Choosing which school a local school board should close

✔ Picking a city in which to hold a scholarly convention

✔ Deciding whether to publish a famous manuscript or donate it to a university library

Every topic can be argued equally well in either direction. The object is to convincingly construct an argument for one side or the other.

When you write your LSAT essay, keep in mind your likely audience. The people who read these essays are usually law professors on the admissions committees of their respective law schools. They're academics, so write as if you were writing something for school. Be intelligent, thoughtful, organized, and lucid. Don't be too conversational, don't use slang, never use sarcasm, and be very careful with humor. You don't want to annoy your reader with a flippant tone.

Walking through a Practice Essay

Here's a Writing Sample topic of the type that appears on the LSAT:

Marilyn, a widow, wants to buy a dog, and is trying to decide between two. Write an argument for Marilyn's choosing one dog over the other, keeping in mind the following goals:

Marilyn wants a dog to guard her house.

Marilyn wants a dog that will be affectionate and inexpensive to feed.

The first dog is a German Shepherd. This dog is large and strong and well trained, and is particularly recommended for use as a guard dog. It weighs 85 pounds and eats several pounds of dog food a day. It is friendly enough but not particularly affectionate or devoted to humans.

The second dog is a Pekingese. This dog is small and has a long, silky coat, and is an excellent lap dog. It forms a strong attachment with one human caretaker and is a devoted companion. At 20 pounds, this dog does not require much food. Its small stature makes it somewhat ineffective as a guard dog, though it will growl aggressively when angered.

Organizing your argument

Take up to five minutes to think about how to answer this question and make an outline. Pick a side — either side, though you probably feel more strongly about one or the other. If you have a real preference, go with it. If you don't, just pick a side to argue. Both sides have good and bad points, so either one lends itself to a good, strong essay.

When you organize your thoughts, think about how to transition from one thought to another. The best essays flow smoothly from sentence to sentence, and from paragraph to paragraph. Try to connect the end of one sentence to the beginning of the next, and the end of one paragraph to the beginning of the next one. Use words such as *also, in addition, despite, nevertheless,* and other conjunctions to lead the reader along gently.

Setting priorities

Choosing a side is simply a matter of setting priorities. For example, in the dog case, if you decide that companionship is what Marilyn needs, choose the Pekingese. If, on the other hand, you think she needs a guard dog more than a lap dog, select the German Shepherd.

Here's one way you can organize the essay about the dog singing the praises of the Pekingese:

Introduction: The widow should pick the Pekingese because companionship is more important to her well-being than guarding.

Paragraph 2: Pekes are excellent companions, and widows living alone need companions.

Paragraph 3: Pekes are inexpensive to feed, and a widow on a fixed income should make this a priority.

Paragraph 4: Pekes aren't the best guard dogs, but they can bark and growl ferociously, and anyway, the widow's need for a guard dog is overstated.

Conclusion: The widow really ought to pick the Peke over the German Shepherd.

Never use slang or super-casual language in your actual essay. It looks unprofessional. In your outline, though, using slang is okay. So, for example, I use the phrase "and anyway" in Paragraph 4 of the outline, which is fine here, but don't put it in your actual essay.

Or you could come down on the side of the German Shepherd:

Introduction: The widow should pick the German Shepherd because her primary need is security, and the Shepherd would also be a decent companion.

Paragraph 2: Shepherds are the best guard dogs.

Paragraph 3: A Shepherd would actually make a good pet.

Paragraph 4: Dog food isn't all that expensive, anyway.

Conclusion: The widow really ought to pick the Shepherd over the Peke.

Either way is fine as long as you do a good job with the thinking and writing.

Making an outline

After you pick your side, jot down a quick outline on the test booklet. There are lots of ways to write this kind of essay, but during the LSAT really isn't the best time for you to get creative. If you follow the same basic structure every time, you'll get a serviceable essay every time — it won't be great literature, but it'll do the job.

Plan on making your essay five paragraphs long — an introductory paragraph, three body paragraphs, and a conclusion paragraph. The following points tell you what to do with these paragraphs:

- ✓ **Make the introduction about three or four sentences long.** Start it by stating your position in your first sentence, such as, "The widow should choose the Pekingese." Follow that with one or two sentences that discuss the goals your party wants to achieve; focus on the ones that your choice would meet.

  The last sentence of the first paragraph should include the word "because." This is going to be your *thesis sentence,* the one that explains why you have chosen the side you have. For example, it could read "Because the Pekingese would make the best companion and also be somewhat effective as a guard dog, the widow should choose it."

- ✓ **Write your first two body paragraphs to explain the reasons why the side you have chosen is best, and compare its advantages to the disadvantages of the other side.** Make each of these paragraphs three or four sentences long — you don't have space for more than that.

✔ **Use the fourth paragraph to discuss disadvantages of the side you have chosen.** No argument is perfect, and pointing out the failings of your side yourself is better than waiting for an opponent to spot them. If you do this, you can then argue that they're not really disadvantages at all. Minimize your side's weaknesses at the same time as you acknowledge them. In the same paragraph, you may want to point out the apparent advantages of the other side, but solely so you can explain why the other side's strengths aren't in fact strengths at all.

One effective way of writing is to start each paragraph with a sentence that first states a disadvantage of your choice but then follows it with an advantage. Use the remaining sentences in the paragraph to back up the advantage. That way, the last thing the reader encounters is an advantage.

✔ **Draft your last paragraph to be your conclusion where you sum up your argument and state for the last time why the side you have chosen is the best.** Don't repeat your thesis statement verbatim, but do say something that leaves your reader with a positive sense of your argument. One or two sentences are enough. Don't skip a conclusion; you want to let your reader off smoothly with a definite sense of finality. Remember, this is the last thing the reader will see; you want it to leave a good impression.

Many people find conclusions difficult to write. They don't have to be. All you really have to do is restate the thesis in a more high-handed way. You may feel silly making a blanket pronouncement, but don't. Your conclusion probably doesn't sound nearly as silly as you think it does.

This structure is very basic. You can probably think of other ways to approach the Writing Sample, and if you enjoy doing that sort of thing, go right ahead. Otherwise, follow this outline and you'll always be able to toss off a decent short essay. It doesn't need to be brilliant; it just needs to be coherent and mistake-free.

Another way to organize the essay is to write it in four paragraphs. Paragraph 1 is the introduction and Paragraph 4 is the conclusion. In Paragraph 2, discuss all the advantages of your choice. In Paragraph 3, discuss all the disadvantages of the other choice.

The key to good writing is simplicity. Say what you have to say in the simplest way possible — that way, you can be sure that your readers will understand you. Use short words instead of long ones. Contrary to what many people believe, using longer words doesn't make your prose look more intelligent. (You don't want your essay to sound like an LSAT Reading Comprehension passage, do you?) The LSAT isn't the right place for creativity or artistry. You can deviate from this structure if you want to, but you don't have the time or space to do very much with it.

You absolutely must observe grammatical rules when writing. You also must write out all words — no abbreviations. If you're out of practice in writing by hand, spend a little time refreshing your technique before plunging into an actual LSAT.

One topic, two different essays

When it comes to the Writing Sample, it really doesn't matter which side you pick. Either one works. Just pick a side and argue your heart out. (Doing so is actually kind of a luxury — lawyers don't get to choose the side they represent in a case.)

The pro-Pekingese approach

Say you decide to argue for the Pekingese, using the outline from the "Organizing your Argument" section. Here's how the essay could go:

Marilyn should choose the Pekingese to be her canine companion. She's a widow living alone on a fixed income, and what she needs most is a friendly dog that won't eat her out of house and home. Because the Pekingese will be more affectionate than the German Shepherd as well as being more friendly to her pocketbook, and because its barking would in fact make it an effective guard dog, it would be the best choice.

Every week the television news runs stories about the dangers of old people living alone; they suffer depression, don't eat enough, and decline much faster than their biology would dictate. The news has also run stories on the benefits of pets to old people; people with pets take much more interest in life and remain healthier themselves. A widow needs an affectionate companion, and the Pekingese would be the best choice for companionship.

Widows are also prone to financial hardship. They must often make their husband's pensions and social security stretch for years without much additional income. The last thing Marilyn needs is a dog who would be a major expense to her. The Pekingese would be very cheap to keep, unlike the German Shepherd.

A Pekingese is a small dog, and therefore wouldn't be the most effective dog for home defense. Realistically, though, Marilyn has little need of a guard dog; people tend to exaggerate the likelihood of their homes being invaded, which is really a very uncommon event. In addition, the Pekingese could actually pass muster as a guard dog. A Pekingese can bark and growl ferociously, alerting Marilyn to potential intruders and frightening off criminals who hear it. An angry Pekingese might be all the defense she needs if a stranger called with mischief on his mind; the Pekingese has a growl much bigger than its stature and teeth.

Marilyn most needs a loving pet that won't eat all her money. A Pekingese would meet her needs perfectly, providing companionship for a reasonable price and actually guarding her home quite well. For this reason, she should choose the Pekingese.

Going with the German Shepherd

What if you decide that the German Shepherd is the better choice? Bigger teeth, fiercer growl, and all that? That's fine. Here's an example of how you could argue that point:

Life is very unsafe for older women living alone. A widow like Marilyn is virtually defenseless against burglars and ne'er-do-wells. She needs a dog that will make her feel safe. She also needs a dog for company. Because the German Shepherd is by far the better dog for striking fear in the hearts of criminals and would also make a fine companion, Marilyn should choose it.

German Shepherds make excellent guard dogs. They're large, imposing, intelligent, and have lots of big teeth that they're not afraid to use. The police often use German Shepherds for work with criminals because they are so well suited to this task. These qualities would make the German Shepherd an excellent choice as a guard for Marilyn.

This German Shepherd will also make an excellent companion. It won't curl up in her lap while she watches television, but it will spend every possible minute in her presence. She will get exercise by taking it for long walks, which will improve her health and her bone density, possibly forestalling osteoporosis and hip fractures. And because the German Shepherd is more intelligent than a Pekingese, Marilyn will find it easier to keep out of trouble in and out of her house.

The only drawback to the German Shepherd is its size and appetite. This is a minor consideration; even the most expensive dog food is hardly ruinous, and Marilyn can always buy food in bulk at a discount warehouse, achieving substantial savings.

Marilyn's needs are clear: safety and companionship. The German Shepherd is the better choice on both counts.

Do your best to make your essay fill the entire lined box. If you leave space, try to keep it down to one or two lines at most. Really, you don't have much space to fill, and you should be able to think of ample content to write in two-thirds of a page, even under serious time constraints. That way, if an admissions officer looks at your essay in order to compare you to another similar candidate, at least your Writing Sample will be as long as anyone else's could possibly be.

Considering Essay Practice

I can't honestly tell you to devote much of your LSAT practice time to the Writing Sample; if your time is limited, spend most of it studying sections that get scored.

Nevertheless, the Writing Sample is actually most representative of the work you'll do in law school, where exams expect you to write coherent and detailed essays in a limited amount of time. When you apply to law school, part of your application is a "personal statement," which is an essay on some topic written by you, all by yourself, and practicing for the LSAT Writing Sample can't hurt your abilities there. Furthermore, writing well is a valuable skill that you're probably going to need for the rest of your life. If nothing else, you need it to write e-mails that don't annoy their recipients.

That's why you should practice writing. Of course handwriting is somewhat important here — an LSAT oddity — but the crucial thing is how you organize your argument. If you're confident of your ability to do that, great. Otherwise, practice building arguments. Do it in your head, do it in e-mails, do it at the dinner table with your parents or partner (you probably have plenty of disagreements anyway — that's a great opportunity to improve your skill at arguing). Try your hand at a few practice essays. Get comfortable with expressing yourself quickly and clearly. It'll be worth it in the long run.

Chapter 19

Practice Writing Samples

In This Chapter

▶ Trying out two LSAT Writing Sample topics
▶ Looking at possible responses

*N*ow you have your chance to try writing LSAT-style Writing Sample essays. Grab some ruled paper and plan to use about two-thirds to three-quarters of the page. (Look at the Writing Samples in the practice tests in Chapters 20 and 22 to see how much room you should give yourself.) Remember, there's no right or wrong answer. Just pick a side and defend it well. After the two sample topics, I include two possible responses for each. My answers aren't right or wrong. Read them to get an idea of how you could organize your essays.

Topic 1: Choosing a Law School

This first topic deals with picking one law school over another. Don't forget to set up your argument before you start writing.

A senior in college plans to attend law school the following year. She has been accepted by several law schools, and has narrowed her choice down to two of them. Write an argument for selecting one law school over the other, keeping two guidelines in mind:

> She wants to go someplace where she can pursue her main interest, environmental law and the preservation of resources, and she would like her school to have a friendly atmosphere with close relationships between professors and students.

> She wants to borrow as little money as possible and to find a lucrative job as soon as she graduates.

Law School A is a small school attached to a state university in a fairly undeveloped state known for its liberal tendencies. Because of its small size and relaxed atmosphere, students and faculty get to know one another very well. It has one of the best environmental law programs in the country; graduates of this program usually do find jobs that let them protect the environment, but it sometimes takes them several months to find work and the jobs usually do not pay as well as private law firms. Because the student comes from another state, the tuition would be very expensive and she would have to take out a substantial loan to pay it.

Law School B is a larger law school that is part of a well-known and prestigious private university. The tuition is about the same as the tuition at Law School A, but Law School B has offered the student a partial scholarship that would cover about one-third of her costs. This law school is known for its stressful atmosphere; students compete with one another viciously, and professors have no time to socialize with students because they are constantly working on their own research. Law School B has an excellent job placement record, and nearly all its graduates accept high-paying jobs at private law firms. Law School B offers courses in environmental law, but is not especially know for its environmental program.

Sample answer: Choosing Law School A

Here's a possible argument for choosing Law School A:

Law School A would be a better choice for this student. The student wants to specialize in environmental law and to attend school in a collegial atmosphere. These priorities should come ahead of her desire to economize, and should not interfere with her wish to find a lucrative job. Because Law School A has one of the best environmental law programs in the country, as well as one of the friendliest atmospheres of all law schools, the student would be much happier in the present and more satisfied with her career in the future if she chooses to go to law school there.

Law school A has one of the best environmental law programs in the country. The student is very interested in a career that would let her help protect the environment and preserve natural resources, and attending Law School A would make it very easy for her to spend the rest of her life doing this. Although she could study some environmental law at Law School B, the program there is not nearly as concentrated on the preservation side of environmental law, and she might feel somewhat isolated if she tried to pursue her interest in an environment that does not value environmentalism.

Law School A also has a friendly atmosphere that would make the student's law school experience more pleasant and ultimately more satisfying than Law School B would. At Law School A, she could form deep relationships with both students and faculty that would make it easier for her to learn more about her chosen field and find compatible colleagues for her future work life. Bonds that she forms during law school will benefit her for the rest of her career.

It is true that Law School A will be slightly more expensive than Law School B because Law School A has not offered the student a scholarship. That small difference in money is not enough to justify choosing a law school that will not offer her the opportunity to pursue her goals. It is also true that Law School A does not place nearly as many of its graduates in law firms that pay high salaries, so it might take the student slightly longer to pay off her student loans. Nevertheless, it is more important that the student be able to study and find a job in a field that interests her than that she be able to make a lot of money quickly.

Both schools have advantages, and the student probably would be successful if she attended either one. Nevertheless, because it would provide her a pleasant law school experience studying a field that most interests her, followed by a satisfying career in that field, Law School A would be a much better choice for this student than Law School B.

Sample answer: Fighting for Law School B

If you prefer Law School B, here's an example of how you can state that argument:

The student should choose Law School B. Law School B is much more prestigious than Law School A, which will provide the student with more opportunities after she graduates. It has offered her a partial scholarship, which will decrease her financial burden upon graduation, and it is more likely to provide her with a lucrative job once she completes school. Because Law School B offers this prestige and financial advantage without preventing the student from pursuing environmental law, the student should choose to go there.

First, a degree from a well-known law school is a valuable commodity. Future employers are extremely impressed with credentials such as a degree from Law School B. A degree from this school will allow the student to pursue employment anywhere and in any field, and will not restrict her to specialized environmental employers. The student wants to find a job that will pay her well, and a degree from Law School B would be the best way to ensure that she does.

Second, law school is very expensive. If the student accepts the partial scholarship from Law School B, she will be able to pay off her loans in a much shorter period of time than she would if she had to take out loans for the full amount of tuition, as she would if she attended Law School A. That means that she would be financially free much sooner, and if she wanted to, would be able to leave her lucrative law firm job to take a lower-paying job in an environmental agency, thereby combining financial success and career satisfaction.

Third, although Law School B is known for its stressful atmosphere, spending three years in a less enjoyable law school is a small sacrifice to make for a scholarship and a degree that will allow her to pursue employment anywhere and in any field. Even though Law School B's environmental law program is not as complete and well-known as that at Law School A, that does not mean the student will not be able to specialize in environmental law if she chooses. She might also find that her interests really lie elsewhere, and she will be in a better position to pursue them if she attends a school that does not specialize entirely in one area of the law.

Although Law School A does offer some benefits, Law School B would be a much better choice for this student. It would provide her with prestige, financial independence, and an excellent job, without taking anything away from her environmental aspirations. She should therefore choose Law School B.

Topic 2: The Sporting Goods Store

This topic deals with whether the state should fund a large sporting retailer to come to the area.

A small southern town is trying to decide whether or not to provide financial incentives to a large national retailer that wants to open an outlet there. Town business leaders are considering offering funds raised by state taxes to pay for the construction of the store. Write an argument either supporting or protesting offering the financial incentives, keeping two guidelines in mind:

The town wants to create jobs and bring tourist dollars to the area.

The town wants to avoid putting local merchants out of business.

Town business leaders want to use state taxes to pay for the construction of the national retailer's multimillion-dollar facility right next to an exit from the Interstate highway. The facility would include a giant sporting goods store, several restaurants, and a hotel. It would create at least 300 new jobs, and the town hopes that it would also attract tourists who otherwise would not bother leaving the highway. If the town does not provide the tax funds, the retailer will probably take its business elsewhere.

Local merchants in the town don't want to use state funds to finance the construction of the major retailer's facility. They claim that local retailers already provide all the goods that would be available at the new store, and they fear that the new store would deliberately cut its prices in order to drive them out of business. They believe it would be wrong for the state to fund the construction of a store for an out-of-town retailer when it does not provide the same service to local businesses. They insist that the town should treat the out-of-town retailer the same way it treats local merchants, and if the national retailer takes its business elsewhere, so much the better for local businesses.

Sample answer: Use the state funds

Here's a sample answer that argues for using the state funds:

The benefits of bringing this large national retailer to the town are tremendous, and the town should do whatever is necessary to persuade it to come. If that means the town's leaders must offer to pay for the construction of the facility out of state tax funds, then they should do it because the benefits of having the retailer move in far outweigh the cost of using state money to build the store.

The retailer would build a huge multimillion-dollar facility just off an interstate exit. This would make that exit into a major destination; people who would otherwise never consider stopping in the town would now have a reason to get off the highway and spend their money there. Once these people have stopped, it will be easier to convince them to stay a while and spend even more money, perhaps on amenities that already exist in town, away from the interstate.

Introducing the retailer would create hundreds of new jobs. First, construction workers would have ample employment. Second, all the facilities that would be part of the retailer's complex — the sporting goods store, the several restaurants, the hotel — would require a large number of employees. These would be good, stable jobs, and the local economy needs that.

The town already has several sporting goods stores and of course hotels and restaurants, but they are not all located in one convenient place; people must drive around to get to them, and they will never attract anyone from out of town. The local merchants already have a loyal local clientele, and it's not likely that that will change; regardless, it is unfair to force local customers to pay high prices for goods that the major retailer can sell for less.

Bringing the major retailer to town would be a win-win situation for nearly everyone. The town should bend over backwards to persuade it to come; spending tax money to build the facility would be an investment with huge payoffs in the near future.

Sample answer: Don't use state funds

Here's a sample answer for the other side:

Offering to pay for the construction of this retailer's facility is a terrible idea. Because the potential consequences to the town's local merchants are horrific and the likely economic benefit to the town of the retailer's locating there is unproven at best and negligible at worst, the town should definitely not subsidize the construction of the store with state funds.

The town should not pay to construct the national retailer's monstrous facility because to do so would be extremely unfair to local merchants. Local merchants have to pay their own way; no one has ever offered to build facilities for them. To add insult to injury, if the town does decide to use state taxes to build the complex, then local merchants will in effect be forced to finance the construction of a major competitor.

Countless towns have proven that introducing large national retailers with big-box stores is devastating for local merchants. The national retailers carry a larger variety of merchandise with prices set specifically to drive local merchants out of business. There is no reason to assume this retailer would be different. If this retailer comes to town, customers will flock there to do their business, abandoning the merchants who already operate in the heart of town. As for tourists, perhaps a few interstate travelers will get off the highway to do a little shopping or have a quick meal, but they are unlikely to stay very long or venture into town. Nothing about a big-box sporting goods store will impress them with "local color."

Although this retailer would provide a certain number of jobs, they would be low-paying jobs in an isolated area around a remote interstate exit. They would come at the cost of the jobs that already exist with the town's local sporting-goods merchants. All profits would leave the state to go to corporate headquarters, leaving the town with a hefty construction bill and 300 minimum-wage jobs with no security.

If the national retailer is serious about coming to this town, it can pay its own way like any other honorable vendor. There's no sense in the town's subsidizing its own economic destruction.

Part VI
The Real Deal: Full-Length Practice LSATs

In this part . . .

Okay, here you go — time to take an LSAT or two and see how you do! This part contains two complete LSATs, including Writing Sample (but not including the extra "testing" section that you'll get with the real LSAT). If you want to see how your LSAT abilities measure up, take a test in the allotted time, add up the number of answers you get right, and check your score.

Section I

1. Ⓐ Ⓑ Ⓒ Ⓓ Ⓔ
2. Ⓐ Ⓑ Ⓒ Ⓓ Ⓔ
3. Ⓐ Ⓑ Ⓒ Ⓓ Ⓔ
4. Ⓐ Ⓑ Ⓒ Ⓓ Ⓔ
5. Ⓐ Ⓑ Ⓒ Ⓓ Ⓔ
6. Ⓐ Ⓑ Ⓒ Ⓓ Ⓔ
7. Ⓐ Ⓑ Ⓒ Ⓓ Ⓔ
8. Ⓐ Ⓑ Ⓒ Ⓓ Ⓔ
9. Ⓐ Ⓑ Ⓒ Ⓓ Ⓔ
10. Ⓐ Ⓑ Ⓒ Ⓓ Ⓔ
11. Ⓐ Ⓑ Ⓒ Ⓓ Ⓔ
12. Ⓐ Ⓑ Ⓒ Ⓓ Ⓔ
13. Ⓐ Ⓑ Ⓒ Ⓓ Ⓔ
14. Ⓐ Ⓑ Ⓒ Ⓓ Ⓔ
15. Ⓐ Ⓑ Ⓒ Ⓓ Ⓔ
16. Ⓐ Ⓑ Ⓒ Ⓓ Ⓔ
17. Ⓐ Ⓑ Ⓒ Ⓓ Ⓔ
18. Ⓐ Ⓑ Ⓒ Ⓓ Ⓔ
19. Ⓐ Ⓑ Ⓒ Ⓓ Ⓔ
20. Ⓐ Ⓑ Ⓒ Ⓓ Ⓔ
21. Ⓐ Ⓑ Ⓒ Ⓓ Ⓔ
22. Ⓐ Ⓑ Ⓒ Ⓓ Ⓔ
23. Ⓐ Ⓑ Ⓒ Ⓓ Ⓔ
24. Ⓐ Ⓑ Ⓒ Ⓓ Ⓔ
25. Ⓐ Ⓑ Ⓒ Ⓓ Ⓔ
26. Ⓐ Ⓑ Ⓒ Ⓓ Ⓔ
27. Ⓐ Ⓑ Ⓒ Ⓓ Ⓔ
28. Ⓐ Ⓑ Ⓒ Ⓓ Ⓔ
29. Ⓐ Ⓑ Ⓒ Ⓓ Ⓔ
30. Ⓐ Ⓑ Ⓒ Ⓓ Ⓔ

Section II

1. Ⓐ Ⓑ Ⓒ Ⓓ Ⓔ
2. Ⓐ Ⓑ Ⓒ Ⓓ Ⓔ
3. Ⓐ Ⓑ Ⓒ Ⓓ Ⓔ
4. Ⓐ Ⓑ Ⓒ Ⓓ Ⓔ
5. Ⓐ Ⓑ Ⓒ Ⓓ Ⓔ
6. Ⓐ Ⓑ Ⓒ Ⓓ Ⓔ
7. Ⓐ Ⓑ Ⓒ Ⓓ Ⓔ
8. Ⓐ Ⓑ Ⓒ Ⓓ Ⓔ
9. Ⓐ Ⓑ Ⓒ Ⓓ Ⓔ
10. Ⓐ Ⓑ Ⓒ Ⓓ Ⓔ
11. Ⓐ Ⓑ Ⓒ Ⓓ Ⓔ
12. Ⓐ Ⓑ Ⓒ Ⓓ Ⓔ
13. Ⓐ Ⓑ Ⓒ Ⓓ Ⓔ
14. Ⓐ Ⓑ Ⓒ Ⓓ Ⓔ
15. Ⓐ Ⓑ Ⓒ Ⓓ Ⓔ
16. Ⓐ Ⓑ Ⓒ Ⓓ Ⓔ
17. Ⓐ Ⓑ Ⓒ Ⓓ Ⓔ
18. Ⓐ Ⓑ Ⓒ Ⓓ Ⓔ
19. Ⓐ Ⓑ Ⓒ Ⓓ Ⓔ
20. Ⓐ Ⓑ Ⓒ Ⓓ Ⓔ
21. Ⓐ Ⓑ Ⓒ Ⓓ Ⓔ
22. Ⓐ Ⓑ Ⓒ Ⓓ Ⓔ
23. Ⓐ Ⓑ Ⓒ Ⓓ Ⓔ
24. Ⓐ Ⓑ Ⓒ Ⓓ Ⓔ
25. Ⓐ Ⓑ Ⓒ Ⓓ Ⓔ
26. Ⓐ Ⓑ Ⓒ Ⓓ Ⓔ
27. Ⓐ Ⓑ Ⓒ Ⓓ Ⓔ
28. Ⓐ Ⓑ Ⓒ Ⓓ Ⓔ
29. Ⓐ Ⓑ Ⓒ Ⓓ Ⓔ
30. Ⓐ Ⓑ Ⓒ Ⓓ Ⓔ

Section III

1. Ⓐ Ⓑ Ⓒ Ⓓ Ⓔ
2. Ⓐ Ⓑ Ⓒ Ⓓ Ⓔ
3. Ⓐ Ⓑ Ⓒ Ⓓ Ⓔ
4. Ⓐ Ⓑ Ⓒ Ⓓ Ⓔ
5. Ⓐ Ⓑ Ⓒ Ⓓ Ⓔ
6. Ⓐ Ⓑ Ⓒ Ⓓ Ⓔ
7. Ⓐ Ⓑ Ⓒ Ⓓ Ⓔ
8. Ⓐ Ⓑ Ⓒ Ⓓ Ⓔ
9. Ⓐ Ⓑ Ⓒ Ⓓ Ⓔ
10. Ⓐ Ⓑ Ⓒ Ⓓ Ⓔ
11. Ⓐ Ⓑ Ⓒ Ⓓ Ⓔ
12. Ⓐ Ⓑ Ⓒ Ⓓ Ⓔ
13. Ⓐ Ⓑ Ⓒ Ⓓ Ⓔ
14. Ⓐ Ⓑ Ⓒ Ⓓ Ⓔ
15. Ⓐ Ⓑ Ⓒ Ⓓ Ⓔ
16. Ⓐ Ⓑ Ⓒ Ⓓ Ⓔ
17. Ⓐ Ⓑ Ⓒ Ⓓ Ⓔ
18. Ⓐ Ⓑ Ⓒ Ⓓ Ⓔ
19. Ⓐ Ⓑ Ⓒ Ⓓ Ⓔ
20. Ⓐ Ⓑ Ⓒ Ⓓ Ⓔ
21. Ⓐ Ⓑ Ⓒ Ⓓ Ⓔ
22. Ⓐ Ⓑ Ⓒ Ⓓ Ⓔ
23. Ⓐ Ⓑ Ⓒ Ⓓ Ⓔ
24. Ⓐ Ⓑ Ⓒ Ⓓ Ⓔ
25. Ⓐ Ⓑ Ⓒ Ⓓ Ⓔ
26. Ⓐ Ⓑ Ⓒ Ⓓ Ⓔ
27. Ⓐ Ⓑ Ⓒ Ⓓ Ⓔ
28. Ⓐ Ⓑ Ⓒ Ⓓ Ⓔ
29. Ⓐ Ⓑ Ⓒ Ⓓ Ⓔ
30. Ⓐ Ⓑ Ⓒ Ⓓ Ⓔ

Section IV

1. Ⓐ Ⓑ Ⓒ Ⓓ Ⓔ
2. Ⓐ Ⓑ Ⓒ Ⓓ Ⓔ
3. Ⓐ Ⓑ Ⓒ Ⓓ Ⓔ
4. Ⓐ Ⓑ Ⓒ Ⓓ Ⓔ
5. Ⓐ Ⓑ Ⓒ Ⓓ Ⓔ
6. Ⓐ Ⓑ Ⓒ Ⓓ Ⓔ
7. Ⓐ Ⓑ Ⓒ Ⓓ Ⓔ
8. Ⓐ Ⓑ Ⓒ Ⓓ Ⓔ
9. Ⓐ Ⓑ Ⓒ Ⓓ Ⓔ
10. Ⓐ Ⓑ Ⓒ Ⓓ Ⓔ
11. Ⓐ Ⓑ Ⓒ Ⓓ Ⓔ
12. Ⓐ Ⓑ Ⓒ Ⓓ Ⓔ
13. Ⓐ Ⓑ Ⓒ Ⓓ Ⓔ
14. Ⓐ Ⓑ Ⓒ Ⓓ Ⓔ
15. Ⓐ Ⓑ Ⓒ Ⓓ Ⓔ
16. Ⓐ Ⓑ Ⓒ Ⓓ Ⓔ
17. Ⓐ Ⓑ Ⓒ Ⓓ Ⓔ
18. Ⓐ Ⓑ Ⓒ Ⓓ Ⓔ
19. Ⓐ Ⓑ Ⓒ Ⓓ Ⓔ
20. Ⓐ Ⓑ Ⓒ Ⓓ Ⓔ
21. Ⓐ Ⓑ Ⓒ Ⓓ Ⓔ
22. Ⓐ Ⓑ Ⓒ Ⓓ Ⓔ
23. Ⓐ Ⓑ Ⓒ Ⓓ Ⓔ
24. Ⓐ Ⓑ Ⓒ Ⓓ Ⓔ
25. Ⓐ Ⓑ Ⓒ Ⓓ Ⓔ
26. Ⓐ Ⓑ Ⓒ Ⓓ Ⓔ
27. Ⓐ Ⓑ Ⓒ Ⓓ Ⓔ
28. Ⓐ Ⓑ Ⓒ Ⓓ Ⓔ
29. Ⓐ Ⓑ Ⓒ Ⓓ Ⓔ
30. Ⓐ Ⓑ Ⓒ Ⓓ Ⓔ

Chapter 20

Some Rainy-Day "Fun": LSAT Practice Exam 1

● ●

You're ready to take a crack at a full-blown practice LSAT exam. You're feeling good and ready to go (well, maybe not, but you're at least smart enough to know that this practice is good for you).

For best results, try to take this practice exam under simulated LSAT conditions.

1. **Find a quiet place to work, where you won't be distracted or interrupted.**

2. **Use the answer grid provided and mark your answers with a No. 2 pencil.**

3. **Set your watch or alarm clock for 35-minute intervals.**

4. **Do *not* go to the next section until the time allotted for the current section is up.**

5. **If you finish early, check your work for that section only.**

6. **Don't take a break during any one section.**

7. **Give yourself exactly one 10-minute break between sections III and IV.**

When you complete the whole test, check your answers with the answer key at the end of this chapter. A sample scoring chart is provided.

The answer explanations to all questions are in Chapter 21. Go through the explanations to all the questions, even the ones you answered correctly. The answers are a good review of the techniques I discuss throughout the book.

Section 1

Time: 35 minutes

26 Questions

Each group of questions in this section is based on a set of conditions. In answering some of the questions, it may be useful to draw a rough diagram. Choose the response that most accurately and completely answers each question and blacken the corresponding space on your answer sheet.

Questions 1–7

A college fraternity participates in a beach volley-ball tournament. The fraternity's team consists of five players: Biff, Chas, Deke, Marc, and Trip. Each game pits two players from this fraternity against two players from a rival fraternity (there are two players to a side), so for every game, the fraternity must supply a pair of players. Each player in this fraternity plays in at least one game. No pair of players plays more than one game together. The following conditions apply:

> If Biff plays with Marc for one game, then he cannot play with Chas.
>
> Any player who plays with Deke for one game must also play with Marc for one game.
>
> Trip plays in only one game.
>
> Deke does not ever play with Marc.

1. Which one of the following could be a complete and accurate list of the pairs of players that play in the tournament?

    (A) Biff and Chas; Biff and Deke; Biff and Marc; Chas and Marc; Marc and Trip

    (B) Biff and Chas; Biff and Deke; Biff and Trip; Deke and Marc

    (C) Biff and Chas; Chas and Deke; Chas and Marc; Marc and Trip

    (D) Biff and Marc; Biff and Trip; Chas and Deke; Chas and Marc; Marc and Trip

    (E) Biff and Deke; Biff and Marc; Chas and Marc; Deke and Trip

2. At most how many pairs of players could play together?

    (A) three

    (B) four

    (C) five

    (D) six

    (E) seven

3. Which one of the following could be true?

    (A) Biff and Chas play a game together, and neither Biff nor Chas plays with anyone else.

    (B) Biff and Marc play a game together, and neither Biff nor Marc plays with anyone else.

    (C) Biff and Trip play a game together, and neither Biff nor Trip plays with anyone else.

    (D) Chas and Marc play a game together, and neither Chas nor Marc plays with anyone else.

    (E) Marc and Trip play a game together, and neither Marc nor Trip plays with anyone else.

4. If exactly three players play games with Biff, then which one of the following could be an acceptable pairing of players?

    (A) Biff and Chas

    (B) Chas and Deke

    (C) Chas and Trip

    (D) Deke and Trip

    (E) Marc and Trip

Go on to next page

5. If four of the players play with the remaining player, then which of the following players must pair up for a game?

    (A) Biff and Deke

    (B) Biff and Trip

    (C) Chas and Deke

    (D) Deke and Trip

    (E) Marc and Trip

6. Which one of the following pairs of players CANNOT play together?

    (A) Biff and Deke

    (B) Biff and Marc

    (C) Biff and Trip

    (D) Chas and Trip

    (E) Deke and Trip

7. If Marc is the only player to play with Biff, then which one of the following could be true?

    (A) Chas plays exactly one game.

    (B) Marc plays exactly one game.

    (C) Deke plays exactly two games.

    (D) Mark plays exactly two games.

    (E) Chas plays exactly four games.

Go on to next page

Questions 8–12

A wrangler at a dude ranch in Colorado is taking a family of six on a trail ride through the mountains. She has selected six horses and allocated them to the participants based on age, size, and disposition. The six horses include two feisty mares, two placid geldings, and two small Shetland ponies. The trails are narrow, so the horses must walk single file. In determining the order of horses, the wrangler must observe the following rules:

> Either the first or second horse must be a gelding.
>
> The last horse cannot be a mare.
>
> The third horse cannot be a pony.
>
> The wrangler can never put two horses of the same type immediately next to one another.

8. Which one of the following statements CANNOT be true?

   (A) The first horse is a pony.

   (B) The first horse is a mare.

   (C) The second horse is a gelding.

   (D) The third horse is a mare.

   (E) The fifth horse is a pony.

9. If the third and fifth horses are the same type, then which one of the following statements must be true?

   (A) The first horse is a pony.

   (B) The second horse is a gelding.

   (C) The fourth horse is a pony.

   (D) The fifth horse is a mare.

   (E) The last horse is a gelding.

10. If the third horse is a gelding, which one of the following must be true?

    (A) The first horse is a gelding.

    (B) The second horse is a pony.

    (C) The fourth horse is a mare.

    (D) The fifth horse is a pony.

    (E) The last horse is a mare.

11. Which of the following pairs of horses MUST be of different types?

    (A) the first and third horses

    (B) the first and fourth horses

    (C) the second and fourth horses

    (D) the second and last horses

    (E) the third and last horses

12. If the wrangler replaces one of the mares with a third pony, and the other rules still apply, then which one of the following is a complete and accurate list of the positions that must be occupied by ponies?

    (A) second

    (B) fourth

    (C) second, fourth

    (D) fourth, sixth

    (E) second, fourth, sixth

Go on to next page

Questions 13–19

A fantasy gaming team has seven members: Brunhild, Cayenne, Maev, Roxanne, Solomon, Yorick, and Zilla. They each get to participate in exactly one of three fantasy gaming tournaments. The three tournaments are held in Fargo, Little Rock, and Omaha. In deciding who attends which tournament, they must observe the following rules:

Yorick cannot attend the tournament in Fargo.

Cayenne must attend the tournament in Fargo.

Brunhild and Roxanne must attend the same tournament.

Solomon and Yorick cannot participate the same tournament.

Maev and Zilla cannot participate in the same tournament.

Exactly half as many team members attend the tournament in Omaha as attend the tournament in Fargo.

13. If Brunhild and Yorick attend the same tournament, then which one of the following could be true?

(A) Brunhild attends the tournament in Fargo.

(B) Maev attends the tournament in Fargo.

(C) Roxanne attends the tournament in Omaha.

(D) Solomon attends the tournament in Little Rock.

(E) Yorick attends the tournament in Omaha.

14. Which one of the following could be true?

(A) Roxanne is the only team member who attends the tournament in Little Rock.

(B) Solomon is the only team member who attends the tournament in Omaha.

(C) Solomon is the only team member who attends the tournament in Fargo.

(D) Exactly two team members attend the tournament in Little Rock.

(E) Exactly three team members attend the tournament in Fargo.

15. If exactly one team member attends the tournament in Little Rock, then which one of the following must be true?

(A) Brunhild attends the tournament in Fargo.

(B) Maev attends the tournament in Omaha.

(C) Solomon attends the tournament in Fargo.

(D) Yorick attends the tournament in Omaha.

(E) Zilla attends the tournament in Omaha.

16. Each of the following could be a complete and accurate list of the team members who attend the tournament in Omaha EXCEPT:

(A) Brunhild and Roxanne

(B) Maev and Solomon

(C) Maev and Yorick

(D) Solomon and Zilla

(E) Yorick and Zilla

17. Which one of the following could be a possible allocation of team members to tournaments?

(A) Brunhild: the tournament in Omaha; Maev: the tournament in Fargo; Solomon: the tournament in Little Rock

(B) Brunhild and Maev: the tournament in Omaha; Yorick: the tournament in Little Rock

(C) Brunhild, Solomon, and Zilla: the tournament in Little Rock

(D) Maev: the tournament in Little Rock; Yorick and Zilla: the tournament in Fargo

(E) Roxanne, Solomon, and Zilla: the tournament in Fargo

Go on to next page

18. Which one of the following must be true?

    (A) Brunhild, Cayenne, and Maev do not all attend the same tournament.

    (B) Cayenne, Yorick, and Zilla do not all attend the same tournament.

    (C) Brunhild and Maev attend different tournaments.

    (D) Cayenne and Maev attend different tournaments.

    (E) Maev and Yorick attend different tournaments.

19. Which one of the following could be a complete and accurate list of the team members who do NOT attend the tournament in Fargo?

    (A) Solomon, Yorick

    (B) Yorick, Zilla

    (C) Brunhild, Roxanne, Yorick

    (D) Maev, Solomon, Yorick

    (E) Roxanne, Yorick, Zilla

Go on to next page

<u>Questions 20–26</u>

A gourmet ice-cream parlor offers a super-deluxe banana split intended to be shared by a group of people. They make it in a special long dish that contains five individual cups, side-by-side in a straight line. Each cup can hold one or two scoops of ice cream. A group of teenagers comes in and orders one of these banana splits; they request seven scoops of ice cream, three chocolate and four vanilla. Each scoop gets a topping on it; two scoops get sprinkles, and five scoops get nuts. Due to personal dislikes, mild allergies, and the likelihood that adjacent ice creams will leak into one another, the teenagers specify the following rules:

> A cup containing a scoop of vanilla with nuts cannot be immediately next to a cup containing a scoop of chocolate with sprinkles.

> No cup can contain both vanilla and chocolate ice cream.

20. Which one of the following could be a complete and accurate arrangement of ice cream flavors and toppings in the five cups?

  (A) 1: two scoops of vanilla with sprinkles; 2: nothing; 3: one scoop of chocolate with nuts; 4: one scoop of chocolate with nuts; 5: one scoop of chocolate with nuts, two scoops of vanilla with nuts

  (B) 1: one scoop of vanilla with sprinkles, one scoop of vanilla with nuts; 2: two scoops of vanilla with nuts; 3: one scoop of chocolate with sprinkles; 4: one scoop of chocolate with nuts; one scoop of chocolate with nuts

  (C) 1: one scoop of vanilla with nuts, one scoop of vanilla with sprinkles; 2: one scoop of vanilla with nuts, one scoop of vanilla with sprinkles; 3: one scoop of chocolate with sprinkles; 4: one scoop of chocolate with nuts; 5: one scoop of chocolate with nuts

  (D) 1: nothing; 2: two scoops of vanilla with nuts; 3: two scoops of chocolate with nuts; 4: two scoops of vanilla with sprinkles; 5: one scoop of chocolate with nuts

  (E) 1: two scoops of vanilla with nuts; 2: one scoop of vanilla with sprinkles; 3: one scoop of chocolate with nuts; 4: one scoop of chocolate with nuts, one scoop of chocolate with sprinkles; 5: one scoop of chocolate with nuts

21. Which one of the following CANNOT be false?

  (A) At least one cup contains nothing but one scoop of chocolate ice cream.

  (B) At least one cup contains nothing but one scoop of ice cream with sprinkles.

  (C) At least one cup contains nothing but one scoop of ice cream with nuts.

  (D) At least one scoop of vanilla ice cream has sprinkles.

  (E) At least one scoop of chocolate ice cream has sprinkles.

22. What is the maximum number of cups that could contain exactly one scoop of ice cream?

  (A) one

  (B) two

  (C) three

  (D) four

  (E) five

23. If the third cup has no ice cream in it, and no cup containing a scoop of vanilla is immediately adjacent to another cup containing a scoop of vanilla, then which one of the following could be false?

  (A) Exactly one cup contains exactly one scoop of ice cream.

  (B) No scoop of chocolate is in a cup immediately next to a cup containing a scoop of vanilla.

  (C) None of the scoops of chocolate have sprinkles on them.

  (D) None of the cups contain exactly one scoop of vanilla.

  (E) All the scoops of vanilla are in the second and fourth cups.

Go on to next page

24. If two scoops of chocolate with sprinkles are in the fourth cup and at least one scoop of vanilla with nuts is in the second cup, then all of the following must be false EXCEPT

    (A) A scoop of chocolate with nuts is in the first cup.

    (B) A scoop of chocolate with nuts is in the second cup.

    (C) A scoop of chocolate with nuts is in the fourth cup.

    (D) A scoop of chocolate with nuts is in the fifth cup.

    (E) Two scoops of ice cream are in the fifth cup.

25. If each of the scoops of chocolate ice cream is in its own cup and all the scoops of vanilla have nuts on them, then which one of the cups CANNOT contain vanilla ice cream?

    (A) the first cup

    (B) the second cup

    (C) the third cup

    (D) the fourth cup

    (E) the fifth cup

26. Each of the following could be a complete description of the contents of the first and second cups EXCEPT:

    (A) 1: two scoops of chocolate with nuts; 2: one scoop of vanilla with nuts

    (B) 1: one scoop of vanilla with sprinkles, one scoop of vanilla with nuts; 2: one scoop of vanilla with sprinkles

    (C) 1: nothing; 2: one scoop of chocolate with nuts

    (D) 1: one scoop of chocolate with sprinkles; 2: one scoop of vanilla with sprinkles

    (E) 1: one scoop of vanilla with sprinkles; 2: nothing

STOP You may check your work on this section only. Do not go back to any previous section.

Section 11

Time: 35 minutes

25 Questions

Directions: Read the passage and choose the best answer. Some questions may have more than one answer that looks right. Select the one that answers the question most completely. Don't assume anything that isn't directly stated, and don't let your imagination run wild; all the information you need is in the arguments and the answer choices.

1. Tempest: I bought two urns from an auction at Christie's. Christie's advertised them as dating from the Louis XV period of the late 18th century. I now believe that they actually date from the late 19th century and are worth much less than I paid for them. Several antiques experts agree with me. Therefore Christie's advertised them falsely and should refund my purchase price.

   Which one of the following, if true, most seriously weakens Tempest's argument?

   (A) The auction catalog described the urns as "A Pair of Louis XV Porphyry and Gilt-Bronze Two-Handled Vases."

   (B) Dating antiques is an extremely and imprecise art, and often several experts will disagree about the date of origin of the same item.

   (C) Scientists have performed tests on the bronze linings of the urns, but they have not produced conclusive results as to the dates of the vases.

   (D) Christie's states in its auction catalogs that all buyers should consult outside specialists before bidding on antiques, especially in the case of extremely valuable items.

   (E) The experts who Tempest hired to date the urns are known as some of the best in their field.

2. The state should continue to use the death penalty to punish the most extreme criminals. The death penalty is the only way to provide closure for the families of victims. People who commit cold-blooded, premeditated murders are incorrigible. Anyone whom a jury convicts of committing a truly heinous crime deserves to be executed by the state.

   Which one of the following, if true, most weakens the argument?

   (A) Surveys of the families of murder victims show that the surviving relatives overwhelmingly support the death penalty.

   (B) It is far cheaper simply to execute convicted criminals than it is to maintain them in maximum-security prison for life, with no chance of release or parole.

   (C) Recent studies have shown that a large proportion of criminals sentenced to death are later shown to be innocent of their crimes.

   (D) Modern methods of execution such as lethal injection are much less unpleasant to watch than earlier methods such as the electric chair or hanging.

   (E) Many states that had moved away from supporting the death penalty are now moving in the other direction, and the number of executions has increased dramatically in recent years.

Go on to next page

3. The top-ranking, highest-paying law firms select their new associates exclusively from top-ten law schools. Therefore, if a student doesn't get into a top-ten law school, he or she shouldn't bother attending law school at all.

The reasoning in the argument is most vulnerable to criticism on the grounds that the argument

(A) promises students that if they attend a top-ten law school they are guaranteed a position at a top-ranking law firm

(B) suggests, without offering evidence, that the legal education provided by lower-ranking law schools is inadequate

(C) fails to criticize the biased recruiting practices of top-ranking law firms

(D) assumes that the only reason anyone would attend law school is to acquire a job at a top-ranking, high-paying law firm

(E) misrepresents the relationship between law school and future employment

4. Exterminator: In the summer, we implement a large-scale mosquito abatement program to protect the population from West Nile virus. In addition to spraying insecticide and larvicide to kill mosquitoes, we also collect dead birds and test them for the virus. We have not found the virus in any birds tested this year, so we expect that we will not see an outbreak of West Nile virus this summer.

The conclusion drawn by the exterminator follows logically if which one of the following is assumed?

(A) Mosquitoes transmit the virus to birds by biting them, which is the same way humans catch the virus, but birds are much more susceptible than humans to dying from West Nile virus.

(B) The massive spraying of insecticide and larvicide will kill enough mosquitoes that they will not be able to transmit the virus effectively.

(C) Birds are an indicator species of West Nile virus; the virus always appears in birds before humans start catching the disease.

(D) It is possible to have an outbreak of West Nile virus among humans even if no birds die of the virus, though that would be an unusual scenario.

(E) The insecticide and larvicide used to kill the adult and larval mosquitoes do not have a deleterious effect on the health of birds that eat mosquitoes.

5. Editorialist: Conservative legislators and religious groups want to ban all research involving undifferentiated stem cells, fearing that this would be akin to abortion because it would destroy an embryo's chances at life. They could not be more wrong; stem cells are not embryos and can never develop into human beings. Stem cell research could lead to all sorts of promising treatments for diseases such as Alzheimer's, diabetes, and some kinds of cancer.

Which one of the following is most strongly supported by the information above?

(A) The editorialist believes that stem cell research offers many powerful benefits and that the arguments of its detractors are invalid because they misunderstand the nature of stem cells.

(B) The editorialist believes that because stem cells sometimes come from embryos, using them in research will inevitably result in the destruction of embryos that could become people.

(C) The editorialist believes that religious groups should not be allowed to influence legislators on scientific matters because they refuse to accept scientific fact when it contradicts their religious beliefs.

(D) The editorialist believes that the legislature should pass a law allowing stem cell research but also pass another law banning the use of stem cells acquired from aborted embryos.

(E) The editorialist believes that stem cell research offers many potential benefits but that it should be banned because those benefits are outweighed by costs.

6. Scientists have concluded that a pickled human heart long believed to be the heart of king Louis XVII of France is indeed his heart, and not that of a commoner substituted for the royal boy. Louis XVII's parents, Marie Antoinette and Louis XVI, fell to the guillotine during the French Revolution, and Louis XVII was thrown into prison, where he died at the age of ten. His heart was removed and preserved. Many people believed, however, that the young king had been spirited away and the boy who died in prison was an imposter put there in Louis's place. Scientific evidence now shows that the child who died in prison was indeed Louis XVII.

Which one of the following, if true, most strongly supports the statement above?

(A) At that time in France, it was traditional to remove and preserve the hearts of royal corpses, a service that was never done with the bodies of commoners, which indicates that the heart must have had a royal owner.

(B) Scientists examining the heart have concluded that it must have belonged to a male between the ages of eight and twelve.

(C) DNA samples taken from the heart and from hair cut from Marie Antoinette's head when she was a child prove that the heart and hair came from people who were very closely related.

(D) The doctor who removed Louis XVII's heart preserved it in a jar of alcohol, which was so effective as a preservative that the heart's valves and muscles are still in good condition and can be easily examined by scientists.

(E) Scientists examining the heart have determined that it came from a child who suffered great physical privation in the years just prior to his death; in particular, its undeveloped muscles suggest that the owner of the heart did not engage in much physical activity for several years.

Go on to next page

7. Emilio: Every child should be encouraged to play a single team sport at a high level, perhaps on a select traveling team that plays year-round. If a child does not play on an elite team at a young age, he will not have a chance to play on his high school varsity team, and will thus forego any opportunity to win college scholarships for athletics.

Julienne: Parents should encourage their children to play a wide variety of sports. Sports teach children teamwork, leadership, and encourage them to develop physically; most of all, sports should be fun. Children who specialize in one sport too early miss out on the chance to develop a wide range of skills, are more prone to injuries, and usually don't enjoy themselves as much as those who play a variety of sports. Also, there are so few athletic scholarships available, there is very little point in counting on one.

Emilio and Julienne disagree about whether

(A) sports teach children teamwork and leadership

(B) children who play a single sport on an elite team enjoy themselves

(C) parents should encourage their children to participate in organized sports

(D) early specialization in a single sport is beneficial or harmful to children

(E) children below high school age should be participating in organized sports

8. In order to preserve the flavor of food for the longest time, a home freezer should maintain a temperature of no more than 0° Fahrenheit. Even food that is kept frozen at the proper temperature will last no more than a year. For every five degrees of temperature above zero, the life of food is cut in half. Most home freezers maintain a temperature of about ten degrees.

If the statements above are true, which one of the following would also have to be true?

(A) Most home freezers can store food for no more than three months.

(B) Most homeowners don't know the temperature of their freezers.

(C) Frozen foods can still be safe to eat even when they have lost their optimum flavor.

(D) Commercial freezers stay colder than home freezers.

(E) Most food in home freezers has been kept past the point at which its best flavor begins to deteriorate.

Go on to next page

9. Ichthyologist: I have discovered a new kind of mollusk that lives deep in the ocean. All animals that live in the deep sea are predators who eat other animals. Therefore, this new mollusk must be a predator.

Which one of the following exhibits a pattern of reasoning most similar to that exhibited by the argument above?

(A) A yoga enthusiast discovers a new yoga studio. All yoga studios employ experienced and highly trained instructors. Therefore the yoga enthusiast will be able to find a good instructor.

(B) A coach finds a talented new basketball player in Croatia. All Croatian basketball players are tall and hardworking. Therefore this new basketball player is tall and hardworking.

(C) A gardener discovers a new variety of tomato in his garden. All tomatoes are members of the same family as potatoes and eggplants, the nightshade family. Therefore this tomato must be a member of the nightshade family.

(D) A jeweler finds a perfect sapphire. All sapphires are very hard and durable. Therefore this sapphire must be hard and durable.

(E) A botanist finds a new kind of cactus in the driest part of the desert. All plants that live in the dry desert are extremely efficient at collecting and retaining water. Therefore, this new cactus must be extremely efficient at collecting and retaining water.

10. Counselor: People should always pick their battles. By arguing only about issues that truly matter to them and ignoring the ones that don't, they maximize chances of getting what they want and avoid antagonizing friends and relatives unnecessarily.

Which one of the following best illustrates the proposition above?

(A) A brother and sister have to share a car. The brother never fills the tank with gasoline, always driving it until it's nearly empty and then waiting for his sister to fill it up. She yells at him every time she has to visit a gas station.

(B) A wife wants her husband to wash the dishes, take out the garbage, and make the bed in the morning, but she knows he won't do all three; she most dislikes taking out the garbage herself, so she makes a point of asking him to do that many times and ignores the dishes and bed. After a few weeks, he promises to take the garbage out every week and does so.

(C) A test-prep teacher teaching an LSAT course wants to improve her students' scores in both Logical Reasoning and Analytical Reasoning, but doesn't have time to do a thorough job on both, so she spends half her time on Logical Reasoning and half on Analytical Reasoning. As a result, the students do moderately but not spectacularly well on both sections.

(D) A bride's mother wants her to have a big wedding in a church followed by a large reception, but the bride wants a small, less formal wedding with just a few guests. They can't agree, so the bride and groom decide to elope instead and the mother is terribly disappointed.

(E) A father wants his son to win an athletic scholarship, and insists that his son spend hours every afternoon working out and practicing sports. Despite the son's strenuous efforts, he fails to win an athletic scholarship. Because he is a good student, though, he does win an academic scholarship.

Go on to next page

11. People who live in poverty often have little money to spend on food, and as a result are often afflicted with malnutrition. Ironically, these same people have very high rates of obesity.

   Which one of the following best resolves the apparent paradox above?

   (A) Obesity is becoming a serious problem all over the world and at all levels of income.

   (B) People who live in poverty do not understand the basic rules of nutrition.

   (C) American citizens have gotten out of the habit of cooking family meals, and as a result fewer and fewer people know how to prepare healthy foods such as vegetables.

   (D) The cheap foods that make up the majority of the diets of the poor people are full of calories but devoid of essential nutrients.

   (E) Recent statistics show that processed foods and fast food make up almost half the diet of a large number of people in the United States.

12. Most players of video games are male. Therefore video game manufacturers should not bother making any games aimed at girls or women.

   Which one of the following employs a flawed argumentative strategy that is most closely parallel to the flawed argumentative strategy in the argument above?

   (A) Most avid cyclists are male. Therefore bicycle manufacturers should make most of their bike frames to fit men.

   (B) Most Americans now have cellular telephones. Therefore most Americans should not bother to maintain normal land-based telephones.

   (C) Most people use Windows computers. Therefore software producers should not bother to make any software for MacIntosh computers.

   (D) Most lawyers need glasses or contact lenses. Therefore optometrists should aim some their advertising at the legal profession.

   (E) Most Labrador retrievers are easy to train. Therefore a person who wants an obedient dog should consider getting a Labrador retriever.

13. The legislature should pass a law banning the use of cell phones by people who are driving a moving car. Drivers talking on cell phones are distracted by their phone conversations and cannot give their full attention to driving their vehicles. Banning the use of cell phones by drivers will make the roads safer.

   The legislator's argument depends on assuming which one of the following?

   (A) A study by a sociologist has shown that the use of cell phones is occasionally a contributing factor in traffic accidents.

   (B) It is the proper role of the legislature to enact laws that protect the safety of drivers and passengers in automobiles.

   (C) Drivers who hold their cell phones in their hands are more distracted than drivers who use a hands-free headset or speaker phone while driving.

   (D) Because drivers talking on cell phones are distracted, they are more prone to getting into accidents and thus make the roads more dangerous.

   (E) Many drivers engage in behavior that distracts them from their driving, such as eating, fiddling with the radio, reading maps, and talking on cell phones.

14. Partner: Attorney A and Attorney B each wrote a brief arguing the same side of a case. Attorney A spent 8 hours writing his brief. Attorney B spent 12 hours writing her brief. Therefore Attorney B's brief is better than Attorney A's brief.

   The reasoning in the partner's argument is flawed because the argument

   (A) equates time spent on a job with quality without examining the products to verify the quality

   (B) criticizes Attorney B for taking too long to write her brief

   (C) fails to explain why the partner believes Attorney B's brief is better than Attorney A's brief

   (D) takes for granted that tracking time spent on work is the best way to ensure quality work

   (E) fails to identify the topic of the brief

Go on to next page

15. High school student: Insects are defined as animals with six legs, an outer skeleton, and wings. Ants are insects, but most ants don't have wings. Therefore ants can't be insects.

    A reasoning flaw in the high school student's argument is that the argument

    (A) ignores the possibility that some ants have wings

    (B) misstates the definition of an insect

    (C) fails to mention that insects have a three-segmented body, and both legs and wings are attached to the middle section, or thorax

    (D) exaggerates the importance of wings to ants

    (E) assumes incorrectly that all individuals of a species must display all the characteristics of a category in order to belong to that category

16. This store is having a sale in which all their merchandise is 25 percent off. I plan to buy many things, because the more I spend, the more I will save.

    The argument is vulnerable to criticism on which one of the following grounds?

    (A) It assumes erroneously that the same discount of 25 percent will apply to all the merchandise in the store.

    (B) It draws a mistaken correlation between percentage of discount and savings.

    (C) It fails to realize that spending money on discounted items is still spending money, and will result in no savings at all.

    (D) It presupposes that the store has put its merchandise on sale in an effort to attract more customers.

    (E) It neglects to consider that merchandise might be put on sale because it is of poor quality, defective, or unpopular.

17. Christina: The best way for employers to reduce health insurance costs is to implement consumer-driven health plans. These plans have high deductibles, which encourage employees to think twice before seeing a doctor for frivolous reasons. Employers will pay lower premiums for these plans, and can help their employees pay for necessary care by contributing to healthcare savings accounts along with their employees.

    Guthrie: This will reduce healthcare costs only if the real reason for skyrocketing costs is that patients abuse medical care, seeing doctors far too often. Consumer-driven plans run a real risk of increasing healthcare costs in the long run. Patients will be reluctant to seek care for minor problems because it will cost them too much money, and that neglect could result in minor problems turning into major catastrophes that will be very expensive for everyone. Insurers can't assume that healthcare costs are entirely the fault of irresponsible patients.

    This dialog lends the most support to the claim that Christina and Guthrie disagree with each other about which one of the following statements?

    (A) Employers can reduce healthcare costs by encouraging their employees to lose weight and do other things to care for their own health.

    (B) Increasing healthcare costs are mainly due to patients seeing doctors more often than necessary, for complaints that do not actually need medical attention.

    (C) Health insurance companies make it very difficult for smaller employers to buy affordable coverage for themselves and their employees.

    (D) High deductibles are effective at deterring people from seeking medical attention for all but the most serious concerns.

    (E) Healthcare savings accounts offer employees a way to save pretax income for anticipated medical expenses.

Go on to next page

18. Context is everything. For example, on an Internet perfume discussion board, one participant posted the message "Azkaban arrives today!" referring to an extremely popular film about a boy wizard that was opening that day. Another participant responded, "Where can you buy it?" evidently assuming that "Azkaban" must refer to a new perfume. She quickly realized her mistake, but because the reference to the movie was out of context, she could not immediately place it.

Which one of the following most accurately expresses the main conclusion of the argument?

(A) Internet discussion boards are not a reliable source of information.

(B) Even well-known and widely available information, provided out of context, can be misleading.

(C) People should always be very careful to state their topic precisely.

(D) Participants on perfume discussion boards do not know much about popular movies.

(E) The names of perfumes are so fanciful it's easy to confuse them.

19. Divemaster: Some scuba divers fill their tanks with nitrox instead of air; nitrox is a combination of nitrogen and oxygen that contains more than the percentage of oxygen usually contained in air. Nitrox aficionados claim that the additional oxygen makes diving safer; they can stay down longer, decompress faster, dive again after a shorter surface interval, and feel less fatigued after extended diving than if they were breathing plain air. On the other hand, divers using nitrox face some dangers and limitations, particularly the risk of convulsions and death at depths that are safe for divers using air.

Which one of the following, if true, most helps to reconcile the divemaster's two claims?

(A) Oxygen that is too concentrated becomes toxic to humans; the higher concentration of oxygen in nitrox becomes toxic when it is compressed at depths that do not result in the same problem for divers breathing air.

(B) Divers who use nitrox are likely to stay underwater too long, lulled into a false sense of security by their breathing gas.

(C) Divers who use air pay more attention to training and safety procedures, and as a result experience accidents resulting in fatalities much less often than divers using nitrox.

(D) All divers face the rare but real risk of receiving a tank with contaminated air inside it; this can occur when bacteria grow inside a compressor, and occasionally results in diving fatalities.

(E) Divers who use nitrox tend to be slightly older and more experienced than divers who use air; they are more likely to dive regularly, take frequent training courses, and buy the most up-to-date and technologically advanced equipment.

Go on to next page

20. Many Americans do not take all of the vacation time to which they are entitled by their jobs. There are several reasons for this; they might feel that they are indispensable at work, fear the resentment of coworkers, or dread discovering that their workplaces can actually function perfectly well without them. This is a mistake; vacation time gives workers a chance to rest, recover, and gain perspective that in turn can lead to more creativity and better performance at work.

The claim that many Americans do not take all the vacation time to which they are entitled plays which one of the following roles in the argument?

(A) It is a recommendation of a policy that the American workplace should implement.

(B) It is evidence of the author's claim that vacation time gives workers a chance to rest.

(C) It is the conclusion of the argument.

(D) It is a statement of a principle that the author wishes all people would observe.

(E) It is a statement of fact that the author introduces in order to argue that it is bad practice.

21. A large southern state university has changed its teaching practices. Formerly, most introductory courses were taught by instructors without PhDs; now all introductory classes will be taught by professors with PhDs. That will mean class size will increase from 44 students per class to 600 per class, but overall the students' learning experiences should improve.

Which one of the following is an assumption required by the argument?

(A) Requiring professors with PhDs to teach all introductory classes will mean that the university must hire more faculty with doctorates.

(B) Students tend to participate in smaller classes more than they do in large lectures, even when the lectures are supplemented by weekly discussion sections.

(C) Major private universities already use this format, in which professors with PhDs teach all introductory classes as large lectures.

(D) A class taught by a PhD, even a giant lecture with hundreds of students, is a better teaching environment than a smaller class taught by an instructor without a PhD.

(E) Services that rank colleges and universities usually consider the percentage of classes taught by PhDs when computing ranks, and this change should increase the universities' ranking.

Go on to next page

22. Griselda: The United States should remember that it is part of a global community and that its actions affect other nations. It is very important for the United States to avoid alienating the citizens of foreign countries; ultimately, that is the best way to assure national security.

Theodore: The good opinion of foreign countries is largely irrelevant to U.S. national security concerns. The United States should always act in its own best interest, regardless of what other nations think. If that means sending troops off to war without the approval of the rest of the world, then so be it.

Which one of the following is most strongly supported by the conversation above?

(A) Griselda agrees with Theodore that sometimes the United States is justified in sending troops abroad despite the disapproval of other nations, but believes that in most circumstances an international consensus is desirable.

(B) Theodore believes that the proper response to threats from abroad is a show of military strength.

(C) Theodore and Griselda both believe that the opinion of the international community is important, but disagree about the proper response to actions that threaten U.S. national security.

(D) Griselda believes that the United States should follow the dictates of the United Nations on all matters of national security and foreign intervention, particularly when it comes to sending troops to other countries.

(E) Griselda and Theodore disagree about whether the United States should respect the opinions of other nations when making decisions that affect national security, such as sending troops to fight wars in foreign nations.

23. Obstetrician: Children born to mothers who drink heavily during pregnancy often have severe birth defects and mental retardation caused by prenatal exposure to alcohol. Pregnant women should never consume alcohol because it will cause their children to be born with these serious problems.

The reasoning in the obstetrician's argument is most vulnerable to criticism on the grounds that the argument

(A) assumes that consuming any amount of alcohol, large or small, during pregnancy will cause birth defects and mental retardation

(B) suggests that pregnant women should be prevented from drinking during pregnancy

(C) presumes that the state's interest in the health of unborn children is greater than the rights of pregnant women to behave as they choose

(D) fails to provide evidence proving the link between heavy drinking and birth defects

(E) blames mothers for causing their children's problems

Go on to next page

24. An ounce of prevention is worth a pound of cure; it is always cheaper to head off problems before they start than to fix them once they have occurred.

Which one of the following most closely conforms to the principle above?

(A) A homeowner spent hours preparing the soil for his lawn and garden, and as a result of his preparation, his grass was green and lush and his flowers bloomed with abandon.

(B) A state school board insisted that all students in public schools show evidence of vaccination against measles before being allowed to attend classes.

(C) A pre-law student spent several weeks studying for the LSAT, and as a result received an excellent score that, combined with the grades she had earned from years of diligent study, earned her admission to a top law school.

(D) A town that offered free prenatal care to low-income pregnant women found that it more than recouped its costs from the money it did not have to spend on treating medical problems of both mothers and infants.

(E) A woman who spent several months dieting and exercising and finally achieved her ideal body weight continued to watch what she ate and to exercise regularly in order to avoid gaining weight again.

25. Psychologist: Patients who feel they have a good relationship with their doctors generally show more improvement in their health than those who feel that their doctors ignore their concerns. Patients who like their doctors show improved physical and emotional health, are less anxious about their symptoms, and are more likely to follow doctors' prescribed regimens.

Which one of the following, if true, would provide the most support for the psychologist's assertion?

(A) Patients are more likely to sue a doctor for malpractice if they believe that the doctor ignored them or failed to listen while they explained their symptoms.

(B) When a patient begins to describe symptoms to a doctor, the average physician interrupts him or her after only 18 seconds of speech.

(C) Studies done by medical researchers show that good communication between physicians and patients results in lower blood sugar levels in diabetic patients, reduced pain in cancer patients, and lower blood pressure in those suffering from hypertension.

(D) Medical schools and health insurers have spent years trying to improve doctor-patient communication, but so far they have met with little success.

(E) Doctors who work in stressful environments are much less likely to take the time to listen to patients than doctors in more relaxed settings.

STOP You may check your work on this section only. Do not go back to any previous section.

Section III

Time: 35 minutes

25 Questions

Directions: Read each passage and answer the questions that follow it. Some questions may have more than one answer that looks right. In that case, pick the one that answers the question most completely and correctly. Don't assume anything that isn't stated in the passage or the questions. All the information you need to answer the questions is contained in the passage, questions, and answer choices.

Line Recumbent bicycles, invented in the mid-1800s, dropped out of sight during most of the 20th century due to a historical accident. In 1934, a second-rate French bicyclist rode a recumbent
(05) in a race and not only won but broke several speed records. The Union Cyclist International banned recumbents from competition, ruling that bicycle racing should be about the talent of the rider, not the advantages of a particular bicycle
(10) design. This decision produced an unintended result; bicycle manufacturers stopped designing and producing recumbent bicycles and instead focused on trying to improve the inherently inefficient diamond frame, which has remained essen-
(15) tially unchanged since 1885.

Conventional diamond-frame bicycles were designed based on the position a person assumes when riding a horse: upright with head high and legs low. Recumbents, on the other
(20) hand, are designed to maximize aerodynamic efficiency and comfort. A recumbent rider sits back on a seat resembling a lawn chair, with his legs in front. This position is extremely comfortable; recumbent riders never suffer the saddle
(25) sores or aching hands and necks of upright bicyclists, who report three times more overuse injuries and pain than riders of recumbents. Recumbents are also aerodynamically efficient. A recumbent rider's legs are within the frame of his
(30) body, so he presents less frontal area to the wind than the rider of an upright bicycle, thereby minimizing wind resistance. This permanent aerodynamic tuck affords the rider a 15-percent speed increase over an upright bicycle. Adding a fair-
(35) ing, a kind of windshield, can increase speed a

further 15 percent. All bicycling land-speed records have been set on recumbents; a recumbent was the first bicycle to break 65 mph on a flat track, and low-racer recumbents are now setting world records over 80 mph. (40)

The popularity of recumbents has surged recently, bringing with it a flood of new bicycle designs. One major difference in types of recumbent is the length of the wheelbase. Short wheel-
base bikes place the rider's feet in front of the (45) front wheel, an extremely aerodynamic riding position that allows for high speeds. Long wheelbase bikes place the front wheel ahead of the rider's feet; these bikes are very comfortable for long distance touring. Recumbent cyclists must (50) also choose between two steering types. Above-seat-steering places the riders hands at chest height, within the frame of his body, which improves aerodynamics. Below-seat-steering allows the rider to hang his arms from his shoul- (55) ders to steer, which is more comfortable. Manufacturers have also been experimenting with different materials. Most recumbents are still made from heavy but inexpensive steel, but a few high-end models are now made from light- (60) weight titanium or carbon fiber.

Some riders fear they will not be able to climb hills on recumbents, but most experienced recumbent riders find that they can equal their performance on an upright bike on grades of up to 12 (65) percent. Climbing fast requires a high power to weight ratio and a fast cadence, of about 70 to 80 rpm. Riders can improve their climbing by lifting weights to build strength and by learning to downshift early in their attack of a hill. (70)

Go on to next page

1. Which one of the following most accurately expresses the main idea of the passage?

   (A) The Union Cyclist International banned recumbent bicycles from competitions because they feared that allowing recumbents would turn bicycle racing into a design competition rather than a test of training, endurance, and skill.

   (B) Recumbent bicycles have become more popular recently after years of neglect, and this surge in popularity has brought with it a proliferation of recumbent bicycle designs, each of which offers benefits to speed or comfort.

   (C) Recumbent bicycles have a much more aerodynamic profile than upright bicycles, especially when used with a fairing, which explains why recumbent bicycles are faster than upright diamond-frame bicycles with identical riders under identical conditions.

   (D) Recumbent bicycles, which were banned from competition in the 1930s and have thus been neglected for much of the 20th century, offer many advantages over upright bicycles and come in many designs.

   (E) The permanent aerodynamic tuck of a recumbent rider allows recumbent bicycles to move faster than upright bicycles under equivalent conditions, which accounts for recumbents' breaking several world speed records.

2. According to the passage, why are recumbent bicycles faster than upright bicycles?

   (A) The seating position places the cyclist in a permanent aerodynamic tuck, with arms and legs contained within the rider's torso profile, thereby creating less wind resistance than an upright rider.

   (B) Most recumbent bicycles are made from high-tech super-light materials such as carbon fiber and titanium, which makes them lighter and stronger than upright diamond-frame bicycles.

   (C) Recumbents are designed to maximize aerodynamic efficiency and comfort through the use of ergonomic seating and fairings, which reduce wind resistance.

   (D) Bicycle manufacturers have been experimenting with recumbent frames since they were first invented in the mid-1800s, which has resulted in greater refinement of construction techniques than are available for upright bicycles.

   (E) Recumbents can have two different steering configurations, which makes them faster than upright bicycles, which have only one basic steering structure.

Go on to next page

3. According to the passage, why did the Union Cyclist International ban recumbents from competition?

   (A) A second-rate cyclist won a race on a recumbent and the other competitors petitioned the cycling organization to outlaw recumbents, despite the obvious aerodynamic advantage offered by recumbent bicycles.

   (B) After several cyclists set records on upright bicycles, the organization decided that upright bikes were far superior to recumbents and should therefore be the only vehicles allowed in bicycle racing.

   (C) Bicycle manufacturers petitioned the Union Cyclist International to standardize the bicycle types that were allowed in racing in order to achieve a monopoly on the racing bike market.

   (D) In 1934, a second-rate cyclist on a recumbent attracted too much press attention due to his unusual and eye-catching bicycle, and the organization decided to ban recumbents to focus attention back on the more talented cyclists.

   (E) After a second-rate cyclist won a race and broke several records on a recumbent, the UCI decided that recumbents offered too much mechanical advantage and that in order for races to reflect actual ability all riders should use the same kind of bicycle.

4. Which one of the following is NOT mentioned in the passage as an advantage of recumbent bicycles over upright bicycles?

   (A) Recumbent bicycles are more comfortable than upright bicycles, which allows cyclists to ride them for longer periods than they would on upright bicycles.

   (B) Recumbent bicycles are lighter than upright bicycles, which gives them an advantage at hill climbing.

   (C) Recumbent bicycles minimize the frontal profile of the cyclist, improving aerodynamics.

   (D) Recumbent bicycles can be 15 percent faster than upright bicycles on the same terrain.

   (E) Recumbent cyclists report many fewer overuse injuries than upright cyclists.

5. What is the primary purpose of the last paragraph?

   (A) to argue that, contrary to what they might expect, cyclists can climb hills well on recumbent bicycles, and to suggest ways to improve climbing performance

   (B) to prove that recumbents are as fast on hills as upright bicycles because a cyclist with a high power-to-weight ratio on a recumbent can climb hills just as well as he could on an upright bicycle

   (C) to describe the ideal cadence a recumbent cyclist should use on a grade of up to 12 percent

   (D) to dispute the contention that recumbent bicycles lose their aerodynamic advantage when climbing hills by offering anecdotal evidence of recumbent cyclists who are strong climbers

   (E) to recommend that recumbent cyclists interested in improving their hill-climbing speed lift weights to increase their strength and minimize the weight of their bikes

6. According to the passage, which one of the following recumbent bicycles would be fastest ridden by the same rider under the same riding conditions?

   (A) a short wheelbase bike with above-seat-steering

   (B) a short wheelbase bike with below-seat-steering

   (C) a short wheelbase bike with above-seat-steering and a fairing

   (D) a long wheelbase bike with below-seat-steering and a fairing

   (E) a long wheelbase bike with above-seat steering

Go on to next page

7. The author would be most likely to agree
    with which one of the following statements?

    (A) A rider on a recumbent bicycle with
        above-seat-steering should be able to
        climb faster than a rider on an upright
        bicycle of the same weight.

    (B) In the near future, more cyclists will be
        riding recumbents than are riding
        upright bicycles as more people dis-
        cover the aerodynamic and comfort
        advantages of recumbent bicycles.

    (C) A cyclist who wants to make his recum-
        bent bicycle faster by reducing its
        weight should consider installing a fair-
        ing on it.

    (D) An aerodynamic tuck on an upright
        bicycle offers as much aerodynamic
        advantage and comfort as the ordinary
        riding position on a recumbent bicycle.

    (E) A cyclist who wants to maximize speed
        and comfort and is not interested in
        racing should choose a recumbent over
        an upright bicycle.

Go on to next page

Line Migratory bird populations have dropped sharply in recent years, largely due to habitat loss. Migratory species travel thousands of miles between North American breeding grounds and (05) winter territories in Central America and the Caribbean, and the loss of any part of this habitat can be disastrous for them. The Migratory Bird Conservation Commission works with the U.S. Fish and Wildlife Service to preserve U.S. (10) habitats for migratory birds, especially waterfowl, by purchasing or leasing land and water used by the creatures and establishing wildlife refuges on it. The Commission is a Cabinet-level organization chaired by the Secretary of the (15) Interior and staffed by members of the U.S. Fish and Wildlife Service's Division of Realty. Its members include two Senators, two Congressmen, the Secretary of Agriculture, the Administrator of the Environmental Protection Agency, and repre- (20) sentatives from each state.

The Commission was established in 1929. Since that time, it has helped the Fish and Wildlife Service purchase, lease, or get easements to more than 4.5 million acres of habitat (25) crucial to migratory birds, which are managed as part of the 93-million-acre Wildlife Refuge System. When the Commission identifies a likely area, it sends experts to assess the biology and ecology, existing land uses and values, the area's (30) economy, and the needs of the local people. After the Commission approves the boundaries of a potential refuge, its representatives contact the landowners within the area to see if they will sell their land. The Commission usually pur- (35) chases the property at fair market value but will also lease land or make other arrangements such as a life-use reservation, which allows the owner to continue living on the property for the rest of his life. Although the Fish and Wildlife Service (40) does have the power to condemn property, it rarely does this, preferring to work with willing sellers or to leave property in private hands.

The Commission and Service add to their collection of protected waterfowl habitat every year. (45) For example, in 2000, the Commission spent more than $6.3 million to acquire 6,500 acres of important habitat and to protect an additional 1,000 acres. This territory included 632 acres for the proposed Cat Island National Wildlife Refuge in (50) Louisiana, 2,251 acres of the Great Dismal Swamp National Wildlife Refuge in North Carolina and

Virginia, and 2,250 acres of the Cokeville Meadows National Wildlife Refuge in Wyoming. The Commission chose this habitat because of its location along migratory waterfowl flyways, (55) travel corridors that birds follow on spring and fall migrations.

The Commission gets most of its funding from the sale of Migratory Bird Hunting and Conservation Stamps, better known as Duck (60) Stamps, which waterfowl hunters must purchase as hunting permits. The Commission receives additional funding from the Wetlands Loan Act, import duties on arms and ammunition, the sale of refuge admission permits under the Emergency (65) Wetlands Resources Act, the sale of rights-of-way across national wildlife refuges, disposals of refuge land, and reverted Federal Aid funds.

8. Which one of the following most accurately states the main idea of the passage?

(A) The Migratory Bird Conservation Commission assists the U.S. Fish and Wildlife Service in identifying potential wildlife refuges and negotiating with the owners to purchase that land.

(B) The Migratory Bird Conservation Commission, along with the U.S. Fish and Wildlife Service, identifies and preserves large amounts of habitat crucial to the survival of migratory waterfowl, funding its activities mainly through sales of Duck Stamps.

(C) The Migratory Bird Conservation Commission spent $6.3 million in 2000 to buy a vast amount of land along migratory waterfowl flyways, which are crucially important to ducks and geese migrating in the fall and spring.

(D) The Migratory Bird Conservation Commission sells Duck Stamps to hunters as its main source of revenue; it uses this money to buy land.

(E) Migratory bird populations have dropped in recent years due to habitat loss, which the Migratory Bird Conservation Commission and the U.S. Fish and Wildlife Services are trying to counteract.

Go on to next page

9. According to the passage, which one of the following is NOT a goal of the Migratory Bird Conservation Commission?

    (A) Helping the U.S. Fish and Wildlife Service purchase, lease, or get easements to habitat that is important to migratory waterfowl

    (B) Establishing wildlife refuges along migratory waterfowls flyways

    (C) Negotiating with landowners to purchase or lease property or otherwise acquire rights to property on amicable terms

    (D) Selling Migratory Bird Hunting and Conservation stamps to people who want to hunt waterfowl

    (E) Breeding migratory waterfowl in special nurseries and releasing the young birds into the wild in an effort to bolster wild populations.

10. According to the passage, all of the following could be sources of funding for the Commission EXCEPT:

    (A) the sale of rights-of-way across national wildlife refuges

    (B) import duties on arms and ammunition

    (C) reverted Federal Aid funds

    (D) the sale of Migratory Bird Hunting and Conservation Stamps

    (E) the sale of hunting leases

11. Which one of the following is most likely the author's overall purpose in the passage?

    (A) to describe the organization and actions of a facet of the federal government that has as its goal the protection of migratory birds

    (B) to impress readers with the importance of the Migratory Bird Conservation Commission to migratory bird populations and argue that the government should increase funding for conservation and habitat preservation

    (C) to praise the actions of the Commission and the Fish and Wildlife Service in acquiring property for conservation purposes, especially the Commission's preference acquiring property from willing sellers instead of through condemnation

    (D) to analyze the history of the Migratory Bird Conservation Commission since its establishment in 1929 and explain how it decides which parcels of land to purchase for conservation

    (E) to generate support for the Commission and encourage readers to take an interest in habitat preservation

Go on to next page

12. The author describes the territory purchased by the Commission in 2000 primarily in order to

    (A) argue that $6.3 million to acquire 6,500 acres of land was a fair price given that the purchased land includes 632 acres in the proposed Cat Island National Wildlife Refuge in Louisiana, and 2,251 acres of the Great Dismal Swamp National Wildlife Refuge in North Carolina and Virginia

    (B) complain that in 2000 the Commission didn't purchase nearly enough territory due to a lack of funding

    (C) describe to readers the sort of land that constitutes migratory waterfowl flyways, which are travel corridors that birds follow on their spring and fall migrations

    (D) inform readers of the locations of the new wildlife refuges, which were selected by the Commission after assessment of biology and ecology, existing land uses and values, economic considerations, and the needs of the local people near the new refuges

    (E) provide a concrete example of the amount and type of habitat that the Commission regularly purchases for the Wildlife Refuge System

13. What does the author mean by the phrase "the Service does have the power to condemn property" in Lines 39 and 40?

    (A) The U.S. Fish and Wildlife Service has the power to declare land unfit for human habitation.

    (B) The U.S. Fish and Wildlife Service has the power to declare land environmentally devastated due to pollution and human construction.

    (C) The U.S. Fish and Wildlife Service has the power to take private property from its owner for public use, providing the owner fair compensation for the value of the property.

    (D) The U.S. Fish and Wildlife Service has the power to lease private property from landowners and include it in the Wildlife Refuge System.

    (E) The U.S. Fish and Wildlife Service has the power to change the zoning of pieces of property, preventing landowners from using it for specified purposes.

Go on to next page

Line "Power" is a generic term, which must be distinguished from the more specific term "authority." When party A gets party B to do what party B would not otherwise have done, party A has
(05) exercised power. Power takes many forms and appears variously in the histories of Alexander the Great and his time. Alexander enjoyed military power and delegated a portion of it to his general Antipater. Antipater in turn used the
(10) coercive power afforded him by his army in Greece to install friendly governments and forestall concerted action against Macedonia. The politicians and public speakers in the Greek states demonstrated powers of persuasion that at differ-
(15) ent times affected the course of events differently. All this is not in itself particularly interesting — after all, only those with some degree of power become actors in political histories. More interesting is the particular manifestation of power
(20) that we call authority.

Authority is a kind of power, but not all power is authoritative. Authority is a matter of speaking; it is a "discursive function." Authority describes the ability to command effectively, for
(25) even when we speak of someone "acting" authoritatively, we actually mean "causing others to act by virtue of one's authoritative speech." As such, authority implies an asymmetry in the relationship between speaker and listener. Because
(30) authority demands obedience, it is associated with coercive power, and because it operates in discourse, it is associated with persuasive power. Yet these associations are uneasy. The command, "Don't move or I'll shoot" is discursive and
(35) demands obedience, but while it shows that the speaker is in a position of power, it does not suggest a position of authority. Likewise, a well-argued case may effect its desired result, but argument presupposes a certain equality between
(40) speaker and listener.

Authoritative speech relies for its effect on the identity of the speaker, her or his relationship with the audience, and the audience's perception of the speaker. Coercion and persuasion may sup-
(45) port this relationship, as the listeners assume either that dire consequences will result from disobedience, or that there must be good reasons for obedience, reasons which could be given. But for us to see authority in action, both coercion
(50) and persuasion must remain in the background, occulted. If the listener demands a reason for a command or asks about the consequences of disobedience, the speaker's authority falters. At this point authority may give way to persuasion (if

the speaker argues in favor of the command), or (55) naked force (if the speaker threatens), or it may be reasserted by invoking the privileged, authoritative position of the speaker: "Because I said so!"

Alexander himself enjoyed many kinds of authority at different times: as acclaimed leader, (60) first among equals, of the Macedonians, as presider over the Treaty of Common Peace in Greece, as Great King in Persia, and as an earthly divinity at first to the Egyptians (who were used to such things) and later to many Greeks. Other (65) Macedonians also held authority, at various times, either by association with Alexander or according to their own abilities and positions.

14. Which one of the following most accurately states the central idea of the passage?

(A) Power and authority are the same thing, but are spoken of differently depending on whether the person exercising power is a political leader or not.

(B) Power is a kind of authority that comes from persuasive speech and the threat of coercive force.

(C) Authority is a kind of power that does not explicitly depend for its effect on persuasion or coercion.

(D) Alexander was unique among ancient kings in exercising power and authority, but his general Antipater was also powerful.

(E) Alexander exercised power among the Greeks, but relied on authority to govern Macedonians, Persians, and Egyptians.

15. The primary function of the second paragraph of the passage is to

(A) discuss the use of authority by Alexander the Great

(B) explore aspects of the concept of authority and its uneasy association with coercive power

(C) imply that without coercive power there is no authority

(D) criticize scholars who have suggested different definitions of authority

(E) suggest that a speaker's authority falters if listeners question it

Go on to next page ⟹

16. What does the author mean by the word "occulted" in Line 51?

    (A) expressed

    (B) understated

    (C) hidden

    (D) magical

    (E) accosted

17. According to the passage, what is the difference between power and authority?

    (A) Authority is a generic term for creating an effect through persuasion, while power involves coercive force.

    (B) Power is a generic term for the ability to make someone do something; authority is a particular form of power, the ability to command without explicit persuasion or coercion.

    (C) Authority is exercised by virtue of political office, while power requires military command.

    (D) Power exists in the eyes of the governed, while authority resides in the one employing it.

    (E) Power is a generic term for the ability to make someone do something; authority is a particular form of power, the ability to command by using both persuasion and coercion at the same time.

18. According to the passage, what happens when a listener questions a speaker's authority?

    (A) The speaker's authority becomes weaker, whereupon he can resort to persuasion or force, or reassert his authority by invoking his privileged position.

    (B) The speaker's power falters, but he retains authority as long as the conversation continues.

    (C) The listener and speaker change roles, with the listener becoming the one with access to authority.

    (D) The speaker necessarily has to rely on coercion to assert authority.

    (E) Both power and authority vanish from the relationship, which becomes one of mutual negotiation.

Go on to next page

Line   In 1897, the explosion of the *USS Maine* in the Havana harbor ignited a war between the United States and Spain over Cuba. The U.S. Navy had just constructed the *USS Oregon,* one of the first

(05) true battleships, and believed that this new ship was an important and necessary weapon in the ensuing conflict. But there was one problem — the *Oregon* was stationed in San Francisco, far from Cuba. The voyage around South America,

(10) more than 12,000 miles in all, gave the United States 67 days to worry whether or not their flagship could arrive in time.

    The Oregon eventually arrived and did play a pivotal role, but military strategists in the United

(15) States were left thinking: What would the U.S. Navy have done had it not been able to transport its ship quickly enough? What would happen in future conflicts if a more powerful enemy were to attack and there were no ships in the area to

(20) repulse them? The impossibility of sailing north of North America and the distance of the voyage around South America effectively divided the U.S. Naval forces into two fleets. Such a division was costly, inefficient, and ultimately less powerful

(25) than a fleet that could unify on demand. If the Oregon had been able to somehow pass through the Americas in a narrow point in Central America, the distance between the coasts could be cut by two-thirds.

    Two decades later, the questions were

(30) answered. The U.S. ships based in California and Hawaii who set out for Europe to transport soldiers to fight in World War I found their trips greatly shortened by a passage through the isthmus of Panama, which cut nearly a month off the

(35) trip from one ocean to the other. Since 1914, the Panama Canal has provided U.S. Naval forces with a guaranteed shortcut that has conferred a great tactical advantage in all interocean conflicts.

    In addition to its role in ensuring security, the

(40) Panama Canal bears enormous economic significance for the United States and the world market. More than 100 million tons of U.S. cargo passes through the Canal every year, comprising 14 percent of American international seaborne trade.

(45) Japan, the second heaviest user of the Canal, receives the most of its grain imports and sends the majority of its automobile exports through the Canal. The relative importance of this trade route is even greater for many South American

(50) economies; more than 50 percent of Ecuadorian international trade passes through the Canal, as does more than 40 percent for Chile and Peru. The Canal, by drastically reducing the distance cargo must travel, allows merchants to profit

(55) from shipments that would not be economically feasible if sent by another route.

19. Which one of the following most accurately expresses the main point of the passage?

(A) Before the Panama Canal was built, it took more than two months to move a navy ship from California to the Atlantic; after the Canal was opened, the same trip took about one month.

(B) During World War I, the U.S. Navy quickly learned to exploit their new passage through the isthmus of Panama, which made it easy for them to transport troops from the west coast and Hawaii to the European theatre of war.

(C) The Spanish-American War was the impetus that persuaded the Roosevelt administration to construct the Panama Canal, intended to be a marine shortcut between the Atlantic and Pacific Oceans.

(D) The Panama Canal is important to the military, but its real significance is economic, especially for nations in South America.

(E) The Panama Canal, built as a result of military strategists worried about transporting Navy ships from one ocean to another, not only expedited military transport but also made it easier to move cargo between the oceans, opening a wealth of economic opportunities.

Go on to next page ⟩

20. According to the passage, what was the logistical problem that inspired the construction of the Panama Canal?

    (A) The U.S. Navy could not realistically build enough ships to man fleets in both the Atlantic and the Pacific oceans.

    (B) U.S. merchants on the east coast could not profitably sell their goods to markets on the Pacific because it was too expensive and time-consuming to ship them there.

    (C) Spain launched an attack on U.S. forces in Cuba by destroying a U.S. ship in the Havana harbor and the U.S. Navy did not know if the *USS Oregon* would reach Cuba in time to fight.

    (D) Without the canal, the only way to transport boats from the Atlantic to the Pacific was to sail them around the entire continent of South American, which took more than two months.

    (E) After the Spanish destroyed the *USS Maine* in 1897, the U.S. Navy had no major ship in the Atlantic to offer a counterattack to the massive Spanish presence near Cuba.

21. What does the author mean by the phrase "effectively divided the U.S. Naval forces into two fleets" in Lines 22 and 23?

    (A) The commanders of the U.S. Navy wanted to keep half their ships in the Pacific and half in the Atlantic in order to have fleets in both oceans all the time.

    (B) The U.S. Navy was unable to use all of its ships in the same conflicts because it took far too long to sail ships from the Atlantic to the Pacific and vice versa.

    (C) Ships based in the Pacific could not sail around South America in time to play effective roles in conflicts in the Atlantic.

    (D) The U.S. Navy had intended the *USS Maine* to be the flagship of its Atlantic fleet, and when it was destroyed in Cuba in 1897, the Navy had great difficulty moving its Pacific battleship, the *USS Oregon,* into the Atlantic.

    (E) The Navy built all of its battleships, such as the *USS Oregon,* in California, on the assumption that the Pacific theatre would have more need of battleships than the Atlantic theatre.

22. What does the author imply might have happened if the *USS Oregon* had not arrived in Cuba in time?

    (A) The Panama Canal might not have been built.

    (B) American ships other than the *USS Maine* could have been destroyed.

    (C) Spain could have won the fight for Cuba.

    (D) San Francisco might have been left without a ship to defend it.

    (E) The Navy might not have had a chance to test out its new battleship.

23. The passage mentions each one of the following functions of the Panama Canal EXCEPT:

    (A) It has transformed Panama into a major player in world trade.

    (B) Fourteen percent of U.S. seaborne trade passes through the canal.

    (C) Japan imports most of its grain and exports most of its automobiles through the canal.

    (D) The U.S. Navy uses it to transport ships from the Atlantic to the Pacific and vice versa.

    (E) It facilitates a large proportion of the trade of several South American nations.

Go on to next page

24. The primary purpose of the second paragraph is to

(A) analyze the thinking of military strategists who worried about what would have happened had the *USS Oregon* not reached Cuba in time and what might happen in future conflicts if there were no battleships in the immediate vicinity of an act of foreign aggression

(B) explain the role of the *USS Oregon* in the war with Spain over Cuba and the effects of its performance on the thinking of military strategists

(C) weigh the costs and benefits of travel through the Panama Canal and compare them to those of sailing around South America

(D) discuss various possible alternatives to the construction of the Panama Canal that the U.S. military strategists considered at the time, such as sailing north of North America

(E) describe the drawbacks of sending ships around South American and the reasoning that led to the decision to build the Panama Canal

25. Which one of the following is most likely the author's overall purpose in the passage?

(A) to argue that the U.S. Navy was severely hampered by the geographical necessity of sailing around South America before the building of the Panama Canal, and that the United States was therefore justified in digging a canal through a foreign nation

(B) to describe the history behind the construction of the Panama Canal and the canal's importance to world trade and the U.S. military

(C) to present the history of the founding and creation of the Panama Canal as an illustration of American exercise of imperial power in the early 20th century

(D) to tell the story of the military's role in the construction of the Panama Canal and the Panama Canal's subsequent role as a facility used by both military and commercial shipping concerns

(E) to explain why the explosion of the *USS Maine* in 1897 was the precipitating event in the design and construction of the Panama Canal

STOP You may check your work on this section only. Do not go back to any previous section.

Section IV

Time: 35 minutes

24 Questions

Directions: Read the passage and choose the best answer. Some questions may have more than one answer that looks right. Select the one that answers the question most completely. Don't assume anything that isn't directly stated, and don't let your imagination run wild; all the information you need is in the arguments and the answer choices.

1. Curmudgeon: Why should I have to pay taxes for public schools? I don't have children who can attend those schools, so I shouldn't have to pay for something that can never benefit me.

   Which one of the following is an assumption required by the curmudgeon's argument?

   (A) In a democracy, it is essential that all citizens have at least a basic education to enable them to choose candidates and vote intelligently.

   (B) People who do not have children attending public schools cannot benefit in any way from the existence of public schools.

   (C) People who do have children in public schools are reaping an undeserved benefit from the tax dollars of other citizens.

   (D) It is in the interest of the state to encourage people to have children because these children form the next generation of citizens.

   (E) It is much cheaper to pay for 12 years of education for a child than it is to pay for 12 years of incarceration for a convicted criminal.

2. Magazine: Scientists have found that people fall asleep faster when they go to bed with warm feet that cool off as they lie still, for instance if they warm their feet with socks before going to bed and then remove them when they lie down to sleep to let their feet cool off again. That means that anyone with insomnia should try wearing socks to bed.

   The reasoning in the magazine's argument is flawed because the argument

   (A) concludes without justification that the technique of warming feet and then letting them cool is a valid approach to preventing sleeplessness

   (B) implies that the same advice will work for all sufferers of insomnia, regardless of the cause

   (C) assumes that the research on warm feet that cool off leading to sleep is accurate because it came from scientists, without investigating the source of the information further

   (D) misinterprets the results of the research by failing to note that the sleep technique suggested by scientists requires the sleeper to remove the socks before trying to sleep in order to allow the feet to cool off

   (E) criticizes those suffering from insomnia for not taking well-known steps to solve their problem

Go on to next page

3. Everyone knows that mothers love their babies more than anything else in the world, and that mothers are the ones who should raise their children. No one can do the job of raising a child as well as that child's mother, so all mothers should stay home to care for their young children.

The reasoning in the argument is most vulnerable to criticism on the grounds that the argument

(A) discounts evidence indicating that not all mothers love their babies wholeheartedly

(B) fails to consider that many children thrive in daycare

(C) belittles the fact that many women have to work to help support their families

(D) is based on a generalization that is not supported with evidence

(E) suggests that fathers, grandparents, and other close relatives are inadequate caretakers

4. Researchers in Germany have discovered that dogs can understand human language quite well, comprehending a vocabulary as large as that understood by other intelligent animals such chimpanzees, dolphins, and parrots. Many dogs, such as the border collie named Rico, can understand more than 200 words and are capable of learning new ones.

If all of the statements above are true, which one of the following must also be true?

(A) Many dog owners spell words that their dogs recognize, such as *bath,* instead of saying them out loud because they know their dogs will understand the words and overreact.

(B) Dogs can learn words only if their human trainers consistently use the same words for the same objects.

(C) Intelligent animals such as chimpanzees are capable of understanding more than 200 words.

(D) Dogs in Germany understand more human words than dogs in other countries.

(E) Animal trainers use the same training methods and vocabulary when training various intelligent animals, including dogs, chimpanzees, dolphins, and parrots.

5. The recipe says to bake this pie for 40 minutes at 250 degrees. I can bake it in half the time if I double the temperature, so I'm going to bake it for 20 minutes at 500 degrees.

Which one of the following is most closely parallel in its flawed reasoning to the flawed reasoning in the argument above?

(A) The label on the aspirin bottle says to take one aspirin every four hours. My headache is very bad, so I'll take two aspirin every four hours.

(B) The directions on the bag of cat food say to give a nine-pound cat one cup of food every day. My cat weighs 13 pounds, so I'll give her one and a half cups of food every day.

(C) My neighbor wants me to give her plant one gallon of water every day. I won't have to water it as often if I give it more water each time, so I'm going to give it two gallons of water every other day.

(D) The hair highlighting kit says to leave the bleach on my hair for twenty minutes and then wash it out. I want my hair to be very blonde, so I'm going to leave the bleach on my hair for forty minutes.

(E) The express train goes twice as fast as the local train but costs twice as much. I want to reach my destination quickly, so I'll pay twice the price of the local train to ride the express.

Go on to next page

6. Businessman: It makes absolutely no sense for businesses to engage in charitable giving or socially conscious activities that do not maximize profits. The whole purpose of a business is to maximize profits for its owners and/or shareholders.

   The reasoning in the argument is most vulnerable to criticism because the argument fails to consider the possibility that

   (A) the IRS allows businesses to deduct some of the money they spend on charitable contributions

   (B) charitable giving can increase a business's goodwill, which can potentially increase profits

   (C) not every business owner believes that the single and entire purpose of the business is maximizing profits for owners and shareholders

   (D) an increasing number of investors seek out socially conscious mutual funds

   (E) some businesses that spend a good portion of their profits on charity still make a large profit overall

7. Nutritionist: The United States is currently facing an epidemic of obesity. Average weights have increased in all populations and at all ages. This is almost certainly due to the pervasiveness of fast food, which every citizen is consuming in larger quantities than two decades ago.

   Which one of the following, if true, would most call into question the nutritionist's explanation of the obesity epidemic?

   (A) Though average weights have increased, the weight gain has occurred exclusively among people who were already overweight; thin people have not gained weight, despite the fact that they, too, are consuming more fast food than was the case two decades ago.

   (B) The increase in average weights has reached down into populations of children, resulting in incidences of Type 2 Diabetes, which formerly was considered an exclusively adult disease, occurring in people under the age of 14.

   (C) Some nutritionists believe that some of the weight gain among Americans is due to the substitution of high fructose corn syrup for sugar in most soft drinks.

   (D) Many school districts have ended physical education programs in recent years, citing lack of funding and the need to spend most school time on academic subjects rather than sports and exercise.

   (E) At the same time as the overall population has grown heavier, the ideal of beauty has grown thinner, with near-anorexic young women setting an impossible standard of attractiveness.

Go on to next page

8. All human beings are primates. All primates are mammals. All mammals are vertebrates. Therefore all human beings are both mammals and vertebrates.

   Which one of the following arguments is most similar in its pattern of reasoning to the argument above?

   (A) All dogs are canines. All canines are mammals. All canines are vertebrates. Therefore dogs are both mammals and vertebrates.

   (B) All flies are insects. All insects are arthropods. All arthropods are invertebrates. Therefore all flies are both arthropods and invertebrates.

   (C) All whales are cetaceans. All cetaceans are mammals. All mammals have mammary glands. Therefore all whales have mammary glands.

   (D) All snails are mollusks. All mollusks have shells. All oysters are bivalves. All bivalves have shells. Therefore all creatures with shells are bivalves and mollusks.

   (E) All gorillas are primates. All chimpanzees are primates. All primates are vertebrates. Therefore all gorillas and chimpanzees are vertebrates.

9. Sergeant: Ordinarily all soldiers must obey all orders from their superiors. There is an exception, though; when a superior orders a soldier to commit an act that is against the law, then it is permissible for the soldier to refuse to carry out the order.

   Which one of the following judgments conforms most closely to the principle stated by the sergeant?

   (A) It is permissible for a soldier to refuse to obey an order to torture and abuse prisoners of war because that would violate national and international law.

   (B) It is permissible for a solder to refuse to obey an order to fire on the enemy because the soldier believes it would be immoral to kill other humans.

   (C) It is permissible for a soldier to refuse to obey an order stationing him in another country because he does not believe that the military should be in that country.

   (D) It is permissible for a soldier to refuse to obey an order to imprison an enemy soldier because the soldier believes that such imprisonment should be against the law.

   (E) It is permissible for a soldier to refuse to obey an order to bomb a town because the soldier knows that civilians would be among the casualties.

Go on to next page

10. Legal theorist: U.S. courts have struggled since the 1950s to define obscenity, and have for the most part failed to come up with a consistent definition that works reliably. In 1964 Justice Stewart summed up the difficulty of this problem by declining to suggest a definition but stating that for his part "I know it when I see it." Clearly it is impossible to come up with a suitable definition of obscenity, and it is therefore impossible for the states to regulate obscenity without violating the constitutional guarantee of free speech.

    To which one of the following principles does the legal theorist's commentary most closely conform?

    (A) Because it is impossible to define obscenity at the federal level, the states should create their own standards of decency tailored to local community preferences.

    (B) Because it is impossible to define obscenity, it is impossible to pass laws prohibiting it without violating the free speech rights of those producing the material.

    (C) The difficulty of defining obscenity is proof of the fact that courts and legislatures should not be involved in regulating speech of any kind.

    (D) States can create laws regulating obscenity by defining it as anything that appeals to "prurient interests" and is designed solely to incite lust in the people who read it or view it.

    (E) It is easier to define obscenity when children are involved, and the states should be encouraged to pass laws prohibiting child pornography.

11. No employer wants to face the liability it would incur if a drug-using employee made a serious mistake on the job. The best way to avoid this situation is require all employees to have their urine tested before hiring, and then to perform urine tests on all employees at random times. These urine tests help employers determine which of their employees are regular users of serious drugs such as cocaine, methamphetamines, heroin, and cocaine.

    The argument is vulnerable to criticism on all of the following grounds EXCEPT:

    (A) Testing a strand of hair is a much more reliable method of identifying those who use serious drugs regularly; residue of illicit drugs remains in hair for three months.

    (B) Urine tests cannot spot cocaine, heroin, or methamphetamines that were taken more than one or two days previously, so it is fairly easy for weekend drug users to avoid detection.

    (C) Drug testing costs the American workplace many millions every year and only catches a handful of people who have consumed less serious drugs such as marijuana.

    (D) Most consumers want to feel sure that the employees of businesses they patronize are not abusing serious drugs on the job.

    (E) It is easy for employees to cheat on urine tests by purchasing urine from businesses that sell it specifically to help people pass workplace drug tests.

Go on to next page

12. Albert, a careful shopper, bought a pair of shoes from a well-known catalog, choosing the catalog based on its guarantee. This guarantee stated that the seller would take back any item of merchandise and provide the buyer either a replacement item or a full refund, at any time and for any reason. Over the next twenty years, Albert acquired seven pairs of shoes from the catalog by returning the shoes whenever they wore out and requesting a replacement pair, and never paid for a pair of shoes other than the original pair. When his wife criticized him for taking advantage of the catalog company, he replied that he had done nothing wrong.

    Which one of the following principles, if established, most helps to justify Albert's position?

    (A) A buyer and a seller enter into an unwritten contract when the seller offers an item for sale and the buyer agrees to purchase it for the seller's stated price.

    (B) A customer should not take unfair advantage of a catalog's goodwill gesture, and should understand that an unconditional guarantee is not meant to be identical to a lifetime guarantee.

    (C) A seller should not make promises that it does not intend to keep, because there will always be customers who try to get the maximum value of every dollar by abusing sellers if necessary.

    (D) It is the seller's responsibility to set prices for its merchandise that are sufficient to cover its expenses and generate a profit.

    (E) A seller is obligated to observe the terms of the contract of sale, even if this works to the seller's own disadvantage.

13. Abelard: The city should provide more money for public schools. More money would allow the schools to hire more teachers and reduce class sizes from 30 to 25 children, which would result in a better education for all students.

    Heloise: I don't believe hiring more teachers and reducing class sizes will benefit students. Good teachers should be able to teach as many students as they are given. A class of 30 students isn't too large for a good teacher to handle.

    Which one of the following, if true, most undermines Heloise's objection to Abelard's analysis?

    (A) Schools in Japan typically have between 40 and 45 students per classroom, and the Japanese educational system is widely believed to be excellent.

    (B) A school district in another state reduced class sizes from 30 to 25 students; within a year average test scores had increased by 25%.

    (C) Teachers like smaller classes better than larger ones because smaller classes are easier to manage.

    (D) Many taxpayers want to spend as little as possible on public schools.

    (E) Private schools often limit classes to 18 or fewer students.

Go on to next page

14. In 2003, luggage belonging to 2.2 million passengers failed to arrive at the destination at the same time as the passenger. Travelers should never check their bags when they fly on commercial airlines.

Which one of the following, if true, most weakens the argument?

(A) Airlines advise passengers to pack a small carry-on bag containing essential medicines, eyeglasses or contact lenses, toiletries, and a change of clothes.

(B) When a traveler loses his luggage, he must sometimes hastily buy clothes for business meetings, resulting in great expense.

(C) It is not always possible to buy new clothes to replace those that were packed in lost luggage; for example, passengers who arrive at their destination during a national holiday might have to wait a day or two for shops to open.

(D) Most holiday travelers plan to shop at their destinations anyway, and losing luggage is a good excuse to buy new clothes.

(E) Despite the large number of lost bags, in fact airlines only lose the bags of 4 out of every 1000 passengers, so the odds of arriving without checked luggage are very low.

15. LASIK, or Laser-Assisted *In Situ* Keratomileusis, is a surgical procedure used to correct vision problems such as nearsightedness. In the procedure, a surgeon cuts a flap from the surface of the patient's cornea, uses a laser to reshape the middle portion of the cornea, and then replaces the flap. In most cases, LASIK can correct a patient's vision to near 20/20, eliminating the need for corrective lenses. Patients should be warned, though, that no doctor can guarantee a good result, and they do run the risk of side effects, including loss of vision, severe dry eyes, glare or haloes that impair night vision, and loss of depth perception.

Which one of the following is most strongly supported by the information above?

(A) Some patients who undergo LASIK find that they can no longer drive a car at night.

(B) It is very important that a prospective LASIK patient find a surgeon who is experienced in using the LASIK machinery.

(C) Patients who need reading glasses before undergoing LASIK often still need them after the procedure.

(D) Even if a patient achieves 20/20 vision after LASIK, his or her eyesight can still change with age, resulting in imperfect vision once again.

(E) LASIK is usually successful at improving a patient's vision, but it does not always result in perfect uncorrected eyesight and can create new problems for the patient.

Go on to next page

16. Brightly-lit high-rise buildings kill approximately one billion birds every year. The birds, flying on their migratory paths, become captivated by the lights in the building and fly toward them; they then either crash into the glass, which is invisible to them when interior lights are on, or they fly around and around the source of light until they are exhausted and tumble to the ground. On some mornings, janitors of high-rise buildings must shovel piles of dead birds from the sidewalk. A simple solution is very effective at combating this problem; if a building's residents simply turn off all interior lights at night, no birds will be attracted to it and die.

    If all the statements above are true, then which one of the following must be false?

    (A) Turning on the lights inside a building makes it easier for birds to see the glass windows and avoid flying into them.

    (B) Many tenants of high-rise office buildings habitually leave their interior lights and signs lit up all night.

    (C) In Chicago, two years after most tenants of high-rises agreed to turn off their lights at night, bird mortality fell by 80 percent.

    (D) Rare species such as Kirtland's warbler are vulnerable to running into lighted buildings, which will speed up the eventual extinction of the species.

    (E) Birds running into buildings is only a problem during the birds' migrations between their northern and southern territories, just a few weeks out of the year.

17. Americans today blame outsourcing of jobs to foreign countries for high unemployment today, complaining that companies are taking jobs from U.S. citizens and sending them to other nations where labor is less expensive. Statistics issued by the Labor Department, however, indicate that only 9 percent of layoffs are due to outsourcing, and of that 9 percent, nearly three-quarters of the jobs are moved to other locations within the United States, not to foreign nations.

    The statements above, if true, most strongly support which one of the following?

    (A) Americans who are laid off from their jobs are right to blame the government for encouraging businesses to look abroad for cheaper labor.

    (B) It makes sense for companies to relocate their factories overseas if the labor there costs much less than comparable labor in the United States; this maximizes profits, lowers prices, and provides opportunities for citizens in developing nations.

    (C) Outsourcing of jobs to foreign nations is an inevitable consequence of globalization, as are layoffs of American workers who do jobs that can be performed much more cheaply in other countries.

    (D) Outsourcing to foreign countries is not nearly as important a cause of layoffs as many Americans mistakenly believe.

    (E) Outsourcing of jobs to other locations within the United States does not disrupt the national economy but does benefit one local economy at the expense of another.

Go on to next page

18. In many nations throughout the world, child labor is still prevalent. In some countries, more than half of the children under 14 work full-time, often in dangerous conditions. This causes a cycle of poverty that is terrible for the economic development of the countries; child labor is the result of poverty, but it also causes poverty to continue.

Which one of the following, if true, contributes most to an explanation of the cycle of poverty described above?

(A) Without a social safety net, poverty-stricken families have no alternative but to send their children to work in menial jobs.

(B) Many developing nations do not have enough schools to educate all of the children born there, so parents choose to send their children to work instead.

(C) Girls who are forced to work as children tend to grow up with health problems that affect the health and prosperity of their own children.

(D) Children who work cannot go to school, and without an education they cannot get high-paying jobs as adults, so their own children are forced to work instead of attending school.

(E) In some developing nations, the middle and upper class depend on a plentiful supply of cheap servants, usually in the form of young girls from poor families.

19. California has passed a law that will require car manufacturers to drastically reduce the fossil-fuel emissions from automobiles in the next five years; these requirements are far stricter than those imposed by the federal government. Seven other states on both coasts have also passed laws ordering reduced emissions, and several others have announced plans to follow suit. This is excellent news for environmentalists, who praise these states' efforts to slow global warming.

Which one of the following is an assumption required by the argument?

(A) States on the coasts are more likely to be interested in environmental issues.

(B) Reducing fossil-fuel emissions will slow global warming.

(C) Car manufacturers could have reduced emissions long ago but did not because the law did not force them to.

(D) Individual states have environmental priorities that are different from those of the federal government.

(E) Environmentalists have lobbied car manufacturers to reduce emissions.

Go on to next page

20. Philip: Hybrid cars are the best response to the impending energy crisis. They are powered by a combination of gasoline and electric power; the gasoline engine recharges the battery when it runs, resulting in an extremely efficient use of fuel. They get excellent mileage, have good power, and are very comfortable.

Ryan: Instead of developing hybrid cars, car manufacturers should have kept making small, light, fuel-efficient gasoline-powered cars. Fuel-efficient cars from the 1970s got better gas mileage than today's hybrids, and did not come with the added burden of a complex battery that will inevitably become a problem when it comes time to dispose of it.

Ryan responds to Philip by

(A) denying the existence of the problem that hybrid cars are intended to ameliorate

(B) using an analogy to compare modern hybrid cars to fuel-efficient gasoline-powered cars from the 1970s

(C) challenging the validity of Philip's information

(D) arguing that an old technology was superior to a new technology that will probably result in heretofore unforeseen problems

(E) providing an example of a situation in which hybrid cars do not get good mileage

21. Legislator: Our state is deeply interested in maintaining the integrity of families. We believe families are the building blocks of our state, and we want to do everything we can to support them. In order to help families stay intact, we have designed a brochure that will be distributed to all new mothers and to girls and young women who seek birth control at publicly funded clinics. This brochure will emphasize the importance of the family and inform women that they should finish school, find a job, and get married before having children.

The reasoning above is flawed because it fails to recognize that

(A) many women do not want to be married

(B) no one reads pamphlets given by the state

(C) the main problem facing single mothers is lack of financial support from the fathers of their children

(D) families do not consist of only females, and if the state is to take measures to improve the family it needs to address men as well

(E) girls who are seeking birth control at publicly funded clinics are not the teenagers most likely to get pregnant

Go on to next page

22. Stuart and Steve each drove from Yokohama to Tokyo. Stuart drove his car. Steve drove a small motor scooter that could not go more than 25 kph. They both drove the same route, which had a speed limit for cars of 60 kph. Despite the fact that Stuart's car moved faster than Steve's scooter, they both arrived at their destination at the same time.

Which one of the following, if true, most helps to explain why Stuart and Steve arrived in Tokyo at the same time?

(A) Steve did not drive faster than 25 kph, but he did sometimes drive on the shoulder to pass stopped cars.

(B) The traffic between Tokyo and Yokohama was so bad that Stuart could not go faster than 25 kph.

(C) Stuart drove the speed limit when he could.

(D) Stuart and Steve could see one another on the road for most of the drive.

(E) Stuart had to stop at 74 red lights, and Steve had to stop at 68 red lights.

23. Judge: The defendant has admitted that he is prone to road rage, which is why he attacked the driver at the red light. In addition to a fine and community service, I am going to sentence the defendant to yoga classes, which will help him bring his anger under control and head off any future incidents such as this one.

Which one of the following is an assumption on which the judge's argument depends?

(A) Practitioners of yoga never attack fellow drivers.

(B) Fines and community service are not sufficient penalty for road rage.

(C) Yoga will be effective at helping the defendant control his anger, which will prevent him from experiencing outbursts of road rage in the future.

(D) It is improper for judges to introduce new penalties that are not an ordinary part of criminal sentencing.

(E) The defendant's road rage was justified but still inexcusable.

24. At least 29 million people used online matchmaking and dating services last year and that number is expected to increase in the near future, but such services come with several caveats. Far more men than women visit dating sites, which makes it easy for women to find partners but much harder for men. It's easy for users to lie and claim to be single when in fact they are not. The sites can't guarantee that no sexual predators will try to use the service. And because users must rely on the honesty of fellow participants in describing themselves, some hopeful daters receive unpleasant shocks when meeting their correspondents for the first time.

Which one of the following most accurately expresses the main conclusion of the argument?

(A) Women who use online dating services face much better odds than men of finding a partner.

(B) Online dating can be very dangerous because the dating services can't effectively bar sexual predators from participating.

(C) Despite the popularity of online dating services, participants should realize that such services come with many potential pitfalls.

(D) Online dating services should insist that no one who is married or otherwise attached to a partner participate in their programs.

(E) In the next five years, millions of people will seek out online matchmaking services, type in their personal data, send in photographs of themselves, and peruse the vital statistics of other people using the same service.

STOP You may check your work on this section only. Do not go back to any previous section.

Writing Sample

Two sisters are planning a horseback riding vacation in August between one sister's taking the MCAT and beginning the fall semester, which gives them two weeks to work with. They must choose between two trips, one in Ireland and one in the Dominican Republic. Write an essay in favor of choosing one destination over the other based on the following considerations:

- ✔ The sisters want to spend as many days as possible riding horses.
- ✔ The sisters want to improve their riding skills through instruction by qualified teachers.

The riding vacation in Ireland would place the sisters on fine, well-trained horses in the hands of excellent riding instructors. Every morning the sisters would spend two hours in the ring, working on equitation skills and jumping, and then every afternoon they would go for a trail ride through the countryside. They could expect their riding skills to improve a great deal, although they would not have much free time to simply ride around on their horses. Due to price constraints and the pre-med sister's schedule, if the sisters go to Ireland they will be able to spend only one week there.

If the sisters choose the vacation in the Dominican Republic, the favorable exchange rate and cheaper air fares would allow them to stay for two weeks. They would ride horses every day with an experienced guide who would take them on trails in the mountains, through sugar cane fields, and on the beach. They would also be allowed to ride freely as much as they wanted. The guide in the Dominican Republic is not a qualified equitation teacher, and he would not instruct the sisters on riding technique beyond the basics of handling the horses safely.

STOP You may check your work on this section only.
Do not go back to any previous section.

Answer Key for Practice Exam 1

Section I	Section II	Section III	Section IV
1. C	1. D	1. D	1. B
2. C	2. C	2. A	2. D
3. C	3. D	3. E	3. D
4. B	4. C	4. B	4. C
5. C	5. A	5. A	5. C
6. E	6. C	6. C	6. C
7. D	7. D	7. E	7. A
8. E	8. A	8. B	8. B
9. D	9. E	9. E	9. A
10. A	10. B	10. E	10. B
11. E	11. D	11. A	11. D
12. D	12. C	12. E	12. E
13. B	13. D	13. C	13. B
14. B	14. A	14. C	14. E
15. A	15. E	15. B	15. E
16. A	16. C	16. C	16. A
17. C	17. B	17. B	17. D
18. B	18. B	18. A	18. D
19. D	19. A	19. E	19. B
20. D	20. E	20. D	20. D
21. A	21. D	21. B	21. D
22. C	22. E	22. C	22. B
23. E	23. A	23. A	23. C
24. D	24. D	24. E	24. C
25. C	25. C	25. B	
26. E			

Computing Your Score

Add up the total number of correct answers from each section; if you got everything right, you should have a raw score of 100.

Section I __

Section II __

Section III __

Section IV __

Now compare your raw score to the following chart. That would be your LSAT score if this were a real LSAT. It's not, so whatever you get on this test should just give you an idea of your abilities.

Raw Score	LSAT Score	Raw Score	LSAT Score	Raw Score	LSAT Score	Raw Score	LSAT Score
98-100	180	97	179	96	178	95	177
94	176	93	175	92	174	91	173
90	172	89	171	88	170	87	169
86	168	84-85	167	83	166	82	165
80-81	164	79	163	77-78	162	75-76	161
74	160	72-73	159	71	158	69-70	157
67-68	156	66	155	64-65	154	62-63	153
60-61	152	59	151	57-58	150	55-56	149
54	148	52-53	147	50-51	146	48-49	145
47	144	45-46	143	44	142	42-43	141
40-41	140	39	139	37-38	138	36	137
34-35	136	33	135	31-32	134	30	133
29	132	27-28	131	26	130	25	129
23-24	128	22	127	21	126	20	125
18-19	124	17	123	16	122	15	121
0-14	120						

On the real LSAT, there will be an extra experimental multiple-choice section thrown in the mix, but you can't identify it. It looks just like the rest, and it doesn't count toward your final score.

Wrong answers don't subtract from your raw score on the LSAT. So, if you run out of time, make sure you bubble in an answer for each question! You may get some right just by sheer luck!

Chapter 21

Practice Exam 1: Answers and Explanations

. . . .

*I*n this chapter, you can find the answers and explanations to the test in Chapter 20. This chapter doesn't contain sample answers for the Writing Sample, mainly because there would be no point; you need to practice writing for yourself, and I don't want you to mistakenly think there's some "perfect" essay. Besides, it's not scored, anyway.

Section 1

If you like to work these problems by picking your favorite one first, the best criterion for choosing a favorite is number of questions — the problem with the most questions had the most points attached to it. Assessing a problem's difficulty is nearly impossible before you start, and often the problems that look hard initially turn out to be easy. Maximize your investment of time — pick a problem with seven questions before you work one with only five.

<u>Questions 1–7</u>

Think about what you know from the related facts in the problem. You know that every guy plays once. You know that the same pair of guys can't play together more than once. You don't know how many games the fraternity will play; that depends on who gets paired with whom.

This game doesn't really lend itself to a set diagram; there are too many possible scenarios to draw them all out. But that doesn't mean you can't make yourself some concrete notes and at least start diagramming possibilities — that's just part of your pre-question preparation. Start your notes by abbreviating all the guys: B, C, D, M, and T. You could try jotting down all the players and drawing lines between them, showing who does and doesn't play together, but that would get awfully complicated.

Jot down the rules in shorthand and try to make some deductions. Use arrows or something similar to mark down who plays with whom. See Chapter 4 for more information on that, and Chapter 5 for some examples.

If B -> M, B x> C

If -> D, -> M

T -> |

D x> M

Now, what can you deduce? Well, if T can play only one game, then he can't ever play with D, because that requires him to play another game with M. You could write that T x> D. Otherwise it looks as if T could play with B, C, or M. Create some quick lists to look at your possibilities.

How many games can B play? Three is the maximum. B could play with both D and M, which would eliminate C, and then partner B with T for T's sole game. If B plays those three games, then C would have to play a game with either M or with both D and M. Those possibilities are charted as #1 and #2. What about C? Well, C could potentially team up with each of the other players. But if he did that, then each of them would play one and only one game and C would play four. Why? If C plays with B, then B can't play with either D or M because that violates a rule. If C plays with D, he must play with M. D and M can't play together, T can play only once, and there aren't any other possibilities. Look at list #3 to see that scenario. What about D? Well, D can't play with either T or M, which leaves B and C, so D can play two games at most. How many games could M play? M can't play with D, but he can play with B, C, and T, so he functions similarly to B. If D and M maximize their games, you could have a scenario like that drawn in List #5.

Lo and behold, this can actually turn into a decent diagram; you have several possible scenarios pairing players with one another. Be aware that this might not be all possible scenarios (okay, it isn't); this is enough for you to work with, though, and you want to get going on the questions.

#1	#2	#3	#4	#5
B D	B D	B C	C B	D B
B M	B M	B T	C M	D C
B T	B T	C D	C T	M B
C D	C M	C M	C D	M C
C M				M T

1. **(C).** Look for rule violations and eliminate wrong answers. First and easiest: Look for any answers that have Trip playing more than once, which eliminates (D). Next, look for any answers that have Biff playing with both Marc and Chas; that knocks out (A). Now, does an answer have Deke and Marc playing together? Yes, (B) does, so cross it off. Last, does a choice have someone playing with Deke but not with Marc? Yep. (E) has Deke playing with Trip, which is clearly impossible. That leaves (C); run through it to make sure it works. It has Biff playing with Chas but not with Marc, so that's fine. Trip plays once, with an allowable partner. Chas plays with both Deke and Marc. It all checks out, so (C) is correct.

2. **(C).** If you already did the deductions in the previous diagram, you're ahead of the game here, and getting to the right answer is short and sweet. You already know the largest possible number of pairs is five, (C).

If you haven't gotten this far yet, then here's your opportunity to get to work. Try to come up with a scenario that gives you the largest possible number. Try pairing Biff with Deke, which requires Biff to play a game with Marc as well. If Biff plays with Marc, then he can't play with Chas, so that's out, but he can still play with Trip. Now Chas has to play with someone; he can't play with Biff or Trip, but he can play with Deke and Marc. That gives you Biff paired with Deke, Marc, and Trip, and Chas paired with Deke and Marc, which is five pairings, and no more possibilities there because Trip can't play more than once, and Deke can't play with Marc. That's possibility #1 in your diagram. Can you improve on that? Try pairing Biff with

Deke and Marc. Then you can have Chas play with Deke and Marc as well, and let Trip play with Marc. That still gives you only five pairs — scenario #4 in the diagram. If you pair Chas with Biff, then you end up with only four pairs: Biff with Chas and possibly Trip, and Chas with Deke and Marc, and Trip if Biff doesn't pair with him; that's even worse — look at list # 3. The only way to maximize pairings is to have at least two players both play with Deke and Marc; the only way to do so is if both Biff and Chas pair with Deke and Marc, and that leaves Trip to make a fifth pair. Five is the maximum number of pairs of players, so the answer is (C).

3. **(C).** Test the possibilities. If Biff and Chas play together, then Trip can play with Marc, which leaves Deke with no partner because he can't pair up with either Trip or Marc, so (A) is wrong. If Biff plays with Marc, then Chas could play with Trip but that would once again leave Deke out in the cold. Chas can't play with Deke without also playing with Marc, which would be impossible, so (B) is wrong. If Biff and Trip play together, then Chas could play with Deke and Marc. That would work, giving everyone at least one game and violating no rules, so (C) could be right. If Chas and Marc play together, you once again run into the Deke rule; no one can play with Deke without also playing with Marc, so (D) is impossible. If Marc and Trip play together, that causes the same problem — anyone who plays with Deke must also play a game with Marc, so (E) is wrong. (C) is the correct answer.

4. **(B).** The quick approach to answering this question is to look at the lists you made in preparing to work this problem. Look at Lists #1 and #2, each of which has Biff playing three games. (B), Chas and Deke, is the only answer that could work according to either of those lists, so it must be right.

   Here's a more detailed explanation: In order for Biff to play three games, he must play with Deke and Marc, which means he can't play with Chas, so he must also play with Trip. You can eliminate (A) immediately because Biff and Chas can't play together. You can also eliminate any choice that has Trip playing with someone other than Biff, which knocks out (C), (D), and (E). That leaves (B). Double-checking, it would be perfectly acceptable for Chas to play games with both Deke and Marc, so (B) is fine. (Wasn't that easier than you thought it would be?)

5. **(C).** Before you started on the questions, you worked out which player can pair up with the other four players: Only Chas can do this, and if he does, no one else gets to play more than once. That means (C) is the only possible answer.

6. **(E).** You also worked this one out before embarking on the problems. Remember that Trip can play only one game, and anyone who plays with Deke is committed to playing a game with Marc, too; that means Trip can never play a game with Deke. The answer is (E).

7. **(D).** For this to work, Chas must play with both Deke and Marc. Then either Chas or Marc could play with Trip. That means Marc must play with both Chas and Biff, and Chas must play with both Marc and Deke. Deke can't play with Trip or Biff, so Deke can play only one game. Chas and Marc each play either two or three games; one of them plays two, and the other plays three, but you can't tell which one from the given information. That means the correct answer is (D). The diagram of the two possible arrangements looks like this:

Scenario #1   Scenario #2

B M   B M

C D   C D

C M   C M

C T   M T

Questions 8–12

Well, this pattern looks fairly straightforward — all you have to do is put the horses in order. First, write out your numbers, 1 to 6, to mark the places of the horse participants. Now abbreviate the horses: m, g, and p, for mares, geldings, and ponies. Write in what you know about their placement, marking the positions that must or must not contain particular horses:

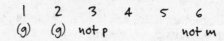

That's your permanent diagram. Be sure you give yourself a little room under it to jot down possibilities.

Instead of writing "not p" for the third horse, you could also write a "p" with an x through it, or write in the horses that could occupy that spot (g, m). How you write your notes doesn't matter as long as it doesn't take long and it makes sense to you.

Now think a moment. If the third horse can't be a pony, then it must be a gelding or a mare. If the sixth horse can't be a mare, it must be a gelding or a pony. Now remember that the wrangler can't put two horses of the same type next to each other. For example, it means that the first and second horses can't both be geldings, and so positions 3 to 6 must contain one gelding. This rule affects all your computations, so keep it at the front of your brain and be sure to give it a prominent place in your diagram. You could note this: 3-6 = 1 gelding. You could develop more possibilities now, but you don't really need to as long as you have your rules where you need them.

8. **(E).** The most straightforward approach to this question is simply to plug in each possibility. Try (A). If the first horse is a pony, then the second one must be a gelding, and the third must be a mare; if the sixth horse is a gelding, then the fourth can be a pony and the fifth a mare (pony, gelding, mare, pony, mare, gelding). That works. Now (B). You can do that one m, g, m, p, g, p. That works. Try (C). It works fine if you just used the same order that worked in (A). The same thing goes for (D). That leaves (E), but try it out anyway just in case. If the fifth horse is a pony, then the last one must be a gelding because it can't be a mare. The fourth horse must be a mare because it's next to a pony and you need your other gelding for one of the first two slots. Then you run into a problem: The third horse can't be a pony because of the rules, it can't be a mare because it would be next to a mare, and it can't be a gelding because you already used your spare gelding. The fifth horse can't be a pony, so (E) is your answer.

9. **(D).** Okay, if the third and fifth horses are the same type, what must they be? They can't be ponies because the third horse can't be a pony. They can't be geldings, because you have only one gelding to use in the last four spots. So they must be mares. Your answer must be (D). The other answers all could be true, but they don't have to be; work them out if you want to.

10. **(A).** This question is easy, or it should be if your diagram looks right and you understand the rules. If the third horse is a gelding, then what happens to the lineup? You know the first or second horse must be a gelding; you know a gelding can't be next to another gelding; and you know the third horse is a gelding, so the first horse must be the other gelding. That's (A). You can test the other answers if you want, but (A) is the only one that must be true.

If you have perfectionist tendencies, be careful to not overwork a problem. After you know a solid "fact," check the choices to see if you can already answer the question. Do yourself a favor and save time by not squeezing every last possibility out of a question before looking at the choices.

Did that seem too easy? Don't let it get to you. If a question seems absurdly easy, there's a good chance that it really is. That's not a problem and it's nothing to worry about.

11. **(E).** You could plug the same horse into all those pairs and see what you get, but there's a faster way to work this one. Look at your diagram. You know the third horse can't be a pony, and you know the sixth horse can't be a mare. You also know they both can't be geldings, because you need one gelding to occupy the first or second position. So there's no way the third and sixth horses can be the same type. That's (E).

If you want to test the possibilities, do it this way: Make both members of the pair the same kind of horse and see if they work out. First (A): You already know that both the first and third horses can be geldings (see Question 10), so that's wrong. Try (B). If you make the first and fourth horses geldings, you could have the lineup gelding, pony, mare, gelding, mare, pony, which is legitimate. Now (C). If you make both the second and fourth horses ponies, you get gelding, pony, mare, pony, mare, gelding. That's fine. (You can also make them both geldings, but that would be overkill.) Try (D). You could have mare, pony, gelding, mare, pony, gelding, which is fine. Now (E). Make them both geldings; that leaves no gelding for the first or second spot, which doesn't work.

12. **(D).** Don't you hate it when the rules change? Still, though, just think of the poor wrangler. Anyway, here's how to work this one. In order to accommodate three ponies and still keep them separated from one another (pony rivalry?), you have to put one right in the middle, in position three or four; but you can't put a pony third, so it has to be fourth. Then you need a pony on either end. Toward the front, make the pony either first or second, as long as a gelding takes the other spot. In back, you have to put the third pony in the sixth position, at the end of the line. So the spots that must be occupied by ponies are the fourth and the sixth positions, choice (D).

You probably noticed that several of the answer choices included *second* but none included *first*. That wording may have confused you a bit, making you think that maybe you didn't understand the rules as well as you thought and maybe a pony did have to be second, though you sort of thought it could be first, too. It was supposed to confuse you. Don't let it — you're at least as smart as this test.

Questions 13–19

Wow, this problem is complicated! You have seven players, each of whom you have to match with one of three locations. The problem would be easier if it told you exactly how many people go to each tournament, but it doesn't. That number can change depending on who goes where.

When in doubt, always start with what you know. First, make your list of abbreviations. Your players are B, C, M, R, S, Y, and A. Your places will be f, l, and o. Make the places lowercase so you don't mix them up with people.

Now write the rules in shorthand. You could write them like this:

$$Y \neq f \text{ (this is the same as } Y = l \text{ or } o)$$

$$C = f$$

$$B = R$$

$$S \neq Y$$

$$M \neq Z$$

$$Zo = f$$

That's a lot to work with. You can start making some conclusions at this point. If twice as many people go to Fargo as go to Omaha, then there are two possibilities: Either one person goes to Omaha and two to Fargo, leaving four to go to Little Rock; or two people go to Omaha, four go to Fargo, and one goes to Little Rock. That's useful. Write that down in a little template, adding the very useful permanent information about C always going to Fargo and Y never going to Fargo:

f[C] _ (not Y)   f[C] _ _ _ (not Y)

l: _ _ _ _   l _

o _   o _ _

After you have this framework in place, plugging in possibilities is simple. You can make a few deductions just by looking at these diagrams. For example, if B and R must attend the same tournament, then their possible locations are quite limited. They can fit only into locations with at least two open slots, and even then you have to allow space for the people that have to be separated. So realistically, B and R can either attend the conference in Little Rock when it has four slots, or the conference in Fargo when it has four slots. That's good to know. (What about the two slots allocated to Omaha in the second scenario? B and R can't have them; you have two pairs of members that have to be split up — S and Y, and M and Z — and Little Rock has only one slot open, so you need an Omaha slot for one of those pairs.) Update the diagram with this info:

f[C] _ (not Y)   f[C] [B] [R] _ (not Y)

l [B] [R] _ _   l _

o _   o _ _

Now *that* is a diagram! And instead of an unlimited number of scenarios, you now have two discrete possibilities, each of which is nearly half complete. That's good. Get going on those questions.

When all's said and done, this problem actually isn't all that hard. After you get your information plugged into a workable diagram, spotting the correct answers is really pretty simple. And it has seven questions — a virtual bonanza of points. That's why choosing your problems based on the number of questions rather than apparent difficulty is better.

13. **(B).** How can Brunhild and Yorick attend the same tournament? They can do only that if they both attend the tournament in Little Rock; the other possibility is Fargo, but Yorick can't go to Fargo. That leaves one slot open in each of the cities to be occupied by Maev, Solomon, and Zilla. Now go through the answer choices and strike off the four that are impossible. (A) is wrong because Brunhild must be in Little Rock. (B) could be true; Maev could take the open slot in Fargo. (C) is wrong because Roxanne is with Brunhild in Little Rock. (D) is wrong because Solomon can't attend the same tournament as Yorick, and Yorick must be in Little Rock. (E) is wrong because Yorick must be in Little Rock. That leaves (B) as the only possible answer. The diagram could look like this:

f[C] M (not Y)

l [B] [R] Y _

o _ _

14. **(B).** You can eliminate several answers just by looking at your permanent diagram. (A) can't be true, because Roxanne can't attend a tournament without Brunhild. (C) is wrong because either two or four people must go to Fargo. (D) and (E) are wrong because there is no way that either two people could go to Little Rock or three to Fargo. So could (B) work? Yes, it's possible for the team to send only one member to Omaha, and there's no reason it can't be S. (B) is correct.

15. **(A).** You don't have to do much to figure out the answer to this one. If one member goes to Little Rock, then four go to Fargo and two to Omaha. Who has to go to Fargo in that scenario? Cayenne, Brunhild, and Roxanne. It looks like (A) is your answer. Skim the other choices anyway — they're all possible, but none of them is required by the rules. (A) is correct.

16. **(A).** Do the answers list anyone who can't go to Omaha? Yes, (A) includes Brunhild, who is always stuck with Roxanne and thus can never sample the delights of Nebraska's capital. Look over the other choices to see if anyone is prohibited from attending the Omaha tournament. They all look fine, and they're all pairs, which is certainly possible. (If any choice had three members, that would have been a dead giveaway wrong answer, but then the Brunhild answer would have to change.) So (A) is correct.

17. **(C).** You could jot down the answer choices into your diagram to see which one works, but there's a quicker way — look for rule violations. You don't have to bother with (A) or (B); Brunhild can't go to Omaha. (C) doesn't obviously violate anything yet, so skip it for the moment to see if (D) and (E) have clear problems. (D) does; Yorick can't go to Fargo. (E) doesn't work either because if Roxanne is in Fargo, Brunhild must be, and so must Cayenne because Cayenne always goes to Fargo. That leaves (C) as the only legal possibility. Test it out completely just to be sure. If you put Brunhild, Roxanne, Solomon, and Zilla in Little Rock, then Yorick can go to Omaha, and Maev can go to Fargo, which separates the incompatible people and keeps Yorick away from Fargo. That works, so (C) is right.

18. **(B).** Again, look for rule violations. (A) is wrong because Brunhild and Cayenne can attend the same tournament, and there's no reason why Maev can't attend with them (as long as they go to Fargo and Roxanne goes with them). (B) does have to be true; in the scenario in which four members go to Fargo, three of the slots are already spoken for by Cayenne, Brunhild, and Roxane, which doesn't leave room for both Yorick and Zilla to attend, too. Check the other answers just to be sure. All are possible, but none of them must be true. You can put Maev and her various partners together, but you can also separate them. (B) is correct.

19. **(D).** What's the first thing you know about the team members who don't go to Fargo? Their numbers: Either two people go to Fargo and five go elsewhere, or four go to Fargo and three go elsewhere. That means any answer that doesn't have either three or five choices is wrong; eliminate (A) and (B) now. (C), (D), and (E) all have three people listed, which means you're looking at the four-people-in-Fargo scenario, which means Cayenne, Brunhill, and Roxanne *must* go to Fargo. (C) and (E) are both wrong because they both include Roxanne. That leaves (D). Could (D) work? Sure. Send Zilla to Fargo, send Solomon to Little Rock, and send Yorick and Maev to Omaha and you've observed all rules. (D) is correct. The diagram could look like this:

$$f:[C]\ [B]\ [R]\ Z\ (not\ Y)$$

$$l: \underline{S}$$

$$o: \underline{Y}\ \underline{M}$$

Questions 20–26

What a weird ice cream parlor. I guess they line the big dish with bananas and then put the ice cream on top. And why don't the rules mention how many of the vanilla scoops get nuts, and all that other stuff you want to know?

They don't mention that stuff because that's what you're supposed to figure out. This problem has plenty of shifting players. You have to consider the five cups — that's your unchanging framework — your flavors, your toppings, and which is next to which. The flavors, toppings, and arrangements can change depending on what you put where.

So start with what you do know. You have five cups in a row, so write the numbers 1 through 5 across the page. You don't really know where the row begins or ends; that means you could number just as well from right to left as from left to right. It's totally arbitrary. Now next to these numbers (not below them — that's where you plug in data) write down your two sets of variables, (ice cream flavors and toppings). Doing so gives you something like this:

$$1 \quad 2 \quad 3 \quad 4 \quad 5 \qquad CCCVVVV$$
$$ssnnnnn$$

When you plug in possibilities, it'll probably be easier to write the flavors in one row and the toppings in another, below it. See the explanation for Question 21 for an example of how this diagram could look.

The rules don't give you any permanent homes for these ice creams or toppings. Either flavor of ice cream can get either topping. What you must remember to do is to account for every flavor and every topping. Every possible scenario must include four vanillas, three chocolates, two sprinkles, and five nuts. When you plug in data, if possible include both flavor and topping (for example, vanilla with sprinkles would be Vs, and chocolate with nuts would be Cn). Write the rules in shorthand, like this: Vn <-x-> Cs; no VC in same cup.

Before you start, think a little bit. You know every cup can hold up to two scoops. With only five cups and seven scoops, at least two cups will have two scoops. Does every cup need a scoop of ice cream in it? Not necessarily. You don't know how many teenagers are sharing this frozen monstrosity; maybe there are only four of them, and each one gets his or her choice in an individual cup, leaving one cup empty. Here's another thought: You can't mix flavors in one cup, but you can mix toppings. So you can put two scoops of vanilla in one cup, and top one with nuts and one with sprinkles.

This kind of problem can be tricky because developing a permanent drawing is impossible. Fret not, though; all you need to do is keep those rules in mind. This problem may be easier than you think.

20. **(D).** Look for obvious rule violations. (A) has three scoops in cup 5; no good. (B) has a vanilla with nuts in cup 2 next to a chocolate with sprinkles in cup 3; that doesn't work. (C) has three scoops with sprinkles; you can only have two, so that's wrong. (D) may be the answer; you have four vanillas, three chocolates, five nuts, two sprinkles, and you don't have either vanilla and chocolate intermingled in the same cup, or vanilla with nuts next to chocolate with sprinkles. That looks good. (E) has four scoops of chocolate, which is too many. (D) is the answer. Just as an example, here's how the diagram of (D) could look:

$$1 \quad 2 \quad 3 \quad 4 \quad 5$$
$$VV \quad CC \quad VV \quad C$$
$$nn \quad nn \quad ss \quad n$$

21. **(A).** First, note that you're looking for something that can't be false, which is another way of saying that it must be true. Now consider the answers. (A) looks correct right off the bat. If you have seven scoops of ice cream, and the most scoops you can put in the same cup is two, and three of those scoops are chocolate, and you can't put vanilla and chocolate in the

same cup, then inevitably at least one cup will contain nothing but one scoop of chocolate ice cream and its topping. That's an obvious correct answer, and you can save time by spotting it and moving on. Just for the sake of study, consider the other answers. Each of them is in fact possible, but doesn't necessarily have to be the case. This ice cream sundae is pretty flexible. Remember, an answer that COULD be true but isn't necessarily true isn't good enough; it MUST be true in order to be correct. (A) is correct.

22. **(C).** You already know the answer can't be (D) or (E). You run out of cups before distributing all seven scoops. (C), three, looks like a good answer; test it to see if it's possible. If you put two scoops of vanilla with nuts in cups 1 and 2, then a scoop of chocolate with nuts in cup 3, followed by single scoops of chocolate with sprinkles in cups 4 and 5, that would give you three cups each containing exactly one scoop of ice cream. You don't need to bother with (A) and (B). (C) is correct.

23. **(E).** Think through this one first. If the third cup is empty, that leaves you only four cups to hold all seven scoops of ice cream. Because you have four scoops of vanilla, you're going to have to have two cups that each contain two scoops of vanilla, which leaves one cup with one scoop of chocolate, and one cup with two. In order to separate the two cups of vanilla, you have to put one on either side of cup three (either cup 1 or cup 2 will hold 2 scoops of vanilla, and cup 4 or cup 5 will hold the other two). The chocolate scoops will occupy the cups not occupied by vanilla. You won't be able to put sprinkles on a scoop of chocolate; there's no way you can avoid putting chocolate and vanilla in adjacent cups, and some of the vanilla must have nuts on it. Here's one way you could arrange the sundae:

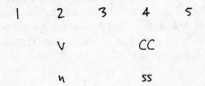

Now look at the answers. You're looking for something that isn't necessarily true, though it could possibly be. (A) is true; one cup contains one scoop of chocolate. (B) must be true; there's no way to arrange this sundae without putting a scoop of chocolate immediately next to a scoop of vanilla. (C) must be true; you can't put sprinkles on any of the chocolate scoops because they all have to be next to scoops of vanilla. (D) must be true. (E) is the only answer that doesn't have to be true. The vanilla scoops could be in the second and fourth cups, but they could also be in the first and fifth, or the first and fourth, or the second and fifth. (E) is the correct choice.

24. **(D).** Here's how your initial diagram could look:

```
      1    2    3    4    5

           V         CC

           n         ss
```

Test the possibilities. You're looking for a scenario that doesn't violate any rules; four of the choices do. Try (A). If you put chocolate with nuts in cup 1, then you have a problem because you have to put a vanilla with nuts in either cup 3 or cup 5, if not both, but both of them are adjacent to the chocolate with sprinkles in cup 4, so (A) doesn't work. (B) is just plain wrong, because vanilla is already in the second cup and you can't put chocolate there. (C) is also wrong, because that puts three scoops in one cup. Now (D); could you put a scoop of chocolate with nuts in cup 5? Sure, then you could fit two scoops of vanilla with nuts in both cups 1 and 2 and satisfy all the rules. (D) looks like your answer, but check (E) anyway. Could you put two scoops of ice cream in cup 5, like (E) suggests? No. The two scoops would have to be vanilla because you only have one scoop of chocolate left, and they would have to have nuts on them because the two orders of sprinkles have already been used up, and they would be next to chocolate with sprinkles, which is forbidden, so (E) must be false. (D) is correct. Here's how the diagram for (D) could look:

1	2	3	4	5
VV	VV		CC	C
nn	nn		ss	n

Another way to answer 24 is to incorporate the rules and deduce. As it happens, there is only one possible arrangement of the ice cream and toppings: 1: VnVn; 2: VnVn; 3: empty; 4: CsCs; 5: Cs. This question is easy once you figure that out!

25. **(C).** If each scoop of chocolate gets its own cup, then the four scoops of vanilla must occupy only two cups. The scoops of vanilla each have nuts on them, which means two of the scoops of chocolate have sprinkles on them, and therefore can't be next to vanilla. There's only one way to ensure that vanilla with nuts doesn't get put next to chocolate with sprinkles: Separate them with the one remaining scoop of chocolate, which must have nuts on it. That scoop of chocolate with nuts has to go in the center cup, cup 3. Then you could put the vanilla in cups 1 and 2 and the chocolate with sprinkles in cups 4 and 5; or the vanilla could go in cups 4 and 5 and the chocolate with sprinkles in cups 1 and 2. Cup 3 is the only place vanilla can't go, so the answer is (C). Here's the diagram:

1	2	3	4	5		1	2	3	4	5
C	C	C	VV	VV		VV	VV	C	C	C
s	s	n	nn	nn	OR	nn	nn	n	s	s

26. **(E).** Test these possibilities out on your diagram. All you really have to do is sketch in the contents of the first two cups and then mentally see if you can fill in the rest; you don't need to plot out the whole thing if you can see how to work it out easily. (Yes, I know I ordinarily say to diagram everything; in this case, though, it's quicker to run through the possibilities in your head, at least for most of the answers. If you get confused, though, by all means keep writing everything down. All I'm suggesting is that if you can work part of a problem mentally without getting confused and without hurting your accuracy, it's okay to do it and it will save you time.) Try (A). (A) works fine. If you put the sprinkles on two of the remaining three scoops of vanilla, distributing the rest of the ice cream would be easy. Now (B): This one is also easy, because all the sprinkles are on the vanilla, you don't run into pesky rules about neighboring scoops. And (C): You may actually want to draw this one out, because the answer allocates only one scoop of ice cream. This scenario works fine if you allocate the scoops like this: 1: empty; 2: Cn; 3: VsVs; 4: CnCn; 5: VnVn.

1	2	3	4	5
x	C	VV	CC	VV
x	n	ss	nn	nn

Now try (D): Sure, (D) works. You don't have any chance of a chocolate with sprinkles being put next to a vanilla with nuts, so you can just distribute the rest of the scoops as you see fit. That leaves (E), which looks like this:

```
  1    2    3    4    5

       V    ×

       ×    ×
```

Uh oh. You run into a problem here. The problem isn't the sprinkles; you could put them on another scoop of vanilla. The problem is that you have three cups left and you need four: two for vanilla and two for chocolate. You have three scoops left of each of them, but because you can't put vanilla and chocolate together, you would have to have one cup with a single scoop of vanilla and one cup with a single scoop of chocolate. That's impossible with only three cups. (E) is your answer.

Section 11

1. **(D).** You want to weaken the argument. Tempest claims that her urns aren't 18th century, based on expert opinions, and therefore Christie's advertised them falsely. To weaken this conclusion, look for evidence that would suggest Christie's didn't advertise falsely. (A) doesn't work. The catalog does indeed say the urns are 18th century. (B) doesn't really address the issue of whether Christie's advertised the urns falsely. If it's difficult to date antiques accurately, it would be entirely possible for different experts to date the urns differently. (C) is of no use at all for strengthening or weakening Tempest's argument. (D) is a very good answer. If Christie's told Tempest upfront that she shouldn't rely exclusively on the claims in their catalog, then she can't blame the auction house if she didn't have her urns assessed before purchasing them. (E) is all very well for the experts, but still doesn't prove or disprove that Christie's lied. (D) is correct.

2. **(C).** This is a weaken question. The argument's conclusion is that those convicted of heinous crimes by juries deserve the death penalty, because bad criminals are incorrigible and the families of victims need them to die for closure. Note, though, that the conclusion says "anyone whom a jury convicts," which isn't necessarily the same thing as an "extreme criminal." What if someone is convicted wrongly? (A) doesn't weaken the argument. The author uses family feelings as evidence to support the conclusion. (B) is an advantage of using the death penalty, and doesn't hurt the argument. Cost, by the way, doesn't enter into the argument at all. (C) does weaken it. If large numbers of convicts are in fact innocent, then they're not incorrigible extreme criminals, and don't deserve to be executed. (D) is evidence of how pleasant the death penalty can be, and doesn't hurt the argument. (E) likewise doesn't harm the author's point. If many states are increasing executions, it must be popular. (C) is the only choice that weakens the argument.

3. **(D).** What's wrong with this argument? It suggests that there's no point in attending any law school that's not in the top ten, because those are the only schools that lead to jobs in high-paying firms. So, is that the only reason to go to law school? (A) is wrong because the argument doesn't promise anything. (B) doesn't work because the argument doesn't address quality of education. (C) is wrong because nothing in the argument implies that the author thinks top firm recruiting practices are good or bad — there aren't any value judgments here, so you can't attack them. (D) is your answer. Surely some people can think of reasons to attend law school that go beyond finding a job in a top-ranking law firm. (E) isn't true. You can't identify any misrepresentation based on the information contained in this argument. (D) is correct.

4. **(C).** The exterminator's conclusion is that there will probably not be an outbreak of West Nile virus this summer, based on the fact that no one has found dead birds carrying the virus. That would only be good evidence if the virus almost always appears in birds before attacking humans, so that's the assumption you're looking for. (A) doesn't work because it doesn't

quite address the point; the fact that birds are more susceptible to dying from West Nile doesn't do anything to further the exterminator's conclusion. (B) doesn't establish a connection between virus, birds, and humans. (C) is a good answer. If birds are an indicator species, and the virus hasn't killed any birds yet, that would be good evidence that an outbreak among humans is unlikely. (D) is confusing because it looks as if it could be possible to have human West Nile without first spotting the virus in birds, though it would be odd, and that would fit with the exterminator's argument, but that doesn't really lead from the evidence to the conclusion the way (C) does. (E) is kind of random; the effect of insecticide on birds isn't the point at all. (C) is the correct answer.

5. **(A).** The editorialist argues that stem cell research could be beneficial and that it's not akin to abortion because stem cells aren't embryos. (A) looks like a statement she would agree with. (B) is the opposite of what the editorialist thinks; she claims that stem cells aren't and can never be embryos. (C) may be something the editorialist would agree with, but she doesn't say in her argument that religious groups have no business influencing legislation. (D) is wrong because the editorialist never suggests banning research on a particular type of stem cells. (E) is also wrong; the editorialist believes the benefits of the research are such that the research should be legal. (A) is correct.

6. **(C).** Some scientific evidence — DNA or something like that — proving conclusively that the heart was Louis XVII's would support the argument. (A) doesn't necessarily help; an imposter's heart could have been removed and preserved to fool Louis's enemies. (B) is scientific evidence and it tells you the age and sex of the heart's owner, but it doesn't tell you who he was. (C) supports the argument. If Louis's mother and the heart have the same DNA, that would be scientific proof of the heart's identify. (D) is an interesting factoid but doesn't establish that the heart belonged to Louis. (E) could be evidence that the heart belonged to a child who died in prison, but doesn't prove who that child was. (C) is the best support for the conclusion.

7. **(D).** Emilio and Julienne disagree about whether early specialization in youth sports is beneficial or harmful to children. Only Julienne mentions teamwork, leadership, and enjoyment of sports, which eliminates (A) and (B) as bones of contention. They both seem to think that kids should play sports, so (C) is out, and they don't discuss an age below which play sports at all, so (E) is out. (D) looks like the answer; Emilio thinks early specialization is good, and Julienne thinks it's bad.

8. **(A).** Okay, if food at 0° lasts a year, food at 5° should last six months and food at 10° should last three months. That looks like (A). (B) isn't necessary to the argument, though it might be true. The argument doesn't address taste, only safety, so (C) doesn't work. (D) isn't a necessary implication of the argument as presented. It may be true, but nothing in the argument tells you anything about commercial freezers. Likewise (E) — no information tells you about how long most people keep food in their freezers. (A) is best.

9. **(E).** The pattern goes like this: mollusk = deep; deep = predator; mollusk = predator. You could rewrite that A = B; B = C; A = C. (A) goes like this: Enthusiast finds studio; studio = good instructors; enthusiast finds good instructors. That's not quite the same. (B) goes player = Croatia; most Croatian players = tall and hardworking; player = probably tall and hardworking. This choice is very close but it isn't right. The topic of the first sentence is "mollusk" and the topic of the second sentence is "all animals"; (B) would work only if the second sentence started with a larger category, such as "all Croatians," but making it "all Croatian basketball players" makes it too specific. See if you can find a better answer. (C) goes like this: tomato = garden; tomato = nightshade; tomato = nightshade. That's not much of a conclusion. (D) is like this: perfect sapphire; sapphire = hard and durable; perfect sapphire = hard and durable. That just restates the obvious. (E) goes: cactus = desert; desert = efficient with water; cactus = efficient with water. That duplicates the pattern stated in the argument, so (E) is correct.

10. **(B).** Look for an answer that involves someone choosing one battle out of several possible ones and winning it. (A) is no good because the sister doesn't pick her battle and never gets her brother to fill the tank. (B) looks like a good choice. The wife chooses one task out of several and manages to get her husband to do the job she cares about most. (C) illustrates the

dangers of trying to fight two battles at once, so it's wrong. (D) is an example of someone not fighting a battle at all and running away instead. (E) doesn't really fit at all, because there's no real choice of battles. (B) is the best answer.

11. **(D).** Look for an answer that shows why people who spend little on food get fat. Make sure there's a connection between money and food. (A) is just a truism and explains nothing. (B) is a possibility but doesn't really work because not understanding the rules of nutrition could just as easily lead to starvation. (C) doesn't focus on poor people so it doesn't explain why they in particular are malnourished and obese. (D) does resolve the paradox. If the food they can afford is full of calories, it'll make them fat, and if it's devoid of nutrients, it can hurt their nutrition. (E) doesn't address poor people, so it doesn't work. (D) is the answer.

12. **(C).** The reasoning goes like this: Most players = male; manufacturers shouldn't bother with females. (A) goes: most cyclists = male; manufacturers should concentrate on males. That's not right. (B) goes: most Americans = cell phones; most Americans shouldn't bother with landlines. That's not right. (C) goes: most users = Windows; producers shouldn't bother with MacIntosh. That looks right. (D) goes: most lawyers = glasses; optometrists should bother with lawyers. That's wrong. (E) goes: Labs = easy to train; person who wants obedient dog should consider Labs. That doesn't work. (C) is correct.

13. **(D).** You're looking for an assumption. The conclusion is that if drivers can't talk on cell phones, the roads will be safer; that means the author thinks the use of cell phones by drivers makes the roads dangerous because those drivers are distracted. (Yes, that's obvious, but the author doesn't explicitly say what the connection is, so it's an assumption.) (A) is tricky and looks like it could be the right answer but it's not. The legislator's argument doesn't depend on one particular study by a sociologist — which would be a very specific assumption that would be fairly unusual for someone to make. See if you can find a better answer. (B) is wrong; obviously the author does assume that this is the legislature's job, but it's not really the main point and doesn't specifically connect cell phone use with danger. (C) doesn't work; the author isn't concerned with distinctions between types of cell phones. (D) is something the author assumes — it explains the connection between cell phones and distracted drivers and dangerous roads. This is a better answer than (A) because it's a more reasonable assumption and fits the total argument better; (A) focuses on occasional wrecks, but (D) gets right to the point of overall road safety. (E) distracts attention from the author's point about cell phones; yes, those other behaviors can also distract drivers, but he's talking about phones exclusively. (D) is the right answer.

14. **(A).** The partner draws a direct correlation between time spent on a task and quality of work, which isn't in fact a foregone conclusion. (A) looks like a good answer. The partner's reasoning is flawed because he's assuming the work that took longer is better without reading the briefs to compare them. (B) is wrong. He's not criticizing attorney B and if anything is happy with her performance. (C) doesn't work because the partner does explain why he thinks attorney B's brief is better. (D) doesn't quite work because this argument isn't about keeping track of time as a concept. (E) is irrelevant. (A) is correct.

15. **(E).** The student assumes that because most ants don't have wings, ants as a group can't be insects. The flaw is that he reasons backwards, thinking that if all members of a species don't fit all of a group's characteristics, then the species can't belong to that group. (A) is wrong because he admits that some ants do have wings. He gets the definition of an insect right, so (B) is wrong. (C) is just more detail about insects; adding those details doesn't affect the flaw in his reasoning. (D) doesn't work because he doesn't mention the significance of wings to ants. (E) is the best answer.

16. **(C).** Ah, the more you spend the more you save; or, maybe the more you spend the more you spend. Spending money, even at a discount, is spending, not saving. (A) is wrong. All the merchandise is 25 percent off, so the speaker isn't wrong about that. She makes no mistake about percentage of savings, so (B) is wrong. (C) is an area in which she is vulnerable to criticism; she doesn't save anything if she spends money. (She may get better prices on items she would have bought anyway, thereby paying less than she might have, but she's still spending, not saving.) (D) and (E) don't work because the reasons for the sale aren't relevant here. (C) is correct.

17. **(B).** Christina thinks consumer-driven health plans save money and Guthrie disagrees. Christina thinks these plans help because they'll keep people from going to the doctor more than they need to, while Guthrie isn't so sure that's the problem. (A) doesn't enter into the conversation so you don't know whether they agree or disagree about it. (B) looks like a good possibility; they do disagree on whether patient behavior is the main reason for rising costs. (C) can't work because they don't discuss business sizes. (D) is an area where they do agree; they both think high deductibles will keep people away from the doctor. (E) isn't the point at all and Guthrie doesn't mention it. (B) is correct.

18. **(B).** The argument concludes that meaning of language often derives from context, and that people may not recognize simple concepts out of context. (A), though possibly true, isn't the conclusion. The speaker isn't debating the reliability of Internet information. (B) does look like the conclusion. (C) isn't really right because the speaker isn't giving advice but merely commenting on a phenomenon. (D) is wrong because the participants obviously do know about popular movies. (E) isn't the point at all; the argument isn't really about the names of perfumes, but about confusion of the meaning of words depending on context. (B) is correct.

19. **(A).** On the one hand, nitrox is safer than air. On the other, it's more dangerous than air. What's the difference? Note the last sentence, in which the divemaster describes nitrox's hazards. He says nitrox is dangerous "at depths that are safe for divers using air." So the apparent discrepancy must be due to nitrox's behavior at depths, and something about going deep makes it dangerous. (A) looks like a very good explanation for this phenomenon. If oxygen gets dangerous when compressed, that explains the nitrox hazards are at depths that don't make air especially hazardous. The divemaster never mentions anything about different behavior by nitrox divers, so you can't assume (B) or (C) is the explanation. (D) sounds like a real hazard but it's not specifically connected with nitrox use, because all divers face this risk. (E) would, if anything make nitrox sound even safer, and doesn't begin to explain why it's more dangerous than air in some circumstances. (A) is correct.

Did you eliminate answer choices you are sure are incorrect? Doing so helps you spot the right answer choice.

20. **(E).** The claim in question is a statement of fact in the first sentence that the speaker explores more thoroughly, concluding with the statement that it's a mistake. She's not suggesting that it's a good thing, so (A) and (D) are wrong. It's not evidence, so (B) is wrong. Her conclusion is that not taking vacation is a mistake, so (C) is wrong. It is a statement of fact and the speaker does try to argue that not taking vacation is bad practice, so (E) is correct.

21. **(D).** The author concludes that having classes taught by PhDs instead of instructors improves students' learning experiences, so she must assume that PhDs are somehow better at teaching than instructors. (A) isn't her assumption; in fact, it sounds as if the university won't be hiring more faculty if its increasing class size so drastically. (B) contradicts the author's conclusion, assuming (of course) that student participation is a good thing. (C) is interesting information but isn't essential to the conclusion. (D) looks like the right answer. The author does seem to think that a class taught by a PhD is somehow superior, which explains why she thinks the change would benefit students. (E) explains why the university might want to increase classes taught by PhDs, but it doesn't explain how that would benefit students. (D) is correct.

When doing assumption, strengthen, and weaken questions, remember to zero in on the conclusion. The assumption is always tightly bound with the conclusion supported by the evidence.

22. **(E).** Griselda cares what other countries think of the United States.; Theodore doesn't. Griselda doesn't say anything that would give the impression that she thinks the United States sometimes should send out troops despite international disapproval, so (A) is wrong. (B) is right as far as Theodore goes, but it doesn't address Griselda, so see if you can find something better. (C) is wrong. Theodore doesn't think the international community's opinion is important. (D) is also wrong. Griselda doesn't mention the United Nations, so you can't assume that she thinks this. (E) is correct because it sums up the conversation nicely.

23. **(A).** The obstetrician draws a connection between alcohol consumption and pregnancy that may not be entirely justified by the facts. Heavy drinking might always be bad, but he provides no additional information to show that light drinking is equally bad or will definitely cause birth defects. (A) looks like a good answer. The obstetrician is assuming that any amount of alcohol is equally deleterious, when in fact he has only connected birth defects with heavy drinking. (B) isn't as good. The doctor doesn't mention prevention or suggest that women be forcibly stopped from drinking, merely that they shouldn't. (C) doesn't work because the doctor doesn't mention the state or its interest in unborn children. (D) isn't really a flaw. The argument isn't really harmed by the lack of evidence here, and presumably the doctor could furnish some. (E) isn't a flaw in the argument because if heavy drinking caused the birth defects in question, then the mothers did cause their children's problems. (A) is the best answer.

24. **(D).** Look for an answer in which someone's preparation prevents a problem that otherwise would have occurred. (A) doesn't work because the homeowner isn't preventing a problem here. (B) doesn't work because there's no mention of measles being prevents. (C) is an example of preparation, not prevention. (D) does conform to the principle; money spent on prenatal care prevents postnatal medical expenses. (E) doesn't work quite as well; the cure comes first, followed by the prevention. (D) is the best answer.

25. **(C).** The psychologist claims that patients do better when they like their doctors, so look for evidence to support that. (A) doesn't help. It illustrates the danger of people not liking their doctors, but doesn't prove the psychologist's point. (B) is evidence of how the average doctor doesn't have a good relationship with patients. (C) does support the conclusion, providing plenty of evidence of the health benefits of good patient-doctor relationships. (D) doesn't support the conclusion at all, and is instead more evidence of poor doctor communication skills. (E) doesn't prove the point, either. (C) is correct.

Section III

1. **(D).** Think what this passage is about. You know it's about a kind of bicycle called a recumbent that is designed differently from a regular bicycle, which the passage refers to as an "upright" bicycle. It mentions a bit about the history of recumbents, why they were banned from competition, describes the advantages of recumbents, spends a paragraph on different recumbent designs, and then concludes with a paragraph on how to improve recumbent hill-climbing. It's mostly informative, but the author definitely has an agenda — notice how she dwells on the advantages of recumbents.

   (A) is definitely wrong. The UCI's decision is only a minor part of the entire passage, not the main idea. (B) isn't the main idea, either. Although the author does mention that recumbents have surged in popularity, which has generated new design interest, that's not the main idea of the whole passage; instead, it's kind of the main idea of the third paragraph. (C) is true and is one of the author's points, but it's not her main idea, which has to apply to the entire passage. (D) looks like the right answer. It sums up the gist of the entire passage pretty well and doesn't add anything that the passage doesn't say. (E) is true and is also one of the author's points, but it doesn't sum up the main idea of the entire passage. (D) is correct.

2. **(A).** The passage makes it clear that aerodynamics are the reason for recumbent speed. Look for an answer that emphasizes the aerodynamic advantages of recumbents. (A) looks good, but check the others. (B) is wrong because the author explicitly says that most recumbents are made of steel, *not* of lighter materials. (C) is a bit tricky because recumbents do maximize aerodynamics, and fairings and seat position do play a role in aerodynamics, but the main way that recumbents maximize aerodynamics is through an aerodynamic tuck. The author clearly states that fairings are optional, so you can't assume that fairings are responsible for the aerodynamic improvement. (D) doesn't really work because you know that bicycle manufacturers neglected recumbents for most of the 20th century. (E) doesn't work either; it's not specifically steering that makes recumbents faster, and one steering configuration is known to be faster than the other. (A) is the right answer.

3. **(E).** The UCI (incidentally, "Union Cyclist International" is a French name, though all the words are also English; the English version would be International Cycling Union) banned recumbents after a lousy cyclist won a race on one, proving that his bike was faster than the other bikes because he himself wouldn't have won on an upright bike. (A) is wrong because the passage says nothing about other cyclists petitioning anyone. (B) is totally wrong because the author never mentions anyone setting records on upright bikes. (C) isn't in the passage. (D) starts off promising with the mention of the second-rate cyclist, but then veers into nonsense about press attention, so that's no good. That leaves (E), which is the correct answer.

4. **(B).** Do this one by process of elimination. If you prefer, mark the passage where you find answer choices that do appear. (A) is mentioned; the author mentions comfort several times. (B) looks wrong. The author says that recumbents are heavier than uprights, not lighter, so this answer certainly isn't one of the advantages she lists. (C) is in the passage as an advantage; so are (D) and (E). (B) is correct.

5. **(A).** Before predicting the right answer, you may want to quickly skim this paragraph. Now, in your own words, why did the author write this paragraph? The last paragraph contains the author's discussion of climbing on recumbents. She mentions that some cyclists believe that recumbents are slow at climbing, claims that they aren't, and offers a suggestion or two of ways recumbent cyclists can improve their climbing prowess. (A) matches up with that description quite well. (B) is wrong though it may be a bit confusing; the author does say that recumbent cyclists can climb hills well, but she isn't proving anything, just making a statement that she could back up with evidence if she chose to, though she doesn't. (C) isn't exactly right. The author does discuss cadence, but that's not her primary purpose in writing the paragraph. (D) doesn't work because although the author does dispute the contention that recumbents can't climb, she doesn't offer anecdotal evidence; the claim that "most experienced recumbent riders" climb well isn't anecdotal evidence — you would need some actual examples of fast riders for this answer to be right. (E) is wrong; the author does recommend weight-lifting, but that isn't the main point of the paragraph. (A) is correct.

6. **(C).** To answer this question, you have to use information from the passage. The third paragraph discusses the different designs of recumbent bikes: Short wheelbase is faster than long wheelbase and above-seat-steering is faster than below-seat-steering. If you go up to the second paragraph, you find mention of fairings, which can increase speed. So your fastest bike would be a short wheelbase bike with above-seat-steering and a fairing. That's (C).

7. **(E).** You can't predict the answers to this one, so just read through the choices and see which one jives with what the author seems to believe. (A) doesn't really work because the author probably wouldn't make such a blanket statement. She's precise in her numbers, and not likely to make a blanket statement like that, with no consideration for different riders. (B) is wrong because although the author mentions that recumbents have become more popular, nowhere does she mention absolute numbers of recumbent cyclists as compared to upright cyclists. For all you know, recumbent cyclists comprise a mere 1 percent of the cycling population. Because she hasn't mentioned this topic, you can't assume she'd agree. (C) is wrong. A fairing would make a recumbent faster but by improving aerodynamics, not by reducing weight; if anything, the fairing would increase weight. (D) is wrong. Even if the author conceded that a tucked position on an upright bike is as efficient as the normal position on a recumbent, she would never agree that it was as comfortable as sitting back in a recumbent seat. (E) is correct; the author's points are that recumbents offer both speed and comfort, though it's true that you can't enter them in most bike races.

8. **(B).** This passage describes an organization of the federal government, explains what it does, and identifies its funding sources. (A) looks like it could be the answer, but see if there's a better one. (B) is better than (A) because it provides a more complete summary of the passage's contents. (C) is true but it's not the main idea. (D) likewise is information found in the passage, but it's definitely not the main point. (E) may be tempting because the first line mentions declines in populations of migratory waterfowl, but the passage as a whole doesn't focus on these declining populations, instead describing the actions of the Commission. (B) is the best choice.

9. **(E).** To answer this one, you have to go through all the answer choices and mark off the ones that do appear in the passage. (A) is a goal of the Commission, as is (B), (C), and (D). (E) isn't; nowhere in the passage does the author mention breeding waterfowl.

10. **(E).** This one is another question where you have to eliminate all answer choices that appear in the passage. The last paragraph contains information on how the Commission funds its purchases. (A) through (D) all appear there. (E) doesn't. As far as you know from this passage, the Commission doesn't sell hunting leases.

11. **(A).** The author doesn't display any real agenda beyond informing the reader about the Migratory Bird Conservation Commission — this passage isn't really a critique or praise or anything else obviously biased. (Remember, though, even the most "objective" of reading passages has an agenda of some sort.) (A) looks like a good answer; check the others to see if there's a better one. (B) is wrong. The author doesn't suggest that the Commission should have its funding increased. (C) is wrong because the author isn't really praising the Commission's work. (D) doesn't quite work because it leaves out some major portions of the passage. (E) might work, except that the author isn't really trying to drum up support. (A) still works best.

To save time, quickly glance at the first words in each choice. You can quickly eliminate choices that are clearly wrong. Was the author's main purpose to describe? Impress? Praise? Analyze? Generate support? That first word should give you a major clue of the right answer before you read the entire choices.

12. **(E).** The information about that massive purchase of land is in the passage as an example of something the Commission has done. (A) doesn't work because the author doesn't have any real argument to make; he's not obviously trying to persuade the readers of any point. (B) isn't right because the author isn't complaining, just stating facts. (C) might work, but it's not exactly right. The author isn't describing the land that the Commission acquired. (D) isn't quite right. Though the author does list the locations of these parcels of land, that's not the primary purpose of the paragraph. (E) looks like the best answer.

13. **(C).** The word "condemn" in this context refers to the government's ability to take property from private landowners if it's needed for some public purpose, of course providing compensation to the landowner (this process is known as *eminent domain*). Now, even if you didn't already know that use of the word *condemn,* you could figure it out from context, at least the part about taking the property from private landowners. You couldn't necessarily figure out that compensation is part of the deal, but you don't need to know that to answer the question. The full sentence in question reads "Although the Fish and Wildlife Service does have the power to condemn property, it rarely does this, preferring to work with willing sellers or to leave property in private hands." The preceding sentence discusses ways in which the Commission and the Service acquire property, by buying, leasing, or getting easements to it. That should give you a clue that "condemn" must mean some other way of acquiring property, and that it's incompatible with purchasing from a willing seller or allowing the owner to retain it but grant the Service access to it. The most likely remaining option is simply taking the property from an unwilling seller. Even though you don't know for sure that compensation is part of the taking of property, (C) is the only answer that fits the bill based on its mention of taking property; don't worry about the compensation aspect because you know (C) must be right.

Now that you've worked that out, go through the choices. (A) doesn't work because the Service doesn't want the land for human habitation. (B) likewise doesn't fit; the land probably is environmentally fine, or it wouldn't make good wildlife habitat. (C) looks like a good answer. (D) is true but it can't be what condemn means because the author already mentioned leasing as one of the desirable options. (E) likewise doesn't work, because the passage is concerned with land acquisition, not land use and zoning. (C) is correct.

14. **(C).** This passage is tough. A bit of strategy: You will of course have read the questions before tackling the reading, and you'll have noticed that this passage only has five questions. In this situation, you may be well served by postponing this reading until the end. It's not worth as many points as the others, and it's harder to understand. Often it doesn't matter whether or not you work the passages in order, but readings like this can really bog you down.

For a clue as to its topic, read the last sentence of the first paragraph, a common place to put a thesis: it's about "the particular manifestation of power that we call authority." This is an excerpt from a much longer piece on Alexander the Great, which is why Alexander appears in this passage, but Alexander isn't actually the focus of the passage; authority as a subcategory of power is.

Now, what's the central idea? The author is arguing that authority is a kind of power that relies for its effect on the speaker's ability to command and get people to obey him, and doesn't depend on coercion or persuasion. Read through the answer choices and see if you can find one that fits. (A) doesn't work; the author has said that authority is a kind of power, which means they can't be the same thing. (B) is backwards — authority is a kind of power. You don't need to bother with the rest of the answer, which is also wrong. (C) looks good. The author has said that "authority is a kind of power" and "for us to see authority in action, both coercion and persuasion must remain in the background," which adds up to (C). (D) doesn't work; though the author mentions Alexander, he's really incidental to this discussion and even more so is his general, Antipater. (E) is wrong, too. In the last paragraph, the author describes Alexander's exercise of authority, but not of power. (C) is correct.

15. **(B).** The second paragraph contains a discussion of authority and the relationship implied in any situation in which one person has authority over another. (A) is wrong. Alexander doesn't appear in this paragraph. (B) looks good — the author does mention "coercive power" and uses the word "uneasy" to describe relationships in which one person has authority over another. (C) isn't right. The author may in fact suggest that coercive power is essential to authority, but that's not the point of the entire paragraph, and is never really directly stated. (D) is wrong. The author doesn't mention other scholars or their interpretations anywhere. (E) is a statement that appears in the third paragraph, not the second, and it isn't the point there either. (B) is the best answer.

16. **(C).** The sentence in question reads: "But for us to see authority in action, both coercion and persuasion must remain in the background, occulted." If something is in the background, you're not supposed to see it, or at least not focus on it. (C), "hidden," would make sense in this context. The other choices don't. The only other choice that may make some sense is (B), but "hidden" makes much more sense than "understated." Incidentally, although the word *occult* can refer to magic, *occulted* in this context has nothing to do with magical topics, so (D) is way out there. (C) is correct.

17. **(B).** The definition of power appears in the first paragraph, and the definition of authority appears in the second. Note the author's use of the word "generic" to describe "power." Skimming the answers, (B) and (E) look like possibilities. (B) looks right and (E) looks wrong; the author says that authority is a kind of power and that it shouldn't depend on outright coercion or persuasion. (A) is wrong because both authority and power can involve persuasion and coercion. (C) doesn't work because nowhere does the author suggest that authority goes with politics and power goes with the military. (D) is likewise wrong. (B) is the best answer.

18. **(A).** Here's what the author says: "If the listener demands a reason for a command or asks about the consequences of disobedience, the speaker's authority falters. At this point authority may give way to persuasion, or naked force, or it may be reasserted by invoking the privileged, authoritative position of the speaker." (A) looks like it matches up pretty well with that. (B) is wrong because the speaker doesn't necessarily lose power but may lose authority. In addition, you should automatically be suspicious of extreme wording such as "loses all power." (C) is just plain wrong. (D) isn't right either, because the speaker could also use persuasion or reinvoke his authority. (E) definitely isn't right. (A) is the best answer.

19. **(E).** This passage is a short history lesson on the Panama Canal — the events that preceded its construction and the worries they caused, and then the effects on the world after it was operational. (A) isn't the main point, though it is a factoid you can figure out from the passage. (B) isn't the main point, either; the passage isn't only about the U.S. Navy's use of the

canal during World War I. (C) sums up the first half of the passage, but doesn't do justice to the whole thing. (D) is a conclusion that the author doesn't state. (E) is the best answer; it sums up the passage nicely.

20. **(D).** Why did the United States decide it needed the Panama Canal? The only way to get ships from the Atlantic to the Pacific or vice versa was to sail around the entire continent of South America. The narrow *isthmus* of Panama (an isthmus is a little strip of land with ocean on either side of it) was an obvious place to construct a passage to shorten the trip. (A) isn't right; the navy had no desire to build two complete fleets. (B) is true, but the passage gives the impression that the impetus behind the construction was military, not commercial. (C) is misleading because it's the event that starts off the passage, but you're looking for a logistical problem, and having a ship blown up doesn't fit that category. (D) looks right. The problem was indeed that it took too long to move ships from one ocean to another. (E) is similar to (C), in that it mentions the event that begins the passage and led to worry by military strategists, but the single instance of lacking a ship wasn't the logistical problem that led to the digging of a major canal. (D) is correct.

21. **(B).** Here's what the passage says: "The impossibility of sailing north of North America and the distance of the voyage around South America effectively divided the U.S. Naval forces into two fleets. Such a division was costly, inefficient, and ultimately less powerful than a fleet that could unify on demand." What that phrase means, then, is that without a shortcut between oceans, the navy essentially had to keep one fleet in the Pacific and one fleet in the Atlantic; ships couldn't realistically sail to help one another because the trip took so long. (A) is wrong. Naval commanders certainly wished they could mobilize their entire fleet in the same place at the same time. (B) looks correct. (C) doesn't work; the *USS Oregon* did in fact make it to Cuba in time to play a pivotal role. The problem was that the navy couldn't count on this happening in the future, but the trip wasn't impossible. (D) isn't right; it describes one incident that exemplified the two-fleet problem but doesn't sum up the phrase in question. (E) doesn't work either because the author never mentions air power. (B) is right.

22. **(C).** After the *USS Maine* blew up, the navy wanted to send its brand spanking new battleship to Cuba, but the author points out that they had to wait 67 days for it to get there, biting their nails the whole time. Why were they nervous? Spain and the United States were fighting over Cuba. The author doesn't say exactly what was going on, but you can assume that if the *USS Oregon* hadn't arrived on time, Spain would have taken Cuba. (In fact, Cuba had started a war for independence from Spain, and the United States sent the *Maine* to assist the Cubans. After the war, Cuba was independent. But you don't need to know that to answer the question.) Skim the answers; (C) looks exactly right. (A) may be true, but the author doesn't imply it. (B) is wrong because although the loss of more ships would have been undesirable, that wasn't the nation's primary concern. (D) is irrelevant. You don't have any reason to assume San Francisco needed defense. (E) may also work, but that's hardly what the passage suggests the navy was worried about (surely they would have found another opportunity to use the *Oregon*). (C) is the best answer.

23. **(A).** Read through the passage and mark off the answer choices that you find. (B), (C), (D), and (E) are all in there, mostly in the last paragraph. Conspicuously absent from the author's discussion of the canal's impact is its effect on its home nation, Panama. (A) is the answer.

24. **(E).** In the second paragraph, the author discusses the concerns and desires the navy had that led to the construction of the Panama Canal. (A) is wrong because even though the thinking of military strategists on the subject of the Spanish-American War does appear, that's just a piece of evidence that backs up the main point of the paragraph. (B) is misleading because the paragraph starts off with the *Oregon*'s contribution, but the battleship never appears again in that paragraph so it's not the primary purpose. (C) is wrong. The action in the second paragraph occurs before the canal was built, so it can't mention costs and benefits of traveling through it. (D) is wrong. There weren't any effective alternatives to the canal. (E) is correct. The military couldn't help but notice that South America was awfully big and time-consuming to sail around, and reasoned that a canal through Panama would speed things up nicely.

25. **(B).** This is an analytical history passage, describing events and interpreting the forces behind the decisions of the time. (A) isn't right. The author doesn't really get into the business of justifying U.S. actions in building the canal. (B) looks good. (C) is wrong because the passage never mentions imperialism. (D) is wrong because the author doesn't really get into the military's role in the construction of the canal. The passage skips from military strategists worrying in the late 1800s to the use of the canal in World War I, and you never find out about the details of construction. (E) is wrong, too, because explosion of the *Maine* is just incidental to the story, not the author's primary concern. Notice that you don't see anything about the *Maine* after the first paragraph. (B) is the best answer.

Section IV

1. **(B).** The curmudgeon assumes that the only way a person can benefit from public schools is by having children who attend them. (A) is wrong. Although (A) is a possible benefit from public education, it goes too far from the curmudgeon's basic assumption. Remember to stay close to the text — an assumption is the most basic piece of evidence that bridges the stated evidence to the conclusion. (A) is a step beyond the assumption and makes another assumption — that education is necessary to vote intelligently — but the curmudgeon never mentions voting or democracy in his argument. (B) looks like the right answer; he does believe a childless person can't benefit from public schools. (C) is probably something he would agree with, but it's not the assumption that ties together his thesis and conclusion; he mentions nothing about other people getting undeserved benefits. (D) is totally wrong and has nothing to do with the argument. (E) is a point that someone arguing with the curmudgeon might bring up, but it's not the curmudgeon's assumption. (B) is the only correct answer.

When you look for assumptions, stay as close to the text as possible. You need to find only the one necessary assumption that bridges the gap between evidence and conclusion — anything else is too far away. Don't let your imagination lead you astray.

2. **(D).** The conclusion leaves off the crucial step of removing the socks when going to bed to allow the feet to cool off — that's its mistake. (A) is wrong because the magazine does have justification in the form of scientific research. (B) isn't true; the magazine only suggests that insomniacs try wearing socks, not that it would be a cure-all. (C) isn't a flaw in reasoning; people believe scientists all the time. (D) looks like the best answer. The magazine does misinterpret the results, and should have added that for the technique to work properly, the feet must first be warmed and then be allowed to cool off, such as by removing socks. (E) is wrong because the magazine doesn't criticize insomniacs. (D) is the answer.

Careful reading is the strategy for Question 2. Be careful about the language being used and don't fill in the gaps yourself. Look at what the text says!

3. **(D).** Well, if that's not an overly broad prescriptive statement, I don't know what is. The "everyone knows" is a bad start, there's no evidence to support the claims, and the whole thing is a gross generalization. (A) is wrong because the speaker offers no evidence, so he can't discount it. (B) isn't really something you can criticize. It may be something to bring up in an argument, but bringing in outside information as a subject of criticism isn't fair. (C) is wrong; the argument doesn't address women in the workplace. (D) looks right and is a generalization; the author offers no evidence in support of the conclusion. (E) is wrong. The author doesn't mention a relative other than mothers. (D) is the best answer.

4. **(C).** Did you take a good look at the question before you started reading the argument? You're looking for something that *must* be true. It may be helpful to underline that word so that you know what the right answer will look like. Now that you know what you're looking for, do some quick thinking before going on to the answer choices. What *must* be true? You

want to think actively about this before going to the answer choices. You may think something like, if dogs can understand as much as chimps, dolphins, and parrots, and dogs can understand 200 words, then chimps, dolphins, and parrots can understand 200 words. (A) may be true, but it doesn't have to be based on the information contained in the argument. There's no way you can get to (B) from the argument, which doesn't address training techniques. (C) looks like a logical conclusion and a good answer. If you take another look at the argument, you can indeed infer this to be true. (D) misses the point. The researchers may have been in Germany, but the animals could be from anywhere. (E) isn't an assumption you can make because the author never mentions training methods, only results. (C) is right.

5. **(C).** Yikes; burnt pie. The reasoning in the argument goes like this: 40 min at 250 = 20 min at 500. You want to find an answer that results in more or less an identical equation, in which one quantity is doubled while the other is halved. (A) is like this: 1 aspirin every 4 hours; I'll do 2 aspirin every 4 hours. That's wrong. (B) goes: 9 lbs gets 1 cup; 13 lbs gets 1.5 cups. Seems sensible, and not flawed. But because you're looking for a flaw, this won't work. This answer might look attractive to you because it manipulates the proportions in the directions in a similar way to that in the argument, but remember that the argument messes up that manipulation; the cat-feeder here gets the calculation right. (C) goes: 1 gallon every day = 2 gallons every other day. That's very close to the reasoning in the argument, which doubled the temperature and halved the time. (D) is like this: bleach for 20 minutes; I'll do bleach for 40 minutes. The quantity of bleach isn't affected, so that's wrong (and never do that to your own hair!). (E) goes: twice as fast and twice the cost; I want that so I'll take it. That doesn't work at all. (C) is the best answer.

6. **(C).** Anytime you make a statement about the "whole purpose" of something, you run into trouble; someone can always argue that some other purpose exists. What if some business owner doesn't think maximizing profits is his only purpose? (A) is wrong because the businessman isn't concerned with deductions; they're nice but they don't maximize profits. (B) isn't quite right; goodwill may help with profits, but quantifying it is hard so you can't say for sure that charitable giving could help profits. Remember the argument says "maximize" profits, and "potentially increasing" profits isn't the same thing. (C) looks right. If a business isn't founded for the sole purpose of maximizing profits for shareholders, then the businessman's argument has a weak point. (D) is nice, but the argument isn't about investors and mutual funds. (E) is also nice, but the fact remains that a business that has spent profits on charity isn't as profitable as it may have been. (C) is the best answer.

7. **(A).** The nutritionist blames fast food for the obesity epidemic. Any evidence disproving a connection between fast food and obesity would weaken the argument. (A) looks like it might do that; if everyone is eating more fast food than before but only certain people are getting fatter, then eating fast food alone can't be the cause. None of the other answers address the fast food–obesity connection, so (A) must be the answer.

8. **(B).** This one lends itself to being written as an equation: H = P; P = M; M = V; H = M and V. Try writing the answers as equations to see if one comes out like that. (A) goes like this: D = C; C = M; C = V; D = M and V. That's *so* close but not quite there; canines appear twice at the beginning of a sentence, which ruins this one. (B) goes: F = I; I = A; A = I; F = A and I. That looks identical to the argument, so it's a good answer. (C) goes: W = C; C = M; M have mammary glands; W have mammary glands. Nope. (D) goes like this: S = M; M have shells; O = bivalves; bivalves have shells; creatures with shells = bivalves and mollusks. Totally wrong. (E) goes: G = P; C = P; P = V; G and C = V. That's not it. (B) is correct.

If you find it confusing using different letters as variables, you can also use A, B, C, and D for each of the players in the equations. So the argument would go: A = B; B = C; C = D; A = C and D. (A) would go: A = B; B = C; B = D; A = C and D. You can do this with all the choices and it might make the equations look clearer to you.

Write the equations one on top of the other, which makes the logical differences between them stand out very clearly.

9. **(A).** Look for an answer in which a soldier refuses to carry out an order he knows is against the law. (A) looks right. Torture violates the law, so a soldier can legitimately refuse to carry out torture orders. (B) isn't right. Soldiers aren't allowed to refuse orders that are simply against their own consciences. (C) is wrong. A soldier's belief that the military shouldn't be involved in a particular conflict isn't the same as an actual law. (D) is wrong for the same reason. (E) is also wrong. In order for the answer to be right, it has to say that the action is against the law, not simply against an individual's conscience or moral beliefs. (A) is the right answer.

10. **(B).** The commentary's conclusion is that defining obscenity without violating free speech guarantees is impossible. (A) isn't the theorist's point; he doesn't mention the different roles of federal and state governments. (B) looks like a good answer. (C) is wrong. The theorist doesn't suggest that courts and legislatures ignore all speech, just obscenity. (D) contradicts the theorist's conclusion. He thinks defining obscenity is impossible, so the suggested definition would inevitably have flaws. (E) doesn't work because the theorist doesn't mention using different standards for children and adults. (B) is correct.

11. **(D).** Make sure you know what you're looking for: Look for the one answer that _doesn't_ hurt the argument. It doesn't necessarily have to strengthen the conclusion, but it can't weaken it. What's the conclusion? That the best method to avoid drug-using employees from making mistakes on the job is to administer random urine tests. Just go down the list and eliminate any answer choice that does weaken the link from evidence to conclusion. The last choice standing is right! (A) weakens the argument that urine tests are the best method by suggesting hair tests are better. (B) weakens the argument by suggesting that urine tests can't spot drugs taken more than a couple of days ago. (C) weakens the argument by suggesting that drug tests are expensive and mostly useless. (D) doesn't weaken the argument. If consumers want their places of business to be drug-free, it's in employers' interest to test for drug use among employees. (E) weakens the argument. If it's easy to cheat on urine tests, they can't be very effective. (D) is the best answer.

12. **(E).** Albert would argue that he was acting as the catalog told him he could act and therefore isn't taking unfair advantage of the seller. In other words, he is abiding by the terms of the agreement, as is the seller, so he isn't taking advantage of the company. (A) states only that buyers and sellers enter unwritten contracts during transactions, but that doesn't justify Albert's actions, at least not all the way; look for something better. (B) is wrong. Albert is taking advantage of the seller's goodwill, by all evidence with the seller's consent. (C) could work, but Albert isn't abusing the seller or even taking undue advantage, not with seven pairs of shoes in 20 years; see if there's something better. (D) doesn't justify Albert's position, though it's a reasonable warning to merchants. (E) is the best answer. When Albert bought the shoes, the sale contract stated that he could have them replaced at any time, so he's only observing the contract's terms, as in fact the seller is. (E) is the best answer.

13. **(B).** Heloise doesn't believe that reducing class size makes any difference. See if you can find an answer providing evidence that it does. (A) actually helps Heloise make her point. If the Japanese thrive on very large classes, size may not be a problem. (B) does undermine her position. If reducing class sizes made a sizable difference in a short time, maybe it is valuable. (C) doesn't really undermine her point. Teachers may like small classes better, but that doesn't mean they're better for students. (D) would, if anything, help her point, though it's really irrelevant to the issue of student performance. (E) could undermine her point if it went further, but the mere fact that private schools limit class size tells you nothing about the performance of the students. (B) is the best answer.

14. **(E).** That's a lot of lost luggage, but maybe the problem isn't as serious as the numbers make it look. (A) doesn't weaken the argument; if anything, it strengthens it. If airlines warn passengers to pack carry-ons, they must expect luggage to get lost. (B) doesn't weaken it; lost luggage can certainly be inconvenient. (C) likewise doesn't weaken the argument for the same reason. (D) doesn't really weaken the argument; although some travelers may not mind having to go shopping, many do. (E) does weaken it. If the odds of losing luggage are that low, then checking bags is fairly safe. (E) is correct.

15. **(E).** The argument is about the benefits and risks of LASIK. (A) isn't a conclusion you can reasonably draw from the facts; though the passage says night vision can be impaired, the argument says nothing about it being so bad as to prevent driving. (B) doesn't work; the passage doesn't address the differences in doctors. (C) isn't supported by the passage. It tells you nothing about reading glasses, and in fact suggests that most patients need no glasses afterward. (D) isn't in the passage either; it doesn't address aging. (E) makes the most sense. According to the passage, LASIK has many benefits but some real risks. That actually makes a pretty good conclusion, summing up the information rather nicely. (E) is the right answer.

16. **(A).** You can't predict this answer, so dive in. (A) looks like the right answer; the passage tells you that birds *can't* see glass when lights are on inside. (B) is probably true, if birds are running into buildings in record numbers. (C) could be true, based on the information in the passage. (D) could certainly be true. (E) is true; the passage says this problem occurs during migration. (A) is the only necessarily false statement and is therefore correct.

17. **(D).** The argument suggests that outsourcing to foreign countries isn't nearly the problem many Americans think it is. (A) is wrong. The passage doesn't think anyone should blame the government for letting jobs go overseas. (B) doesn't work because the passage doesn't suggest that businesses should look overseas for labor. (C) is wrong. Although this may be true, that's not what the passage says. (D) looks right; that's exactly what the argument suggests. (E) may be true, but it's not the main point of the argument. (D) is the answer.

18. **(D).** First, be sure of what the question is asking. You're looking for an explanation of a phenomenon. If child labor is both a problem of poverty and a cause of poverty, there must be some sort of vicious cycle going on, probably caused by the fact that people are working as children and passing their disadvantages on to their own children. (A) is only a partial answer, and introducing the social safety net is irrelevant. (B) doesn't make sense. It sounds as if parents have a choice of whether to send their kids to school or work. Look for something better. (C) may be true, but it doesn't totally explain how child labor and poverty feed on one another. You want a tighter explanation. (D) explains the phenomenon best; that's a real circular problem, with uneducated children unable to earn much which forces their own children to be uneducated child laborers. (E) doesn't really explain the cycle of poverty. (D) is the best answer.

19. **(B).** The environmentalists like the emissions-reduction laws because they think that will slow global warming. The last sentence is the only place where global warming is mentioned, so the assumption must be that reducing emissions slows warming. (A) is wrong because the author says nothing about coastal states being environmentally conscious. (B) looks exactly right. (C) doesn't come up. (D) is interesting, and the author does touch on this, but it's not the assumption that leads from argument to conclusion. (E) isn't something you can conclude from the information given. (B) is correct.

20. **(D).** Philip thinks hybrids are the greatest thing since sliced bread, but Ryan's not so impressed. He thinks older technology was a better solution than heavy, complicated hybrids and their weird batteries. Ryan doesn't deny the existence of the problem, so (A) is wrong. He uses no analogy, so (B) is wrong. He's not challenging Philip's information, so (C) is wrong. He is arguing that older technology was superior to hybrids, so (D) looks good. He doesn't suggest that hybrids don't get good mileage, so (E) is wrong. (D) is the best answer.

21. **(D).** Pro-family brochures distributed only to women? Though many women may not want to get married, that's not the main flaw in the reasoning, so (A) is wrong. (B) may be true, but not because of flawed reasoning. (C) may also be true, but the legislator isn't thinking only of single mothers. (D) does name a flaw; any efforts to improve the family need to recognize that women aren't the only people in them. (E) may well be true, but it's not the main reason the thinking is flawed. (D) is the best answer here.

22. **(B).** Maybe Stuart's car spent more time stopped. (A) explains how Steve kept moving but doesn't account for Stuart's slow performance. (B) could well offer an explanation; if the traffic was terrible, Stuart couldn't go any faster than Steve. (C) doesn't help explain matters. If Stuart was driving 60 mph, he should have arrived sooner, unless he couldn't do that often,

but the answer doesn't tell you that. (D) doesn't help; the guys could see one another, but why? (E) is amusing, but still doesn't answer the question. Stuart stopped more, but he should have been able to drive faster when he was moving. (B) makes the most sense.

23. **(C).** This judge must be assuming that yoga helps with anger management. (A) is unlikely. The judge says that yoga can help control anger, but not that yoga practitioners never attack drivers. (B) isn't the reason for the sentence of yoga. The judge is trying to improve the man's behavior, not just impose a more serious sentence. (C) looks like a good answer because the judge clearly assumes that yoga is good for preventing road rage. (D) can't be right, because the judge is introducing an unusual penalty. (E) is wrong. The judge doesn't give the impression that road rage is justified in this case. (C) is correct.

24. **(C).** To predict the conclusion, think about where the evidence is leading you. Try to compose a sentence that would follow the last sentence in the argument, beginning with the word "therefore." The argument's conclusion is that online dating must be approached with caution. (A) isn't the conclusion, but a piece of evidence the author mentions. (B) isn't the conclusion, though the author does suggest that sexual predation may be a danger. (B) is more of a detail than a general conclusion of the entire prompt. (C) looks like a good answer; it summarizes the author's argument pretty well. (D) isn't the author's point; he's not recommending that online dating services take any specific actions. (E) is more information about online dating and not a conclusion at all. (C) is right.

Section I

1. Ⓐ Ⓑ Ⓒ Ⓓ Ⓔ
2. Ⓐ Ⓑ Ⓒ Ⓓ Ⓔ
3. Ⓐ Ⓑ Ⓒ Ⓓ Ⓔ
4. Ⓐ Ⓑ Ⓒ Ⓓ Ⓔ
5. Ⓐ Ⓑ Ⓒ Ⓓ Ⓔ
6. Ⓐ Ⓑ Ⓒ Ⓓ Ⓔ
7. Ⓐ Ⓑ Ⓒ Ⓓ Ⓔ
8. Ⓐ Ⓑ Ⓒ Ⓓ Ⓔ
9. Ⓐ Ⓑ Ⓒ Ⓓ Ⓔ
10. Ⓐ Ⓑ Ⓒ Ⓓ Ⓔ
11. Ⓐ Ⓑ Ⓒ Ⓓ Ⓔ
12. Ⓐ Ⓑ Ⓒ Ⓓ Ⓔ
13. Ⓐ Ⓑ Ⓒ Ⓓ Ⓔ
14. Ⓐ Ⓑ Ⓒ Ⓓ Ⓔ
15. Ⓐ Ⓑ Ⓒ Ⓓ Ⓔ
16. Ⓐ Ⓑ Ⓒ Ⓓ Ⓔ
17. Ⓐ Ⓑ Ⓒ Ⓓ Ⓔ
18. Ⓐ Ⓑ Ⓒ Ⓓ Ⓔ
19. Ⓐ Ⓑ Ⓒ Ⓓ Ⓔ
20. Ⓐ Ⓑ Ⓒ Ⓓ Ⓔ
21. Ⓐ Ⓑ Ⓒ Ⓓ Ⓔ
22. Ⓐ Ⓑ Ⓒ Ⓓ Ⓔ
23. Ⓐ Ⓑ Ⓒ Ⓓ Ⓔ
24. Ⓐ Ⓑ Ⓒ Ⓓ Ⓔ
25. Ⓐ Ⓑ Ⓒ Ⓓ Ⓔ
26. Ⓐ Ⓑ Ⓒ Ⓓ Ⓔ
27. Ⓐ Ⓑ Ⓒ Ⓓ Ⓔ
28. Ⓐ Ⓑ Ⓒ Ⓓ Ⓔ
29. Ⓐ Ⓑ Ⓒ Ⓓ Ⓔ
30. Ⓐ Ⓑ Ⓒ Ⓓ Ⓔ

Section II

1. Ⓐ Ⓑ Ⓒ Ⓓ Ⓔ
2. Ⓐ Ⓑ Ⓒ Ⓓ Ⓔ
3. Ⓐ Ⓑ Ⓒ Ⓓ Ⓔ
4. Ⓐ Ⓑ Ⓒ Ⓓ Ⓔ
5. Ⓐ Ⓑ Ⓒ Ⓓ Ⓔ
6. Ⓐ Ⓑ Ⓒ Ⓓ Ⓔ
7. Ⓐ Ⓑ Ⓒ Ⓓ Ⓔ
8. Ⓐ Ⓑ Ⓒ Ⓓ Ⓔ
9. Ⓐ Ⓑ Ⓒ Ⓓ Ⓔ
10. Ⓐ Ⓑ Ⓒ Ⓓ Ⓔ
11. Ⓐ Ⓑ Ⓒ Ⓓ Ⓔ
12. Ⓐ Ⓑ Ⓒ Ⓓ Ⓔ
13. Ⓐ Ⓑ Ⓒ Ⓓ Ⓔ
14. Ⓐ Ⓑ Ⓒ Ⓓ Ⓔ
15. Ⓐ Ⓑ Ⓒ Ⓓ Ⓔ
16. Ⓐ Ⓑ Ⓒ Ⓓ Ⓔ
17. Ⓐ Ⓑ Ⓒ Ⓓ Ⓔ
18. Ⓐ Ⓑ Ⓒ Ⓓ Ⓔ
19. Ⓐ Ⓑ Ⓒ Ⓓ Ⓔ
20. Ⓐ Ⓑ Ⓒ Ⓓ Ⓔ
21. Ⓐ Ⓑ Ⓒ Ⓓ Ⓔ
22. Ⓐ Ⓑ Ⓒ Ⓓ Ⓔ
23. Ⓐ Ⓑ Ⓒ Ⓓ Ⓔ
24. Ⓐ Ⓑ Ⓒ Ⓓ Ⓔ
25. Ⓐ Ⓑ Ⓒ Ⓓ Ⓔ
26. Ⓐ Ⓑ Ⓒ Ⓓ Ⓔ
27. Ⓐ Ⓑ Ⓒ Ⓓ Ⓔ
28. Ⓐ Ⓑ Ⓒ Ⓓ Ⓔ
29. Ⓐ Ⓑ Ⓒ Ⓓ Ⓔ
30. Ⓐ Ⓑ Ⓒ Ⓓ Ⓔ

Section III

1. Ⓐ Ⓑ Ⓒ Ⓓ Ⓔ
2. Ⓐ Ⓑ Ⓒ Ⓓ Ⓔ
3. Ⓐ Ⓑ Ⓒ Ⓓ Ⓔ
4. Ⓐ Ⓑ Ⓒ Ⓓ Ⓔ
5. Ⓐ Ⓑ Ⓒ Ⓓ Ⓔ
6. Ⓐ Ⓑ Ⓒ Ⓓ Ⓔ
7. Ⓐ Ⓑ Ⓒ Ⓓ Ⓔ
8. Ⓐ Ⓑ Ⓒ Ⓓ Ⓔ
9. Ⓐ Ⓑ Ⓒ Ⓓ Ⓔ
10. Ⓐ Ⓑ Ⓒ Ⓓ Ⓔ
11. Ⓐ Ⓑ Ⓒ Ⓓ Ⓔ
12. Ⓐ Ⓑ Ⓒ Ⓓ Ⓔ
13. Ⓐ Ⓑ Ⓒ Ⓓ Ⓔ
14. Ⓐ Ⓑ Ⓒ Ⓓ Ⓔ
15. Ⓐ Ⓑ Ⓒ Ⓓ Ⓔ
16. Ⓐ Ⓑ Ⓒ Ⓓ Ⓔ
17. Ⓐ Ⓑ Ⓒ Ⓓ Ⓔ
18. Ⓐ Ⓑ Ⓒ Ⓓ Ⓔ
19. Ⓐ Ⓑ Ⓒ Ⓓ Ⓔ
20. Ⓐ Ⓑ Ⓒ Ⓓ Ⓔ
21. Ⓐ Ⓑ Ⓒ Ⓓ Ⓔ
22. Ⓐ Ⓑ Ⓒ Ⓓ Ⓔ
23. Ⓐ Ⓑ Ⓒ Ⓓ Ⓔ
24. Ⓐ Ⓑ Ⓒ Ⓓ Ⓔ
25. Ⓐ Ⓑ Ⓒ Ⓓ Ⓔ
26. Ⓐ Ⓑ Ⓒ Ⓓ Ⓔ
27. Ⓐ Ⓑ Ⓒ Ⓓ Ⓔ
28. Ⓐ Ⓑ Ⓒ Ⓓ Ⓔ
29. Ⓐ Ⓑ Ⓒ Ⓓ Ⓔ
30. Ⓐ Ⓑ Ⓒ Ⓓ Ⓔ

Section IV

1. Ⓐ Ⓑ Ⓒ Ⓓ Ⓔ
2. Ⓐ Ⓑ Ⓒ Ⓓ Ⓔ
3. Ⓐ Ⓑ Ⓒ Ⓓ Ⓔ
4. Ⓐ Ⓑ Ⓒ Ⓓ Ⓔ
5. Ⓐ Ⓑ Ⓒ Ⓓ Ⓔ
6. Ⓐ Ⓑ Ⓒ Ⓓ Ⓔ
7. Ⓐ Ⓑ Ⓒ Ⓓ Ⓔ
8. Ⓐ Ⓑ Ⓒ Ⓓ Ⓔ
9. Ⓐ Ⓑ Ⓒ Ⓓ Ⓔ
10. Ⓐ Ⓑ Ⓒ Ⓓ Ⓔ
11. Ⓐ Ⓑ Ⓒ Ⓓ Ⓔ
12. Ⓐ Ⓑ Ⓒ Ⓓ Ⓔ
13. Ⓐ Ⓑ Ⓒ Ⓓ Ⓔ
14. Ⓐ Ⓑ Ⓒ Ⓓ Ⓔ
15. Ⓐ Ⓑ Ⓒ Ⓓ Ⓔ
16. Ⓐ Ⓑ Ⓒ Ⓓ Ⓔ
17. Ⓐ Ⓑ Ⓒ Ⓓ Ⓔ
18. Ⓐ Ⓑ Ⓒ Ⓓ Ⓔ
19. Ⓐ Ⓑ Ⓒ Ⓓ Ⓔ
20. Ⓐ Ⓑ Ⓒ Ⓓ Ⓔ
21. Ⓐ Ⓑ Ⓒ Ⓓ Ⓔ
22. Ⓐ Ⓑ Ⓒ Ⓓ Ⓔ
23. Ⓐ Ⓑ Ⓒ Ⓓ Ⓔ
24. Ⓐ Ⓑ Ⓒ Ⓓ Ⓔ
25. Ⓐ Ⓑ Ⓒ Ⓓ Ⓔ
26. Ⓐ Ⓑ Ⓒ Ⓓ Ⓔ
27. Ⓐ Ⓑ Ⓒ Ⓓ Ⓔ
28. Ⓐ Ⓑ Ⓒ Ⓓ Ⓔ
29. Ⓐ Ⓑ Ⓒ Ⓓ Ⓔ
30. Ⓐ Ⓑ Ⓒ Ⓓ Ⓔ

Chapter 22

Some More Rainy-Day "Fun": LSAT Practice Exam 2

. . . .

*R*eady for another practice test? Sure you are!

Like the previous practice exam in Chapter 20, I set this one up like a real LSAT. For best results, try to take this practice exam under simulated LSAT conditions.

1. **Find a quiet place to work, where nothing can distract or interrupt you.**

2. **Use the answer grid provided and mark your answers with a No. 2 pencil.**

3. **Set your watch or alarm clock for 35-minute intervals.**

4. **Don't go to the next section until the time allotted for the current section is up.**

5. **If you finish early, check your work for that section only.**

6. **Don't take a break during any one section.**

7. **Give yourself exactly one 10-minute break between sections III and IV.**

The answer explanations to all questions are in Chapter 23. Go through the explanations to all the questions, even the ones you answered correctly. The answers are a good review of the techniques I discuss throughout the book.

When you complete the whole test, check your answers with the answer key at the end of this chapter. Count the number of answers you answered correctly in each section; add those together to compute your raw score. Use the following worksheet.

Keep in mind that this practice exam isn't an official LSAT. Although it serves as good practice for your test-taking technique and has the advantage of detailed explanations of all answers in the following chapter, don't assume that your score on this test is exactly the score you can expect when you take a real LSAT. LSAT PrepTests are still the best practice for that, but even they can't duplicate the stress you'll feel on test day and, therefore, still can't tell you what score you'll receive when you take the LSAT for real.

Section 1

Time: 35 minutes

24 Questions

Directions: Read the passage and choose the best answer. Some questions may have more than one answer that looks right. Select the one that answers the question most completely. Don't assume anything that isn't directly stated, and don't let your imagination run wild; all the information you need is in the arguments and the answer choices.

1. Consumer Review: This mail-order catalog claims that its customers save money by buying clothing through it, but the economy it promises is illusory, because it only occasionally marks down its normal prices.

   Which one of the following is an assumption on which the consumer review's argument depends?

   (A) This catalog's competitors mark down their normal prices more frequently and by greater amounts.

   (B) This catalog affords economy only when its normal prices are marked down and is otherwise more expensive.

   (C) This catalog marks its normal prices down by smaller amounts than do its competitors.

   (D) The competitors have lower normal prices.

   (E) Consumers should make purchases by mail order only when the normal prices are marked down.

2. The archaeological findings at level IVa of this bronze-age settlement in Turkey show how the settlement met its end. The village was surrounded by a thick defensive wall. The findings include a large number of clay vessels sunk in the ground as though for long-term storage of food during a siege. A number of bronze arrowheads were found, and at least one of the structures seems to have suffered a fire. Therefore it is clear that this settlement was destroyed in war, either with its neighbors or foreign invaders.

   Which one of the following most accurately describes a flaw in the argument?

   (A) The argument is a circular one, with the premises anticipating the conclusion.

   (B) The evidence is varied, but the conclusion is unified and therefore suspect.

   (C) The argument depends on intermediate conclusions, which make the final conclusion invalid.

   (D) The argument makes a historical conclusion but nowhere gives any dates to support it.

   (E) None of the pieces of evidence point directly to the conclusion, and all of them could lead to different conclusions.

Go on to next page

3.   Oceanographer: The size of oceanic waves is a function of the velocity of the wind and "fetch," the length of the surface of the water subject to those winds. The impact of waves against a coastline is a function of the size of the waves and the shape of the sea-bottom. The degree of erosion to which a coastline is subject is a function of the average impact of waves and the geologic composition of the coastline.

If the oceanographer's statements are true, which one of the following must be true?

(A) The "fetch" of winds is related to the shape of the sea-bottom.

(B) The size of oceanic waves will not fluctuate far from an average, for any given stretch of ocean.

(C) The degree of erosion to which a coastline is subject is related to the shape of the sea-bottom.

(D) The size of oceanic waves is related to the shape of the sea-bottom.

(E) The average velocity of the wind in an area plays no role in the degree of erosion to which a coastline is subject.

4.   Historian: It is nearly impossible for a historian to assert that one historical event or circumstance caused another. Given any coherent historical narrative, the sequence of events makes the notion of causation a tempting trap; a subsequent event can seem a necessary outcome of those that preceded it. But this is a mere consequence of the backward-looking perspective of the historian's art. That one event did in fact happen, and that other events did in fact happen prior to it, does not make the subsequent event inevitable or a direct outcome of those that went before.

The claim that "this is a mere consequence of the backward-looking perspective of the historian's art" plays which one of the following roles in the historian's argument?

(A) It is used to identify the theoretical imperative that is the concern of the argument.

(B) It is an illustration of a premise that is used to support the argument's conclusion.

(C) It is used to support indirectly a claim that the argument in turn uses to support directly the conclusion.

(D) It is used to explain a consideration that might be taken to undermine the argument's conclusion.

(E) It is the conclusion that the argument aims to support.

5. Despite five consecutive years in which global consumption of grain has been greater than global production, it is unlikely that we are facing a near-term crisis in the food supply. The average shortfalls have been mainly due to reduced output from farms in China, which is moving from a policy of central control over agricultural production to a more market-driven model. Therefore, if demand for grain continues to fall short of supply, we should expect to see Chinese production of grain increase dramatically.

Which one of the following principles most helps to justify the reasoning above?

(A) Global markets respond more slowly than regional markets, so local rates of production usually change more rapidly than the global average.

(B) When agricultural production is centrally controlled, it is unable to respond to changing demand by adjusting rates of supply.

(C) Average shortfalls are most readily remedied by local increases in production.

(D) When agricultural production is market driven, it is likely to respond to rising demand by increasing production.

(E) Centrally controlled agricultural production has been shown to be more inefficient than market-driven models.

6. Economist: Health insurers are largely immune to the factors that are limiting profit in many sectors of the healthcare economy. Consumers have shown a willingness to pay almost any price for health insurance premiums. Capital demands, which are the responsibility of doctors and hospitals, are increasing dramatically, even as cost-containment measures, largely encouraged by the insurers and their friends in government, have forced new levels of fiscal discipline upon hospitals and doctors. Patients still need MRIs and buildings to put them in, but hospitals are limited in how much they can charge patients for the use of these facilities.

Which one of the following most accurately describes the role played in the Economist's argument that "patients still need MRIs and buildings to put them in"?

(A) It is a specific example of a general condition described in the course of the argument.

(B) It is used to counter a consideration that might be taken to undermine the argument.

(C) It is used to support indirectly the claim made by the argument.

(D) It describes a social side effect of the benefit with which the argument is concerned.

(E) It introduces the conclusion that the argument intends to support.

Go on to next page

7. As peer-to-peer (PTP) filesharing networks flourished, the ability of consumers to download music without paying seriously damaged the prosperity of the recording industry. The numbers speak for themselves. During this time, revenues from sales of CDs in the United States fell by tens of millions of dollars a year, despite the fact that prices for individual CDs kept pace with inflation. It is clear, then, that PTP filesharing was killing the recording industry.

The argument depends on assuming which one of the following?

(A) That all sharing from PTP networks violates copyright.

(B) That there are no other explanations for the decreasing revenues from CD sales.

(C) That the musicians and producers have a right to profit from distribution of music.

(D) That people who download music would otherwise have purchased it on CD.

(E) There is a complex relationship between filesharing and the market in music, both online and on CD.

8. Engineer: In any complex machine on which human life depends, critical systems must have many layers of built-in redundancy. So in designing airplanes, whose control surfaces depend on hydraulic systems for their movement, engineers must include multiple independent redundant systems of hydraulic lines, each capable of giving the pilot control of the airplane's control surfaces. More redundancy is always better than less, so if an airplane design is deemed relatively safe with three redundant hydraulic systems, it must be deemed safer with four, and safer still with five.

The engineer's argument is most vulnerable to criticism on the grounds that it

(A) assumes that redundant systems will not be subject to simultaneous failure

(B) fails to take into account any practical factors that might limit the number of redundant systems or practical trade-offs involved in increasing levels of redundancy

(C) focuses on one area — movement of the control surfaces — without taking into account other important considerations of safety

(D) is limited to a single kind of engineering project, and may not be applicable as a general rule

(E) gives no comprehensive criteria for judging relative levels of safety, according to which we could evaluate its claim the increasing redundancy yields increasing safety

Go on to next page

9. It's a terrible idea to force businesses to furnish employees with paid leave for family concerns, such as paternity leave or leave to care for a sick child. If a business allows employees to take this time off, the workers will take advantage of the privilege and come to work as little as possible. This will destroy productivity and workplace morale.

Which one of the following, if true, most seriously weakens the argument?

(A) European countries guarantee employees generous family leave and paid vacation time, but the European standard of living is slightly below that of the United States.

(B) Most male workers refuse to take paternity leave even though it is allowed under federal law and their employees encourage it; they fear angering coworkers and harming their chances for promotion if they take time off for what is still seen as a frivolous reason.

(C) The FMLA requires employers to grant employees 12 weeks a year of unpaid leave for family purposes; though employers save money because the leave is unpaid, they often must spend money to find a replacement for the employee who takes time off.

(D) In some workplaces, the loss of a single employee at a busy time of year can be devastating, even if that employee plans to return after a few weeks; allowing family leave can overwhelm the employees who stay on the job.

(E) Allowing employees to take leave for family matters reduces absenteeism, improves morale, and surprisingly increases productivity because the employees who are granted leave tend to work much harder and more efficiently when they come back to work.

10. Casino gambling tends to be detrimental to individuals who live in the county where the casino is located, but paradoxically it benefits businesses in those same counties. Individual bankruptcy rates in counties with casinos are more than double the national average. Bankruptcy rates for businesses in the same counties are 35% lower than the national average.

Which one of the following, if true, most helps to explain the apparent paradox described above?

(A) Businesses are profiting from casino gambling because they take in money from gamblers; local individuals go bankrupt because they lose money gambling.

(B) Casinos are known to take advantage of gamblers by setting odds in such a way that the casino will always make a profit.

(C) Counties with casinos have many business opportunities for entrepreneurs who want to open hotels, restaurants, and other services businesses.

(D) Gambling functions as an addictive disease in many people; they find themselves unable to stop gambling even when they are seriously in debt and must borrow money to continue.

(E) Counties that vote to allow casinos to open generally are poor counties with high unemployment and low levels of education.

Go on to next page

11. Social Services worker: We approve of the government's new policy on food stamps. Instead of issuing actual stamps, the government now provides recipients with debit cards that they can use to buy groceries. Each month their accounts will be electronically credited with their allowance, and they can spend the money just as if it were in a bank account but only on specific approved items. This prevents the inconvenience and embarrassment associated with food stamps, which will increase the number of qualified recipients who actually buy food with their allowance and prevent fraud that was a problem associated with the paper coupons.

   All of the following, if true, help to support the position of the Social Services worker EXCEPT:

   (A) In communities that use the food stamp debit cards, participation in food stamp programs has increased 74 percent since changing to cards from coupons.

   (B) Paper food stamp coupons have long been abused by people who trade them for drugs or weapons at several cents on the dollar.

   (C) The food stamp program is meant to improve nutrition among people with low incomes, and the government has long wanted to make sure it was used to buy food.

   (D) People used to have to pick up their paper coupons at a government office once a month, which proved too inconvenient for many people who lacked transportation or free time.

   (E) Some food stamp recipients say they prefer the paper coupons because they can't tell how much money they have in their debit card accounts.

12. Primatologist: We have discovered a new kind of primate in Madagascar, the fat-tailed lemur. These lemurs hibernate, sleeping in holes in trees for up to seven months out of the year. Winter temperatures in Madagascar rarely drop below 86 degrees, so these lemurs are not hibernating to escape the cold, but perhaps conserving energy during the dry season when food is scarce. This is the first time anyone has found an animal that hibernates during hot weather, disproving the common belief that only animals in cold climates hibernate.

   Which one of the following most accurately describes the role played in the primatologist's argument by the assertion that this is the first time anyone has found an animal that hibernates during hot weather?

   (A) It challenges the long-held belief that primates never hibernate.

   (B) It accuses scientists who have studied hibernation in the past of wrongfully assuming that hibernation only occurs in cold weather.

   (C) It indicates that this discovery is very important and perhaps even revolutionary because it disproves a long-held theory about hibernation.

   (D) It calls into question the assumption that this behavior is true hibernation and suggests that it might be something else.

   (E) It sets up a rival theory so that the primatologist can disprove it.

Go on to next page

13. Director: I've decided to cast the famous American actor Burt Lancaster as the prince in my epic film of the Sicilian classic novel *The Leopard*. I want him for his star appeal and his massive dignity. The film will be in Italian, but Lancaster cannot speak Italian, so I will let him speak his lines in English and then have an Italian actor dub them in Italian. The result will be a seamless Italian film with a famous actor to help sales.

Which one of the following is an assumption on which the director's argument depends?

(A) Italian audiences will refuse to see a film of an Italian classic that does not use an Italian actor in the title role.

(B) The other actors in the film might object to playing their scenes with a character who cannot speak their language.

(C) In order to increase sales, it is more important to have a famous actor in the title role of a film than to have an actor who can actually speak the language of the film.

(D) It would be impossible to teach Lancaster enough Italian to allow him to deliver his lines in the correct language.

(E) Lancaster would feel uncomfortable working with a director and crew who did not speak English.

14. Alberto: We should eradicate mosquitoes from the earth. Mosquitoes cause a great deal of harm to humans, transmitting serious diseases such as malaria, dengue fever, and encephalitis, and they don't do anything desirable. Ecologists have found that the loss of a single species from an ecosystem doesn't usually harm the rest of the ecosystem, so eradicating mosquitoes wouldn't harm the environment, which of course would be undesirable.

Which one of the following, if true, would most weaken Alberto's argument?

(A) Mosquito-born diseases such as malaria are responsible for millions of deaths and millions of dollars of lost productivity every year.

(B) One inevitable consequence of restoring wetlands to their original state is an increase in mosquito populations.

(C) Mosquitoes have historically kept human and other animal populations down by spreading disease among them.

(D) Many animals eat mosquitoes and other flying insects.

(E) The only substances that could eradicate all mosquitoes would also kill off many birds and beneficial insects.

Go on to next page

15. Public parks are intended for use by all citizens equally. But when groups such as schools or churches use a park for parties or other organized events, they bring large numbers of people to the park at one time. Therefore there should be strict rules against large groups using public parks.

The argument's reasoning is vulnerable to criticism on the grounds that the argument presumes, without giving warrant, that

(A) large groups of people might be noisy or become violent.

(B) individuals have complained about large groups of people using public parks.

(C) public parks are designed with use by organized groups in mind.

(D) members of organized groups, like other individuals, pay taxes that support public parks.

(E) large numbers of people coming to a park prevent individuals from enjoying use of the park.

16. Employers have recently begun to offer their employees the opportunity to save money for future healthcare or family care expenses in flexible spending accounts, or FSAs. These accounts allow employees to set aside pre-tax salary income for specific expenses, which can result in a substantial savings on income tax. Surprisingly, though, very few employees have taken advantage of FSAs.

Which one of the following, if true, contributes most to an explanation of why few employees have chosen to save money in FSAs?

(A) Insurance companies have started to offer employees debit cards to go with FSAs, which makes it much easier for workers to use FSAs to pay their costs.

(B) Most employers who offer FSAs have about 20 percent workforce participation.

(C) Employees can use funds saved in FSAs to pay for over-the-counter drugs and other healthcare costs that are not covered by insurance.

(D) Funds saved in FSAs must be spent during the plan year or forfeited, which makes employees reluctant to place money in them.

(E) Employers who move to consumer-driven healthcare plans with high deductibles are finding that more of their employees choose to open FSAs.

Go on to next page

17. Many Latin American countries established democratic governments in the past decade. Recently, however, six elected heads of state have been ousted during violent revolutions. A majority of people in those countries, dissatisfied with continuing poverty, have stated that they would install a dictator if he promised to improve economic conditions.

The statements above, if true, most strongly support which one of the following conclusions?

(A) Two hundred twenty million Latin Americans, nearly half the population of the region, live in grinding poverty without many of the basic necessities of life.

(B) The governments of these countries, though democratically elected, are plagued by corruption and graft.

(C) A majority of residents of these six Latin American countries do not believe that democracy is without question the best form of government for them.

(D) Weak governments in Latin America are one of the reasons drug trafficking and illegal immigration to the United States have increased in the last decade.

(E) Some citizens of Latin American countries have expressed the opinion that rule by organized crime is preferable to democratically elected leadership.

18. Years ago people enjoyed homemade eggnog and cookie dough made with raw eggs without fear, but today raw eggs are spoken of as a biohazard, a potential hotbed of salmonella waiting to cause disease and death with the slightest contact. In previous decades, salmonella was generally found on the outside of eggshells, mainly from the eggs having come in contact with the waste products of the chickens who laid them. More recently, however, a growing number of chickens are themselves infected with salmonella, thus allowing the bacterium to be present inside the egg itself. So where once simply washing uncracked eggs protected diners from illness — usually some form of gastrointestinal distress, only rarely fatal — now only cooking eggs thoroughly can guarantee a safe dining experience.

Which one of the following most accurately expresses the main conclusion of the argument?

(A) Salmonella poisoning is on the increase, but is rarely fatal.

(B) That the relationship between salmonella and eggs has in fact changed over the years, justifying the recent caution with which people regard raw eggs.

(C) Some caution is merited when handling raw eggs, although the facts behind salmonella and eggs do not merit extreme levels of caution.

(D) The risk of food-poisoning from eating raw eggs is related to the conditions under which the eggs are produced, which have changed over time.

(E) The caution with which people regard their food is related to a better understanding of the science behind food poisoning.

Go on to next page

19. Software engineers know that a poorly written application can consume more memory than it should, and that running out of memory can cause an application to crash. However, if a crashing application causes the whole operating system to crash, the fault lies with the operating system.

    Which one of the following, if all of them are true, is LEAST helpful in establishing that the conclusion above is properly drawn?

    (A) Operating systems with generous amounts of memory are less susceptible to crashing, even when applications are poorly written.

    (B) Operating systems can isolate the memory used by individual applications, even when an application uses a lot of memory.

    (C) It is possible for an operating system to monitor an application's consumption of memory and to take action when that gets too high.

    (D) Techniques for programming operating systems to catch and handle memory errors are well defined and well known among programmers.

    (E) Since it is possible for many applications to run simultaneously under a single operating system, the operating system should have a well-defined method of managing memory consumption.

20. The document was published under a license that allows others to copy it and disseminate it as long as they do so for noncommercial purposes only. Company A included copies of the document in a training manual that they marketed and sold, arguing that the license was invalid. However, even if the license were proved invalid, the copyright was still valid, leaving Company A with no rights to use the document in any way at all.

    Which one of the following statements best illustrates the principle illustrated by the argument above?

    (A) The warranty on the laptop computer claimed to be rendered void if the user opened the case. But the manual that came with the laptop included instructions for opening the case to upgrade the computer's memory. Consumers successfully argued that those instructions constituted an endorsement of users' opening the case and that, therefore, the warranty was not void.

    (B) When the 13-year-olds were caught trying to enter an NC-17 movie at a multiplex, they argued that the cashier at the ticket-counter had sold them tickets for that movie. The manager explained that the cashier's error did not change the rules of age-limits and movie ratings.

    (C) A restaurant was fined by the Alcoholic Beverage Commission for serving distilled liquors when its license covered only beer and wine. The restaurant's manager argued that they had applied for the proper license and expected to receive it within days. The ABC countered that a license was valid only from the moment the restaurant posted it on the premises.

    (D) Ted's parents gave him permission to drive the car, but only over to Alice's house. When his mother saw the car parked at the mall, some miles away, Ted argued that Alice was not at home. Ted's mom pointed out that he ought, upon discovering that fact, to have driven straight home.

    (E) The celebrity sued the magazine for publishing photographs of him sunning himself in his back yard, which was enclosed by a high fence. The magazine claimed that he was a public figure and did not, therefore, have the same rights to privacy as normal citizens. The celebrity claimed that the extensive fence around his yard justified his privacy rights when behind it, despite his prominent stature in the eyes of the public.

Go on to next page

21. Scholar: Greek epic poetry emerged as an art form before any of it was ever written down. Singers developed a specialized vocabulary that allowed them to compose poems about the heroes of the Trojan War as they sang them. These poems were neither made up from scratch as the singer sang, nor were they fixed texts that were memorized and repeated verbatim. Even after written texts were created that captured these orally-composed poems, the tradition continued to evolve, with written texts of the same poem differing from place to place and from time to time, according to the circumstances of their production and the interests of their creators and their intended audiences.

    If the scholar's statements are true, which one of the following must be true?

    (A) That each written edition derived from the first written version of an orally composed epic.

    (B) That any single written edition of a Greek epic cannot claim to represent the "original" version.

    (C) That the poems inevitably grew longer and more narratologically complex over the centuries.

    (D) That the tradition of composing epics orally died away as the poems came to be written down.

    (E) That the older editions were less likely to have been influenced by local politics than subsequent editions.

22. Curator: This museum does not grant people the right to use images of items in its collection in online publications. We are obliged to do everything in our power to ensure the continued appeal of visiting our collection in person.

    The Curator's argument depends on assuming which one of the following?

    (A) Taking photographs of art objects, especially using a flash, can damage the objects by accelerating the fading of paint.

    (B) The museum sells pictures of its collection in its gift shop, which is an important source of income for the museum.

    (C) Images placed online are easily copied and reused by other people.

    (D) The quality of most electronic images, especially those online, falls short of the professional standards of the museum.

    (E) If people see online images of items in the museum's collection, they will no longer be interested in seeing the collection with their own eyes.

23. Career counselor: Many large international companies have changed their practices regarding international assignments. There is much more emphasis on helping spouses of expatriate employees to adjust to the foreign environment. This has reduced premature returns by 67 percent.

Which one of the following is an assumption upon which the career counselor's argument depends?

(A) Most expatriate employees go abroad with their spouses, and spousal and marital difficulties were formerly responsible for a large number of premature returns.

(B) When an employee is assigned to a foreign assignment for a year or less, his or her family sees the assignment as an adventure and spends most of the time in a "honeymoon" period.

(C) Expatriate employees work long hours and travel a great deal, and their children make new friends at school, but spouses often have no friends and no work to support them while they're abroad.

(D) The majority of international assignments today last for less than a year, but ten years ago 70 percent of them lasted much longer than one year.

(E) Many companies now offer expatriate spouses language training, career guidance, and assistance in finding homes and schools.

24. Traveler: When I flew to Boston on Tuesday, I checked my suitcase but carried my computer on the plane with me, just to make sure it would arrive with me. It was a good thing I did, because when I arrived in Logan Airport my bag was nowhere to be seen; neither were any of the other checked bags from my flight. We trooped to the help desk en masse, and I approached the clerk first. I spoke politely and was very understanding, while my fellow passengers behind me stomped impatiently and heaped abuse on her. As a result, she was very helpful to me, but she also took her time, rewarding me for my politeness and punishing the other passengers who were so rude by making them wait for her assistance.

Which one of the following principles most helps to justify the reasoning above?

(A) A stitch in time saves nine.

(B) Don't price an unborn calf.

(C) Don't put all your eggs in one basket.

(D) Neither a borrower nor a lender be.

(E) You catch more flies with honey than you do with vinegar.

STOP You may check your work on this section only. Do not go back to any previous section.

Section 11

Time: 35 minutes

26 Questions

Directions: Read each passage and answer the questions that follow it. Some questions may have more than one answer that looks correct. In that case, pick the one that answers the question most completely and correctly. Don't assume anything that isn't stated in the passage or the questions. All the information you need to answer the questions is contained in the passage, questions, and answer choices.

Line   *Black Apollo,* by Kenneth Manning, describes the life of Ernest Everett Just, one of the first black scientists in America. Manning recounts Just's impoverished origins in South Carolina, his
(05) adaptations to a white educational system, and his professional careers as a zoology professor at Howard University and as an embryologist at Wood's Hole Biological Laboratories. Despite countless difficulties imposed upon him by a
(10) world in which a black person was not supposed to practice science, Just became an internationally esteemed biologist. His story is one of courage, determination, and dedication to science. But Manning's goals are more far-reaching
(15) than to simply tell a story or describe one man's life. After all, while Just was a brilliant biologist, he was ultimately not pivotal to the development of either science or race relations in the 20th century. The issues brought out in his story, however,
(20) are pivotal. A comprehensive appreciation of the conditions that Just faced in his daily work offers a powerful lens by which to examine the development of science and racial boundaries in America.
    Manning wrote *Just's* story as a biography.
(25) In some respects, biography does not seem to be a promising medium for great historical work. Biographies simply tell a story. Most students receive their introductions to the history of science in the worshipful biographies of past scien-
(30) tific giants. Benjamin Franklin and Albert Einstein offer excellent examples to young students of how scientists contribute to society. Biographies are popular for children's reading lists (and best-seller lists) because they have simple subjects,
(35) can present clear moral statements, and manage

to teach a little history at the same time. This simplicity of form, however, does not preclude the biography from being a powerful medium for historical work and social commentary.
    The biography yields *particular* rewards for (40) the historian of science. One of the central principles of history of science, indeed a central reason for the discipline, is to show that science is a product of social forces. This principle implies that historians and sociologists have insights on (45) the practice of science that scientists, to whom the subject would otherwise fall, are less likely to produce. Moreover, if society does influence science, then it behooves historians to explain how such an important process works. The human (50) orientation of the biography makes it an excellent medium in which historians can do this work. Were a researcher to investigate the development of scientific theory solely by reading the accounts written of a laboratory's experiments — by look- (55) ing only at the "science" — the researcher would likely see a science moved by apparently rational forces toward a discernible goal. But this picture is incomplete and artificial. If that researcher examines science through the people who gener- (60) ated it, a richer mosaic of actors emerges. The science biography has the potential to reveal both the person through the science and the science through the person. From these perspectives, the forces of politics, emotions, and eco- (65) nomics, each of which can direct science as much as rational thought, are more easily brought to light. *Black Apollo* is a riveting example of what a historian can accomplish with a skillful and directed use of biography. (70)

Go on to next page ⟹

1. Which one of the following most accurately states the main point of the passage?

   (A) Ernest Everett Just was an extremely important biologist during the 20th century, both because of his contributions to the field of embryology and because of his race.

   (B) Scientists tend to ignore the social, historical, and political forces that surround all scientific research and discovery, which makes their interpretations of scientific events incomplete.

   (C) Biographies are a popular genre for children's books because they can tell discrete stories in an accessible fashion, incorporating scientific knowledge into a person's life and thereby making it more interesting to readers.

   (D) Biography is a powerful tool for a historian of science, who can use the genre to explore the effects of politics, economics, and emotions on the direction of scientific development; *Black Apollo* is an example of biography used in this way.

   (E) Kenneth Manning wrote *Black Apollo* to criticize racial prejudices and to prove that Ernest Everett Just could have been much more successful if he had not been the victim of discrimination.

2. According to the passage, the main goal of the discipline called history of science is to

   (A) illuminate the effects of social forces on scientists in a way that scientists themselves are unlikely to do

   (B) explain scientific discoveries in a manner that is easily understood by non scientists

   (C) write biographies of important scientific figures that portray their work against a social and political background

   (D) influence scientific research by identifying the most important scientific contributions in history

   (E) provide an academic discipline that allows people without scientific inclinations to study science painlessly

3. What is the primary purpose of the second paragraph?

   (A) to describe the many things Ernest Everett Just accomplished despite the racial prejudice he faced

   (B) to suggest that biography is really too simple a historical form for the historian of science to use to convey complex ideas

   (C) to explain why biography is both a popular historical genre and a powerful medium for explaining the significance of scientific discoveries

   (D) to argue against using biographies to teach children about scientific figures from the past

   (E) to advocate increased teaching of the sciences in schools and universities

4. The author of *Black Apollo* would be most likely to agree with which one of the following statements?

   (A) One of the best ways to come to an understanding of the realities of race relations and scientific development in the 20th century is to read an in-depth account of the life of one of the people who lived and worked in that world.

   (B) The goal of a historian of science is to glorify the accomplishments of his historical subjects, embellishing them if need be.

   (C) A scientific historian should pay close attention to the social and literary aspects of a scientific biography and play down the actual science because readers can turn to scientific reports to get that information.

   (D) Ernest Everett Just was the most important black biologist, and in fact one of the most important biologists, of the 20th century.

   (E) Biography is too limited a genre to allow a historian of science to do justice to a topic, but it is useful occasionally because most readers find biographies more accessible than other historical formats.

Go on to next page

5. According to the passage, why is Ernest Everett Just significant enough to warrant a biography?

   (A) Just was one of the first professional black scientists in the United States.

   (B) Just grew up in poverty but overcame this initial adversity to attend Howard University and then become a professional scientist.

   (C) Just was a biologist whose work was known and respected internationally.

   (D) Just's daily experiences illuminate the conditions characterized by both scientific research and racial relations during his lifetime.

   (E) Just became a college professor and an embryologist at Wood's Hole Biological Laboratories.

6. What does the author mean by the phrase "simplicity of form" (Line 37)?

   (A) the simple language used by many biographical writers

   (B) the easy-to-read page design used by most publishers of biographies

   (C) a writing style that is easy for schoolchildren to read and understand

   (D) the clear moral judgments that accompany the account of the subject's life

   (E) the standard format of a biography, which follows the course of the subject's life

Go on to next page

Line   Sodium lauryl sulfate (SLS) is an emulsifier
and surfactant that produces lather and foam
which can dissolve oil and dirt on skin and hair.
SLS and another similar detergent, sodium laureth
(05) sulfate (SLES), are commonly used as foaming
agents in cleaners, shampoos, and toothpaste.
Both of these substances are derived from
coconut oil. They make liquid and paste cleansers
more effective at cleansing because they allow the
(10) cleanser to disperse more readily over the object
being cleaned and make it easier to rinse the
cleanser away. SLS and SLES have been used for
years in numerous products sold to consumers.
Other foaming agents are available but SLS and
(15) SLES have remained popular because of their low
cost, effectiveness, lack of taste and odor, and
long history of safe use.
    There are a few minor risks associated with
the use of SLS and SLES. They will burn human
(20) eyes, a phenomenon well known to anyone who
has ever gotten a drop of shampoo in his or her
eye. A high enough concentration of SLS will burn
skin if it remains in contact with the skin for a
long time, though normally this is not a problem
(25) because the products containing SLES or SLS are
diluted with water and quickly rinsed away. SLS
in toothpaste can cause diarrhea in someone who
swallows a large quantity of it, but it is not known
to be toxic if ingested in small quantities.
(30)   Many people have become afraid of SLS and
SLES in recent years, largely as a result of widespread rumors circulated on the Internet that
blame SLS and SLES for causing numerous ailments in humans, including hair loss, dry skin,
(35) liver and kidney disease, blindness in children,
and cancer. SLS has been called "one of the
most dangerous substances used in cosmetic
products." Rumors warn that SLS and SLES can
react with other ingredients in products to
(40) form nitrates, which are potential carcinogens.
Detractors of SLS and SLES point out that these
substances are used in cleansers intended for the
floors of garages and bathrooms and in engine
degreasers. This is true; it is also true that house-
(45) hold and garage cleaners are not sold for cosmetic use, come with warnings of possible skin
and eye irritation, and are perfectly safe to use
for their intended purposes.
    These Internet warnings of the dangers of
(50) SLS and SLES are absurd and unsubstantiated.
The FDA has approved the use of SLS and SLES
in a number of personal care products. The
Occupational Safety and Health Administration,
the International Agency for Research on Cancer,
(55) and the American Cancer Society have all done
extensive research on SLS and SLES and concluded that they do not cause cancer.

7. Which one of the following best summarizes
the main idea of the passage?

(A) There are a few minor risks associated
with the use of SLS and SLES, but
consumers should feel safe in using
products containing these substances
because the FDA has approved them
for use in personal care products.

(B) Manufacturers of shampoos and tooth-
pastes include the artificial chemicals
SLS and SLES in their products because
they are cheap and effective surfactants,
despite the known dangers associated
with them.

(C) SLS and SLES are detergents that are
commonly used in personal care products because they are effective and
safe, despite unsubstantiated rumors
to the contrary.

(D) Widespread rumors circulated on
the Internet blame SLS and SLES for
numerous ailments in humans, but
these rumors are unsubstantiated, as
proven by research done by the FDA,
the American Cancer Society, and other
scientific organizations.

(E) It's entirely possible to use SLS and
SLES in both personal care products
such as shampoos and industrial products such as engine degreasers because
at lower concentrations the substances
are perfectly safe to use on human skin.

8. According to the passage, what are some of
the household products that commonly
contain SLS or SLES?

(A) shampoo, mouthwash, sunscreen,
hair dye

(B) shampoo, toothpaste, bathroom cleaners, engine degreasers

(C) toothpaste, engine degreasers, engine
lubricants, garage cleaners

(D) mouthwash, facial moisturizers, baby
wipes

(E) bathroom and kitchen cleaners, laundry detergents, fabric softeners

Go on to next page

9. Why does the author mention the FDA in the last paragraph?

    (A) To point out that the FDA has approved the use of SLS and SLES in personal care products.

    (B) To suggest that the FDA has the best interests of consumers at heart.

    (C) To imply that the FDA's opinion that SLS and SLES are safe for use in personal care products excuses manufacturers from testing their personal care products for safety.

    (D) To protest the FDA's approval of the use of SLS and SLES in personal care products.

    (E) To criticize people who claim that SLS and SLES are dangerous despite the FDA's approval of the substances in personal care products.

10. According to the passage, what are some of the known risks of SLS exposure?

    (A) cancer, blindness, cataracts, dry skin, diarrhea

    (B) burning eyes, burned skin after long exposure, liver disease, kidney disease

    (C) skin irritation, eye irritation, hair loss, diarrhea if ingested in large quantities

    (D) burning eyes, burned skin after long exposure, diarrhea if ingested in large quantities

    (E) diarrhea, skin irritation after extended exposure, eye irritation, cataracts, bladder cancer

11. Which one of the following best describes the organization of the passage?

    (A) A list of known risks of exposure to SLS and SLES; a list of unsubstantiated risks of exposure to SLS and SLES; a conclusion stating that SLS and SLES are perfectly safe.

    (B) A description of several common surfactants and the way in which they work; several anecdotal accounts of injuries and illnesses allegedly caused by SLS and SLES; a call for the government to ban the use of SLS and SLES in consumer care products.

    (C) A description of the chemical composition of SLS and SLES; a list of evidence against the use of SLS and SLES in personal care products; a proposal to manufacturers suggesting that they use only naturally-occurring substances in their products.

    (D) An overview of the many uses of SLS and SLES; an explanation of why manufacturers use these substances in both consumer care and household cleaning products; a criticism against people who spread rumors over the Internet; praise for the FDA.

    (E) A description of SLS and SLES and their uses; known risks of SLS and SLES; criticisms aimed at SLS and SLES by detractors on the Internet; evidence that SLS and SLES are perfectly safe and the rumors are preposterous.

Go on to next page

12. The primary purpose of the third paragraph is

    (A) to criticize makers of personal cleansing products for including harsh chemicals in their shampoos, toothpastes, and other offerings

    (B) to describe the way SLS and SLES work and explain why they are commonly used in various foaming products

    (C) to warn readers of the dangers associated with exposure to SLS and SLES, which include cancer, skin irritation, blindness, and kidney and liver ailments

    (D) to propose other naturally-occurring substances that manufacturers could substitute for SLS and SLES in their products

    (E) to explain why some people fear SLS and SLES, and to list the diseases that Internet rumors have linked to the substances

13. It can be inferred from the passage that the author would be most likely to agree with which one of the following statements?

    (A) It's silly for people to be afraid of substances that have been deemed safe by the FDA and several other major organizations and that have a long history of safe use simply on the basis of unsubstantiated rumors.

    (B) Consumers can trust the FDA to make sure that all consumer products are safe because the FDA is funded by tax dollars and takes seriously its mission to ensure the health of American citizens.

    (C) The Internet isn't a very reliable source of information on the hazards associated with common consumer products, but information posted on the Internet by the FDA, OSHA, and the American Cancer Society is generally reliable.

    (D) SLS and SLES are cheap and effective surfactants and emulsifiers, but they aren't especially safe to use in products intended for direct physical contact with human skin.

    (E) If enough concerned consumers protest the inclusion of SLS and SLES in personal care products, they can probably persuade manufacturers to use all-natural ingredients, but there's no reason for them to do this because SLS and SLES are safe.

Go on to next page

Line   The disabled in the United States have made a good deal of progress since the 1927 case *Buck v. Bell*. That case centered around Carrie Buck, a mentally retarded female inmate at the Virginia
(05) Colony for Epileptics and Feebleminded, the daughter of a fellow inmate and the mother of a child who appeared likely to spend her life in the institution as well. The commonwealth of Virginia had passed a law, the Virginia Statute
(10) for Eugenical Sterilization, which allowed doctors to sterilize the disabled, beggars, criminals, alcoholics, and other unfortunates, in order to prevent them from passing their traits on to children who would likely become wards of the
(15) state. The Supreme Court ruled that this law was constitutional — Justice Oliver Wendell Holmes wrote in his opinion "three generations of imbeciles are enough" — and Carrie Buck was sterilized.
(20)   By the 1960s, the disabled had begun to fight back against such coercive and disrespectful laws. Employing tactics that had worked in the civil rights movement, the disabled and their advocates insisted that their basic rights were
(25) being denied and that they had the right to decide how to take care of themselves. Starting in the late 1960s, Congress passed a series of laws designed to help the disabled live in society as equal citizens. The Architectural Barriers Act of
(30) 1968 required federally owned buildings to eliminate structures that were impossible for the disabled to negotiate. The Urban Mass Transit Act of 1970 required all new buses to have wheelchair lifts. The Rehabilitation Act of 1973 removed fed-
(35) eral funding from any institution that discriminated against the disabled. The Education for All Handicapped Children Act of 1975 guaranteed all disabled children free and appropriate public education.
(40)   All of these laws were precursors to the Americans with Disabilities Act, passed in 1990. This law, which applies to all employers with 15 or more employees, prohibits any discrimination against qualified people with disabilities in all
(45) employment matters. Employers cannot discriminate during hiring, firing, promotion, pay, training, or any other aspects of employment. Under the terms of the ADA, a "qualified" person is anyone who can perform the essential functions
(50) of a job, if necessary with reasonable accommodation; that accommodation can include making facilities accessible, revising job descriptions, or changing training requirements to make it possible for the disabled to participate. Employers do
(55) not have to accommodate all possible disabilities, especially if that would be very expensive or difficult, but they do have to allow the disabled to participate if possible.

In the 2004 decision *Tennessee v. Lane*, the U.S. Supreme Court ruled that disabled people can sue states under the ADA for failing to make (60) their courthouses wheelchair-accessible. This case involved several disabled plaintiffs who claimed that they did not have reasonable access to the state's courts. In writing the court's opinion, Justice Souter noted that the government (65) has a duty to respect the dignity of all people, and that judges have historically been some of the worst offenders against the disabled — a far cry from *Buck v. Bell*.

14. Which one of the following titles most accurately describes the contents of the passage?

    (A) "*Buck v. Bell*: Eugenics in American History"

    (B) "Disability Activism and the Civil Rights Movement: a Comparison"

    (C) "Disability Law and the Supreme Court"

    (D) "The Americans with Disabilities Act: A Step Forward for the Disabled"

    (E) "Disability Law: From Forced Sterilization to Workplace Accommodation"

15. The author quotes the words of Oliver Wendell Holmes in Line 17 in order to

    (A) illustrate the attitude of national leaders toward people with disabilities

    (B) imply that Justice Holmes was unusually insensitive toward disabled people

    (C) criticize the Commonwealth of Virginia for being insensitive toward the mentally retarded

    (D) defend Justice Holmes from accusations of prejudice against the disabled because he was simply enforcing state law

    (E) suggest that the Supreme Court of the 1920s was biased against the disabled

Go on to next page

16. According to the passage, the ADA requires employers to do all of the following EXCEPT:

    (A) treat the disabled just like other applicants and employees in all employment matters

    (B) ignore disabilities when choosing applicants to interview if the disabled applicants are qualified and could perform the job in question with reasonable accommodations

    (C) revise job descriptions, rearrange facilities, reschedule work shifts, or whatever other reasonable actions would make it possible for the disabled to work

    (D) build whatever additional facilities are necessary to make it possible for disabled people to work at a particular workplace

    (E) provide reasonable accommodations for disabled employees

17. The function of the second paragraph is to

    (A) compare and contrast the disability rights movement with the civil rights movement

    (B) explain the functioning of the Education for All Handicapped Children Act

    (C) tell the story of Carrie Buck, who was involuntarily sterilized by the state of Virginia

    (D) describe the legislative improvements to the rights of the disabled created by legislation of the 1960s and 1970s

    (E) draw a link between disability legislation of the 1960s and the 1970s and the Americans with Disabilities Act

18. The author mentions the civil rights movement in the second paragraph in order to

    (A) imply that disability rights activists were more motivated to improve their living conditions than civil rights activists

    (B) suggest that civil rights legislation paved the way for later disability rights legislation

    (C) criticize the lawmakers of the 1960s and 1970s for caving in to unreasonable demands from both the civil rights and the disability rights movements

    (D) inform the reader of the type of tactics used by the disabled and their advocates to demand rights of their own

    (E) introduce an account of the sit-in used by the disabled to force the administration to enact the Rehabilitation Act of 1973

19. Which one of the following best describes the author's view of disability law?

    (A) It makes it possible for the disabled to live lives virtually undistinguishable from those of people without disabilities.

    (B) It has improved living conditions for the disabled tremendously since the 1920s.

    (C) It does not impose an undue burden on state governments and employers.

    (D) It is better than it was fifty years ago but still has ample room for improvement.

    (E) It has forced employers to interview disabled workers and seriously consider them for positions.

Go on to next page

Line   Public education as it is currently known was a creation of a German government worried about the dangers of workers' uprisings that was then transformed by Enlightenment and
(05) Romantic educational theories into an institution genuinely concerned with developing human minds. Before the 1700s, there was no public education in Europe. Parents who wanted their children to be educated paid for private schools or
(10) private tutors. The rest of the children in Europe worked. Many of them worked alongside their parents in spinning factories producing thread for Germany's burgeoning textile industry. The textile mill owners blatantly exploited their work-
(15) ers, which led to increasing levels of unrest on the part of the peasants. During the 1750s, King Frederick II asked his minister of Silesia, Ernest Wilhelm von Schlabrendorff, to find a way to channel the energy of restless peasants into
(20) something that would be less dangerous to the throne than riots.

    Schlabrendorff suggested that the king could mold a compliant citizenry if he created a system of state-run schools. These schools could teach
(25) the children of the peasantry that their lot was ordained by god, that they should not try to improve it, that the government was good to them, and that they should not question authority, along with reading, writing, and arithmetic.
(30) School would be compulsory, and children who did not attend could be punished by truant officers. This would shift children's primary loyalty from their parents and families to the state; their parents would be powerless against the truant
(35) officers, and thus would be forced to send their children to school whether they wanted to or not. Aristocrats liked this idea. They liked the thought of schools making peasants more docile and patriotic, and they appreciated the way state-
(40) run schools would teach children of lower social classes to accept their position in life. In 1763, Frederick gave Schlabrendorff the go-ahead to start opening schools, and soon every child in Silesia between the ages of 7 and 15 was attend-
(45) ing school. These earliest schools, called *Spinnschulen,* combined work with education. Children took classes in the mornings and spun thread in the afternoons.

    By the 1800s the Spinnschulen had metamor-
(50) phosed into full-day schools with state-certified teachers who taught a state-approved curriculum, and Germany became a hotbed of educational theory, much of it influenced by 19th-century Romanticism that directly contradicted the princi-
(55) ples that had led to the foundation of public

schools in the 1700. Johann Bernhard Basedow used the work of Enlightenment scholars to argue that education should be a holistic pursuit, incorporating physical movement, manual training, realistic teaching, and the study of nature. (60)
Friedrich Froebel invented kindergarten in the mid-1800s, creating a "children's garden" based on the belief that children are naturally creative and productive and developed special toys designed to teach specific skills and motions. Wilhelm von (65)
Humboldt specialized in secondary and university educational theory, insisting that advanced students should pursue independent research and prizing above all three educational principles: self-government by teachers, unity of teaching, and (70)
academic freedom.

20. The passage is primarily concerned with discussing which one of the following?

(A) the use of public schools to disseminate political messages, as exemplified by German public schools in the 18th and 19th centuries

(B) the exploitation of the working class by German aristocracy in the 18th century and the use of public education to justify this practice

(C) the philosophical origins of public schools in 18th century Germany and the transformation in educational thinking in the 19th century

(D) the thinking of German educational theorists and their influence on modern educational practices

(E) the role of Frederick II's minister of Silesia and the German aristocracy in the creation of public schools in Germany

Go on to next page

21. The passage suggests which one of the following about the owners of textile mills in the 1700s?

    (A) They wanted their child workers to have the benefit of an education, so they opened schools within their factories and required all young workers to attend classes.

    (B) They paid children less than adults and so they preferred to hire young workers whenever they could.

    (C) They were indifferent to the well-being and needs of their workers, caring only to maximize production and profits no matter what it cost their employees.

    (D) They were all aristocrats who believed their authority was divinely ordained, and that as a result of this divinely ordained position, they had a duty to care for the less fortunate people in their communities by providing work and education for them.

    (E) They were uniformly patriotic and supported the authority of their king without question and supported the opening of Spinnschulen because this would allow peasants to be taught the same patriotic ideals they held so dear.

22. According to the passage, how did 19th century schools differ from 18th century schools?

    (A) Eighteenth century schools were intended to make textile mills run more efficiently, by making workers become more skilled at their jobs; 19th century schools were no longer attached to textile factories.

    (B) Eighteenth century schools were concerned primarily with teaching working-class children to accept their fate and love their ruler; 19th century schools began to focus on developing the full human potential of students.

    (C) Eighteenth century schools were open only to children of the aristocracy whose parents could pay their tuition. By the 19th century, schools were open to all free of charge but poorer students had to pay their way by working in spinning factories in the afternoons.

    (D) Eighteenthcentury schools were designed to instill patriotic ideals in the peasantry and make them docile and compliant; 19th century schools instead tried to develop all children into free thinkers.

    (E) Eighteenth century schools were not appealing to parents, who often tried to keep their children out of school and as a result were punished by truant officers; 19th century schools, on the other hand, were appealing to both parents and children because educational philosophers believed a more pleasant environment was more conducive to education.

23. What does the author mean by the phrase "increasing levels of unrest" in Line 15?

    (A) riots and other forms of violence against the owners of textile factories by peasants unhappy at their treatment

    (B) political speeches and demonstrations by politicians trying to earn the working-class vote

    (C) aggression from neighboring countries looking to invade Germany

    (D) religious turmoil between Catholics and Protestants

    (E) juvenile delinquency and vandalism by unemployed and uneducated young men

Go on to next page

24. According to the passage, what did German aristocrats think about the idea of creating public schools?

(A) They feared that educating the working classes would make them less docile and accepting of their position in life and more likely to rise up and overthrow the nobles.

(B) They disliked the idea of paying taxes to support public schools and resented the king and Schlabrendorff for forcing this expense on them.

(C) They appreciated Schlabrendorff's brilliance in concocting an idea that would both make the peasantry more compliant and simultaneously produce more workers for the spinning factories.

(D) They approved of disseminating religious education to the masses because this would make the citizenry more compliant and less likely to engage in workers' rebellions.

(E) They liked the idea because it would make the peasantry more docile and more accepting of their fate, which would help keep the aristocracy safe in their prosperity.

25. According to the passage, what was the purpose of using truant officers to keep children in school?

(A) to ensure that all children received the full education that was their right, even if their parents wished instead to keep them working at home

(B) to take away the authority of parents and replace it with state power over children and citizens

(C) to assist parents in making sure that their children attended school as required by catching and punishing children who failed to attend

(D) to indoctrinate children and their parents with political messages designed to help the aristocracy

(E) to assist the king and his administration in molding a compliant citizenry through a system of state-run schools

26. Which one of the following best summarizes the views of 19th century educational thinkers?

(A) The function of state-run schools is to instill obedience, patriotism, and docility in the working classes; wealthy children whose parents can afford to pay can have a more liberal education from private tutors.

(B) The most important subject for children to learn is religion, which is why schools should be run by the Church and should include all aspects of worship and theology.

(C) Most people cannot adequately educate their children on their own, but the state has an interest in an educated citizenry, so it is the government's job to provide public education and see that people send their children to school.

(D) People learn best in an environment that respects their individuality, affords them freedom, and incorporates a variety of aspects of learning, such as physical movement, manual skills, and independent exploration.

(E) A child's best and first teacher is his or her mother, so mothers should be encouraged to teach their children at home; this produces better results than public schools and is much cheaper for the state.

STOP You may check your work on this section only.
Do not go back to any previous section.

Section III

Time: 35 minutes

25 Questions

Directions: Read the passage and choose the best answer. Some questions may have more than one answer that looks right. Select the one that answers the question most completely. Don't assume anything that isn't directly stated, and don't let your imagination run wild. All the information you need is in the arguments and the answer choices.

1. Economist: On average, the more a person donates to a religious group, the less likely that person is to participate in religious activities, including weekly or daily religious services. For every one percent increase in a person's donations, there is a one percent decrease in his participation. Therefore we can assume that people who donate the largest amounts to their churches are the least likely to attend services.

   Which one of the following statements, if true, most seriously weakens the economist's argument?

   (A) Conservative Protestants tend to continue attending services even when they donate large amounts.

   (B) Many religious people claim that they feel more comfortable skipping services if they give more money to their churches.

   (C) The same phenomenon has been observed in all denominations of Christians and in Jewish congregations.

   (D) One of the causes of the Protestant Reformation in the 1500s was the Church's practice of granting indulgences to parishioners who donated money.

   (E) The bigger a check a parishioner writes, the more likely he is to skip services the following weekend.

2. Geneticist: The odds of a child being born with Down syndrome increase dramatically when a woman reaches the age of 35. By the age of 49 a woman has a one in four chance of conceiving a child with such abnormalities. Yet the vast majority of Down syndrome children are born to mothers under the age of 35.

   Which one of the following, if true, most helps to reconcile the geneticist's two claims?

   (A) The number of women having babies in their forties has increased in the last decade.

   (B) Down syndrome is one of the most common birth defects.

   (C) Many mothers decide to abort fetuses that are diagnosed with chromosomal abnormalities in prenatal tests.

   (D) New tests can now identify fetuses affected with Down syndrome in the first trimester.

   (E) Most babies are born to mothers under the age of 35.

Go on to next page

3. Shoe company: Our shoes are masterpieces of podiatric design. We use wide toe boxes to give toes room to spread naturally. Our footbeds support the entire foot, toe, arch, and heel. Slightly raised heels and a curved sole alleviate fatigue and facilitate walking. The materials we use in soles are excellent shock absorbers. We guarantee that your feet will love our shoes or your money back.

   The claim that "we guarantee that your feet will love our shoes or your money back" plays which one of the following roles in the argument?

   (A) It infers from the information preceding it that advanced podiatric design is essential to comfortable shoes.

   (B) It implies that if a consumer purchases these shoes and they hurt her feet, the company will refund her purchase price.

   (C) It suggests that all customers who buy these shoes are satisfied with their purchases.

   (D) It criticizes the design of most mass-produced shoes, which are much more likely to cause foot problems.

   (E) It argues that only shoes designed by certified podiatrists can guarantee healthy and pain-free feet.

4. The administration has issued new regulations restricting travel to Cuba and limiting the amount visitors can spend there. Only Cuban-Americans are allowed to visit Cuba, they can visit only once every three years for 14 days, they may bring only $300 in cash to the country, and they may not bring back to the United States any merchandise purchased in Cuba. This should hasten the fall of Cuba's repressive dictatorship, which should benefit all Cuban people.

   Which one of the following, if true, most weakens the argument?

   (A) Many Cubans depend on cash and goods brought to them by relatives who previously could visit once a year and bring in $3,000; without that money, they will suffer financial hardship.

   (B) U.S. citizens who are not Cuban-American will not be allowed to visit Cuba at all, though the administration will make a few exceptions for journalists.

   (C) Cuba's government is led by the communist Fidel Castro, who has been in control of the island nation since 1959.

   (D) Critics of the law have accused the administration of pandering to the demands of the powerful Cuban-American lobby in Florida.

   (E) The Treasury Department believes that Castro's regime receives a great deal of financial support from infusions of cash brought into the country by Cuban-Americans.

Go on to next page

5. Airline: We have reduced the number of seats available to frequent-flier customers wishing to exchange 25,000 miles for basic tickets, but we have increased the number of premium seats that require 50,000 miles. We believe customers will appreciate this because the premium seats offer more flexibility than the basic seats.

The reasoning in the argument is most vulnerable to criticism on the grounds that the argument

(A) suggests that customers with more frequent-flier miles deserve more access to seats than those with fewer frequent-flier miles

(B) criticizes customers who use frequent-flier miles to purchase seats for their inflexibility

(C) neglects to mention that airlines dislike awarding frequent-flier seats because they cut into profit margins

(D) assumes without offering evidence that customers value flexibility enough to pay double the frequent-flier miles for it

(E) disingenuously encourages people to use their frequent-flier miles to upgrade to first class instead of purchasing coach class tickets

6. Sociologist: Women tend to marry up; that is, they marry men who are at least their equals in education, income, and social status. This trend is not as apparent among women with the most education and the highest incomes, who are more likely to marry men of equal status, but it is perceptible among women with less education and lower incomes. The result is that many men, especially poorly educated and poverty-stricken ones, never manage to find wives.

The conclusion drawn by the sociologist follows logically if which one of the following is assumed?

(A) Highly educated women are most likely to marry educated men.

(B) Wealthy men are more physically attractive to women than poor men.

(C) Though there are approximately equal numbers of men and women, women are more likely than men to marry at least once.

(D) Highly educated men still make more money than their female counterparts.

(E) Low-income women are more interested in education than their male counterparts.

Go on to next page

7. Bullying bosses are a common fixture of the workplace. They usually abuse subordinates simply because they enjoy exerting power for its own sake. Subordinates who are abused by their bosses typically perform their jobs as usual and almost never lodge formal complaints, preferring to complain in sessions with coworkers in which they discuss their bosses' misdeeds.

   Which one of the following best illustrates the proposition above?

   (A) Boss Maureen blames subordinate Skylar for all of her mistakes, informing clients that she would have gotten work done on time but for his incompetence. Skylar files a complaint with the EEOC and receives a right to sue letter for national origin discrimination.

   (B) Boss Frank makes subordinate David stay late every afternoon, making him do work that he could have done in the morning if he had known about it. David tolerates this for a few months and then accepts a job at a rival company.

   (C) Boss Belinda makes fun of the way subordinate Casey dresses, telling her that no one will ever take her seriously with her budget wardrobe. Casey informs her company's human resources manager of Belinda's comments and is transferred to another department.

   (D) Boss Bill demands that subordinate Paul bill a certain number of hours but fails to provide Paul with enough work. Paul comes to the office every day and pretends to work without accomplishing anything, spending much of his time complaining about Bill to his secretary.

   (E) Boss Stephanie constantly criticizes subordinate Kim's work, correcting it one way one day and then correcting it back to its original state the next. Kim meekly accepts the criticisms, but spends every Thursday evening at a bar with coworkers making fun of Stephanie.

8. In order to earn a graduate equivalency diploma, a student must pass tests on subjects taught in high schools, proving that he or she has mastered them to the degree assumed of a high school graduate. It makes sense for a student to drop out of high school and earn a GED. A GED takes much less time to earn than a high school diploma, and is evidence that the student has learned everything he or she would have learned in high school.

   Which one of the following, if true, most seriously weakens the argument?

   (A) Some GED-prep programs incorporate enrichment activities into their test preparation, such as taking students to art exhibits and theatrical performances.

   (B) Most colleges and universities consider a GED equivalent to a high school degree for admission purposes.

   (C) Many successful businessmen dropped out of high school and earned a GED.

   (D) High school graduates generally have a much higher level of mastery of academic subjects than those who earn GEDs.

   (E) Many GED students are slightly older than high school students, and they often hold jobs in addition to studying to pass the GED tests.

Go on to next page

9. The legislature should ban over-the-counter sales to minors of cold medications containing dextromethorphan, commonly known as DXM. Teenagers have been taking overdoses of these medications to induce a cheap high and hallucinations, but high doses of this drug can cause comas or death. Emergency room visits involving this substance has increased recently as teens research DXM on the Internet. A ban will be the best way to protect our young people.

Which one of the following, if true, most strongly supports the statement above?

(A) Effects of DXM overdoses include high fever, seizures, comas, and death; one 20-year-old man spent four months in a coma after abusing DXM.

(B) DXM is not an addictive substance and will not induce chemical dependency in regular users.

(C) The standard dose of DXM for treating colds is 15 mg; teenagers commonly take 100 mg doses to induce hallucinations and a feeling of unreality.

(D) A ban on over-the-counter sales of cough medicines containing codeine reduced incidences of codeine overdoses by 150% in two years' time.

(E) Between 2000 and 2003, the number of calls to poison control centers about overdoses of DXM more than doubled.

10. Hurricanes start over the ocean and must remain over water to keep their powerful winds moving. They almost always form over warm tropical waters in the late summer and early autumn when the water is warmest. They lose strength when they move onto land and eventually dwindle and die away.

If the statements above are true, which one of the following would also have to be true?

(A) A city on the coast is more vulnerable to being struck by a hurricane than an inland city.

(B) Hurricanes can never strike coastal areas in the northern part of the United States because the water there is too cold.

(C) Most hurricanes begin in the eastern Atlantic and travel westward toward the Americas.

(D) It would be impossible for a hurricane to do much damage more than a few miles from the coast.

(E) Hurricanes that form in the early fall tend to be stronger than hurricanes in the late summer.

11. Parent: I'm not going to have my child vaccinated against common childhood diseases. I fear the side effects of the vaccines. Everyone else has his or her children vaccinated, so I won't have to fear my child catching the diseases the vaccines are designed to prevent.

A reasoning flaw in the parent's argument is that the argument

(A) criticizes parents who do have their children vaccinated

(B) makes an emotional plea against forcing children to undergo injections

(C) attacks government leaders who have insisted on a national vaccination program

(D) implies that other parents aren't as knowledgeable about the side effects of vaccines

(E) assumes that no other parents will take the same stance against vaccination

12. The phrase "under God" in the Pledge of Allegiance is not unconstitutional because throughout our nation's history, various presidents and political leaders have invoked God and the almighty in inaugural addresses, Thanksgiving speeches, and other public statements of national unity. It is therefore not improper to allow public schools to require teachers to lead their students in the Pledge every day; this practice does not force religious beliefs on anyone.

The argument is most vulnerable to criticism on the grounds that it

(A) ignores evidence that many politicians do not invoke God and the almighty in public addresses because they believe it would be an improper exercise of religion

(B) fails to acknowledge that the majority of U.S. citizens approve of including the phrase "under God" in the Pledge

(C) equates freedom of expression by national leaders with proof that requiring students to mention God in the Pledge is not an unjust imposition of religious beliefs

(D) praises teachers who lead their classes in the Pledge of Allegiance for performing an act of patriotism that deserves no reward

(E) assumes that all U.S. citizens believe in the same deity and wish to invoke that deity's protection of the nation and its people

13. Barsad: Europeans work far fewer hours on average than Americans do. Full-time workers in Europe rarely work more than 35 hours a week, and take off between four and six weeks every year. This more humane work pattern is directly tied to the higher income taxes imposed on Europeans; high taxes reduce the take-home profit of working long hours, which takes away any incentive workers might have to put in more time than necessary to achieve a comfortable standard of living.

Preston: Within Europe there is no consistent correlation between higher income taxes and shorter working hours. In Ireland, for example, taxes have hardly risen at all in the last 30 years, but the country's workers have nevertheless decreased their average working hours by 25%.

The dialog above lends the most support to the claim that Barsad and Preston disagree with each other about which one of the following statements?

(A) Europeans value leisure much more than Americans do, as evidence by their shorter work-weeks and much more generous vacation policies.

(B) Europeans work shorter hours than Americans because higher income taxes remove any incentive they might feel to increase their take-home pay by working longer hours.

(C) Higher income taxes in the United States would inspire Americans to cut back on the hours that they work, which would benefit families and equalize wealth in the nation.

(D) Despite the fewer hours they spend at work, Europeans have a standard of living that is no more than 25 percent lower than that enjoyed by Americans.

(E) Some studies have found that there is a correlation between higher taxes and shorter hours, but those studies found that the taxes accounted for only one-third of the difference in hours between Americans and Europeans.

Go on to next page

14. History has shown that people will reduce their consumption of fuel only if they have a financial incentive to do so. For example, in the energy crisis of the 1970s, people drastically lowered their consumption of gasoline. When California suffered its own statewide energy crisis in 2001, the state promised a 20-percent discount on power bills to consumers who reduced their power consumption, and a majority of citizens managed this feat. The government should therefore implement financial incentives to reduce energy consumption, such as taxes on gasoline or rewards for reduced consumption.

Which one of the following is an assumption required by the argument?

(A) The government should not interfere with energy policies and should instead let the market guide consumption.

(B) In some cases, citizens have reduced their power consumption even without incentives.

(C) Policies created during the energy crisis of the 1970s should serve as a model of policies that could address the current energy crisis.

(D) It is desirable to get citizens to use less energy than they currently do.

(E) The federal government should follow California's lead in setting energy policy.

15. Requiring public school students to adhere to dress codes or wear uniforms has many benefits. It cuts down on disciplinary problems, reduces theft, and makes it difficult for wealthy students to make fun of poorer ones because of their clothes. It's true that dress codes reduce individual expression, but a public school doesn't need to be a training ground for nonconformists. A dress code can work, though, only if all students are required to follow it.

Which one of the following is most strongly supported by the conversation above?

(A) The author believes that public schools should be a forum for individual expression.

(B) The author has no objection to enforcing conformity on public school students in the form of dress codes.

(C) The author thinks that the only way to implement a dress code is to assign students an official uniform.

(D) Most parents of public school students like dress codes because it makes it easier and cheaper for them to dress their children for school.

(E) Dress codes reduce theft and other disciplinary problems without necessarily harming individual expression.

16. I bought a pair of glasses from this optometrist. One of the lenses regularly pops out of the frame. Therefore this optometrist doesn't know how to make a good pair of glasses.

The reasoning in the argument is most vulnerable to criticism on the grounds that the argument

(A) does not allow the optometrist a chance to defend himself

(B) does not consider the possibility that the frames themselves might be defective

(C) criticizes the optometrist's use of a particular technique when making glasses

(D) jumps to the conclusion that the defect in the glasses must be due to the optometrist's lack of skill

(E) accuses the optometrist of deliberately sabotaging the glasses

Go on to next page

17. If Person A promises to do something if Person B performs a specific action, and if Person B performs that action, then Person A is obligated to do whatever he or she promised to do.

Which one of the following most closely conforms to the principle above?

(A) A man promises a woman that he will give her an engagement ring as soon as he returns from his military deployment. When he returns, he gives her an engagement ring.

(B) A boss promises his workers a party if they reach a sales goal by the end of the month. They reach their sales goal but the boss decides the party would be too expensive and buys pizza instead.

(C) A seal trainer give her seals fish as a reward whenever they perform their tricks correctly. The seals perform perfectly, and the trainer gives them fish.

(D) A mother threatens to take away her son's toy airplane if he doesn't clean up his room during the next five minutes. He fails to clean up his room, so she takes his toy airplane.

(E) A professor promises a student that he will write a good recommendation for her if she does well in the class. She does poorly, so he writes her a bad recommendation.

18. Zoologist: I have discovered a gene that controls whether an individual is monogamous or not. I took a gene from the monogamous prairie vole and implanted it into its more promiscuous relative, the meadow vole. Thereafter, the meadow voles with the new gene became monogamous.

Which one of the following, if true, would provide the most support for the zoologist's assertion?

(A) Studies on humans and other mammals have shown that receptors for the hormone vasopressin play a role in autism, drug addiction, and the formation of romantic attachments.

(B) Prairie voles typically form life-long partnerships, which scientists have linked to an increased number of receptors for the hormone vasopressin.

(C) Meadow voles live in a harsher environment than prairie voles and can't afford to pass up opportunities to mate as often as possible.

(D) The zoologist used a harmless virus to capture the gene and transfer it into the meadow voles.

(E) Normally male meadow voles will mate with any females who cross their paths, but each of the male meadow voles with the new gene chose a single female partner and refused to mate with any others for the rest of their lives.

Go on to next page

19. An art museum has bought a bronze statue that it believes is a sculpture of the god Apollo by the famous ancient Greek sculptor Praxiteles. Only a few sculptures known to be by Praxiteles still exist today, and many sculptures once thought to be by him were actually copies of his originals made by ancient Romans. It is difficult for scholars to date ancient sculpture accurately, but scholars have found several features of this statue that make it likely that it dates from the era of Praxiteles and it certainly conforms to the sculptor's style.

Which one of the following is most strongly supported by the information above?

(A) The art museum is fairly confident that this statue was made by Praxiteles but admits that there is some possibility it is wrong.

(B) In some cases, museums have purchased sculptures that they believed were ancient works and later discovered that they were made by modern forgers.

(C) After extensive research and investigation, scholars will be able to state conclusively whether or not this statue was made by Praxiteles himself.

(D) The statue is certainly an original Greek bronze statue dating from the late fourth century B.C. or the early third century B.C.

(E) Praxiteles's style is so distinctive that it is readily apparent when a statue is one of his originals as opposed to a copy.

20. Psychologist A: Psychologists should not refer to the people who participate in their experiments as "subjects," which is an extremely impersonal term that could apply as well to rodents. They should instead call them "participants," which implies willing consent, except in the case of infants, who of course cannot consent, and should be called "individuals." This concept has been included in the new guidelines for psychologists conducting research.

Psychologist B: I wish the psychologists' governing body had never decided to change the guidelines. The term "subject" worked for years, and my colleagues and I never felt that the word denied the humanity of the people we studied. We now never know what to call the people we use in our studies and we fear criticism if we inadvertently use the wrong term.

Psychologist A and Psychologist B disagree about whether

(A) a survey of psychological research subjects found that most people preferred to be called "participants"

(B) the psychologists' governing body has the authority to change guidelines on terminology used by researchers

(C) the new terminology guidelines were a valuable and necessary update to the field of psychological research

(D) it is proper to use the same word to refer to human and animal research subjects

(E) the word "subject" implies a passive participant, and the word "participant" implies an active one who has given her consent

Go on to next page

21. Gynecologist: Scottish researchers have developed a test that allows them to predict at what age a woman will experience menopause. The scientists use a model that compares a woman's ovaries to "average" ovaries to see whether her ovaries are aging faster or slower than average. They have discovered that the size of ovaries is directly related to the number of eggs they contain, which in turn is directly related to fertility. This discovery will make a huge difference in how women decide when to have children.

The gynecologist's conclusion follows logically if which one of the following is assumed?

(A) Women with smaller ovaries tend to have less success with assisted reproduction techniques such as in vitro fertilization.

(B) Most women experience menopause around the age of 50, but their fertility starts to decline at the age of 37.

(C) Many women, especially professionals, are unpleasantly surprised to discover that they are no longer fertile by the time they start trying to conceive in their late 30s or early 40s.

(D) The test still can't tell women how likely they are to conceive in the years just prior to menopause.

(E) Every woman is born with several million eggs in her ovaries, which formed while she was a fetus; the number of eggs dwindles over her lifetime, until at menopause she has 1,000 or fewer.

22. School board member: A school in a wealthy suburb and a school in a poverty-stricken part of the inner city received exactly the same funding, and got completely different results. The school in the suburb sent all its graduates to college, but the school in the city sent only 10 percent to college and suffered a 25 percent dropout rate before graduation. Clearly the inner-city school is wasting its money while the suburban school puts its money to good use.

The reasoning in the school board member's argument is flawed because the argument

(A) mistakenly finds a correlation between levels of funding and graduation rates

(B) blames the inner city school for causing its students to fail

(C) fails to acknowledge that there might be reasons for the inner city school's difficulties that are not the result of wasting money

(D) criticizes the administrators of the inner city school for their failure to produce the same graduation rates as the suburban school

(E) jumps to the conclusion that students in the suburbs are more intelligent and harder working than students in the inner city

Go on to next page

23. Motorcyclists are told always to wear helmets when they ride their motorcycles. But helmets only protect riders when they have wrecks, and wrecks occur only once out of every 1,000 rides. Therefore a motorcyclist would be perfectly safe if he only wore his helmet once out of every 1,000 rides.

Which one of the following employs a flawed argumentative strategy that is most closely parallel to the flawed argumentative strategy in the statement above?

(A) My European client calls once a week, always in the evening after everyone has left the office. I'll be sure to get his messages if I turn on my telephone's answering machine once a week.

(B) This sunscreen allows me to stay in the sun 15 times longer than I could without sunscreen. If I apply two coats of it, it will allow me to stay in the sun 30 times longer.

(C) The odds are 1,000 to 1 against winning the big jackpot on this slot machine. If I play the slot machine 1,000 times, I'm sure to win the big jackpot.

(D) Seatbelts protect passengers in automobile accidents, but accidents only occur in one out of every 2,000 car trips. Because drivers are in the car the most, they should wear their seatbelts most often.

(E) Top law schools accept one out of every 20 applicants. Therefore someone who wants to get into a top law school should apply to 20 of them.

24. During the 20th century, the introduction of widespread indoor plumbing and electricity and the invention of machines such as washing machines and dishwashers made it much easier for women to accomplish their daily housekeeping chores. Ironically, by the 1950s, women actually spent MORE time doing housework than they had 40 years earlier, before they had plumbing, electricity, and labor-saving devices.

Which one of the following, if true, most helps to resolve the apparent discrepancy in the passage above?

(A) Standards of cleanliness and cooking became higher as housework became easier; by the 1950s, people expected cleaner clothes and surroundings and more elaborate meals than they had earlier in the 20th century.

(B) Women who had gone to work outside the home during the second world war found housekeeping a poor substitute in the 1950s, which led directly to the feminist movement of the 1960s.

(C) The 1950s were the height of the post-war baby boom, and women had to spend a great deal of their time caring for their many children.

(D) Husbands of the 1950s were highly unlikely to help their wives with housework or cooking, though they did typically care for the car and the yard.

(E) In the 1950s many young families moved to newly built suburbs, in which wives often found themselves isolated during the day while their husbands went to work and their children went to school.

Go on to next page

25. European Union: We have issued new rules regulating the use of regional names on food products. Under these rules, actual geographic origin will take precedence over traditional usage, so a product such as Parmesan cheese can no longer be called that unless it was produced in Parma, Italy.

   American Food Manufacturers Union: This ban is outrageous and unfair to food manufacturers and distributors. Certain regional names have been in common use for centuries and have taken on a generic meaning; all consumers know that the term "Parmesan" refers to a type of cheese, not to the geographical region in which the cheese was manufactured.

   Based on the conversation above, the European Union and the American Food Manufacturers Union disagree on which one of the following points?

   (A) Whether a product such as sparkling wine can be of the same quality whether made in the Champagne region of France or in the Sonoma Valley of California.

   (B) Whether the EU should allow American food products bearing names of European regions to be imported into Europe.

   (C) Whether Americans of European ancestry can still appreciate the nuances in taste that result from manufacturing food products in specific regions famous for them.

   (D) Whether geographical names can be used in a generic sense to connote a type of food or whether they should be used in a strictly geographical sense to connote food made in a particular region.

   (E) Whether it is possible to have an intellectual property right in a geographical name.

STOP You may check your work on this section only. Do not go back to any previous section.

Section 1V

Time: 35 minutes

26 Questions

Each group of questions in this section is based on a set of conditions. In answering some of the questions, it may be useful to draw a rough diagram. Choose the response that most accurately and completely answers each question and blacken the corresponding space on your answer sheet.

Questions 1–5

It's 1848, and a number of women and men are attending the first U.S. convention in support of women's rights in Seneca Falls, New York. Six prominent feminists and abolitionists will speak at this meeting: Susan B. Anthony, Frederick Douglass, Jane Hunt, Lucretia Mott, Elizabeth Cady Stanton, and Martha Wright. Each of them will speak once and only once; only one person can speak at a time. The following rules will determine the order in which they speak:

> One person will speak per hour; the first speaker will begin at 2:00, and the last one at 7:00.

> Neither Frederick Douglass nor Lucretia Mott can speak at 6:00.

> Elizabeth Cady Stanton speaks before either Frederick Douglass or Lucretia Mott, but not before both.

> If Jane Hunt speaks at 2:00, then Susan B. Anthony must speak after Martha Wright.

> If Elizabeth Cady Stanton speaks at 4:00, then Martha Wright speaks at 7:00.

1. Which one of the following could be an acceptable order of speakers?

   (A) Frederick Douglass, Jane Hunt, Elizabeth Cady Stanton, Lucretia Mott, Martha Wright, Susan B. Anthony

   (B) Frederick Douglass, Elizabeth Cady Stanton, Susan B. Anthony, Martha Wright, Lucretia Mott, Jane Hunt

   (C) Jane Hunt, Lucretia Mott, Susan B. Anthony, Elizabeth Cady Stanton, Martha Wright, Frederick Douglass

   (D) Jane Hunt, Martha Wright, Frederick Douglass, Elizabeth Cady Stanton, Susan B. Anthony, Lucretia Mott

   (E) Martha Wright, Elizabeth Cady Stanton, Jane Hunt, Frederick Douglass, Susan B. Anthony, Lucretia Mott

2. If Jane Hunt speaks at 2:00, then which one of the following must be false?

   (A) Susan B. Anthony speaks at 5:00.

   (B) Frederick Douglass speaks at 3:00.

   (C) Lucretia Mott speaks at 3:00.

   (D) Martha Wright speaks at 4:00.

   (E) Martha Wright speaks at 5:00.

3. If Martha Wright speaks at 7:00, then which one of the following must be true?

   (A) Jane Hunt speaks at 4:00.

   (B) Elizabeth Cady Stanton speaks at 4:00.

   (C) Lucretia Mott speaks at 5:00.

   (D) At least one person speaks before Jane Hunt speaks.

   (E) At least two people speak before Frederick Douglass speaks.

4. All of the following speakers could speak at 2:00 EXCEPT:

   (A) Susan B. Anthony

   (B) Frederick Douglass

   (C) Lucretia Mott

   (D) Elizabeth Cady Stanton

   (E) Martha Wright

5. Which one of the following could be an accurate partial schedule of speakers?

   (A) Susan B. Anthony at 3:00, Elizabeth Cady Stanton at 6:00

   (B) Jane Hunt at 2:00, Elizabeth Cady Stanton at 3:00

   (C) Jane Hunt at 2:00, Martha Wright at 7:00

   (D) Martha Wright at 3:00, Elizabeth Cady Stanton at 4:00

   (E) Elizabeth Cady Stanton at 5:00, Martha Wright at 7:00

Go on to next page

Questions 6–12

A ballroom dance club has seven members, four women — Madeleine, Natasha, Olivia, and Phoebe — and three men — Antonio, Bertrand, and Christophe. They have entered a ballroom competition that has five events performed in the order listed: foxtrot, passa doble, rumba, tango, and waltz. Each member of the club competes in exactly one event. They compete either in pairs of one man and one woman or as solo performers. The following rules determine who dances with whom and in which event:

Antonio competes as a solo performer.

Natasha competes as part of a pair.

Olivia competes in the rumba.

Bertrand cannot compete in an event immediately before or immediately after the event in which Christophe competes.

6. If Phoebe is the only member who competes in the foxtrot, and Bertrand competes in the rumba, then which one of the following must be true?

    (A) Antonio competes in the passa doble.

    (B) Antonio competes in the waltz.

    (C) Madeleine competes in the passa doble.

    (D) Natasha competes in the tango.

    (E) Natasha competes in the waltz.

7. If Antonio chooses his event first, what is the maximum number of the remaining events from which Natasha can choose her own event?

    (A) one

    (B) two

    (C) three

    (D) four

    (E) five

8. If solo women compete in the foxtrot and the passa doble, then which of the following members must compete in the tango?

    (A) Antonio

    (B) Madeleine

    (C) Natasha

    (D) Natasha and Christophe

    (E) Phoebe and Bertrand

9. Which one of the following is a complete and accurate list of the members who CANNOT dance solo?

    (A) Bertrand, Natasha, Phoebe

    (B) Christophe, Bertrand, Natasha

    (C) Madeleine, Natasha

    (D) Madeleine, Natasha, Phoebe

    (E) Natasha, Olivia

10. Which of the following is a complete and accurate list of the women who could compete solo?

    (A) Madeleine

    (B) Phoebe

    (C) Madeleine, Olivia

    (D) Olivia, Phoebe

    (E) Madeleine, Olivia, Phoebe

11. If the four women compete in four consecutive events, and Natasha competes in the waltz, then which of the following is a complete and accurate list of the events in which members must compete as solo performers?

    (A) Foxtrot, passa doble

    (B) Foxtrot, tango

    (C) Passa doble

    (D) Foxtrot, Passa doble, rumba, tango

    (E) Tango

12. If the three men compete in the first three events, then which one of the following must be true?

    (A) Bertrand competes in the foxtrot.

    (B) Bertrand and Madeleine compete in the same event.

    (C) Bertrand and Natasha compete in the same event.

    (D) Christophe competes in the rumba.

    (E) Natasha competes in the foxtrot.

Go on to next page

Questions 13–18

Seven famous chefs – Andrea, Berthe, Emilio, Jacques, Kimiko, Marthe, and Nigel — have volunteered their services for a presidential dinner. It will consist of five courses, served in the following order: hors d'oeuvres, consommé, entrée, salade, and dessert. The dinner begins at 7:00 and ends at 10:00; one or two courses will be served each hour, at 7:00, 8:00, and 9:00. These chefs refuse to work with one another, so each course will be prepared by exactly one chef. No chef can prepare more than one course per hour. The following chefs have offered to prepare the following courses:

> Hors d'oeuvre: Berthe, Marthe
>
> Consommé: Andrea, Kimiko
>
> Entrée: Andrea, Nigel
>
> Salade: Berthe, Emilio, Jacques
>
> Dessert: Emilio, Kimiko, Marthe

13. What is the minimum number of chefs who could prepare the entire meal?

    (A) two

    (B) three

    (C) four

    (D) five

    (E) six

14. If the salade is served at 9:00, which one of the following could be a complete list of chefs who prepare a course served at 8:00?

    (A) Andrea and Kimiko

    (B) Berthe

    (C) Emilio and Nigel

    (D) Kimiko

    (E) Marthe

15. Which one of the following CANNOT be a complete and accurate list of the chefs who prepare the meal?

    (A) Andrea, Berthe, Jacques, Kimiko

    (B) Andrea, Berthe, Kimiko, Marthe

    (C) Andrea, Emilio, Marthe, Nigel

    (D) Andrea, Jacques, Kimiko, Marthe

    (E) Berthe, Emilio, Jacques, Marthe

16. Which one of the following pairs of chefs could each prepare two courses served during the same two time slots?

    (A) Andrea and Berthe

    (B) Andrea and Kimiko

    (C) Andrea and Marthe

    (D) Berthe and Emilio

    (E) Kimiko and Nigel

17. Which one of the following pairs of chefs could each prepare a course served at 7:00 and a course served at 9:00?

    (A) Andrea and Kimiko

    (B) Andrea and Marthe

    (C) Berthe and Kimiko

    (D) Berthe and Marthe

    (E) Emilio and Marthe

18. Which one of the following could be a complete and accurate list of the chefs who prepare the meal?

    (A) Andrea, Berthe, Emilio, Nigel

    (B) Andrea, Emilio, Jacques, Kimiko, Nigel

    (C) Berthe, Emilio, Kimiko, Marthe

    (D) Berthe, Emilio, Marthe, Nigel

    (E) Emilio, Jacques, Kimiko, Marthe

Go on to next page

<u>Questions 19–25</u>

On a Friday afternoon, an English literature student rents five film versions of literary classics — *Emma, Great Expectations, Ivanhoe, Middlemarch,* and *Wuthering Heights* — to help him prepare for an exam the following Friday morning. Three of the films are on disc and two are on videotape. The student can watch no more than one film per evening; Thursday is the last night he can watch anything. The student must schedule his film viewing with the following constraints in mind:

Emma is on videotape. *Wuthering Heights* is on disc.

The student must watch *Wuthering Heights* before he watches *Emma.*

The student must watch *Middlemarch* and *Ivanhoe* after he watches *Great Expectations.*

The student's girlfriend wants to watch *Emma* with him, so they have arranged to watch it on Monday.

The student and his roommate are sharing the VCR and DVD players, so he can't watch any two videotapes on consecutive days, or any two discs on consecutive days.

The student must watch a film on disc on Saturday.

19. Which one of the following could be an accurate schedule of the student's viewing of the films?

(A) Friday: *Great Expectations;* Saturday: *Wuthering Heights;* Sunday: *Emma;* Tuesday: *Middlemarch;* Wednesday: *Ivanhoe*

(B) Friday: *Great Expectations;* Saturday: *Wuthering Heights;* Monday: *Emma;* Tuesday: *Middlemarch;* Wednesday: *Ivanhoe*

(C) Friday: *Great Expectations;* Saturday: *Wuthering Heights;* Monday: *Emma;* Tuesday: *Middlemarch;* Thursday: *Ivanhoe*

(D) Friday: *Wuthering Heights;* Sunday: *Great Expectations;* Monday: *Emma;* Tuesday: *Ivanhoe;* Wednesday: *Middlemarch*

(E) Saturday: *Wuthering Heights;* Monday: *Emma;* Tuesday: *Middlemarch;* Wednesday: *Great Expectations;* Thursday: *Ivanhoe*

20. If the student watches *Great Expectations* before he watches *Emma,* then which one of the following statements CANNOT be true?

(A) *Great Expectations* is on disc.

(B) *Ivanhoe* is on disc.

(C) *Middlemarch* is on disc.

(D) The student doesn't watch a film on Sunday.

(E) The student doesn't watch a film on Wednesday.

21. If *Middlemarch* is on videotape, then which one of the following statements could be true?

(A) *Ivanhoe* is on videotape.

(B) The student watches *Emma* exactly three days before watching *Middlemarch.*

(C) The student watches *Great Expectations* exactly one day before watching *Middlemarch.*

(D) The student watches *Ivanhoe* on Wednesday.

(E) The student watches *Middlemarch* on Thursday.

22. Which one of the following statements must be false?

(A) The student watches films on both Friday and Monday.

(B) The student watches films on both Monday and Wednesday.

(C) The student doesn't watch a film on either Friday or Sunday.

(D) The students doesn't watch a film on either Sunday or Wednesday.

(E) The student doesn't watch a film on either Tuesday or Thursday.

Go on to next page

23. If the student watches *Great Expectations* after he watches *Wuthering Heights*, then which one of the following statements must be false?

    (A) The student doesn't watch a film on Friday.

    (B) The student watches *Ivanhoe* before he watches *Middlemarch*.

    (C) The student watches *Great Expectations* before he watches *Emma*.

    (D) *Great Expectations* is on disc.

    (E) *Ivanhoe* is on disc.

24. If the student doesn't watch a film on Wednesday, then which one of the following statements must be true?

    (A) The student watches *Great Expectations* on Friday.

    (B) The student watches *Great Expectations* on Tuesday.

    (C) The student watches *Ivanhoe* on Tuesday.

    (D) The student watches *Ivanhoe* on Thursday.

    (E) The student watches *Middlemarch* on Tuesday.

25. If the student watches *Ivanhoe* before he watches *Middlemarch*, then how many different ways could he schedule his list of films in order to view them all during the week?

    (A) one

    (B) two

    (C) three

    (D) four

    (E) five

STOP You may check your work on this section only. Do not go back to any previous section.

Writing Sample

A third-year law student has just received two job offers, one from a small boutique firm and the other from a large firm. Write an essay in favor of choosing one law firm over the other based on the following considerations:

- ✔ The student wants to work for a firm that will allow him to explore many different areas of practice.

- ✔ The student wants to work for a firm that will give him early responsibility and client contact and possibly advance him rapidly.

The small boutique firm limits its practice to estate planning, tax law, and bankruptcy work. Because the firm has only four attorneys, the students would immediately receive his own clients and his own files. The hiring partner has promised him that the firm will help the student gain proficiency, and if he learns quickly and gets along with his coworkers, he could become a partner in three or four years.

The large firm has teams who handle a wide variety of practice areas, including insurance defense, corporate, employment law, workers compensation, construction litigation, real estate, and healthcare. The firm typically rotates its new associates through all of these areas, allowing them to spend six months to a year working with a particular team before moving to another. By fifth year, most associates have become permanent members of a team; this prepares them for partnership, which is never offered before an associate has worked for the firm for at least seven years.

STOP You may check your work on this section only.
Do not go back to any previous section.

Answer Key for Practice Exam 2

Section I	Section II	Section III	Section IV
1. B	1. D	1. A	1. D
2. E	2. A	2. E	2. E
3. C	3. C	3. B	3. D
4. D	4. A	4. A	4. D
5. D	5. D	5. D	5. A
6. A	6. E	6. C	6. E
7. B	7. C	7. E	7. C
8. B	8. B	8. D	8. A
9. E	9. A	9. D	9. B
10. A	10. D	10. A	10. E
11. E	11. E	11. E	11. B
12. C	12. E	12. C	12. E
13. C	13. A	13. B	13. B
14. E	14. E	14. D	14. A
15. E	15. A	15. B	15. E
16. D	16. D	16. D	16. A
17. C	17. D	17. D	17. C
18. B	18. D	18. E	18. A
19. A	19. B	19. A	19. C
20. D	20. C	20. C	20. A
21. B	21. C	21. C	21. C
22. E	22. B	22. C	22. E
23. A	23. A	23. A	23. C
24. E	24. E	24. A	24. A
	25. B	25. D	25. B
	26. D		

Refer to Chapter 20 for tips on computing your score.

Chapter 23

Practice Exam 2: Answers and Explanations

• •

*T*his chapter has answers and explanations to the multiple-choice sections in Chapter 22. It doesn't contain sample answers for the Writing Sample, mainly because there would be no point. You need to practice writing for yourself, and I don't want you to mistakenly think there's some "perfect" essay. It's not scored, anyway.

Section 1

1. **(B).** The review must be assuming that it's impossible that the prices in this catalog could save customers money without being specially marked down. (A) is wrong because the argument doesn't depend on the behavior of the catalog's competitors. (B) looks correct. The review must assume this catalog's prices are cheap only when marked down. (C) isn't right. Evidently when prices are marked down, they're good. (D) is wrong because this argument isn't about competitors. (E) doesn't work, because the argument doesn't address mail-order purchasing as a whole, nor does it address what the customers *should* do. (B) is correct.

2. **(E).** The conclusion is that the settlement was destroyed in war. The evidence, though, doesn't seem that clear, unless archaeologists see more than the rest of individuals can. (Apologies to any archaeologists out there!) It's not a circular argument, because the author doesn't state upfront that he thinks the settlement perished in war, so (A) is wrong. (B) doesn't work. Yes, the evidence is varied and the conclusion is unified, but that's what conclusions are supposed to do — to bring together varied evidence into a single conclusion. (C) is wrong because it doesn't contain any intermediate conclusions. (D) is wrong because there aren't any historical conclusions. (E) is the best answer; it's by no means certain that these bits of evidence point to one single conclusion. (E) is correct.

3. **(C).** No way to guess the answer beforehand here. (A) doesn't look right. If fetch is the length of the surface of the water, it shouldn't be related to the shape of the sea-bottom. (B) definitely seems wrong, because varying undersea terrain and other factors could result in a wide variety of wave sizes. (C) does make sense because the impact of waves is related to the shape of the sea-bottom, and the coast's erosion is related to the impact of waves. (D) is wrong because the size of waves comes from wind and fetch, not the shape of the bottom. (E) looks wrong, too. Wind velocity creates size of waves, size of waves affects impact, and impact affects erosion, so it doesn't make sense that average velocity of wind would play no role in erosion. (C) is the best answer.

4. **(D).** The historian is arguing that it's a mistake for historians to see one event as an inevitable consequence of another. The phrase in question expresses her belief that historians are prone to interpreting events this way because they spend all their time examining and trying to connect past events. (A) is wrong; a "theoretical imperative" sounds like a requirement, and this statement is an explanation. (B) isn't an illustration of the premise, which would be an example of a historian making this kind of mistake. (C) isn't supporting any claim, so it's wrong. (D) seems to make sense. The historian is explaining that although historians sometimes see events as inevitable consequences of other events, that's just an occupational hazard of the historical profession and not justified. (E) is wrong. The conclusion is that historians can't in fact assert that events follow one another inevitably. (D) is the best answer.

5. **(D).** The speaker is suggesting that a market-driven model will result in China producing more grain than a centrally controlled model. (A) isn't right because it isn't actually about the difference between global and regional markets, but about China's transformation to a market economy. (B) doesn't justify the conclusion, but explains how things worked under China's older system. (C) is wrong because the speaker isn't talking about local production. (D) looks like the right answer. The speaker is basing his conclusion on the principle that a market economy will respond to increased demand with increased production. (E) isn't right. The speaker doesn't mention inefficiency or even compare a market-driven system to a centrally regulated one; he's only interested in the effects of China's transition between the two. (D) is the best answer.

6. **(A).** The economist is arguing that patients need medical care and hospitals, regardless of price; the MRI statement is an example. (A) is a good answer; that phrase is a specific example of the general condition described in the argument. (B) doesn't work because the MRI statement isn't countering an attack. (C) is wrong. The author's claim, or conclusion is that health insurers are still profiting from healthcare while doctors, hospitals, and patients are being increasingly squeezed, but the MRI statement doesn't indirectly support that claim. (D) doesn't work. Patients' needing treatment isn't a social side effect, but a normal event that remains consistent regardless of changing circumstances. (E) is wrong; the MRI statement doesn't introduce the conclusion. (A) is correct.

7. **(B).** To make her conclusion, the author must assume that PTP filesharing was entirely or largely responsible for the drop in sales of CDs. She doesn't mention copyright issues, so (A) is wrong. (B) looks like the right answer. (C) isn't at issue here. (D) might work, except the author might not assume that people who download music would purchase it if they couldn't download it. People may have downloaded far more pieces of music than they would have purchased on CDs. (E) doesn't really fit with the argument, which isn't about complex relationships but about how filesharing has killed the record industry. (B) is right.

8. **(B).** The engineer believes that the more redundant control systems an airplane has, the safer it will be. But what if having so many control systems can cause problems of its own, or costs more than it's worth, either in economic or practical terms? (A) is wrong; the engineer does think that simultaneous failure can occur, which is why he believes multiple systems are necessary. (B) looks like it could be the answer, because it addresses problems involved with redundancy itself. (C) is wrong. The engineer is discussing control surfaces, so he's not obligated to consider other safety considerations. (D) is wrong. The engineer is discussing airplane safety, and isn't obligated to apply these concepts to other projects. (E) is also wrong because the argument doesn't depend on being able to evaluate relative levels of safety. (B) is correct.

9. **(E).** To weaken the argument, look for an answer showing that allowing family leave doesn't hurt productivity or even help it. (A) doesn't affect the argument because standard of living isn't an issue, and it doesn't mention U.S. workplace productivity. (B) could arguably weaken the argument because it shows evidence of workers not abusing the privilege of leave — fathers aren't taking family leave at all, which weakens the conclusion that workers would work less if they had leave. On the other hand, if taking paternity leave angers coworkers, that strengthens the conclusion that family leave hurts workplace morale, so this isn't the best answer. (C) strengthens the argument by showing that FMLA leave costs the employer money. (D) also strengthens the argument by illustrating the destruction caused by one employee leaving for a while. (E) weakens the argument. If employers are worried about productivity and morale, this choice says that allowing leave actually increases productivity and morale. (E) is the right answer.

10. **(A).** Look for an answer that could explain why counties with casinos have thriving businesses but bankrupt individuals. (A) looks right. Businesses take money from gamblers (who aren't all local), and locals give their money to casinos. (B) doesn't help. Casino odds explain why gamblers would go bankrupt, but not why businesses would profit. (C) explains why businesses thrive, but not why individuals suffer. (D) explains gamblers but not businesses. (E) may help explain why individual bankruptcy rates are so high around casinos, but does nothing to explain the profitability of businesses around them. (A) is the best explanation.

11. **(E).** (A) supports the argument by showing how the new debit cards increase participation. (B) supports it by showing how paper coupons were often used for fraud. (C) supports her position because the debit cards can be used only for approved items. (D) supports it because it shows how the cards are much more convenient, which will increase participation. (E) is the only answer that doesn't support the social worker's position, because some participants in the program don't like the cards. (E) is correct.

12. **(C).** This discovery of an animal that hibernates in hot weather could be ground-breaking, especially if previous scientific wisdom held that hibernation only happens in cold weather. (A) is wrong because the belief being challenged isn't that primates never hibernate, but that animals never hibernate in the heat. (B) isn't right because it isn't an accusation of any kind. (C) makes the most sense because it's an important discovery. (D) is wrong. The primatologist never disputes the conclusion that the behavior is in fact hibernation. (E) doesn't work because the primatologist isn't setting up a rival theory in a deliberate ploy to attack it. (C) is right.

13. **(C).** Wow, that's a gamble, casting an English-speaking actor in an Italian movie and letting him speak his part in English while everyone else speaks Italian. But the director must have his reasons; clearly he thinks Lancaster's fame is a more valuable commodity for sales than ability to speak Italian would be. He must not think Italian audiences would refuse to see the film with Lancaster or he would never cast him, so (A) is wrong. (B) may be true but it seems actors' objections aren't the director's concern. (C) is right — the director obviously believes fame is more important to box office success than Italian ability. (D) is beside the point. The director doesn't think coaching Lancaster in Italian is necessary. (E) is also beside the point; maybe Lancaster would feel uncomfortable, but the director isn't concerned about that here. (C) is correct

14. **(E).** Alberto suggests that because losing a single species won't hurt an ecosystem, eradicating mosquitoes will cause no environmental problems. Look for an answer that disproves this. (A) is a reason in favor of eradicating mosquitoes. (B) doesn't strengthen or weaken the argument. (C) is another strike against mosquitoes. (D) may suggest that mosquitoes do play a role in the ecosystem, but by itself it doesn't really hurt Alberto's argument; evidence that mosquitoes are the only thing some birds eat does hurt this choice. (E) does weaken the passage. If the only way to eradicate mosquitoes would inevitably devastate birds and other insects, then Alberto can't suggest that his proposal would have no environmental costs. (E) is right.

15. **(E).** The author assumes that large groups in parks are bad but she gives no reasons for this claim; she just assumes that they're bad and shouldn't be in the park. She implies but doesn't directly state that large groups somehow interfere with all citizens' equal right to the park. (A) is wrong because there is no suggestion that large groups are noisy or violent. She mentions no complaints, so (B) is wrong. (C) goes against her argument, so it's wrong. (D) likewise weakens her argument, so it's wrong. (E) is the only answer that makes sense. If she's assuming that large groups interfere with individual citizens, then they would be a problem. (E) is correct.

16. **(D).** (A) looks like a reason why employees should use FSAs. (B) doesn't explain anything, just describes the problem. (C) is another clear benefit of FSAs. (D) is a drawback of FSAs, and may well explain why few employees use them. (E) doesn't explain why so few employees currently use FSAs. (D) is the best answer.

17. **(C).** It appears from this argument that many Latin American people don't like their democratic governments. (A) supports the argument but isn't really the conclusion. (B) also supports the argument but doesn't conclude it. (C) makes sense as a conclusion; clearly the people aren't impressed with their democratically elected leaders. (D) doesn't stick to the point but introduces a side issue. (E) is evidence that would support the conclusion, but isn't itself a conclusion. (C) is the best answer.

18. **(B).** The argument is about the changed risk of salmonella. In the past salmonella was on only the outside of eggs, but now it's inside the eggs themselves. (A) isn't the main conclusion, and in fact the author doesn't specifically state that salmonella has increased, only that its means of transmission has changed. (B) does make sense as the conclusion. (C) isn't right. The author isn't suggesting that salmonella can't be serious, only that it's rarely fatal. (D) doesn't quite work, because the author doesn't describe any change in egg production, only a change in the chickens producing them. (E) isn't right either. People in the past ate raw eggs safely because the eggs were uncontaminated, not because they were blissfully ignorant that the eggs contained salmonella. (B) is correct.

19. **(A).** Okay, you want to find the four answers indicating that operating systems are responsible for the smooth functioning of applications, and when the operating system fails at this task, then it can crash itself. The best way to do this is by process of elimination. If you can find four answers that show the operating system handling applications, then the answer that's left over should be correct. (B) helps the conclusion because it shows that operating systems are responsible for handling the memory used by individual applications. (C) helps because it shows that operating systems can spot overuse of memory and stop it. (D) helps because it tells you that programmers should know how to program an operating system that can prevent memory errors, which means all operating systems should be able to do this. (E) helps the conclusion because it describes what an efficient operating system should be able to do. (A) is the only answer that doesn't put responsibility for memory management on the operating system; adding memory to the computer evidently can let the operating system off the hook. (A) is the right answer.

20. **(D).** This question is a tough one, requiring lots of reading and thinking. Company A has a limited license to use a product but violates the license, claiming it's invalid. But there's a rule beyond the license that makes Company A's actions wrong even if the license is invalid. Look for an answer that follows this pattern. (A) doesn't work because the consumers end up verifying that the rule voiding the warranty really didn't apply. (B) is wrong because the rule never allowed 13-year-olds into NC-17 movies under any conditions. (C) doesn't work because the validity issue depends on timing. (D) does work. Ted had a limited permission to use the car, and then violates the permission, claiming that it doesn't apply because Alice isn't home, which is equivalent to Company A's argument that the license is invalid. But there's a higher rule beyond the permission, which gives Ted no right to the car at all. (E) doesn't work because there's no permission involved in the first place, limited or otherwise. The celebrity didn't grant permission to the magazine to photograph him in any circumstances, so the pattern is different. (D) is correct.

21. **(B).** The author's conclusion is that texts of poems differed from place to place, due to the changes in oral transmission of the same stories. (A) is clearly wrong because the scholar isn't suggesting that there was one original text of each classical epic. (B) looks right because he is arguing that there can't be any "original" text, but instead many written versions of the same epics. (C) doesn't make sense. The scholar doesn't mention narratological complexity. (D) doesn't work either because the scholar doesn't imply that people stopped transmitting epics orally after the poems were written down, but in fact suggests the opposite, that they continued to compose even after they began transcribing. (E) is totally wrong; there's no suggestion of political influence in this argument. (B) is correct.

22. **(E).** The curator seems to assume that if people see the images online, they won't have any interest in visiting in person. (A) isn't the point because the curator isn't worried about damage from flashes. (B) doesn't work because the curator doesn't mention gift shop sales. (C) isn't his concern. He's not necessarily worried about online distribution. (D) isn't his concern either, because he doesn't mention quality issues. (E) is the best answer. He is worried that online publication of the images will remove incentive to visit the actual museum in person. (E) is correct.

23. **(A).** If helping spouses has improved expatriate retention by such a huge amount, then unhappy spouses must have previously been responsible for lots of premature returns. (A) looks like a good answer. If spouses had trouble, then helping them would improve the situation. (B) is wrong. The argument doesn't depend for its success on length of assignment or families seeing it as an "adventure," though that may improve spousal mood. (C) supports the argument but isn't the assumption on which the conclusion depends. (D) doesn't explain why helping spouses has improved retention. (E) is an example of what companies are doing to help spouses, but not the assumption on which the conclusion depends. (A) is the best answer.

24. **(E).** Now, this is a nice little question — a story and some proverbs. You have to decide which proverb — principle — justifies the traveler's reasoning. A stitch in time saves nine means that early correction of problems prevents them from getting bigger; that doesn't really fit here, so (A) is wrong. Don't price an unborn calf means you shouldn't depend on an event that hasn't yet occurred; that's not right, so (B) is wrong. (C) might work, because the traveler does carry his computer with him, but it's not the best answer. (D) is wrong because he's not borrowing or lending anything. (E) is the best answer; because he was nice (honey) to the clerk (the fly), she was nice to him and punished the other rude (vinegar) travelers by dawdling.

Section 11

1. **(D).** This passage is mainly about the effectiveness of biography as a genre for exploring the history of science and the importance of analyzing scientific discoveries from a historical perspective. The business about *Black Apollo* is just an example the author uses to illustrate his point. So (A) is wrong, because the passage's main point isn't the importance of Ernest Everett Just. (B) is a point the author makes in the last paragraph, but it's not the entire passage's main point. (C) appears in the second paragraph, but once again doesn't cover the whole passage. (D) looks like the right answer; it does sum up the overarching theme of the passage. (E) is wrong because, like (A), it focuses too much on *Black Apollo*. (D) is correct.

2. **(A).** According to the author, "One of the central principles of history of science, indeed a central reason for the discipline, is to show that science is a product of social forces." That makes (A) look like a very good answer. (B) isn't exactly right. The author says people can learn scientific theories by reading the work of the scientists themselves. The drawback is that the picture given by scientists is incomplete because it ignores historical context. (C) isn't exactly right, either. Historians of science do write biographies, but that's not the main reason for the discipline's existence. (D) is wrong because the author never suggests that historians of science want to influence scientific research. (E) is likewise wrong. History of science exists to analyze history, not to make science palatable to non scientists. (A) is right.

3. **(C).** The second paragraph contains a discussion of biography as a historical genre and lists its many advantages. (A) isn't at all the main point. It just barely appears in the paragraph. (B) is wrong; the author does believe biography is a good historical form for the historian of science. (C) looks like a good answer. (D) is incorrect; the author says that biographies are very good for teaching children. (E) never appears anywhere. (C) is right.

4. **(A).** You can't predict the answer here, so just plunge right in. (A) looks pretty good; this is in fact what the author has been saying about history of science. (B) is wrong. The author doesn't think historians should glorify their subjects, and notes that Manning doesn't glorify Just. (C) is also wrong. The author doesn't imply that a scientific history should downplay science simply because it's "history." (D) isn't right. The author explicitly says that Just wasn't the most significant scientist of his time. (E) contradicts what the author says in the second paragraph. (A) is the best answer.

5. **(D).** Here's what the passage says: "A comprehensive appreciation of the conditions that Just faced in his daily work offers a powerful lens by which to examine the development of science and racial boundaries in America." (D) looks like the answer that matches best with this statement. The other answers are all true, but they're also incidental, facts that add up to a bigger picture but by themselves aren't enough to create a significant history.

6. **(E).** A biography is a story of a person's life; the format can't change that much. The author says "Biographies simply tell a story." The phrase "simplicity of form" doesn't refer to language, so (A) is wrong, nor does it mean page design, so (B) is wrong. It doesn't mean simple writing style or moral judgments, so (C) and (D) are wrong. All the author means is that biographies have a standard format, which is fairly consistent from book to book; that makes (E) correct.

7. **(C).** This passage introduces the reader to a couple of detergents commonly used in numerous household products. It describes how they work and mentions a few hazards associated with them. The reason the author mentions those hazards in the second paragraph is to get the facts in ahead of the risks that are solely based on rumor, because her point in the last paragraph is that many of the things people fear about SLS and SLES aren't based in fact. She obviously thinks SLS and SLES are safe as they're commonly used and believes that approval by the FDA and other scientific organizations is sufficient proof of this safety.

   (A) could be a possible answer but it doesn't really cover all of the passage. Look for something with more global application. (B) is wrong. The author clearly doesn't think incorporating SLS or SLES into personal care products is irresponsible or dangerous, and (B) looks like he would think that; the word "despite" is a clue. (C) looks like a better answer than (A) because it incorporates more of the passage's information. (D) is wrong because this passage isn't really about Internet rumors, but about detergents. (E) is wrong. The author doesn't have a problem with using SLS in both shampoo and engine degreasers, but that's not the main point of the passage. (C) is the best answer.

8. **(B).** You have to read carefully to answer this one. Don't assume anything that you can't find in the passage. If you prefer, you can underline or circle substances that the author mentions in the passage in the answer choices — that makes seeing the ones that appear in the text easier. (A) is wrong because the author never mentions mouthwash, sunscreen, or hair dye. (B) looks good. They're all in the passage. (C) is wrong because the passage doesn't mention engine lubricants. (D) is wrong because moisturizer and baby wipes don't appear. (E) is wrong because fabric softener isn't in the passage, though you could probably infer that SLS and SLES are found in kitchen cleaners and laundry detergents. (B) is correct.

9. **(A).** The author says that the rumors about SLS and SLES are absurd and unsubstantiated and "the FDA has approved the use of SLS and SLES in a number of personal care products." That means she's using FDA approval as evidence of the substances' safety. (A) looks like a possible answer, though it doesn't mention that FDA approval implies safety. (B) is wrong because even though the author implies that the FDA has the best interests of the consumers in mind, that isn't the reason why the author mentions the FDA. The purpose of mentioning the FDA is to provide evidence debunking the Internet myths. (C) doesn't work because the author isn't in fact suggesting that FDA approval of putting SLS and SLES in personal care products means that manufacturers don't have to test these products for safety. (D) is wrong; the author isn't criticizing the FDA in any way — quite the contrary. (E) might be confusing because the author is definitely critical of the critics of SLS and SLES, but she's not using her reference to the FDA specifically to criticize them. (A) is the best answer here, so it's correct.

10. **(D).** Read the passage carefully. The answers to this question appear in the second paragraph, *not* in the third paragraph, which lists risks that have not been proven. Skim the answer choices to cross off anything that appears in the second paragraph. (D) is the right answer. Every other choice contains ailments that Internet rumors have associated with SLS and SLES but that haven't been substantiated.

11. **(E).** Look for an answer that could function as an outline for the passage, with all paragraphs in order and nothing extraneous. (A) isn't quite right because it leaves off the subject of the first paragraph. (B) is wrong. The passage doesn't contain any anecdotal accounts of SLS injuries. (C) doesn't work because the first paragraph doesn't describe the chemical composition of SLS and SLES. (D) isn't quite right because it doesn't mention the known and unsubstantiated risks associated with the substances. (E) is the best answer because it follows the structure of the passage closely.

12. **(E).** The third paragraph discusses the Internet rumors that hold SLS and SLES responsible for a host of ailments without providing proof. The author obviously wants to discredit these rumors; that's what the last sentences is all about. She's not criticizing, so (A) is out. She's not describing the substances — that's in the first paragraph — so (B) is out. She doesn't believe these risks are real, so she's not warning anyone of anything, and (C) is out. She makes no proposals of alternate substances, so (D) is out. (E) is the best answer here.

13. **(A).** (A) looks like a good possibility. The author does seem to think it's silly to believe rumors about substances that people have been using safely for years. (B) doesn't quite work. The author does trust the FDA, but makes no mention of its sources of funding or mission. (C) is wrong. The author clearly thinks that some Internet information isn't trustworthy, and she thinks information from the FDA, OSHA, and the American Cancer Society is trustworthy, but she doesn't explicitly say that the information on their Web sites is reliable — maybe she gets her information entirely from print sources. (D) doesn't work. The author does think SLS and SLES are cheap and effective surfactants and emulsifiers, but she doesn't think that they're unsafe to use in products that contact human skin. (E) is wrong. The author probably wouldn't want to prevent manufacturers from using SLS and SLES in their personal care products, but there's no reason to believe that she thinks enough protests could stop this inclusion. She doesn't mention protests anywhere in the passage. (A) is the best answer.

14. **(E).** This passage is a brief history of disability law in the United States, starting with *Buck v. Bell* and ending with *Tennessee v. Lane,* with two paragraphs of legislation sandwiched between the court cases. (A) doesn't quite work because this passage is about more than *Buck v. Bell,* and it never mentions the word *eugenics.* (B) is wrong because the author doesn't really discuss the civil rights movement, so she can't do much comparison of civil rights with disability activism. (C) is wrong because it leaves out the two paragraphs of legislation. (D) is wrong because this passage isn't just about the ADA. (E) is the best answer, encompassing the full range of topics in the passage.

15. **(A).** Obviously Justice Holmes and the leaders of Virginia agreed that disabilities needed to be minimized. (A) looks like a good answer. It nicely sums up the attitudes of national leaders. (B) is wrong. The author doesn't suggest that Justice Holmes was more insensitive than anyone else — he was enforcing a law passed by the state legislature, after all. (C) doesn't work. The author doesn't explicitly criticize Virginia, though you get the impression that she probably would in the right circumstances. (D) is wrong — the author isn't defending or condemning Justice Holmes, simply reporting his famous statement. (E) doesn't work either. The Supreme Court was simply affirming the legitimacy of a state law, and the author provides no evidence to suggest that it was unusually prejudiced against the disabled. (A) is the best answer.

16. **(D).** Read the third paragraph and check off answers as you find them. (A), (B), (C), and (E) are all there. The only one that's not is (D), and it's not required — employers don't have to do whatever it takes to accommodate the disabled, only provide "reasonable" accommodation.

17. **(D).** The second paragraph is primarily a list of legislation benefiting the disabled. (A) doesn't work because the author just mentions the civil rights movement in passing and doesn't indulge in any real comparing and contrasting. (B) is wrong. The passage doesn't in fact describe how that law works. (C) is totally wrong. Buck is up in the first paragraph. (D) looks exactly right. (E) doesn't quite work because the second paragraph doesn't mention the ADA so can't tie it to earlier legislation. (D) is correct.

18. **(D).** The author mentions the civil rights movement because most readers are more familiar with civil rights history than disability activism. Saying that the disabled used tactics borrowed from the civil rights movement suggests various types of peaceful protest that the reader can imagine though the author doesn't describe them here. (A) is wrong because the author isn't concerned with civil rights activists and how they measured up against disability activists. (B) may be true, but the author doesn't suggest it. (C) is wrong. The author doesn't address the issue of whether or not disability accommodations are an undue burden, so you can't assume anything about her opinions there. (D) is a good answer. The author mentions the civil rights movement to give the reader an idea of how disability activists approached their own movement. (E) is completely wrong. The passage doesn't mention the sit-in that brought about the regulations that implemented the Rehabilitation Act (though it's an interesting story). (D) is correct.

19. **(B).** The author likes disability law; she uses language like "designed to help the disabled live in society as equal citizens" when describing laws passed to prevent discrimination. (A) isn't quite right, because the author doesn't suggest that recent legislation makes it possible for disabled people to live just like the non-disabled. The key is the word "indistinguishable," which is impossible in many cases. That is an example of extreme language of which you should be suspicious. (B) does look right. The author does think living conditions have improved tremendously since the days of Carrie Buck. (C) is wrong. The author never mentions the burden on governments and employers. (She could if she wanted to — the ADA and other laws definitely cost money and effort.) (D) doesn't work because the author doesn't mention disability needs that are still unfulfilled, though she probably could if she wanted to. (E) is a statement of fact but doesn't sum up the author's views of disability law as a whole. (B) is the best answer here.

20. **(C).** This passage is about the origins of public education and the changes that occurred in educational philosophy in the first century of public schools; the whole thing is set in Germany. (A) could work but doesn't cover the whole passage, so there's probably a better answer. (B) isn't the passage's primary point. The whole third paragraph gets away from exploitation. (C) looks like a good overarching-theme answer. (D) is wrong because the passage doesn't get into modern educational practices. (E) doesn't cover the whole passage, just a portion of it. (C) is correct.

21. **(C).** The author tells you that textile mill owners exploited their workers badly enough to incite revolts, and that they embraced the concept of schools in the hopes that it would make the workers more docile. (A) is quite wrong. The first schools weren't created to help the students so much as to help the nobles. (B) could well be true but the passage doesn't discuss it. Remember, all correct answers stay close to the text. (C) fits well with what the passage says about the owners. It does appear that they were indifferent to the well-being of their workers. (D) isn't quite right. The passage doesn't specifically tell you that they were all aristocrats, and although some of them may have believed their authority was divinely ordained, you can't assume that of them all; nor is there any reason for you to assume that they cared about nurturing their workers. (E) is wrong. The passage doesn't contain anything about the factory owners being patriotic. (C) is the best answer.

22. **(B).** The difference between centuries was philosophical. Schools in the 1700s were meant for workers and intended to instill patriotism and gratitude toward the government into their students, but schools in the 1800s wanted to develop children to their full potential. (A) isn't right because 18th century schools had nothing to do with efficient textile mills. (B) looks like a very good answer. (C) doesn't work because 18th century schools were for the children of workers, not the aristocracy, and in the 19th century, no one had to spin anymore. (D) is tricky, because it's very close to being correct, but the passage doesn't tell you that 19th century schools wanted to create free-thinking students in general (though academic freedom was prized for advanced students), so it's wrong. (E) may actually be true — it sounds like some parents of Spinnschulen children didn't like the schools, if truant officers were necessary — but that's not the main difference and the passage doesn't really address this point. (B) is the right answer.

23. **(A).** Look at the sentence after the one that mentions increasing levels of unrest. It says that the rulers wanted "to channel the energy of restless peasants into something that would be less dangerous to the throne than riots." So "unrest" must mean riots and other violent uprisings by workers who disliked their lot in life. That would be (A). None of the other answers work. (E) is tempting because it concerns young people and this passage is about schools, but the statement doesn't restrict the violence to young men. (A) is correct.

24. **(E).** According to the passage: "Aristocrats liked this idea. They liked the thought of schools making peasants more docile and patriotic, and they appreciated the way state-run schools would teach children of lower social classes to accept their position in life." (A) is wrong because the schools were intended to do just the opposite; educating workers was supposed to make them more docile, not more violent. (B) doesn't work because the passage never mentions aristocratic resentment of taxes. (C) may be true but the passage doesn't say so; you know nothing of aristocratic opinions of Schlabrendorff himself. (D) is wrong because the passage doesn't tell you that the education would be specifically religious. Teaching children that their "lot is ordained by god" doesn't mean that the entire curriculum was religious. (E) is the most suitable answer to this question.

25. **(B).** The truant officers were meant to take away parental authority over children and replace it with state control. (B) is the most accurate answer. The truant officers weren't there to make sure every child was educated, so (A) is wrong. They didn't help or indoctrinate parents or children, nor did they recruit boys into the army, which nixes (C) and (D). Though they might indirectly have assisted the king and his administration in the compliant-citizen project, which would make (E) a possible answer, that's a bit less specific than the answer given in (B). (B) is correct.

26. **(D).** Nineteenth century educational theorists believed in nurturing innate abilities and using holistic techniques. That's not (A). In fact, (A) is just the opposite of what experts thought in the 1800s. (B) is wrong because nothing in the passage mentions religion. (C) isn't right. The passage never suggests that the state has an interest in an educated citizenry, just an interest in a docile and patriotic one, and that wasn't the prevailing view in the 19th century anyway. (D) looks like a perfect answer to this question. (E) isn't because the passage never mentions mothers as being good teachers of their own children. That makes (D) correct.

Section III

1. **(A).** The economist is using information about a trend to make a generalization that applies to all people. An answer that offers an exception to the rule would weaken the argument, such as evidence of some people who donate a lot and still attend plenty of services. (A) looks like just such an answer. (B) strengthens the argument. (C) shows how the argument applies to many denominations, which doesn't weaken it. (D) is largely irrelevant. (E) is a more detailed restatement of the argument. (A) is correct.

2. **(E).** So the odds go up for older women, but the numbers are bigger for younger women. That must be due to the numbers of women having children. If younger women have more Down's babies despite lower odds, many more of them must be having babies. (A) doesn't reconcile the discrepancy, and if anything would lead you to expect more older women would have Down's babies. (B) doesn't affect the question. (C) doesn't contain any info that would help with the age issue. (D) doesn't work because testing only provides information about which fetuses are affected, not why younger women produce the most Down syndrome children. (E) is the best answer. If the majority of babies are born to women under 35, then it would explain why they also have the majority of Down syndrome babies.

3. **(B).** (A) uses the word "infer" incorrectly. You can infer meaning from something you read, but a text can't infer anything, it can only imply. (Also, there is no reason to assume from the argument that advanced podiatric design is in fact essential to comfort.) (B) looks like a good answer. The guarantee is implying that customers can get a refund if their feet don't love the shoes. (C) is wrong. The argument never says that everyone loves the shoes, and that particular sentence certainly doesn't. (D) is wrong because neither the argument nor the key sentence criticize other shoes. (E) definitely doesn't apply to that sentence, which doesn't mention podiatrists. (B) is right.

4. **(A).** To weaken the argument, look for an answer suggesting that these regulations either won't hasten the fall of Cuba's dictatorship or won't benefit all Cuban people. (A) is an example of how the regulations could hurt Cubans, so (A) looks like a good answer. (B) by itself doesn't weaken the argument but only adds information to the argument. (C) describes Cuba's government but doesn't specifically weaken or strengthen the argument. (D) could arguably weaken the argument but the connection isn't that good because it doesn't show how the administration is wrong about the ban's effects. (E) may strengthen the argument — if Castro is benefiting from visitors, limiting them would hasten his demise. (A) is correct.

5. **(D).** The argument assumes that customers will like this change because they want more flexibility. If they don't in fact want flexibility, the argument becomes weaker. (A) doesn't work because the airline isn't trying to suggest that customers with more miles deserve more seats. (B) is wrong because there's no criticism here. (C) may be a true statement, but because the airline has neglected to mention that frequent-flier awards cut into profit margins, you can't bring that subject up now. Look for an answer that weakens the argument using information that's expressed. (D) looks like a good answer. The airline is simply assuming that customers will appreciate this change, when in fact many of them might prefer to get less flexible seats for fewer miles. (E) doesn't work; the airline isn't encouraging upgrades. (D) is the best answer.

6. **(C).** (A) isn't an assumption but is in fact stated in the argument. (B) isn't necessarily true. The sociologist isn't suggesting that women are choosing these men for their bodies. (C) does play an important role in the argument, because if there are equal numbers of men and women but women are more likely to marry, and you know they marry up, that will leave some men unmarried forever. (It also means that many men must be marrying more than one woman.) (D) may be true but isn't crucial to the argument. (E) isn't something you can assume from what's stated here and is irrelevant anyway. (C) is the best answer.

7. **(E).** You want an answer that shows someone submitting to abuse and then criticizing the boss in private. You can save time by reading the second half of the answer choices. The ones that match the subordinates' behavior are the only ones you read entirely. In this case, (D) and (E) would be in the running. (A) doesn't work because Skylar does take formal action against his boss. (B) is no good because David quits. (C) doesn't work because Casey takes action within her company. (D) is close but it's wrong because Paul doesn't perform his job well. (E) is the best answer.

8. **(D).** The argument suggests that a GED is just as good as a high school education; look for an answer that contradicts that. (A) isn't good. You don't want evidence showing that GEDs really are good. (B) doesn't work. If universities accept GEDs, that's more evidence that they're as good as diplomas. (C) strengthens the argument. (D) does weaken it. If high school students know their subjects better than GED holders, that's a reason to stay in school. (E) doesn't strengthen or weaken the argument. (D) is right.

9. **(D).** Look for an answer that supports the claim that a ban on over-the-counter DXM sales will protect young people. (A) describes bad effects of DXM, but doesn't prove that a ban on OTC sales will help. (B) doesn't help you and is irrelevant to your purpose. (C) is just more information on how teenagers abuse DXM, not how a ban on selling it would help. (D) does support the claim that banning OTC sales would help. It worked with codeine, so it should work with DXM. (E) is evidence of why DXM is dangerous but not why banning OTC sales would work to prevent abuse. (D) is correct.

10. **(A).** (A) looks like a very good answer. If hurricanes need to be over water to maintain their strength, inland cities must be safer from them than coastal cities. (B) doesn't necessarily have to be true. Hurricanes form over tropical water, but the argument doesn't suggest that they can't go into colder water. (C) happens to be true but the argument doesn't mention this fact, so you can't assume it. (D) doesn't follow because the argument says hurricanes lose strength over land, but it never mentions how many miles inland a hurricane would have to move before it loses most of its power to do damage. (E) may be tempting but you can't assume it. The argument presents the two seasons as equivalent, so you can't make distinctions between them. (A) is right.

11. **(E).** This parent assumes his child will be safe from diseases because all other children are vaccinated against them. But what if they aren't? The parent doesn't criticize other parents, so (A) is wrong. He isn't appealing to emotion, so (B) is wrong. He doesn't mention the government, so (C) is wrong. He doesn't mention the knowledge or wit of other parents, so (D) is wrong. But he does assume that everyone else will get their children vaccinated and is counting on that to protect his child. (E) is the best answer.

12. **(C).** The speaker suggests that requiring teachers to lead students in the Pledge with the words "under God" isn't unconstitutional because national leaders mention God all the time, which is a mistake, because the behavior of national leaders doesn't set standards for what is constitutional in schools. (A) is wrong — what other politicians do isn't the issue. (B) doesn't work; whether citizens agree that the words should be in the Pledge isn't the point. (C) looks like a good answer; that's the real problem with this argument, that it confuses the acts of national leaders with proof that something isn't unconstitutional. (D) is wrong because it's not true; the argument doesn't praise teachers. (E) is wrong because it doesn't address the argument's logic. The argument isn't about what people believe, but about the propriety of requiring everyone to make a statement of belief. You can't assume based on what is said that the argument is assuming a uniformity of belief. (C) is the best answer.

13. **(B).** The speakers disagree about whether high income taxes are behind Europeans' shorter work schedules. (A) is wrong because they're not debating Europeans' love of leisure. (B) is the source of disagreement. (C) is wrong. Neither one has suggested that the United States should raise income taxes. (D) doesn't work. They're not comparing European and U.S. standards of living. (E) may be tempting, but it's not the source of disagreement; it works better as evidence in Preston's argument. (B) is the best answer.

14. **(D).** (A) isn't the assumption. The argument suggests that the government should interfere with energy policies. (B) doesn't work because the speaker wants to use incentives. (C) is wrong because the author doesn't ever mention 1970s policies, only that people in the 1970s managed to reduce their energy consumption. (D) does look like an assumption the author makes; he would only suggest the use of incentives to reduce energy consumption if he thought reduced energy consumption was desirable. (E) is wrong. The author mentions California as an example, but isn't specifically suggesting that the federal government follow California's lead. (D) is the best answer.

15. **(B).** The author obviously doesn't think public schools should be a forum for public expression, so (A) is wrong. Clearly conformity isn't anathema to the author, so (B) could be right. (C) isn't right, because the author mentions dress codes in addition to uniforms. (D) is wrong. The argument doesn't contain any evidence about parents' opinions of dress codes. (E) is wrong. The author admits dress codes and uniforms limit individual expression and doesn't care. (B) is the best answer.

16. **(D).** The conclusion is that the optometrist is incompetent; the evidence is that one lens pops out regularly. But that isn't necessarily due to an optometrist's lack of skill. (A) is wrong. Although giving the optometrist a chance to defend himself would be nice, it's not a fault of the argument that the speaker doesn't provide one. (B) is wrong because the author never mentions frames, and nowhere else is the matter of frames introduced. (C) doesn't work. The author doesn't mention any particular techniques. (D) could be the answer. The author does jump to a conclusion here without making a connection between the glasses and the optometrist's skill. (E) is wrong because the author doesn't suggest that sabotage played a role in the bad glasses. (D) is the best answer.

17. **(D).** Look for an instance of someone carrying out a promise in return for a specific act. (A) is wrong because the woman doesn't do anything. (B) is wrong because the boss gives the workers something other than what he promised. (C) is wrong because the seal trainer makes no promise to the seals. (D) actually is right. The mom promises to do something if her son does a particular action; he does it, so she keeps her promise. (E) is wrong because the professor didn't promise a bad recommendation for a bad performance. (D) works the best.

18. **(E).** Look for evidence of the meadow voles' change in behavior. (A) is wrong. This hormone doesn't show that meadow voles can be made monogamous. (B) explains what's up with prairie voles, but not with meadow voles. (C) explains why meadow voles are typically promiscuous. (D) has nothing to do with vole behavior. (E) provides the most support for the assertion that the scientist's work turned promiscuous meadow voles into models of monogamy, so it's correct.

19. **(A).** (A) looks like a good answer. The museum doesn't know for sure that this statue is by Praxiteles, though it has enough evidence to hope it is. (B) doesn't work because the passage never mentions modern forgers. (C) is wrong. The passage says that dating ancient sculptures accurately is difficult, which means they may not ever be able to date this one conclusively. (D) isn't in the passage. (E) is wrong. The passage tells you that plenty of Roman copies have been mistaken for originals. (A) is the best answer.

20. **(C).** Psychologist A likes the change in practices referring to research participants; Psychologist B doesn't because it makes his life complicated. (A) is wrong because they're not arguing about the results of a survey. (B) is wrong because they both seem to agree that the governing body can make these changes. (C) looks right. They do disagree about whether the changes were a good thing. (D) isn't quite right. A mentions animals, but B doesn't address that issue, so you can't say that they disagree about it. (E) is wrong because B doesn't address this subject, so you don't know what he thinks about it. (C) is the best answer.

21. **(C).** The conclusion is that predicting when menopause will occur will make a difference to women planning when to have children, which must mean that not knowing when menopause will occur makes it difficult to plan. (A) is wrong because it doesn't explain why predicting menopause will help anyone. (B) is just general information that's been around for years. (C) could be right — this is an example of women who could benefit from knowing when they will experience menopause. (D) isn't right, though it might be true. (E) is just information about ovaries, not an explanation of how this test will help. (C) is the best answer.

22. **(C).** The school board member assumes that the inner-city schools' poor results are due to its squandering its money, which isn't necessarily the right conclusion; other factors could be involved. (A) is wrong. The member isn't suggesting that funding is tied to graduation rates because both schools got the same funding. (B) is wrong because he's not suggesting that the school made the students fail. (C) looks like a possible answer. He does assume that the school is wasting its money and that's the reason for the students' poor performance. (D) isn't quite right. He's not directing criticism specifically at the administrators. (E) is wrong. He's not suggesting that suburban students are more intelligent or hardworking. (C) is correct.

23. **(A).** The flaw in the argument is the mistaken belief that the odds of an event occurring can tell you how often you need to do a certain act. Odds of 1 in 1,000 don't mean that every 1000th trip will see a certain event, but that any trip out of that 1,000 could see it and you can't predict which one. The reasoning in (A) is similar to this; turning on the answering machine once a week won't necessarily catch a weekly phone call, unless you happen to know which day to expect it, and based on the facts here you don't. (B) is wrong. It's mistaken, but in a different way from the argument. (C) isn't exactly the same as the argument because you're not trying to guess which one of the 1,000 games will result in the jackpot, but instead covering them all. That's actually closer to wearing the helmet for all 1,000 rides on the assumption that one of them will involve a wreck. (D) is totally wrong because the second sentence is nothing like the argument's conclusion. (E) is similar to (C), though the reasoning is wrong; there's no reason to assume that the top law schools won't all pick the same applicants. Anyway, it's not the same as the argument. (A) is the closest and is correct.

24. **(A).** (A) looks like an ideal answer. If standards went up, women could well spend more time on housework even with their labor-saving devices. (B) is irrelevant. (C) looks like it could explain the discrepancy except the argument doesn't mention childcare, only housework. (D) would work if it suggested that pre-war husbands helped their wives, but it doesn't. (E) is irrelevant. (A) is the best answer.

25. **(D).** The two unions disagree about the EU's ban on using regional names for non-regional products, the AFMU claiming that some regional names now have generic, not regional, meaning associated with them. (A) is wrong because they're not arguing about quality. (B) is wrong because they're not discussing imports. (C) totally doesn't work; they're not debating taste buds. (D) does make sense. It looks like the right answer. (E) isn't right because they're not really debating intellectual property law in theory as much as addressing one specific instance of it. (D) is the best answer.

Section IV

If you like to work these problems by picking your favorite one first, the best criterion for choosing a favorite is number of questions — the problem with the most questions has the most points attached to it. Assessing a problem's difficulty is nearly impossible before you start, and often the problems that look hard initially turn out to be easy. Maximize your investment of time — pick a problem with seven questions before you work one with only five.

<u>Questions 1–5</u>

This problem is about as straightforward as you can hope for — a linear setup with single players and one-to-one matching of players with times. Too bad it's only five questions!

To start, make yourself a list of the initials of the participants' last names: A, D, H, M, S, W; this step is especially important in this problem because the participants all have such long names. Write out the speaking times in a row with space under them for plugging in data; go head and note that the 6 o'clock time slot can't contain either D or M. Then write the other rules in shorthand.

$$2 \quad 3 \quad 4 \quad 5 \quad 6 \quad 7$$
$$\text{not } D,M$$

$$S < D \text{ or } M, \text{ but not } D \text{ \& } M$$
$$\text{If } H = 2, W < A$$
$$\text{If } S = 4, W = 7$$

Can you make any deductions from this information? You do know that S must speak no later than 6, because she must speak before D or M but not both, but neither one of them can speak at 6. If D speaks at 4 and M speaks at 7, S must speak at 5 or 6. That's mildly interesting. You also know that if H speaks at 2, then S can't speak at 4, because then W would have a conflict between speaking at 7 (the last slot) and speaking before A. The rules really are quite explicit, so get going on the questions.

Just be aware that the numbering *starts* at 2 p.m. Many hapless students forget that the person speaking at 2 p.m. speaks first!

1. **(D).** Look for rule violations. Jotting down speaking times over the names may help. Remember that the first time slot is 2, so the third person in the list in fact speaks at 4. In (A), Stanton speaks at 4, but Wright doesn't speak at 7, so that's wrong. (B) has Mott speaking at 6, so that's wrong. In (C), Hunt speaks at 2, but then Anthony speaks before Wright, which is wrong. (D) looks okay at first glance, so check (E). (E) is wrong because Stanton speaks before both Douglass and Mott. (D) is correct.

2. **(E).** If Hunt speaks at 2, then Wright must speak before Anthony. That means Stanton can't speak at 4, because if she speaks at 4, then Wright must speak at 7. So Stanton must speak at 3, 5, or 6. Unfortunately none of the answers mention Stanton, so you have to try out the possibilities. Try (A). If Anthony speaks at 5, Wright could speak at 4, Douglass at 3, Stanton at 6, and Mott at 7. That works. That scenario works for (B) and (D), too. If you switch Douglass and Mott, so that Mott speaks at 3 and Douglass speaks at 7, you've also covered (C). That leaves (E), which doesn't work. If Wright speaks at 4, there aren't three times slots after her, and you need three to accommodate Anthony, who must speak after Wright, and Stanton and either Douglass or Mott. Stanton can't speak at 4 because then Wright would have to speak at 7, and she can't speak at 2 because then neither Douglass nor Mott could speak before her. (E) is the only answer that must be false, so it's correct.

3. **(D).** Okay, if Wright speaks at 7, what do you know? You know that Hunt can't speak at 2, because if she did, Wright couldn't speak last; she'd have to speak before Anthony. Does one of the answers say that? Yep. (D) says that one person must speak before Hunt. None of the other answer choices must necessarily be true, so (D) is correct.

4. **(D).** This question is quick. Who must always speak after Douglass or Mott, thereby cutting her out of the first slot? Stanton; she can never speak at 2. The answer is (D).

5. **(A).** This problem is another rule-violation question. Plug the speakers into the suggested time slots and see if they work. (E) doesn't. If Stanton speaks at 5 and Wright at 7, no slot is available for either Douglass or Mott to speak after Stanton, because neither of them can speak at 6. Going back up to the top, what about (A)? That looks possible; put the speakers in the following order: Wright, Anthony, Hunt, Douglass, Stanton, Mott. Hold on to that thought, and try the other choices. (B) doesn't work. Stanton can't speak before both Douglass and Mott, and there's no room for either before her if Hunt speaks at 2. (C) doesn't work. If Hunt speaks at 2, then Wright must speak before Anthony. Anthony can't speak after Wright if Wright speaks last. (D) doesn't work; if Stanton speaks at 4, Wright must speak at 7, so Wright can't speak at 3. That means (A) is the only possible scenario.

<u>Questions 6–12</u>

What a strange ballroom competition, allowing solo competitors in pairs events! Start this one like you always do: Make a list of initials of women and of men, and then write down the events in order. The events are your framework. So you have women: M, N, O, P; men: A, B, C. The events could look like this, with space underneath, and O in the rumba:

Now write the rules in shorthand next to this:

A - solo

N - pair

B <-x-> C

The trick to writing your notes is to make the information immediately recognizable when you look at it. You don't have to do your notes exactly the way I do; what matters is that they work for you, and that you're consistent in how you note information. For example, you could also write these notes in a different sort of shorthand — you could draw a circle around the letter A, to indicate that A is always solo, and you could write the letter B in a pair of parentheses with a space next to it to indicate that it must be part of a pair. For the last rule, you could write "B ___(space) C, or C ___ (space) B." It doesn't matter what you write, as long as you can glance at it and immediately know what it means.

Now think about the requirements. You know that every event must have one member in it; no member competes more than once. Every event with a pair in it must include one man and one woman. What else? Well, if O competes in the rumba, then A can't. If N must be part of a pair, then she must dance with B or C. You know that the maximum number of pairs possible is two, so two women must necessarily compete solo. You also know that the two pair events can't be back to back, because B and C can't dance in consecutive events.

Add this to your main sketch. Write: two pairs, and three solo. Keep track of numbers again. You know that N is paired, which means you only need one more pair!

Keep track of number of spaces and characters! This will be a very helpful strategy which will often lead to important deductions. In this case, the information about numbers tells you exactly how many pairs and solos you'll need.

6. **(E).** Draw this problem out on your chart. If Phoebe dances solo in the foxtrot and Bertrand provides a partner for Olivia, then only one event is left for Christophe to compete in — the waltz. He can't do passa doble or tango without being immediately before or immediately after Bertrand. Natasha must dance with Christophe, because she needs a partner and he's the only one available. So Natasha must dance the waltz. Remember, you have only two pairs, so Natasha must be with Christophe because Olivia and Bertrand are already a couple, and Natasha needs a pair! The answer is (E).

7. **(C).** Well, it can't be four or five, because Antonio dances solo and Olivia has already taken the female slot in the rumba. Could it be three? Try Antonio in the foxtrot. That leaves passa doble, tango, and waltz open. Natasha could feasibly compete in any of those, as long as she dances with Bertrand or Christophe. (C) is the answer.

8. **(A).** If solo women compete in the foxtrot and passa doble, then they must be Madeleine and Phoebe, because Olivia is booked for the rumba and Natasha dances as part of a pair. Antonio must compete in the tango; you know that because Olivia and either Christophe or Bertrand are competing in the rumba, and the only spot left for the other member of the Christope-Bertrand duo is the waltz with Natasha. So the answer must be (A).

9. **(B).** You know that both Bertrand and Christophe must dance with partners because you need two pairs with one man in each, and if Antonio dances solo, then the other two men MUST dance with partners. You also know that Natasha must dance in a pair because it's a rule. You don't need to search any further because none of the answers have more than three members listed, and (B) lists exactly the members you want. So (B) is the answer.

10. **(E).** Well, you know it can't be (A) or (B) because two women must compete solo. Unfortunately none of the other answers include Natasha, who would be a dead giveaway that the answer was wrong. You already know that both Madeleine and Phoebe can compete solo; refer to Question 9 to see one way of working that. Can Olivia compete solo? Sure, if, for example, Phoebe and Christophe dance the passa doble and Natasha and Bertrand compete in the waltz, Olivia is on her own for the rumba. So the correct answer is (E)

11. **(B).** For this one to work, you have to put Antonio in the foxtrot. Bertrand or Christophe must compete in the waltz with Natasha because Natasha needs a partner; the remaining Bertrand or Christophe must dance with either Olivia in the rumba or with Madeleine or Phoebe in the passa doble. That means a solo woman must perform the tango, but you can't tell which of the passa doble or the rumba will be a solo (though one of them will definitely be a solo). So the foxtrot and the tango are the events that *must* have solo performers, and the answer is (B).

12. **(E).** Say Bertrand dances with Olivia in the rumba. Then Christophe must dance with Natasha in the foxtrot, and Antonio competes alone in the passa doble. Or you could switch the places of Bertrand and Christophe, but you must have Natasha in the foxtrot, so the answer is (E).

Questions 13–18

Aren't you glad you're not the official in charge of picking chefs for this dinner? Seven chefs, only five courses — that's at least two disgruntled chefs, if not more. The one who doesn't get to cook for the president may just come after you with a knife for revenge.

Okay, now to organize this puppy. This problem is complicated. You have three categories of information:

- Times the courses can be served
- The courses themselves
- The chefs who can prepare them

To solve these questions, first make a list of initials for courses (h, c, e, s, d) and chefs (A, B, E, J, K, M, N). Two things are going to remain consistent: the order of the five courses and the three serving hours of the dinner. The serving hours stay in one order, but you don't know how many courses will occur at each one (though you do know it'll be one or two, not zero or three). That means that at 7 the kitchen could serve just hors d'oeuvres or it could serve hors d'oeuvres and consommé (which are, by the way, appetizers and a kind of soup). At 8, the kitchen could serve consommé and entrée, just entrée, or entrée and salade. ("Salade" is the fancy French word for "salad," but you already figured that out.) At 9, the kitchen will serve either salade and dessert, or just dessert. Which course happens when depends on the other information in the questions. Assume the kitchen has enough room for two chefs to prepare different courses at the same time without interfering with one another. You can also assume that if two courses occur in one hour, they occur one after the other, not simultaneously. That must be the case if the courses are to occur in order.

Remember to leave your preconceived notions at the door! You might know that salad almost never comes after the entrée in a 5-star restaurant, and of course dessert always comes last, but that's not important here. What's important is what the facts say. (And in Europe, salad usually does come after the entrée, but once again, that's not important here.)

Three scenarios are possible, so make your life easier and just draw three diagrams to illustrate them:

7	8	9		7	8	9		7	8	9
h	ce	sd		hc	e	sd		hc	es	d

When you plug in your data, just write the initials of the chefs under the course they're preparing. Be sure you have enough room.

Now, remember that though the same chef can prepare more than one course, no chef can prepare two courses the same hour. So if both hors d'oeuvres and consommé are served at 7, the same chef can't prepare them both. (Artistic cooking takes too much concentration!) For example, if both consommé and entrée come out at 8, Andrea can't prepare them both, even though he's offered to. (And yes, in this case, Andrea is a guy – he's Italian.)

Make yourself another little set of notes with abbreviations of courses and chefs. Doing so makes reading the abbreviations easier than the text version. Draw this new chart off to the side of your diagrams for quick reference.

h: B, M

c: A, K

e: A, N

s: B, E, J

d: E, K, M

13. **(B).** You already know you can't have more than five chefs because there are only five courses and no chef wants to share glory with another. That means (E) is wrong. You want a minimum number, so start with the smallest choice. Can you schedule a dinner with just two chefs cooking every course? To do that you'd have to find one chef who can cook three courses. Skim through the list to see if you can find any chef whose name appears three times. Nope. No single chef can cook all three courses, so two is impossible. Could you produce the whole dinner with just three chefs? Take, for example, the scenario in which dessert is the only course served at 9. You could come up with a scenario in which Berthe and Andrea cook both courses at both 7 and 8, leaving dessert to a third chef; that scenario would look like this:

7	8	9
h, c	e, s	d
B, A	A, B	E

So you could do the entire dinner with just three chefs. The answer is (B).

14. **(A).** If salade comes at 9, so does dessert, so 8 will see just the entrée or both consommé and entrée. The group of chefs who can prepare these courses include Andrea, Kimiko, and Nigel, which means you can eliminate (B), (C), and (E). Is there any reason you can't serve two courses at 8? No, which means you can eliminate (D), but go ahead and think this one all the way through. There are three ways to do this: c: A and e: N; c: K and e: A; c: K and e: N. One of those choices, Andrea and Kimiko, happens to be an answer: (A) is correct.

15. **(E).** See if you can find an answer choice that leaves off a course or two. (A) could work. You could have 7: h: B, c: A; 8: e: A; 9: s: J, d: K. Here's one possibly for (B): 7: h: B, c: K; 8: e: A; 9: s: B, d: M. (There are a couple of other ways you could arrange these chefs, but you need only one.) For (C) you could do it like this: 7: h: M; 8: c: A, e: N; 9: s: E. d: M. Here's (D): 7: h: M, c: A; 8: e: A; 9: s: J, d: K. That leaves (E). Does leaving out Andrea make such a difference? Yes. Without Andrea and without Kimiko, you have no one willing to make consommé. Nor do you have anyone to make the entrée; Andrea and Nigel are the guys for that, and neither of them is in the list. A superabundance of chefs to make hors d'oeuvres, salade, and dessert doesn't make for a lengthy or complete banquet. That means the answer is (E).

16. **(A).** There are three ways this question could work; the two chefs can prepare the courses at 7 and 8, 8 and 9, or 7 and 9. Take a look at the answer choices; Andrea appears three times, so he's a good one to start with. The only way Andrea can prepare two courses is if he prepares consommé at 7 and the entrée at 8. Is there another cook who could prepare an hors d'oeuvre at 7 and salade at 8? Yes. Berthe could do both, leaving dessert for someone else. See the diagram for Question 13 to see how this works; in that case, Emilio makes dessert, but you don't need to worry about dessert for this question. That means the answer is (A). (Try out the other possibilities yourself; you'll see that they don't work.)

17. **(C).** The only way for this question to work is to have hors d'oeuvres and consommé at 7 and salade and dessert at 9. Look at the list of courses with their corresponding chefs. Is there anyone who can cook hors d'oeuvres and either salade or dessert? Yes. Berthe can do hors d'oeuvres and salade. Is there a chef who can do consommé and dessert? Yes, Kimiko. That's one of the possible answers: (C), and it's correct. None of the other pairs work; test them to see, but (C) is the answer. See the diagram for how that would work.

$$
\begin{array}{ccc}
7 & 8 & 9 \\
h, c & e & s, d \\
B, K & ? & B, K
\end{array}
$$

18. **(A).** This one is just like Question 15 — remember how much fun that was? This one, though, works the other way. Four of the answer choices are wrong and only one is correct; if one course is missing, then the answer is wrong. Try (A). It looks like it should work. Try arranging the chefs like this: 7: h: B, c: A; 8: e: N, s: E; 9: d: E. See the diagram for how that looks. Test the other four to make sure. (B) doesn't work because despite having a roster of five chefs, none of them can make an hors d'oeuvre. (C) has no one to make an entrée. (D) has no one to make a consommé. (E) doesn't have anyone who can make an entrée. So (A) is the only answer that could work.

$$
\begin{array}{ccc}
7 & 8 & 9 \\
h, c & e, s & d \\
B, A & N, E & E
\end{array}
$$

Questions 19–25

This question isn't meant to recommend or condone watching movie versions of literary classics instead of reading the books. Anyway, first step as always: Abbreviate the movies with their initials: E, G, I, M, W. Use lowercase letters to mark film format, "v" for videotape and "d" for disc. So, *Emma* on videotape becomes Ev; *Wuthering Heights* on disc becomes Wd.

The days of the week make the best framework for this problem. Start on Friday and finish with Thursday. Write them across the page with room beneath them. Write in any information you already know about the schedule.

$$
\begin{array}{ccccccc}
F & Sa & Su & M & T & W & R \\
d & & Ev & & & &
\end{array}
$$

Now consider the rules. If E must be on Monday, then W must be on Friday, Saturday, or Sunday. You can't put any two videotapes or two DVDs next to one another, so Sunday can't contain either kind of movie; the student must take that night off. You also know that he must watch W on Saturday, because that's the only way he can watch it before E and observe the rules about discs and videotapes not touching one another. You can draw a further conclusion: If he watches a movie on Friday, it must be a videotape, because if it were a disc, it would violate the rule about no two discs being immediately next to one another. Write in that information:

$$
\begin{array}{ccccccc}
F & Sa & Su & M & T & W & R \\
v & Wd & none & Ev & & &
\end{array}
$$

You also know that G must come before both I and M, though you don't know the order of I and M. There are two ways to make that work — either G is the video on Friday, or it's a disc on Wednesday. If G is a disc on Wednesday, then M and I are videos on Tuesday and Thursday. If instead G is a videotape on Friday, then either M or I is a videotape, and the other of the pair is a disc. In that case, the student would distribute M and I in the proper order between Tuesday and Thursday. Note that the only possible film for Friday is Gv, so if the student watches a film on Friday, that's the one. That means the two possible schedules look like this:

F	Sa	Su	M	T	W	R
Gv	Wd	none	Ev	Id/Md	none	Md/Id
none	Wd	none	Ev	Gd	Iv/Mv	Md/Id

You could also do this chart with two separate rows of information, the first row containing movie name abbreviations and below it a row of abbreviations of formats. If you prefer dividing up your information like that, by all means do so. (See questions 20–26 in Section 1 of the test in Chapter 23 to see how that diagram could work; that question deals with ice cream flavors and toppings.) Your system has to work for YOU, so do what it takes to make everything clear to you, and don't worry about anyone else's preference.

That's a good start. Now answer the questions.

19. **(C).** Look for rule violations. (A) has *Emma* on Sunday, so that's wrong. (B) has *Middlemarch* and *Ivanhoe* on consecutive days, which is impossible because they must both be on disc if *Great Expectations* is on video, so that's wrong. (C) could work, but check the others anyway. (D) has *Wuthering Heights* on Friday, and you need a film on disc for Saturday, so that's wrong. (E) has *Middlemarch* before *Great Expectations,* so that's wrong. That leaves (C) as the only possibility.

20. **(A).** The only way the student can watch *Great Expectations* before *Emma* is to watch it on Friday, because *Wuthering Heights* occupies Saturday and Sunday is off. The film on Friday must be a videotape, because otherwise it would violate the rule about putting films of the same format immediately before or after one another. So *Great Expectations* can't be on disc, and the answer is (A). As for *Ivanhoe* and *Middlemarch,* either one of them could be on disc, you know there's no film on Sunday, and they could take place on Tuesday and Thursday, so the other four answers either must be or could be true. (A) is correct.

F	Sa	Su	M	T	W	R
Gv	Wd	none	Ev	Id/Md	none	Md/Id

21. **(C).** If M is on videotape, then *Great Expectations* and *Ivanhoe* must both be on disc. In that case, *Great Expectations* must be on Tuesday, *Middlemarch* on Wednesday, and *Ivanhoe* on Thursday, with no film on Friday. The diagram looks like this:

F	Sa	Su	M	T	W	R
	Wd	none	Ev	Gd	Mv	Id

Of the answer choices, only (C) is possible. (A) is wrong because *Ivanhoe* is on disc. (B) is wrong because the student must watch *Emma* two days before watching *Middlemarch*. (D) is wrong because the student must watch *Ivanhoe* on Thursday. (E) is wrong because the student must watch *Middlemarch* on Wednesday. But he must watch *Great Expectations* exactly one day before watching *Middlemarch,* so (C) is correct.

22. **(E).** Test the answers, plotting them on your diagram. Try (A). Could the student skip both Friday and Monday? You know he must watch *Emma* on Monday, and he could watch a film on Friday, so that could be true. Now (B). He must watch a film on Monday, and Wednesday can go either way, so that could be true. Try (C). He could take Friday and Sunday off, so that could be true. Now (D). He definitely skips Sunday, and could take Wednesday off if he watches *Great Expectations* on Friday, so that could be true. That leaves (E), and it's the only false statement. The student must watch something on either Tuesday or Thursday. He's already taken Sunday off, and has only one more day off if he wants to watch all five films, so he has to watch something on either Tuesday or Thursday. The answer is (E).

23. **(C).** If the student watches *Great Expectations* after *Wuthering Heights,* then he must watch it on disc on Tuesday, and *Middlemarch* and *Ivanhoe* must fall on Wednesday and Thursday, with the Thursday film on disc and the Wednesday film on videotape — see the diagram for Question 20 for how this could work, and remember you can switch *Ivanhoe* and *Middlemarch.* The student can't watch anything on Friday, so (A) must be true. (B) could be true if *Ivanhoe* is on videotape, which would put it on Wednesday. (C) must be false, because *Emma* must be on Monday and *Great Expectations* must be on Tuesday; that looks like the answer. (D) must be true because *Great Expectations* must be on disc. (E) could be true, because *Ivanhoe* could be on disc. (C) is correct.

24. **(A).** With five movies and seven nights to watch them, the student can take only two nights off. One of those is Sunday. If he also takes Wednesday off, then he has to watch a film on every remaining night, including Friday. The only film he can watch on Friday is the videotape of *Great Expectations.* That means (A) must be true. (B) is false. (C), (D), and (E) are all possible but not necessarily true. (A) is the answer.

	F	Sa	Su	M	T	W	R
	Gv	Wd	none	Ev	Id/Md	none	Md/Id

25. **(B).** The schedule for Saturday, Sunday, and Monday never changes; look at your chart, and you'll see that both possible schedules have the same movies scheduled (or not scheduled) on those days. The day the student sees *Ivanhoe* depends on when he sees *Great Expectations.* If he watches *Great Expectations* on Friday, then *Great Expectations* is a videotape and *Ivanhoe* and *Middlemarch* are both discs. In order to watch *Ivanhoe* before *Middlemarch,* and to avoid viewing two discs on consecutive days, the student must watch *Ivanhoe* on Tuesday and *Middlemarch* on Thursday. If, on the other hand, he watches *Great Expectations* on Tuesday, *Great Expectations* must be on disc and his Thursday movie must also be on disc, while his Wednesday film — in this case *Ivanhoe* — must be on videotape. That's two different schedules; no other arrangements are possible. (See the following diagram for how these two arrangements would work.) So the answer is (B).

	F	Sa	Su	M	T	W	R
#1	Gv	Wd	none	Ev	Id	none	Md
#2	none	Wd	none	Ev	Gd	Iv	Md

Part VII
The Part of Tens

The 5th Wave   By Rich Tennant

"If it's okay for them to ask experimental questions, I figure it should be okay for me to give some experimental answers."

In this part . . .

Now for the fun stuff. You can't have a *For Dummies* book without a Part of Tens! You don't have to work hard to get through these chapters, but they do have some useful information. One chapter lists some tips for doing well on the LSAT, and another lists myths about the LSAT. The last one contains some handy information about different legal-practice areas, for those of you looking ahead to your post-law-school days. Read and enjoy!

Chapter 24

Ten (or So) Habits of Highly Successful LSAT-Takers

. . . .

In This Chapter

▶ Preparing for the test

▶ Taking the test (and no prisoners)

. . . .

Some people just naturally do well on standardized tests. They fly through the SAT (Scholastic Aptitude Test – the one you take to get into college), ace the GRE (Graduate Record Exam – the one you take to get into graduate school), and consider the LSAT easy. What makes them so successful at taking tests in general and the LSAT in particular? These ten (more like 11) habits of highly successful LSAT takers, of course!

Getting a Good Night's Sleep

A sharp brain is a well-rested brain. Studies have shown that people who have a good night's sleep are much better at solving problems than people who are sleep-deprived. People who don't sleep enough are more likely to miss hidden points — clues that lead to those flashes of inspiration that are so useful in problem solving, especially analytical reasoning problems. People who don't sleep enough also have a harder time concentrating, which is important for the entire LSAT. Reading Comprehension passages are intentionally boring — you need all your wits about you to stay focused. (Studies have also shown that a nap in the middle of the day can help your performance in the afternoon and evening, but a siesta won't help you on the LSAT.)

Be careful about using artificial sleep aids the night before the LSAT. Sleeping pills can leave you groggy in the morning, which pretty much cancels out the benefits of a good night's sleep.

Eating Breakfast

Your brain needs fuel to function. Breakfast provides that fuel. Your body also needs fuel. The LSAT is a long test — you're at the testing center for several hours, probably through your customary lunchtime. Don't sabotage your chances by skipping breakfast. (You never know, though — if your stomach growls loudly enough, it may distract your fellow test-takers and hurt their scores. Not that you should try to do something like that.) Something with protein and maybe some fat is best; you don't burn through them as quickly as you would, say, a plain piece of toast. Go easy on the coffee and cola, though; you don't want to be super-jittery and in desperate need of hitting the bathroom.

Planning Ahead

The logistics of taking an LSAT can be daunting. You have to get up on a Saturday morning at an unreasonable hour (unless you take the Monday test), somehow get to the testing site, which is probably in an unfamiliar place, and present yourself in the correct room with the correct paperwork, none of which you habitually carry with yourself. You may need odd supplies, like No. 2 pencils or a stopwatch. Successful LSAT-takers get all this stuff ready before they go — preferably the night before. That way they don't show up without a driver's license and get kicked out before they even start taking the test.

In addition, if you can manage it, you should visit the LSAT testing site at least a day before your test date. Scope out the building, the room if possible, and don't forget to check out parking. Don't assume that you'll be able to find the location on your first try with an online map!

Envisioning Success

Successful LSAT-takers meet the test with confidence, certain that they're equal to the task before them. They go in knowing that they're going to get a great score, and sure enough, they do. Confidence is key. Moving through the questions is a lot easier when you're confident that you're doing the best job you possibly can. Think about what would happen if you spent all your emotional energy fretting about how difficult the questions are and worrying that you're getting them wrong. Not inspiring, is it? Good test-takers don't fuss (leave that to your grandma). They spend their time congratulating themselves on how smart they are and how easy the test is. It really can make a difference.

And for heaven's sake, don't spend your time with your fellow test-takers who either want to gloat at how well prepared they are or worse yet, shoot a shower of bullets at you about how to work this or that LSAT strategy. You may want to bring a portable CD player with you during breaks so that you stay away from group angst.

Guessing Well

Some guesses are inevitable. It's a rare test-taker indeed who is 100 percent sure of the answer to every question. The difference between successful LSAT-takers and everyone else is that the successful folks guess well. They don't guess randomly. Instead, they narrow their possibilities so that they're really choosing the better of two answers, not some random choice of five. Eliminate the obvious duds, and then work with what's left.

Making Notes and Drawings

Many people who do well on the LSAT turn in test booklets filled with notes, underlinings, little sketches, and other marginalia. They don't try to hold all the necessary information in their heads. Instead, they put it on paper in a format that they can use quickly. Jotting down notes and drawings is especially important for the Analytical Reasoning section (*please* don't try to do those problems in your head!), but it also helps for the Logical Reasoning and Reading Comprehension sections. If scribbling down a little equation to symbolize the pattern of reasoning in a question helps you, do it. If it helps you to draw a big box around an important word in a reading passage, do it. No one cares what the test booklet looks like when you're done with it. The booklet isn't your property because you can't take it home, but it is yours to mangle during the test if you so choose.

Concentrating

The LSAT is a test of concentration as much as anything. Law students and lawyers (such as you in the near future) must concentrate on boring, detailed information for hours and days on end. Their grades or their clients' livelihoods depend on it. People who do well on the LSAT are all capable of concentrating on one thing for several straight hours without meaningful interruption. They're also good at switching gears from concentrating on one thing — say, reading comprehension — to something else — such as analytical reasoning — without being nagged by worries about the previous section that is, after all, over and done with. They don't allow their minds to wander to the previous night's party or the current evening's hot date. They don't think about the scratching of other people's pencils or the ticking of the clock. They don't even think much about lunch. They focus on the LSAT and nothing else.

Ignoring Irrelevancies

The LSAT is chock-full of information. You need a lot of that info to answer the questions. You *don't* need it all. Part of the trick to succeeding on the LSAT is separating what you do need to know from what you don't. People who do well on the LSAT are good at winnowing the kernels of information they need from the great pile of irrelevant information. The LSAT-makers toss in lots of facts, opinions, and statements, mainly to make the test exactly the right length, but incidentally to see if you can spot the facts, opinions, and statements that you need to answer the questions. Lawyers have to do this too, so it's a valuable and relevant skill. (Lawyers occasionally participate in a sport called "document review," in which a team gathers someplace and reads the thousands or millions of documents contained in rooms full of boxes. The idea is to spot the few documents that are relevant to the case, while not pulling out any of the million or so that have nothing to do with the matter at hand.)

Staying Relaxed

Okay, maybe "LSAT" and "relaxation" don't belong in the same sentence. It's true, however, that people who do well on the LSAT don't stress out about it. Tension slows down your performance and makes it harder for the thoughts to flow. Effective LSAT-takers don't let any of the petty stresses associated with the test matter too much to them. They don't worry excessively about their answers to previous questions or about the upcoming Analytical Reasoning section. They sit calmly in their seats, read the questions, fill in little dots with their pencils, and consider this experience just another day in their lives. You can't let the LSAT become too big a deal for you — the test senses fear and exploits it.

Managing Your Time Well

You get exactly 35 minutes for every section of the LSAT. (Okay, you get 30 minutes for the Writing Sample section, but whatever.) Every section has more or less the same number of questions. Successful LSAT-takers know approximately how much time they can allocate to any one Logical Reasoning question, any larger Reading Comprehension passage, or any Analytical Reasoning problem. People who aren't quite so successful don't manage their time as well. As a result, they may not finish sections, or they may spend half their time on one quarter of the section and have only half the time to do the last 75 percent of it. At the same time, successful LSAT-takers understand that some questions take a bit longer than others, so they allow a little extra time for longer questions if the questions look like promising sources of points, and the process of solving them is going well. (See Chapter 2 for more on time management.)

Steadily Moving to the Finish

Effective LSAT-takers keep moving. They don't let any one question stop them. They *don't* get bogged down. You know when you're making progress on a question. You also probably have a pretty good idea when you're beating your head against a lost cause (pardon the mixed metaphor). Remember, in order to finish the LSAT, the best approach is to keep on answering questions. Keep moving. Sure, you may really want to crack the code to that first pesky Analytical Reasoning problem, and you may get every question on it right, but that's not going to do wonders for your score if you never get to the other three problems. Admit when you're beaten, guess and move on. Even people who reach the summit of Mount Everest stumble occasionally.

Chapter 25

Ten (Plus One) Myths About the LSAT

People who go to law school tend to be particular and precise about how they do things. They study law school rankings, fret about their grades and LSAT scores, and generally grasp at any apparent "truth" that helps them tackle the daunting process of launching a legal career. That's why myths about the LSAT abound. Nervous would-be law students looking for certainty in an uncertain endeavor try to come up with principles that can guarantee them the results they want. Unfortunately, life isn't certain, and the LSAT is no exception to that rule. This chapter contains some of the most common beliefs, and explanations of why they aren't true.

The LSAT Doesn't Have Anything to Do with Law School

Not true. People may tell you that, and on its face it does seem that Analytical Reasoning and the other sections don't pertain to law school. But think about it; the LSAT-writers have to concoct a test that in about four hours can spot the people who are likely to succeed in the legal education. So they've boiled down law school to its essence, which is the ability to read carefully and apply rules. They realize that what you read in law school and later as a lawyer is often boring, arcane, likely to put a reader to sleep, and extremely complicated, so they've made a test that spots people with the ability to overcome these obstacles. They realize that law students and lawyers have to apply themselves steadily to particular tasks for hours on end, so they've made the LSAT a test of endurance. Really the LSAT is quite impressive when you think of it that way. And the test works — high LSAT scores do in fact match up with good performance in law school. (Also to the Law School Admission Council's [LSAC's] credit, they're constantly working to improve the test and make it more accurate.)

You Can't Study for the LSAT

Not true. This book is all about studying for the LSAT. At the very least, getting familiar with the test's format *before* you sit down to take it for real is bound to make your experience easier; you don't have to waste time reading instructions. At best, studying can make a substantial difference in your score. Analytical Reasoning problems are especially prone to improvement; believe me, I've gotten super-good at those suckers as a result of writing this book! Likewise, Logical Reasoning and Reading Comprehension questions get easier the more you expose yourself to them. Sure, some people start off good at the test, and stay that way, but anyone can improve their score with practice.

You Must Take a Prep Course in Order to Do Well on the LSAT

Nope. Plenty of people ace the LSAT after an hour or two of studying on their own at home. Plenty more do quite well after studying for a few weeks in odd hours. Some people do see dramatic improvements in their scores after taking a prep course. Others see their scores drop. Remember, test-prep companies can't guarantee that you'll do better; they can make promises about refunding your tuition, but they can't buy you an extra ten points on the test. If you think taking a course can help you study, by all means take a course. But if you'd rather save that money for something else (law school, perhaps?) and think you could discipline yourself enough to study sufficiently on your own, then go with your instincts. They're probably right.

If you do decide to study on your own, you can't get better practice materials than actual LSATs, sold as LSAT PrepTests by the LSAC. Try to work through at least two or three of those before you take the LSAT.

Some People Just Can't Do Analytical Reasoning Problems

Not true. Analytical Reasoning problems may be scary, and they may be weird, and they may freak you out the first time you see them, but you can figure out how to do them. They're actually the most teachable part of the LSAT. Studying for a few weeks before the test isn't going to improve your reading speed, and it probably won't improve your vocabulary much, but it can definitely help your ability to work analytical reasoning problems.

When I've taught analytical reasoning in classes, every single student can work the questions. Seriously. Every student in the class can get answers right when they're working together with a teacher and fellow students. Where people fall down is when they're alone, facing the LSAT by themselves. You don't have to let this happen to you. You can figure out how to work analytical reasoning — really. Read Chapters 4 and 5 of this book carefully, work the problems in Chapter 6 and read the corresponding explanations, work the Analytical Reasoning sections in Chapters 20 and 22, and then practice some more by working LSAT PrepTests — the more Analytical Reasoning problems you work, the less scary they become.

You Can Spot Difficult Questions Before You Work Them

Not true. Digesting the material in any LSAT question takes a certain amount of time; that's especially true in the case of the longer questions in the Reading Comprehension and Analytical Reasoning sections. A problem that may look incredibly difficult at first glance may turn out to be incredibly easy after you start on it. I don't care if you skip around while you work the test, but I'd hate to see you waste too much of your precious time on the ultimately fruitless task of rating the questions by difficulty. (After you delve into a question, though, if you discover that it's too difficult, then don't fret; give it your best guess and move on.) See Chapter 2 for a discussion of guessing and test-taking strategies.

B Is the Best Letter to Guess

Not necessarily. The sad fact is that you can't predict what letter is the most prevalent on any given test section. You can test this proposition by reading the answers to several LSATs; the most common letter changes with dismaying regularity. (Though it does seem that (A) and (E) are slightly less common than the middle letters.) What is true about completely random guessing is that you maximize your chances of getting some answers right if you stick to the same letter; statistically you should get about 20 percent right that way. Twenty percent is nothing to strive for, but I suppose it's better than nothing. A better strategy is to guess based on at least some knowledge; you stand a better chance of correctly getting one out of three than one out of five, though you may then have to abandon your chosen "guess letter."

No One Reads the Writing Sample

Would you stake your future law-school career on that belief? Didn't think so. Assume that everyone on every admissions committee is reading every single LSAT essay. They're not, but what if your essay happens to be the one they *do* pull out of the pile for scrutiny? You'd better be prepared. What'll it hurt, anyway? You have to spend 30 minutes of your LSAT experience writing the thing, so you may as well do a good job. You'll have to write essays for the next several years as a law student, if you do go to law school, and then perhaps as a lawyer. You may as well put a little effort into discovering a quick method of cranking out a decent document in limited time.

Finishing a Section Is Better Than Concentrating on Two-Thirds of It

Not true — necessarily. Take the Analytical Reasoning section. You have four problems per section, each with five, six, or seven questions. If you take your time and work the three with the most questions, and because you're taking your time you get most of them right, you're looking at about 75 percent correct — a good score even if you completely ignore one problem. If instead you force yourself to tackle every problem and because you're rushing you miss about half (a typical result), then even though you've finished the section, you get only about 50 percent correct.

A good general rule is, while you're practicing, first try to answer all the questions within the given time. If you score less than 60 percent (or so) correct on a section, you may want to slow down and increase the percentage you get right.

A Great LSAT Score Guarantees Admission to a Great Law School

If only it were so. Alas, a great LSAT score is pretty much a requirement for admission to a top law school, but it just won't guarantee admission. Harvard, Yale, Stanford, and their compatriots at the top of the law school pyramid see so many applicants with scores of 180 that they can afford to toss some in the trash. A 170 won't impress them; they see hundreds of those. What is true, though, is that you need that high score for them even to begin to consider you. This is true of all tiers of law schools; you must achieve a certain score level or they just plain won't let you in. Some schools even use computers to weed out unacceptable applicants, doing some computations that combine LSAT score with GPA to see whom the admissions committee will consider. The moral of this story? Aim high; it never hurts to score higher than you need.

The LSAT Is Used Only for Admissions Purposes

Actually, if your LSAT score is attractive enough to a law school, the admissions folks might give you all sorts of financial perks in addition to looking favorably at your application. For instance, if your LSAT score was off the charts, don't be surprised if you get a notice from a law school allowing you to waive the application fee. In addition, schools may consider your LSAT score when granting merit-based scholarships, which could pay more than 70 percent of your tuition!

The lesson here is even if you're happy with your score, improving it a little more may pay off big time in the end.

Your Score Won't Improve if You Retake the LSAT

It may. It happens often enough that it's something to believe in. You may have a bad day the first time you take the LSAT. Maybe you stayed out too late the night before, or maybe the guy sitting next to you in the classroom had terrible body odor and it distracted you. Or maybe you didn't bother to study the first time around, so you didn't produce a score that represents your true abilities. Plenty of factors can change that can result in a higher score. If you think you can do better given a second chance, look on your first attempt as a practice run and go back and give it another shot.

But be sure that you prepare well for the second test. The LSAT has a high re-test predictability which means that without a significant change in your circumstances (preparation, or maybe you were feeling ill the first time you took it), chances are your score will be very similar to your first try. However, adequate preparation *can* significantly increase your score. Make sure that you get serious about studying and that you chart your progress on real timed practice LSATs published by LSAC. That is the best indicator of your score on test day.

Usually schools average your LSAT score, so for it to make a difference, your score needs to improve quite a lot. For instance, if you got a 145 the first time, and a 155 the second time, your score would be averaged to a 150. But do your homework on this one. A few schools will look at your latest or best score.

Chapter 26

Ten Kinds of Law You Can Practice

So you're seriously considering law school. Have you considered what you would do with a law degree? A degree of Juris Doctor (JD — that's the degree you get when you graduate from law school) can lead down all sorts of roads. A lawyer isn't a multipurpose legal expert; different lawyers specialize in different fields. Don't assume that just because someone is a lawyer he or she can handle any legal task. Just as you'd never go to a plastic surgeon to get a liver transplant, you wouldn't want to hire a criminal lawyer to write your will.

This chapter contains some common areas of legal practice. *Note:* I have room to list only the more common ones. Many specialties aren't listed. Within most of these listed specialties, there are lawyers who are primarily *litigators* — they go to court and talk to judges — and lawyers who specialize in transactional work — they sit in offices, writing documents and negotiating deals. The law offers something for nearly everyone!

Business/Corporate

Some lawyers spend all their time working on behalf of corporations, negotiating deals, writing and reviewing contracts, and handling venture capital, securities, mergers, and acquisitions, commercial paper, and plenty of other big-money topics. Some lawyers work directly for individual corporations as corporate counsel. Others work in firms that do the work for big and small businesses. If you're into deal making and especially like to wear fancy clothes, this field could be for you.

Criminal

Do you want to put bad guys behind bars? Maybe you want to fight to keep wrongfully accused people out of jail? Perhaps what interests you most is the theoretical study of criminal justice, the rationale behind such concepts as the insanity defense, the death penalty, or lengthy incarcerations. These topics all fall under the heading of criminal law. Criminal lawyers include prosecutors, who work for the state prosecuting people accused of crimes, and public defenders, who defend these same people accused of crimes. This field is a great area to pursue if you want to spend a lot of time in court.

Domestic Relations/Family Law

Domestic relations and family law encompass all the messy aspects of family life — prenuptial and postnuptial agreements, divorce, custody, child support, division of marital property, visitation, child abuse, adoption, and so on. Some family lawyers specialize in areas, such as divorces involving wealthy people, though the relatively small number of super-wealthy people in the world limits the number of lawyers who can find work in this area. More typically, family lawyers handle the unfortunate situations confronting everyday people. Many family lawyers work closely with social services, particularly to monitor the welfare of children who may get "lost" in unfortunate family situations.

Employment/Labor

Employment law concerns itself with all aspects of the workplace — compensation, discrimination, sexual harassment, hiring and firing, benefits, and workplace safety. When employees sue employers for wrongful termination or national origin discrimination, employment lawyers get to participate in the fracas.

Labor law isn't the same thing as employment law. Labor law involves labor unions and collective bargaining agreements. Labor law has tons of federal regulation, such as the National Labor Relations Act, and various other state and federal statutes that cover specific industries, such as railroads.

Intellectual Property

Intellectual property includes copyrights, trademarks, and trade names; it also includes patents, though patent lawyers tend to specialize primarily in that area. (Patent law often involves inventions, so many patent lawyers are former engineers or engineering majors.) Intellectual property lawyers help their clients register trademarks, file lawsuits for trademark or trade name violations, watch out for unfair competition, and regularly consider matters such as the value of celebrity endorsements. The Internet has opened up a vast new arena of intellectual property matters, so if you're into software and electronically distributed texts, you may want to pay more attention while you're in intellectual property class.

International

You've heard of the United Nations, but there are hundreds of other less well known international organizations in the world, such as the Association of Southeastern Nations (ASEAN), the Organization of Petroleum Exporting Countries (OPEC), or Mercosur (Southern Cone Common Market — that's in South America). International law comes from all sorts of different sources: Countries enter into treaties and conventions with one another. International organizations such as the International Court of Justice decide some international disputes, and the vague but important principle known as customary international law provides guidance for nations interacting with one another. International lawyers figure out all this stuff. International law is complicated but interesting, and it has a bit of prestige being involved in international affairs, so many people study this field. If you think this field is for you, brush up on your foreign languages; they'll definitely help you find jobs.

Personal Injury/Insurance Defense

Have you been injured in an accident? I hope not, but if you become a plaintiff's attorney and specialize in personal injury cases, you may want to find people who have. Plaintiffs' attorneys file lawsuits on behalf of people who have been injured in some way and hope to recover damages. These lawsuits are usually based on *torts,* which are injuries such as battery, trespass, fraud, products liability, intentional infliction of emotional distress — anything that injures someone but isn't a crime under state or federal law. (This kind of lawsuit is called *civil,* not because the parties are especially polite to one another, but because they're brought by private citizens, unlike criminal lawsuits, which are always brought by the state.)

Of course, someone has to defend the people and companies who get sued in personal injury lawsuits. Defense lawyers rise to the occasion here. In any given year, many personal injury lawsuits are filed against companies with malpractice insurance, and the insurance companies often end up paying for the legal defense — lawyers who defend defendants in certain kinds of personal injury cases are called insurance defense attorneys.

One big difference between plaintiffs' and defense lawyers is in the way they get paid for their work. Plaintiffs' attorneys often collect a *contingency fee,* which is a percentage of whatever amount the plaintiff recovers if he or she wins the lawsuit. If the lawsuit fails, the attorney doesn't get paid. Defense attorneys typically bill by the hour, so the more hours they work on a case, the more they get paid.

Real Estate

If you've ever bought property, like a house, you've probably met a real estate attorney. Real estate lawyers are the folks who oversee *closings,* those quaint ceremonial occasions in which the parties to a transaction sit around a table and pass around myriad forms that everyone has to sign, at the end of which the buyer is poorer and owns the property and the seller is richer and doesn't. Real estate lawyers also do title searches, investigate zoning laws, and come to a deeper understanding of arcane concepts such as the rule against perpetuities (go to law school to figure out that one). Real estate tends to be a fairly stable field that attracts people who want relatively regular hours, though things can get crazy in real estate offices at the end of every month or whenever interest rates do something exciting.

Tax

Ever read the Internal Revenue Code? Become a tax lawyer and you'll experience that sublime pleasure on a daily basis. Tax lawyers almost have to specialize in this one area; the state and federal tax codes are so complex and change so often, being a generalist with a sideline in tax is difficult. Good tax lawyers have mastered a delicate balancing act — making sure that their clients pay exactly as much tax as they need to in order to avoid prosecution, but also ensuring that they don't pay a penny more than they absolutely must. Attorneys who specialize in tax are unusual in that they very often have an advanced legal degree, called a Master of Laws (LLM).

Trusts and Estates/Probate

When people die, they usually leave stuff behind. Trusts and estates is the field of study concerned with how all that stuff gets disposed of, which is a process known as *probate*. Sometimes people die without wills, and it's the lawyer's job to figure out who gets what according to state laws of descent and distribution (I love that phrase). Rich people don't like to let the state decide who gets their money and property, so they usually write wills or create trusts to ensure that particular people get particular things. Lawyers who do estate planning are usually in demand, especially if they combine this specialty with some specialized knowledge of tax laws.

Index

• S •

FOR DUMMIES®

The easy way to get more done and have more fun

PERSONAL FINANCE

0-7645-5231-7

0-7645-2431-3

0-7645-5331-3

Also available:

Estate Planning For Dummies
(0-7645-5501-4)

401(k)s For Dummies
(0-7645-5468-9)

Frugal Living For Dummies
(0-7645-5403-4)

Microsoft Money "X" For Dummies
(0-7645-1689-2)

Mutual Funds For Dummies
(0-7645-5329-1)

Personal Bankruptcy For Dummies
(0-7645-5498-0)

Quicken "X" For Dummies
(0-7645-1666-3)

Stock Investing For Dummies
(0-7645-5411-5)

Taxes For Dummies 2003
(0-7645-5475-1)

BUSINESS & CAREERS

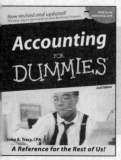

0-7645-5314-3

0-7645-5307-0

0-7645-5471-9

Also available:

Business Plans Kit For Dummies
(0-7645-5365-8)

Consulting For Dummies
(0-7645-5034-9)

Cool Careers For Dummies
(0-7645-5345-3)

Human Resources Kit For Dummies
(0-7645-5131-0)

Managing For Dummies
(1-5688-4858-7)

QuickBooks All-in-One Desk Reference For Dummies
(0-7645-1963-8)

Selling For Dummies
(0-7645-5363-1)

Small Business Kit For Dummies
(0-7645-5093-4)

Starting an eBay Business For Dummies
(0-7645-1547-0)

HEALTH, SPORTS & FITNESS

0-7645-5167-1

0-7645-5146-9

0-7645-5154-X

Also available:

Controlling Cholesterol For Dummies
(0-7645-5440-9)

Dieting For Dummies
(0-7645-5126-4)

High Blood Pressure For Dummies
(0-7645-5424-7)

Martial Arts For Dummies
(0-7645-5358-5)

Menopause For Dummies
(0-7645-5458-1)

Nutrition For Dummies
(0-7645-5180-9)

Power Yoga For Dummies
(0-7645-5342-9)

Thyroid For Dummies
(0-7645-5385-2)

Weight Training For Dummies
(0-7645-5168-X)

Yoga For Dummies
(0-7645-5117-5)

Available wherever books are sold.
Go to www.dummies.com or call 1-877-762-2974 to order direct.

FOR DUMMIES®

A world of resources to help you grow

HOME, GARDEN & HOBBIES

0-7645-5295-3

0-7645-5130-2

0-7645-5106-X

FOOD & WINE

0-7645-5250-3

0-7645-5390-9

0-7645-5114-0

TRAVEL

0-7645-5453-0

0-7645-5438-7

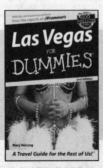
0-7645-5448-4

FOR DUMMIES®

Helping you expand your horizons and realize your potential

INTERNET

0-7645-0894-6

0-7645-1659-0

0-7645-1642-6

Also available:

America Online 7.0 For Dummies
(0-7645-1624-8)

Genealogy Online For Dummies
(0-7645-0807-5)

The Internet All-in-One Desk Reference For Dummies
(0-7645-1659-0)

Internet Explorer 6 For Dummies
(0-7645-1344-3)

The Internet For Dummies Quick Reference
(0-7645-1645-0)

Internet Privacy For Dummies
(0-7645-0846-6)

Researching Online For Dummies
(0-7645-0546-7)

Starting an Online Business For Dummies
(0-7645-1655-8)

DIGITAL MEDIA

0-7645-1664-7

0-7645-1675-2

0-7645-0806-7

Also available:

CD and DVD Recording For Dummies
(0-7645-1627-2)

Digital Photography All-in-One Desk Reference For Dummies
(0-7645-1800-3)

Digital Photography For Dummies Quick Reference
(0-7645-0750-8)

Home Recording for Musicians For Dummies
(0-7645-1634-5)

MP3 For Dummies
(0-7645-0858-X)

Paint Shop Pro "X" For Dummies
(0-7645-2440-2)

Photo Retouching & Restoration For Dummies
(0-7645-1662-0)

Scanners For Dummies
(0-7645-0783-4)

GRAPHICS

0-7645-0817-2

0-7645-1651-5

0-7645-0895-4

Also available:

Adobe Acrobat 5 PDF For Dummies
(0-7645-1652-3)

Fireworks 4 For Dummies
(0-7645-0804-0)

Illustrator 10 For Dummies
(0-7645-3636-2)

QuarkXPress 5 For Dummies
(0-7645-0643-9)

Visio 2000 For Dummies
(0-7645-0635-8)

Available wherever books are sold. Go to www.dummies.com or call 1-877-762-2974 to order direct.

FOR DUMMIES®

The advice and explanations you need to succeed

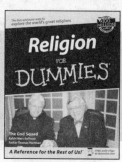

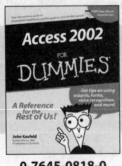

LSAT® For Dummies®

How to Have a Successful Testing Experience

Before the test:

- Register ahead of time — at least two months ahead of the test date because some centers fill up quickly. Check the Law School Admissions Council Web site (www.lsac.org) for official regular and late registration deadlines.

- Start studying early; don't wait until the night before the test. Taking several timed practice tests is the best way to improve your score.

- Make sure you know where to go to take the test. Take a practice drive to the site, if it'll make you feel better, and look for parking.

The night before:

- Set your alarm; give yourself enough time to get there. Plan what to eat for breakfast the next morning — you don't want to walk out the door with an empty stomach.

- If you have time and want a warm-up, work some LSAT sections that you've already taken.

- Assemble the following supplies:

    - Admission ticket

    - Driver's license or other official photo ID (such as a student ID)

    - Coins in case there's a vending machine, or snacks such as nuts, energy bars, or other brain food

    - A list of four law schools you want your scores sent to

    - Several sharp No. 2 pencils and a pencil sharpener

    - A snack

    - A watch with seconds (digital or hand) that doesn't beep

The morning of the test:

- Get to the testing site early enough to park and find your room without panicking.

- Visit the restroom before testing starts.

- Take a deep breath and plunge into the LSAT.

- Feel confident that you have prepared well for the LSAT and are ready to take the test. Envision yourself making a strong performance on the test and picture yourself a soon-to-be winner!

During the test:

- Answer every question — there's no penalty for guessing.

- Fill in the bubbles completely.

- Keep track of your time.

- If you get stuck, guess and move on.

- Keep concentrating, even if you're bored out of your mind.

- Take an occasional short break (no more than 30 seconds, though).

After the test:

- If you want to cancel your score, do it before you leave the test center or within nine days of your test date.

- Wait for your score to arrive; use this time to research law schools or do something fun.

- Repeat the LSAT if necessary.

For Dummies: Bestselling Book Series for Beginners

LSAT® For Dummies®

Cheat Sheet

Tips for Success on Analytical Reasoning

- ✔ Stay calm; keep focused.
- ✔ Work one problem at a time; work the whole problem, and then move on to the next one.
- ✔ Do as much thinking as possible before you tackle the questions.
- ✔ Read the facts carefully.
- ✔ Draw a diagram and rewrite the rules in shorthand.
- ✔ Make connections and deductions.
- ✔ Read the questions carefully.
- ✔ Check all answers; eliminate the wrong ones.
- ✔ Choose an answer and hit the next question.
- ✔ When you finish one problem, forget it, and clear your brain for the next one.

Tips for Success on Logical Reasoning

- ✔ Be quick but careful.
- ✔ Read the question before you read the argument.
- ✔ Read the argument. Identify the conclusion and the key evidence.
- ✔ Try to answer the question in your head before you read the answer choices.
- ✔ Read all the answers and eliminate wrong ones.
- ✔ Choose an answer.
- ✔ Forget about that question and move on to the next one.

Tips for Success on Reading Comprehension

- ✔ Concentrate, concentrate, concentrate — even if you're bored.
- ✔ Work one reading passage at a time; answer all the questions, and then move on.
- ✔ Skim the questions first.
- ✔ Read the passage aggressively; take your time.
- ✔ Focus on the big stuff and gloss over the details, going back to them if the questions ask you about them.
- ✔ Mark important points in the passage, but *don't* mark too much.
- ✔ Think about the passage before you start the questions.
- ✔ Refer back to the passage as often as necessary.
- ✔ If the questions direct you to a specific word or line, read several lines above and below it, so you understand the context.
- ✔ Try to answer questions yourself before reading the answer choices.
- ✔ Don't use any information not contained in the passage — forget what you know or believe about the subject.
- ✔ Read all answers and eliminate the wrong ones.
- ✔ Choose an answer.
- ✔ When you finish a passage, forget it and clear your brain for the next one.

Tips for Success on the Writing Sample

- ✔ Read the question carefully and think for a moment.
- ✔ Pick a side — either side will do. There's no right answer.
- ✔ Take a moment to outline your essay.
- ✔ Write the essay in four or five paragraphs.
- ✔ Explain your position and ward off any potential attacks.
- ✔ Finish the essay smoothly; don't just drop your reader when you reach the end of the page.
- ✔ Write carefully and legibly.
- ✔ Don't end the section early. If you have extra time, proofread!
- ✔ Don't leave more than a line or two blank. Though it isn't scored, it could make or break your entrance into law school if you're being compared with other similar-candidates.
- ✔ Don't sweat this one — it's not scored.

For Dummies: Bestselling Book Series for Beginners